BUENA VISTA IN THE CLUB

Refiguring American Music

A series edited by Ronald Radano and Josh Kun
Charles McGovern, contributing editor

Geoffrey Baker

BUENA VISTA IN THE CLUB

Rap, Reggaetón, and Revolution in Havana

Duke University Press Durham and London 2011

© 2011 Duke University Press
All rights reserved
Printed in the United States of America on acid-free paper ∞
Designed by C. H. Westmoreland
Typeset in Chaparral with Gill Sans by Keystone Typesetting, Inc.
Frontispiece: "Los Paisanos in Buena Vista, Havana," photo by Alex Lloyd.
Library of Congress Cataloging-in-Publication Data appear on the
last printed page of this book.

Para los raperos y raperas de Buena Vista

Revolution is a sense of the historical moment; it is to change everything that needs to be changed; it is full equality and freedom; it is to be treated and to treat others as human beings; it is to emancipate ourselves through our own efforts; it is to challenge powerful dominant forces within and outside the social and national sphere; it is to defend values in which one believes at any cost; it is modesty, unselfishness, altruism, solidarity and heroism; it is to fight bravely, intelligently and realistically; it is never to lie nor to violate ethical principles; it is the profound conviction that there is no force on earth capable of crushing the strength of the truth and ideas.—FIDEL CASTRO

It's true, it's a sense of the historical moment, and it's to change everything that needs to be changed. . . . So who is counterrevolutionary, someone who's pushing for change so that we can move forward, or someone who's kept us frozen in time for fifty years?—EL B OF LOS ALDEANOS

CONTENTS

ACKNOWLEDGMENTS

After seven years of visits to Havana, the list of people who have helped me, in ways large or small, is dauntingly long. I am especially grateful to the following, without whose support or cooperation my research would not have been possible:

Jessel Saladriga Fernández (Mr. Huevo), Randee Akozta, Miguelito, Explosión Suprema, Doble Filo, Rebeld' Malcoms, Papá Humbertico, Hermanos de Causa, Los Aldeanos, Papo Record, Alexánder Guerra, Obsesion, Isnay Rodríguez, Anónimo Consejo, Barón González, Ogguere, El Adversario, DJ Vans, Clan Completo, Omega Kilay, El Discípulo, Anderson, Raudel (Escuadrón Patriota), Rubén Marín, Silvito "El Libre," Yimi Konklaze, DJ Micha, Unión Perfecta, Cuentas Claras, Kumar, El Poeta Lírico, El Enano, Champion Records, Carlos (TC Records), Alexánder Delgado, Nando Pro, El Micha, Jorge Hernández, Triángulo Oscuro, Ariel Fernández, Roberto Zurbano, Rodolfo Rensoli, Jorge Enrique Rodríguez, Williams Figueredo, Fernando Rojas, Alpidio Alonso, Guille Vilar, Lourdes Suárez, DJ Manu, Nehanda Abiodun, Pedro de la Hoz, Yelandi "El Yela," Eduardo Djata, Mercy, Aris, Cintia, Harry Belafonte, Raquel Z. Rivera, Joshua Bee Alafia, Eli Jacobs-Fantauzzi, Jauretsi Saizarbitoria, and Clyde Valentin. My apologies for the inevitable omissions.

Special thanks to Alex Lloyd, Oscar Castillo (Bambú), and Melisa Rivière/Emetrece Productions for allowing me to use their wonderful

ACKNOWLEDGMENTS

photos; to Sophia Blackwell for invaluable editorial assistance; and to Pablo Herrera for many enlightening conversations, opening doors for reggaetón research, and help with translations.

I am grateful to the British Academy, which funded the majority of the fieldwork for this project via its Small Research Grant scheme; Royal Holloway, University of London, for providing me with the sabbatical during which much of this book was written; the Arts and Humanities Research Council, for providing further sabbatical funding via the Research Leave scheme; and Columbia University, for welcoming me as a visiting scholar.

My thanks to all at Duke University Press, especially Valerie Millholland, Miriam Angress, Tim Elfenbein, and Jeanne Farris; to Ron Radano and Josh Kun, editors of the series Refiguring American Music; and to the anonymous readers of my manuscript.

Earlier versions of chapters 1 to 3 were published as "¡Hip Hop, Revolución! Nationalizing Rap in Cuba," *Ethnomusicology* 49, no. 3 (2005), 368–402; "*La Habana que no conoces*: Cuban Rap and the Social Construction of Urban Space," *Ethnomusicology Forum* 15, no. 2 (2006), 215–46; and "The Politics of Dancing: Reggaetón and Rap in Havana, Cuba," in Raquel Z. Rivera, Wayne Marshall, and Deborah Pacini Hernandez, eds., *Reggaeton* (Durham, N.C.: Duke University Press, 2009). My thanks to the relevant publications and editors.

SO I MET WITH FIDEL. We were supposed to have met for roughly forty minutes—a quickie lunch in the Palace of the Revolution. He was having a series of other meetings. And we started to get into some pleasantries and I said, "I've got something I'd like to put before you," and started to talk about hip hop. . . . And I told him that I thought they'd made a big mistake in not recognizing something as global, as powerful, as this art form and that I thought that it would enhance the thinking of young Cubans, give them a platform on which to find international identity and . . . a place in which, as part of a new cultural order, to have a comfort zone in what was going on globally. And that for Cuba not to be part of that was a gross error on their part. I'd not often talked to Fidel Castro that way, only when I felt strongly about something. . . .

And as we got into this conversation, somewhere I saw that Fidel Castro was really caught. He had a number of appointments; the very next appointment from our brief lunch was that he was going to the graduation class of some 4,000 doctors who had taken some special training. . . . And he said, "you're going with me," and I said, "OK, where to?," and he said, "wherever I have to go—this conversation has just begun." And for the next eleven hours I went with him in his car—I call it the Wild West trips—to the next venue; he did his speeches with the university students, he asked me to come and say some words to them and I was amused, I enjoyed it, and I spoke to them, and the minute we got into the car, [puts on Spanish accent, imitating Fidel] "now about this hip hop. . . ."

I could tell that Fidel was excited, I could tell he was hearing something that he needed to hear and wanted to hear.

HARRY BELAFONTE, *singer, actor, and activist,*
on his 1999 meeting with Fidel Castro

INTRODUCTION

Whether or not *Buena Vista Social Club* represents the meaning of life, as Terry Eagleton (2007, 172) implies, it has been hugely influential both in Cuba and around the globe. The 1997 album, a collaboration between the American guitarist-producer Ry Cooder and a number of (mainly elderly) luminaries of Cuban popular music, went on to become the most success ful world-music album of all time, and, along with Wim Wenders's 1999 follow-up documentary of the same name, it changed the way the world saw Cuban music and the way Cuban musicians saw themselves. The rapper Telmary spoke for many young musicians when she ended a concert at La Floridita in London in 2007 with the words "we are here representing the new generation of Cuban music—so that you know that it's not all the Buena Vista Social Club!"[1] Yet Telmary had starred in the 2004 Buena Vista Social Club (BVSC) docudrama "sequel," *Música Cubana*, rapping over one of the original film's hits, "Chan chan." In 2006, her former band, Free Hole Negro—like her, from the Havana barrio of Buena Vista—had released the song "Caballeros para el monte," based on the BVSC track "El carretero," on their rap-fusion album *Superfinos Negros*. These artists were taking their cue from Havana's most famous rappers, Orishas, who included "537 C.U.B.A.," a rap version of "Chan chan," on *A lo Cubano* (1999), thus translating the Buena Vista experience for club-goers around the world within two years of the original album's release. BVSC also reached out into some unlikely spheres of Cuban music: Anónimo Consejo, the epitome of "underground"[2] hip hop in Havana, put out "Aquí sí hay," a cover of "Candela," on their 2008 demo *Los Nuevos Inquilinos*, and even reggaetón, a genre usually considered the polar opposite of Cuban traditional music, got in on the act. The Swedish "Cubatón" project resulted in a docudrama titled "The Children of Buena Vista": the producers marketed Cuban reggaetón by creating a somewhat far-fetched intergenerational tie-in, merging the brash electronic internationalism of its young producers with the global brand recognition of elderly Cuban *soneros*.

The BVSC has framed perceptions and discussions of Cuban music since the late 1990s, whether today's younger musicians identify with it as a source of national pride and/or commercial success; against it, through ironic twists like that of the rap-metaller Mala Bizta Sochal Klu; or both, as in the case of Telmary.[3] Even when trying to break free from it and represent (or re-present) Cuban music in other ways, musicians, producers, and writers know it is the primary lens through which international audiences observe Cuba, and therefore a useful point of reference. Joaquín Borges-Triana saw the award of a Latin Grammy to Orishas in 2003 for their second album, *Emigrante*, as an important moment for alternative Cuban music: "When almost the whole planet associates Cuban music exclusively with the retro phenomenon that is the Buena Vista Social Club, as though musical time in our country had stopped in the 50s, one group of creators is committed to difference."[4] Yet Orishas' first album had included their "Chan chan" cover, while "Mujer," the second track on *Emigrante*, begins with the sound of crackling vinyl, a sonic index of a retro feel. This illustrates the ambivalent yet central position of BVSC in popular music in Havana: while artists and commentators seem eager to escape its orbit, they keep returning to mine it for musical and intellectual reference points. At times, the push and pull of BVSC seems inescapable. Perhaps Terry Eagleton is right.

Buena Vista Social Club to Buena Vista Crew

A notable feature of Wim Wenders's BVSC film is the way it puts a distance between the musical cultures of Cuba and the United States at the same time that it draws them together. Focusing on the musical styles and stars of the 1940s and 1950s, it projects an image of an "island that time forgot" and a musical culture whose isolation ensured a stark difference from that of the United States at the turn of the millennium. Ry Cooder is featured as an explorer who travels through space and time to find a musical "lost world" in Havana; the Cuban musicians who visit New York at the end of the film are captured as bewildered innocents, relics of an earlier age. The first images of the film underline the political division of the early 1960s; the last images show Cooder bridging the divide through music, yet that distance—key to the project's popular and commercial success—is simultaneously underscored by the film's narrative and symbolism. While reflecting a very real gap, the result of political decisions on both sides of the Florida Straits, at the same time the film omits any reference to the historical interconnectedness of the music of the two countries, which can be traced back to the nineteenth century; indeed, the two "symbolic capitals" (Quiroga 2005, 3) of the film—Havana and New York—have particularly intertwined musical histories, of which the exchanges of the BVSC film are just one of many examples.[5] As Lise Waxer (1994, 141) writes: "Havana and New York are seen as two points of creativity in a circular process, each one responding, either directly or indirectly, to changes in the other." Cuban music has repeatedly provided fuel for modern popular music styles in New York, playing a vital role in the development of jazz in the 1940s and the evolution of the characteristic Latin styles of mambo and salsa. The music heard in the Havana social clubs of the 1940s and 1950s, meanwhile, was significantly influenced by North American popular music, especially big band jazz, and much post-1959 music has incorporated elements from U.S. doo-wop, funk, and rock. Havana and New York have long been favorite dance partners, and *Buena Vista in the Club*, like its illustrious forebear, is a transnational story with this axis at its heart.

In the late 1990s, while aging Cuban stars were seducing audiences in New York (once again) with the sounds of *son*, in Havana their grand-children's generation was tuning in to a very different beat, one that had originated in the Big Apple: hip hop.[6] As Wenders's film reveals, the social club of Buena Vista, like other pre-revolutionary black associations, had been closed for decades, yet music had not lost its power to act as a form of social glue. In the 1980s a hip hop scene emerged, initially focused on dance, and over the following decade it became a support network for youths cut adrift by the dislocations of the crisis years after the fall of the Soviet Union and the end of its subsidies to Cuba. Ariel Fernández, one of Havana hip hop's leading voices, described the early 1990s scene as "an alternative space for the youth at the time that was very necessary. There was a lot of frustration, and this place meant that you belonged to something, that you weren't alone" (*East of Havana* n.d., 150).[7] Loose neighborhood groups coalesced, echoing U.S. hip hop posses—indeed, early Havana hip hop fans identified themselves as "East Side" or "West Side," New York or Los Angeles. These morphed into local versions—"Costa Norte" (North Coast) and so on—and then into hip hop collectives like the Buena Vista Crew, El Cartel, and La Comisión Depuradora.[8] These contemporary versions of the social club provided a forum for discussion, an outlet for self-expression, and a focus of identification for young Cubans in the city's barrios, with music still the central factor. Like the members of the pre-revolutionary social clubs, 1990s hip hoppers used musical performance and consumption to create social spaces and a public realm on the urban periphery for those left out by the tourism-driven commercialization of the city center.[9] There may be no formal member-

Buena Vista in the Club. Photo by Alex Lloyd.

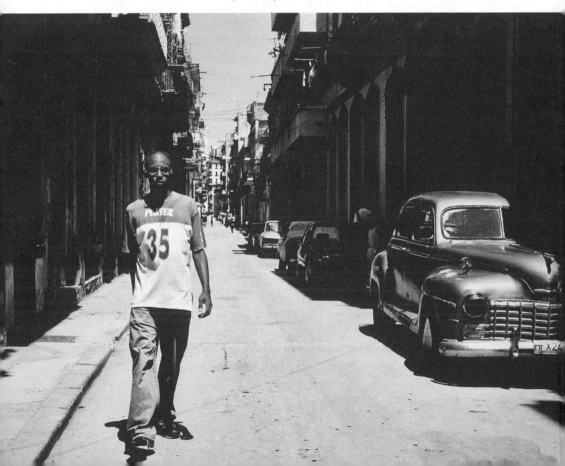

ship, but there is a notable cohesiveness in this tightly knit scene.[10]
Although the hip hop dance scene started out racially mixed, and Havana's first rap stars, SBS, were light-skinned, by the late 1990s a rising
current of negritude, fed by North American visitors, had converted the
hip hop scene into a focal point of Afro-Cuban social and cultural activity,
mirroring the pre-revolutionary social clubs.

Ry Cooder was not the only high-profile American musician visiting
Cuba in 1998, the year that he and Wim Wenders were in Havana making
their film. The same year also saw the creation of the Black August Hip
Hop Collective (BAHHC), a bilateral organization linking Havana with
New York, and the visit to the international Havana hip hop festival of
the first of several delegations of U.S. activists and "conscious" rappers—
including Black Star, Common, The Roots, and dead prez. Simultaneously
with the Wenders/Cooder historical preservation mission, more contemporary cultural connections between Cuba and the United States were
being forged through revolutionary rap. A month after Carnegie Hall
went wild for the old soneros, Mos Def and Talib Kweli stepped onstage at
the Alamar amphitheater in East Havana. North American rappers and
activists provided a major impetus to the Havana scene and ushered in a
boom time for Cuban rap. The presence of these African American musicians in Havana carried echoes of the days when, as the city emerged as
America's playground from the 1930s to the 1950s, figures such as Nat
King Cole, Sammy Davis Jr., and Josephine Baker graced its stages. But
there was also a thread that led back to the post-1959 pilgrimages to
revolutionary Cuba by African American radicals like the civil rights activist Robert Williams and the Black Panthers co-founder Huey Newton.
The visiting hip hop artists and activists of the 1990s revived the transnational cultural and political connections of earlier periods, simultaneously inspiring and taking inspiration from local developments. If
black Cuban musicians had once catalyzed an Africanizing or "Afro-
modernist" movement in New York jazz (Ramsey 2003), black American
rappers returned the favor, fueling a racializing turn in Havana hip hop.

For all the apparent contrasts of young Cuban rappers in baggy jeans
and basketball shirts with elder statesmen like Compay Segundo and
Ibrahim Ferrer, the exchange projects organized by the BAHHC mirror
the BVSC in more ways than one. Both were deeply nostalgic searches for
lost authenticity: Cuba was no longer the source of the new, but rather of
the old that had been lost back home. To the international visitors, the

Havana hip hop scene embodied the lost essence of American hip hop, the old-school vibe of the South Bronx "back in the day." There are close parallels with world-music projects (like BVSC) that are described by Timothy Brennan (2008, 12) as "an escape from the American self." For Brennan, world music is "at least partly about a longing in the metropolitan centers for what is not Europe or North America. . . . It is, among other things, a flight from the self at the very moment that one's own culture is said to have become the global norm, as though people were driven away by the image stalking them in the mirror" (ibid., 16). Similarly, as commercial U.S. hip hop became "the global norm" in the 1990s, some North American hip hop activists and intellectuals began to look to other parts of the globe for sustenance.

The sentiments underlying the simultaneous BAHHC and BVSC projects were thus similar: both resulted from and satisfied the cravings of North American intermediaries who longed for "the *not-here*" (ibid.) and whose nostalgic sensibilities were manifested in neotraditionalism. Dissatisfaction with hypercommercialized U.S. culture drove the search for "authentic" world music and "real" hip hop, both of which were "discovered" in Havana—a discovery that involved a significant dose of invention. In both cases, Cuba's isolation from the United States was seen as having protected it from the ravages of commercialism.[11] Distinguished musicians thus traveled from the United States to Cuba as much to learn as to teach: in both cases there was a sense of pilgrimage, traveling back in time to drink from an unadulterated source.

Havana hip hop drew on both Cuba's cultural creativity and America's historical role in its shaping and global mediation. The Havana hip hop festival began as a local affair in 1995, but its internationalization in the late 1990s led to an influx of overseas documentary makers, who ensured the transmission of Cuban rap as much through film as through music. The arrival of foreign music producers led to several key hip hop compilations aimed at overseas consumers, which helped to create an alternative brand of Cuban hip hop to Orishas in the global marketplace. As with the BVSC, the commodification and transnational mediation of Cuban music by foreign musical "explorers" thus emerges as a central concern. In some cases, recording and filming went hand in hand. The *Cuban Hip Hop All Stars* (CHHAS) project recalls Joaquin Cooder's comment in the BVSC film that the project was the realization of his father's dream of a bizarre band that never existed; as discussed in chapter 4, the CHHAS album

created sounds never previously heard within Havana hip hop, and the
film constructed musical set pieces to support the sound world of the CD
rather than to reflect Havana's daily realities. One might even add that all
this interest in Cuban musicians, both old and young, from foreign producers, filmmakers, and music entrepreneurs has contributed to a widespread hope within Havana's music scenes for a *golpe de suerte* (stroke of
luck) in the form of a foreign impresario willing to fund projects and,
ideally, travel abroad. In both cases, tours and concerts in North America
and further afield—the highest prize available to Cuban musicians—have
resulted from these musical expeditions to Havana. Music documentaries
have also, ironically, served as a stimulus to tourism, the most visible face
of the commercialism whose supposed absence is celebrated in the documentaries themselves. While the scale of the impact of the BVSC on
Cuban tourism was infinitely greater, there is no question that the proliferation of hip hop documentaries—more than twenty-five to date—has
helped to consolidate the scene on Havana's alternative, "nontouristy"
tourist circuit. Hip hop in Havana, like much contemporary Cuban music,
cannot be properly understood without considering the transnational
aspects of its production, circulation, and representation.

"The Way It Was":
An Introduction to Rap and Reggaetón in Havana

It all began when I was a kid with a bunch of antennae,
Clothes hanger wire and a Selena [TV],
I put all that junk out the window and, ay, ay, ay!
Dying to catch '99 [Jamz]!
I caught Soul Train, not fuzzy at all.
Out of the way, mom!
I'm watching a program,
Eyes and ears on stalks.
I copied the steps and then in the barrio
We started battling,
And there were many like me in Havana,
Dancing and listening just to American music.
Dad bought me a tape player
And my first cassette was by Public Enemy.
—ALEXEY RODRÍGUEZ (El Tipo Éste),
"Como fue" (the way it was)[12]

Alexey Rodríguez of Obsesion performing in London. Photo by Alex Lloyd.

The historical interlinkage of Afro-Cuban and African American musicians was curtailed in the aftermath of the 1959 Cuban Revolution. With the imposition of the U.S. embargo in 1962, the exchange of musicians was reduced to virtually zero. However, in the age of mass media, the flow of popular culture continued, despite the best efforts of the Cuban government to limit exposure to U.S. musical influences and the so-called ideological diversionism that might result. Merchant sailors were an important point of contact with outside musical trends, but even more influential were the radio and TV signals beamed across the Florida Straits from Miami and captured on makeshift aerials hoisted on seaside apartment buildings. Alexey Rodríguez's iconic song "The Way It Was" captures the image of young residents of Havana suburbs like Alamar tuning into *Soul Train* and *99 Jamz*, grooving to Earth, Wind and Fire, and marveling at the dance steps of Michael Jackson.[13] This image has entered the lore of Cuban hip hop and is a vital part of the story, revealing rap as the latest manifestation of a Cuban fascination with American music that goes back through funk, soul, and rock 'n' roll to jazz: hip hoppers' parents and grandparents had had their own transnational infatuations.[14] The hip hop kingpin Ariel Fernández told me: "Hip hop didn't come from nothing—it came because it is a tradition that people are always trying to be on top of the new type of music coming from the U.S." His choice of words is revealing: a love of American modernity is a Cuban tradition.

Less well known is the "alternative" origin story of the BVSC. The film plays up Ry Cooder's role as originator of the project, at the expense of local "point man" Juan de Marcos González, who has since attempted to put the story straight. He talked about tuning into Miami radio stations in the 1970s, listening to the funk and soul that would inspire the first generation of Havana hip hoppers, but fixating primarily on Carlos Santana's music (Corbett 2004, 47). Santana's resurrection of Mexican musical history led Juan de Marcos to begin studying traditional Cuban music, which evolved into the creation of the seminal son "revival" group Sierra Maestra, and from there to the BVSC project he organized for Ry Cooder. The origin stories of the son revival and Cuban hip hop—developments that might appear at opposite ends of the musical spectrum—reveal U.S. media broadcasts in an almost identical role as catalyst.

Images and sounds translated far more readily than lyrics, so it is unsurprising that the first shoots of hip hop culture in Havana in the 1980s took the form of dance styles. Many leading figures in the Havana hip hop scene started out as break dancers, frequenting places like the Parque de los Policías in the barrio of Lawton. Alexey Rodríguez went on to become one of Cuba's best-known rappers, but his hymn to the Cuban old school is all about the dance. A nascent form of rapping known as *cotorrear* began to emerge at the end of the decade, but most place its crystallization around 1990, the start of the "Special Period in a Time of Peace."[15] This was the euphemistic name given by the Cuban government to the sudden and profound crisis that engulfed the island with the fall of the Soviet Union and the end of its support for Cuba. It was a time of severe shortages and plummeting living standards. An urgent need for foreign currency ushered in an economic (counter)revolution based on the opening up of Cuba to mass tourism and foreign investment, and the legalization of private possession of dollars. Cuba thus began to operate a dual dollar-peso economy that lasted from 1993 to 2004, when the dollar was replaced by the convertible peso (which did nothing to alter the duality of the economy). Dollars were vital for obtaining most consumer goods and even some domestic staples, yet they were hard for most Cubans to obtain legally: those who had neither one of the few jobs that paid in hard currency nor family members who sent remittances from overseas found themselves suddenly at a disadvantage, and long-suppressed social and economic divisions returned almost overnight. The new dependence on tourism, too, ensured that the harsh burdens of the 1990s were not shared equally across all sectors of society. The underground economy blossomed, further testing the power and legitimacy of the state (Henken 2005; Ritter 2005). The Special Period, the most far-reaching crisis since the 1959 revolution, provides the context in which Cuban hip hop took shape as a cultural phenomenon. Inspired by the militant sounds and images of U.S. rappers like Public Enemy, but also suffering from the sudden unavailability of basic consumer goods, break dancers began to hang up their shoes and instead speak out publicly through rap lyrics about the bewildering changes and hardships that they faced after decades of Soviet-backed stability—scarcity, inequality, corruption, racism, illegal emigration, booming tourism, and prostitution.

While the late 1980s saw the decline and collapse of socialism in the Soviet bloc, it would be a mistake simply to see this as a time when revolution was dying. Rap, a musical form with revolution at its heart, was taking over America and spreading rapidly around the globe. Its most (in)famous group, Public Enemy, known as "the Black Panthers of hip hop," espoused black Marxist philosophies and turned a new generation on to revolutionary figures such as Malcolm X, Huey Newton, and Assata Shakur. Public Enemy, perhaps more than any other group, became the inspiration for rappers around the globe in the early 1990s, as Alexey's song "Como fue" suggests. The Soviet Union might have gone, but Marxist revolutionary ideas were in the air (and on the airwaves). Public Enemy's music, linking hip hop and revolution, provided the catalyst that was later to convert hip hop in Havana from a foreign youth fad to a vanguard manifestation of national culture.

In the early 1990s, the depths of the Special Period, hip hop took a firmer grip on Havana's youth. In 1990, the huge PabExpo hall was divided into sections for dance events, with one dedicated to *moña* (the general term used for African American popular music, including soul, funk, and R&B, as well as hip hop). After PabExpo came the mobile discos that played *música americana* rather than salsa; the best known was at La Piragua on the seafront from 1992 to 1994, a popular space created by the Unión de Jóvenes Comunistas (Union of Young Communists, or UJC) where young *habaneros* gathered to listen to English-language rap and R&B. Smaller venues where hip hop aficionados came together and danced, such as the Casa Estudiantil in 10 de Octubre, emerged around this time, and the longest-running rap show on Cuban radio, *La Esquina de Rap*, had its first incarnation in the early 1990s. The famous *local* at Carlos III and Infanta, known simply as *la moña*, began putting on hip hop in 1994. These popular spaces were primarily for weekend dance events, and local rappers were slower to emerge, with most recalling only isolated freestylers in the early 1990s. But as the audience for hip hop grew, the first rap groups began to make themselves heard, with figures like Rubén Marín (later of Primera Base) and Yrak Saenz (Doble Filo) leading the way. Official attitudes toward hip hop were contradictory at this time; while many spaces were provided by state organizations (such as the UJC and the community cultural centers known as Casas de la Cultura), hip hop fans were often seen as social misfits, supporters of an imperialist cultural invasion from the United States, and they regularly attracted police attention. Music and dance events were broken up, dancers ran to escape arrest—it was, at least in part, a subculture that thrived on the attraction of the forbidden. This paradoxical combination of state support and restriction has characterized the Havana scene ever since.

By 1995 there were enough rap groups in Havana to merit the organization of a hip hop festival in the East Havana neighborhood of Reparto Guiteras by the collective Grupo Uno, led by the cultural promoters Rodolfo Rensoli and Balesy Rivero. The festival became an annual event; it began to grow in size after the organizers shifted the site to Alamar in 1996 and sought logistical help in 1997 from the state organization for youth culture, the Asociación Hermanos Saíz (AHS), which was to become a key player in the story of Cuban rap. The AHS is technically a nongovernmental organization (an NGO), but those who worked for or with the association would always tell me "it is *supposedly* an NGO" or "it is an NGO *in inverted commas*."[16] It has close ties to the political center: it is under the wing of the UJC—one employee described the two as "thumb and nail"—and two of its former presidents, Fernando Rojas and Alpidio Alonso, went on to occupy high political positions.

While other annual events (such as the Rap Plaza festival) and monthly *peñas* (live performances) sprang up across the city, the center of the late 1990s scene was considered to be the distant East Havana suburb of

Alamar, a huge, postrevolutionary housing estate where both the annual festival and regular peñas were held from 1996.[17] As the live rap scene grew, it attracted increasing attention from Cuban youth, intellectuals, and the state. The 1998 festival featured an important speech in defense of hip hop by Ariel Fernández; this statement, published in the UJC magazine *El Caimán Barbudo* (Fernández 1998), eventually brought forth an official response. In 1999 Abel Prieto, the progressive minister of culture, declared rap to be "an authentic expression of Cuban culture" (quoted in Robinson 2004, 119) and added "it's time we nationalize rock and rap" (quoted in Pacini Hernandez and Garofalo 1999–2000, 42). He announced: "We have to support our Cuban rappers because this is the next generation of Cubans and they are saying powerful things with this art. I am responsible for giving this generation the freedom to claim their power culturally" (quoted in Hoch 1999), and that year state funding for the hip hop festival increased significantly.

If this marked a turning point in the recognition of rap as a genuine manifestation of Cuban national culture, the late 1990s were also key years from an international perspective. Negotiations between internationalist figures in the Havana and New York hip hop scenes in 1997–98 led to the creation of the Black August Hip Hop Collective and the visits to the Havana hip hop festival by renowned U.S. conscious rappers; equally crucial was a meeting between Fidel Castro and the musician-activist Harry Belafonte in Havana in December 1999 that evolved into a day-long discussion of hip hop, consolidating its arrival at the highest levels of the Cuban government (see prologue). As foreign hip hoppers, journalists, and activists started appearing at Havana events, the traffic also began to flow in the other direction, as the visiting artists were inspired. Mos Def, who traveled to Cuba in 1998, included the track "Umi Says," set partly in Havana, on his album *Black on Both Sides* (1999). The song alludes to the Elián González case, and its video includes pictures of Cuban demonstrators with signs reading "bring him home." In 1999 Common performed in Havana, where he met the political exile Assata Shakur, something of a cause célèbre in hip hop: she was Tupac Shakur's aunt and godmother, a Black Panther who was given props by Chuck D in Public Enemy's "Rebel without a Pause." Common released "Song for Assata" on *Like Water for Chocolate* (2000). Perhaps more importantly, the American rappers described their trips to Cuba as moving, even life-changing, experiences. The impact of Cuban hip hop on its U.S. counterpart is small but significant, the latest in a line of Afro-Cuban cultural and political influences on African Americans that goes back to the nineteenth century.[18] While many U.S. conscious hip hop fans may not know much about Cuba, their idols like The Roots, dead prez, Common, Talib Kweli, and Mos Def most definitely do, testifying to the mutual influence of U.S. and Cuban hip hop.

The year 1999 also saw the release by EMI of *A lo Cubano*, the globally successful first album by Orishas, a group formed in France by two resident Cuban musicians and two recently arrived members of the Havana hip hop group Amenaza. In the same year, the first compilations of Cuban rap for overseas distribution, *The Cuban Hip Hop All Stars*, *Vol. 1*, and *Cuban Rap Ligas*, were recorded in Havana. While these albums heralded a boom time for Cuban rap both on the island and abroad, it is worth underlining that success came only with substantial foreign involvement and—in the case of Orishas—a permanent move overseas. Beneath the growing international admiration for Cuban hip hop, structural weaknesses remained: though Abel Prieto and even Fidel Castro were taking an interest, and cultural institutions were increasingly opening their doors, the Cuban media and music industry remained largely resistant to rap, obliging ambitious artists to look abroad. While the Havana scene was becoming a hotbed of ideological and artistic activity and inspiring its North American visitors, on the ground opportunities to make money via conscious hip hop were scarce, meaning that its economic underpinnings were insecure and that most rappers remained poor. Havana's socialist context provided hip hoppers with unusual creative opportunities,[19] but there was a chronic lack of material resources in the Special Period. As a result, foreign involvement was to be crucial in the development of the hip hop scene, opening up new prospects but also raising new questions for local artists as the discrepancy between international recognition and local impecuniousness increased.

A pivotal moment in the flow of hip hop from Havana to the world was the official Cuban rap tour to New York in 2001, organized by the International Hip Hop Exchange (which included many of the Black August activists). For the first time, Havana hip hoppers saw where it all began, yet the enthusiastic reception afforded to the delegation ensured that the Cuban visitors did not perceive themselves as inferior to their American hosts. The optimism around the Havana scene was captured in an interview in the documentary *Cuban Hip Hop All Stars*, in which Obsesion talk during their New York trip about the support they are receiving from state institutions; they predict that this tour will mark the start of a new phase in Cuban hip hop. Their words were soon realized, though perhaps not quite in the way they had hoped. The dream of financial betterment led one member of the delegation, Julio Cárdenas, to defect just a few days later, at the end of the tour—a small but psychologically significant incident at a time when Cuban artists were being held up as the past and the future of hip hop.

Obsesion were right that 2002 was to be a pivotal year for hip hop in Havana, but their optimism turned out to be misplaced. In September 2002, the Ministry of Culture created the Agencia Cubana de Rap (Cuban Rap Agency, or ACR) and launched a magazine, *Movimiento: La Revista Cubana de Hip Hop* (movement: the Cuban hip hop magazine). Until that year there had been a thriving and relatively cohesive rap scene, with estimates of two to three hundred groups in Havana at its peak. There had been debates over underground versus commercial directions within the scene, but in reality the limited commercial openings ensured that differences were more imagined than real. With the creation of the ACR, however, an institutional divide emerged between the eight to ten professional groups employed by the agency, which had an explicit commercial orientation, and the dozens of amateur groups supported by the AHS, an organization with a noncommercial ethos. The effect was the consolidation and amplification of the tensions between underground and commercial tendencies.

At this time, the nascent commercialism embodied by the ACR was dramatically reinforced by the emergence of a new musical style in Havana: reggaetón, a Spanish-language hybrid of dancehall reggae, and U.S. rap, with roots in Panama and Jamaica but produced primarily in Puerto Rico. Although the music of reggaetón pioneers like the Panamanians Nando Boom and El General had been known for years in Cuba, it had been more influential in and around Santiago de Cuba, so it is little surprise that the first Cuban reggaetón star, Candyman, emerged from the eastern end of the island. His music began to be heard in the streets of Havana at the start of the new millennium, blasting out from the speakers on the back of bicycle taxis (many of whose drivers are reputedly from eastern Cuba). The consolidation of this new musical wave was marked by the formation of Cubanito 20.02 by former members of the leading rap group Primera Base; within two years they had become the biggest sensation in Cuba, converting the year of their foundation, 2002, into a symbolic watershed of sorts. At its initiation the same year, the ACR included two reggaetón groups, Cubanito 20.02 and Cubanos en la Red, providing a toehold for reggaetón within not just Cuba's music profession but rap's institutional base. Reggaetón soon grew to dominate the agency's output; rap artists began experimenting with the new style as they saw the popularity of Cubanito and Candyman go through the roof. Reggaetón quickly became far and away the most popular music for young Cubans, offering commercial possibilities within Cuba that had never existed for rap and dramatically transforming Havana's soundscape and musical economy. The relationship between reggaetón and hip hop has been fractious; most of the leading *reguetoneros* (reggaetón artists) emerged from the hip hop scene to great acclaim from the general public, but accusations of selling out have proliferated within hip hop circles. In the eyes of many hip hoppers, the combination of rap and reggaetón groups in a single commercial artistic agency damaged the hip hop scene's ideological base, dashing hopes that hip hop would take a leap forward in 2002 and undermining the legitimacy of the agency itself. With the ACR and reggaetón looming large, commercialism was clearly no longer a mirage in the Havana urban music scene.

As a number of first-rank, professional rap artists were moving toward a more commercial or media-friendly stance and style, many amateur rappers were shifting in the other direction, becoming more rebellious, outspoken, and underground. There was another symbolic turning point in 2002: a performance by the rapper Papá Humbertico at the international rap festival which included hoisting a homemade banner with the words *denuncia social* (social denunciation). This act caused consternation among the institutions responsible for the festival. The most obvious consequence was that Papá Humbertico was banned from performing for four months, but several leading figures in the rap scene believe that this was the beginning of the end of the showpiece AHS festival. Similarly, two individuals close to these developments told me that, while the ACR had been in the works for a long time, it was finally inaugurated just weeks after the Papá Humbertico incident as an attempt to bring order to the scene.

It is worth asking why the denuncia social incident carried so much symbolic force—after all, it was simply the name of Papá Humbertico's first demo, and not a particularly outrageous statement in the context of this outspoken youth culture. The reasons are twofold and related: first, it was a visual statement, and second, it was made in front of the world's press. U.S.-based journalists played a significant role in organizing the Black August exchanges, and the booming rap scene and hip hop festivals attracted increasing numbers of representatives of major overseas news organizations, some of them enticed by the notion of a musical counter-revolution in Cuba, ensuring that photographs of Papá Humbertico's banner appeared on newspaper pages and websites around the world the following day. Despite the apparent centrality of the spoken word in rap, visual elements take on greater significance as rap crosses borders, especially linguistic ones. The translation of a few choice lyrics would not have carried the same weight. As it was, Papá Humbertico created an instant global story, and the reaction of the international press, more than any-thing else, concerned Cuban officials and observers (Henríquez Lagarde 2002). This incident is illustrative of two further points. First, perfor-mance context is crucial. Had Papá Humbertico pulled the same stunt at a regular peña, he would probably have received little attention or sanc-tion. Second, the development of Cuban hip hop has been both accom-panied and significantly affected by foreign efforts to document it. The foreign gaze was instrumental in both Cuban hip hop's rise to global prominence and its fall from grace.

How to apportion the blame between reggaetón, the ACR, Papá Hum-bertico, the foreign press, and a lack of common purpose within the rap scene itself is still a matter of debate; less disputed is the fact that Havana hip hop started to go downhill around this time. The last large-scale, summer hip hop festival took place in 2003, and rappers remarked that the audience response was lukewarm in comparison with previous years. The festival was postponed at the last minute in 2004 and suspended by the AHS after the 2005 edition. As reggaetón's popularity soared, a num-ber of leading rap artists switched styles, and hip hop audiences declined substantially; many key hip hoppers left Cuba altogether; and arguments raged over the validity and direction of the ACR, which was derided by those on the inside as well as the outside. El Cartel provided one of Cuban hip hop's strongest artistic statements in 2004, but this effort to organize leading rappers and producers into a collective proved to be a false dawn: the project was short-lived, and half its participants left the island over the next few years. High-profile tours—such as the visit by La FabriK (Obsesion and Doble Filo) to the United States in 2003, which culminated in a performance at Harlem's famous Apollo Theater alongside Havana veterans The Roots, Common, and Harry Belafonte—ensured that Cuban hip hop's stock kept rising overseas, but back home the scene was divided and shrinking.

In 2007, when the live scene was at its nadir, the duo Los Aldeanos, representatives of a new generation of rappers who emerged after the Black August years, brought together dozens of Havana's most talented underground artists under the banner La Comisión Depuradora (the purifying commission) to spark a renaissance with a landmark double album and two famous concerts. Los Aldeanos went on to become the most important figures in Havana's hip hop scene over the following three years, backed up by other members of La Comisión Depuradora. Their path was cleared to a certain extent by the ACR, which sent its groups away on regular provincial tours organized by its parent institution, the Cuban Music Institute (Instituto Cubano de la Música, or ICM). There was a gap in Havana, and Los Aldeanos filled it, but they also brought about significant changes to the scene on both practical and ideological levels. Where leading figures of the late 1990s sought to negotiate with state institutions and forge discourses that were acceptable to officials and hip hoppers alike, Los Aldeanos took a distinct approach. Though they began by using the same routes as other underground groups, finding their feet in legitimate (if alternative) institutional spaces like La Madriguera and Parque Almendares, over time they started to follow an increasingly independent path, using different performance venues and digital technology to connect with a wider audience while reducing their reliance on cultural institutions and the media.[20] They became figureheads of two important tendencies of recent years: first, an increased belief in independence, as the AHS's abandonment of the festival and the bitter history of the ACR led to a loss of faith in state institutions; and second, the need to create a new public after the loss of much of hip hop's core audience from 2003 to 2006. Los Aldeanos began attracting increasing numbers of people who were not primarily hip hop fans, leading to greater social and racial diversity in the scene. Because their seven-year career to date exactly matches the span of my research (2003–10), and because they have become the most popular Cuban hip hop group since Orishas while retaining their place at the heart of the Havana scene, they loom large in the following pages.

The hip hop artists with most appeal in Havana at the time of writing, such as Los Aldeanos, Ogguere, Doble Filo, and El Adversario (in his guise as a sideman to X Alfonso, one of Cuba's most famous fusion musicians), are those who have reached out beyond the hip hop scene to the wider, more heterogeneous alternative-music public. While there are still some artists, activists, and intellectuals who maintain the Black August line of the late 1990s and early 2000s, describing Cuban hip hop as a distinct, coherent sociocultural movement with a strong racial character, a major shift has in fact occurred: many members of the new wave of artists and audiences are light-skinned and disconnected from any unifying hip hop ideology, and most of today's successful artists are closer to the culturally, racially, and politically diverse, almost amorphous, alternative-music sphere than to any supposed hip hop movement. The internationalist, race-based alliances of the Black August years have lost ground to more localized, race-blind interactions with the electronic dance-music and rock scenes, which are predominantly white. For example, the dance-music collective Matraka worked closely with La Comisión Depuradora and orga-nized the Puños Arriba hip hop awards in 2009 and 2010. Around 2000, the highlight of the summer for hip hoppers was the Havana hip hop festival at which local rappers, activists, and fans connected with their foreign counterparts; a decade later, it was Matraka's Rotilla Festival, a three-day beach party at which rappers shared top billing with dance-music DJs. At the *Cuerda Viva* awards ceremony in March 2009, the winners of the 2008 award for best rap demo, Los Aldeanos, handed over the prize to the 2009 victors, Doble Filo: three of the four rappers were light-skinned, as were Doble Filo's DJ (the drum 'n' bass specialist DJ Dark), most members of the rock band (Qva Libre) that collaborated in Doble Filo's performance, and most of the large alternative-music au-dience that cheered both rap groups to the rafters. Things had come a long way from Alamar a decade earlier. One of the aims of this book is to bring these newer but fundamental shifts to the foreground and thereby ad-vance the intellectual framing of Cuban hip hop, which is stuck in a groove laid down over a decade ago.

Representing Cuban Hip Hop

Enough already with your "I'm an anthropologist, I'm a professor,"
With your "Cuban rap has found what was lost in New York."
—RANDEE AKOZTA, "Basta ya" (enough already)

As journalists became a regular fixture at Havana rap festivals starting in 1997, articles on Cuban hip hop began to appear in foreign newspapers and hip hop magazines. Documentary makers from overseas were also drawn to the scene in the late 1990s, with Joe Wentrup's *Más voltaje, más volumen: rap en Cuba* (1997) the first of an extraordinary wave of film production. In the early 2000s, there were sometimes two or three film cameras running simultaneously at rap concerts, and more than two dozen documentaries have appeared to date. Academic researchers formed part of this wave of foreign interest: Deborah Pacini Hernandez and Reebee Garofalo (1999–2000) were first on the scene, and studies by Alan West-Durán (2004) and a number of doctoral students (M. Perry 2004; Fernandes 2006; Boudreault-Fournier 2008; Saunders 2008) soon followed, with further Ph.D. theses by Melisa Rivière and Marie Laure Geoffray close to completion at the time of this writing. All of this interest cemented Cuban hip hop studies as an academic field. These studies have been supplemented by numerous theses at the master's and undergraduate levels at North American universities. Foreign students have thus been a regular presence at Havana hip hop peñas for a decade, and such was the boom of interest that there were sometimes several papers on Cuban hip hop at a single U.S. scholarly conference. Rap did not attract nearly as much attention at home as abroad; although there have been valuable critical contributions by scholars such as Roberto Zurbano, Grisel Hernández, and Joaquín Borges-Triana, and articles by Cuban journalists and cultural commentators in national magazines and newspapers, the local scholarship is far outweighed by the global.[21]

I highlight this point because although I intend this book to be a further contribution to the growing canon on Cuban rap, I will also consider why there has been such an explosion of interest in Cuban hip hop, what forms the resulting documents have taken, and how they have impacted their object of study. To a much greater extent than earlier studies, then, I will focus on the generation of knowledge about Cuban urban music within national and international spheres. The degree of interest in the subject by foreign writers and filmmakers is out of all proportion to its role in the Cuban cultural scene: in terms of audiences and media space, rap has been utterly overshadowed first by timba (Cuban salsa) and then by reggaetón, yet these forms of commercial popular music, the most eagerly consumed by young Cubans, have received considerably less attention from overseas. Cuban rap has excited foreign imaginations in a way that no other musical form other than son—the sound of the BVSC—has done over the last two decades. The enthusiasm for rap and lack of curiosity about reggaetón are revealing of the scholarly agendas that dominate the academic study of popular music, which tend to give greater priority to logocentric, supposedly resistant, niche musical forms than to more widely consumed commercial dance genres (see Coplan 2005, 25).[22] While criticizing sins of omission is often facile, to write about hip hop in Havana in the early 2000s without discussing reggaetón is to present a very skewed picture of urban music. Until now, readers of Cuban hip hop scholarship in English have gotten little idea of the cataclysmic changes that took place in the rap scene during this period. Yet many leading reguetoneros learned their trade in the rap scene, and to relegate them to the margins of scholarly studies of rap or to omit them altogether is to reproduce the ideological position of Havana's underground hip hoppers—that reggaetón is best ignored or dismissed and that it has nothing to do with hip hop—rather than subject that position to the scrutiny that scholars' contributions should properly provide. There are, after all, other ways of looking at the subject: given the number of rappers who have switched styles, hip hop might be seen primarily as a stepping stone to reggaetón, paving the way for the next big musical wave after timba; or hip hop and reggaetón might be regarded as two sides of the same coin since both have deep roots in Jamaica and entail rapping over digitally produced instrumentals.

Underlying foreign representations of urban popular music in Havana and foreign fascination with hip hop is a sensibility that is almost the city's hallmark: nostalgia. Havana is a city in which time seems foregrounded: a "city that time forgot," preserved or merely surviving, full of relics of a past when Havana was the future. As Alexey's song "Como fue" reveals, nostalgia is not a foreign preserve; it is also closely tied both to music and to the rapid changes experienced by habaneros during the Special Period. It is so central to older Cubans' experiences of Havana that its absence provokes anxiety: the novelist Leonardo Padura Fuentes's critique of reggaetón centers on his nostalgia for musical genres capable of evoking nostalgia (see chapter 2). Hip hop, in contrast, is particularly backward-looking music, its spiritual home being 1970s New York, and many of the North Americans who started frequenting the Havana hip hop scene in the late 1990s were from its most nostalgic wing, the New York underground scene. "Como fue," a rose-tinted look to back in the day, synthesizes the nostalgic desires of locals and foreigners, hip hoppers and tourists: it historicizes relatively recent events (Alexey's dancing days were only a decade behind him) and carries the imprint of the late-1990s old-school revival in New York (discussed in chapter 4), even quoting the first U.S. rap hit, "Rapper's Delight." It has one foot in Havana and the other in New York hip hop—two spaces of nostalgia par excellence. A rather more acerbic view can be found in Randee Akozta's "Basta ya" ("Enough already . . . with your 'Cuban rap has found what was lost in New York'"), which suggests that Havana hip hoppers were well aware of the transnational imaginings and projections that focused on their scene, where foreign visitors turned "a loss in the space of the self into a recovery and a hope in the space of the other" (Medina 2007, 9; see chapter 4). Nostalgia has underpinned the interactions between North American and Cuban hip hop artists, activists, and intellectuals, and it has been a productive force on both sides of the Florida Straits, propelling artistic and political activity and generating numerous visual and verbal representations. It is thus an important frame of reference for understanding the body of knowledge produced about Havana hip hop, which has resulted from a confluence of nostalgic strands in music, politics, and scholarship.

There are many accounts of Havana hip hop already in existence—journalistic, academic, and audiovisual. Scholarly studies have focused on the emancipatory discourses of Cuban hip hop, particularly with regard to gender and race (see Armstead 2007 and Zurbano 2009, in addition to those listed above). If I do not discuss gender, it is because this aspect has been well covered by other writers. The topic of race, too, is well-trodden ground in Cuban hip hop scholarship, and thorough, broadly similar expositions can be found in most sources. In this case, I believe the consensus hides as much as it reveals and that a revisionist glance is worthwhile, one which I essay in chapter 4. Race has never been my main focus in researching Cuban hip hop, but questions have arisen as my project has developed. Having initially accepted the position set out in post-2000 academic studies, I found a much broader spectrum of responses to the issue of race than I had expected when I embarked on a series of interviews with hip hoppers in 2008. Not only had the number of light-skinned rappers mushroomed during the course of my research, but also various dark-skinned rappers—whose views I had long taken for granted—revealed skepticism about negritude in the Havana hip hop scene, either rejecting it themselves or questioning the sincerity of others. These responses led me to begin interrogating the academic consensus on race and to wonder whether I had not been the only one taking hip hoppers' views for granted. It seemed that, in promoting Cuban hip hop as an impetus for redefining or revolutionizing blackness in Cuba and as a standard-bearer for North American race studies, many scholars had ignored nuances, complications, and dissenting voices.

My aim is neither to repeat nor to synthesize this literature, but to treat it as part of my broad object of study: the production of knowledge through and around hip hop in Havana. I regard Havana hip hop as a field of debate and negotiation occupied not just by hip hoppers and Cuban state functionaries, but also by foreign activists, writers, and filmmakers. Observation and documentation are part of my story because they are part of the hip hop scene: as a group, we have had a significant influence on the development of that scene and—as Akozta's weary lines in "Basta ya" testify—we can no longer be airbrushed from the picture we create.

My aim in this analysis is to illustrate the importance of foreign, and above all North American, interventions in the construction of Cuban hip hop and to suggest that without these interventions (artistic, activist, and academic), driven by nostalgia for what U.S. hip hop once promised to be and by a particularly North American interest in issues of race, Cuban hip hop might have been a less significant cultural phenomenon than it was on both national and international levels. There may be an interesting story about globalization to be found here: many positive accounts stress local inventiveness in adopting and adapting globally circulating cultural forms, but while Cuban hip hop undoubtedly shows the same, it is also notable that the commonly accepted rise and fall of the Havana scene closely mirrors the ebb and flow of North American interest and presence, which peaked around 2000. In some respects, the blossoming of hip hop in Havana reflects as much a North American urge to find its "not-Us" (not U.S.?) outside its own borders as a Cuban creative reworking. I would also argue that a somewhat hyperbolic tendency in foreign representations of Cuban hip hop has contributed to its success at home and abroad. Robin Moore (1997) has shown how international fascination with Afro-Cuban music in the 1920s and 1930s helped to consolidate its place on the national stage, and there is plenty of evidence that the influx of foreign artists, activists, journalists, scholars, and film-makers in the late 1990s and early 2000s contributed to a sense among Cuban cultural officials and hip hoppers themselves that Cuban rap should be taken seriously.

When anthropologists start not only to feature in local rap lyrics but also to provoke exasperation and when Havana hip hoppers know their foreign counterparts' lines by heart, the symbiotic relationship between academia, activism, and hip hop demands attention. As Murray Forman (2004, 3–4) argues, "research and writing, whether in journalistic or aca-demic contexts, is absolutely part of the wider hip-hop culture," and this is particularly true in the construction of the Havana scene. Foreign docu-menters have been a constant presence there since 1997, and Cuban hip hoppers read articles about themselves, watch documentaries about themselves, and listen to talks at colloquia about themselves. Foreign film-makers and writers have become prime conduits for material resources and overseas travel; we have played an important role in mediating the economic, cultural, and human flows in and out of the Havana scene, transforming it with our purchases, donations, and invitations, and repre-senting it overseas through film screenings and conferences. I thus con-sider researchers and documenters as a subset of the overseas visitors who have been a visible and significant part of the Havana hip hop scene since the late 1990s and have shaped its trajectory and (self-)representation in important ways. While a transnational lens is more or less inevitable in analyzing global hip hop, I am interested not just in the somewhat disem-bodied flows of music and political inspiration but particularly in the physical presence of significant numbers of foreign individuals within the Havana scene, the influence that they have wielded, and their promotion of this scene within and outside the island. In 2008 there was arguably a more coherent "hip hop movement" at Tanya Saunders's El Proyecto event at Lehigh University, Pennsylvania, which brought together émigré Cuban hip hoppers living in the United States and Europe for talks, panels, and a concert, than in Havana itself. Melisa Rivière, another Ph.D. candidate, has managed leading groups Los Aldeanos, Silvito "El Libre," Doble Filo, and Escuadrón Patriota, and she has filmed music videos for Anónimo Consejo and Obsesion. And lest I seem to be washing my hands of the subject, a Cuban rapper defected at an event that I organized in London in 2007. The line between Havana hip hop and researchers from overseas is thus all but nonexistent.

In Los Paisanos' song "Hace tiempo ya," Mr. Huevo raps that "hip hop is created in the streets, not in universities." There is an occasional air of skepticism around the mix of academia and Cuban hip hop: sometimes from Cuban intellectuals (for whom the proliferation of foreign-produced studies can be a source of suspicion), sometimes from rappers (who can feel sidelined by the intellectual activity around the scene), and sometimes from foreign activists (who feel that their grass-roots movement has been hijacked by pointy-headed outsiders). However, critical reflection and intellectual discussion have not been tacked on to Cuban hip hop, but have long been part of it. Knowledge, sometimes referred to as the "fifth element" of hip hop, is particularly important in Havana. Key figures in the hip hop scene such as Pablo Herrera and Roberto Zurbano are academics and have produced scholarly texts on the subject. It was at the University of Havana that Herrera met Pionero Pando, a connection that catalyzed the creation of Orishas, and his experience as a university teacher informed his role as mentor to many leading groups in Havana. The knowledge that he brought came from reading about U.S. hip hop— book learning as much as street knowledge.

Others, such as Ariel Fernández and Rodolfo Rensoli, are perhaps closer to the idea of the organic intellectual. The former, a DJ and promoter, is credited with using his writings to sway the Cuban intellectual and political establishment in favor of rap, and he edited *Movimiento* magazine, with its strong presence of analytical articles by cultural critics and scholars such as Raquel Z. Rivera and Tomás Fernández Robaina. His own contributions to the magazine often stressed the importance of critical, theoretical, and intellectual debate, and he has also spoken at a number of U.S. universities since moving to New York in 2005. More recently, El B and Escuadrón Patriota, two leading voices in the rap scene, told me of the influence on their art of their university studies in psychology. With colloquia, generally lasting two to three days, long forming

Randee Akozta performing in London. Photo by Alex Lloyd.

part of Havana hip hop festivals and symposia, there has been considerable give and take between the intellectual sphere and the Havana scene.

Cuban hip hop may not have been created in universities, but it has
received sustenance there. In recent years, its presence on the international scene has taken place to a significant degree in and via universities:
several events involving Cuban rap artists from the island and the diaspora
have been organized and funded by universities in North America and the
United Kingdom, and the makers of Cuban rap documentaries have priori-
tized universities for their screening tours, illustrating the role of these
institutions as a cradle of alternative cultural, social, and political ideas.
Indeed, for all Randee Akozta and Mr. Huevo's skepticism about profes-
sors and universities, all three artistic invitations to North America and
Europe that they received between 2006 and 2008 were to participate in
university events. Foreign intellectuals have opened doors for Cuban hip
hop and are partners in maintaining its profile in the diaspora.[23]

Havana Hip Hop Outside In and Inside Out

Although the insider-outsider dichotomy is overly stark when dealing with a globalized cultural form like hip hop—especially in the case of the Havana scene, where foreigners have been protagonists—I still regard myself primarily as an outsider: having learned my moves on the (cobbled) streets of Oxford, hip hop concerts were hardly my natural habitat. I am multiply "outside": not Cuban, not even North American (which would be second best, given hip hop's roots); not black or dark-skinned (and therefore something of an interloper, if descriptions of Havana hip hop as a "black space" are taken at face value); not a hip hop head. Certainly I have acquired knowledge, experience, and friendships over seven years that blur this distinction considerably, but this book is a critical analysis of urban music in Havana, not a celebration or a fan's-eye view.

This places me outside the main current of the production of knowledge about Cuban hip hop. As discussed above, the line between those documenting the Havana scene and the scene itself is often blurred or nonexistent; many of those from overseas are artists and/or activists in the spheres of hip hop and identity politics, while Cuban hip hop figureheads such as Pablo Herrera and Ariel Fernández have written their own accounts. This predominance of visions of Cuban hip hop by individuals with some claim to insider status or with activist intentions has had both positive and negative effects: there are undoubtedly facets of Havana hip hop that are more comprehensible to such observers, many of whom have also helped to raise the profile and prestige of the scene; but equally, outsiders are less susceptible to the "curse of fandom"—the risk that "the commitment of (adherence of? advocacy of?) the scholar to 'values' (apparently) inhering in that of which they are writing" (Maxwell 2002, 109) may overshadow the analysis of those values and the context in which they are found. An activist approach brings the possibility of a positive impact on the object of study, and indeed on wider society, while simultaneously rendering the scholarly assessment of both object and impact more challenging. Roberto Zurbano, one of the most perceptive observers of Havana's hip hop scene and a figure of some importance in its history, considers the sympathy for Cuban hip hop on the part of foreign writers and filmmakers as a complicating factor in attempts to document and analyze it; the desire to construct the Havana scene as a movement and to see it thrive have led, in his eyes, to mythification, elision, and to a theoretical disconnect from local realities. Ariel Fernández, an even more central figure, stressed to me the importance of remaining neutral, of observing without romanticism, in order to understand Cuban hip hop.

In an insightful article, Raquel Z. Rivera coins the term "liberation mythologies" in her discussion of the symbolic strategies of African descendants in the Americas: "My understanding of these liberation myths draws from Robert Segal's. . . . definition of myth as a story that may or may not be true. However, what makes 'liberation myths' different from just plain 'myths' is that their purpose is both to describe the world *and* to change it—change, in turn, is defined in terms of personal and collective liberation from oppression, injustice, sadness and/or fear. In other words, the goal of this myth-making is redemption—individual and collective."[24] It is not hard to see how such liberation mythologies might be a powerful resource for artists and activists; what is less clear is the place of myths and myth-making in academic research. Havana hip hop is built on its own freedom myths, which developed in dialogue with North American visitors and provided an impetus to continue in the face of material and political difficulties. The potential problem arises when those who document this scene are invested in these same myths. Liberation mythologies are, then, a double-edged sword in a context in which academia overlaps with art and activism. Rivera, both an artist and a scholar, skillfully negotiates this potential conflict through her reflexivity, managing both to deconstruct liberation mythology and to argue for its value. In Cuban hip hop studies, however, the merging of research and advocacy has led to the blurring of the line between reality and myth, and in some aspects academic studies now perpetuate the mythology rather than analyze it. The motivation may be progressive (as Rivera puts it, "the goal of this myth-making is redemption—individual and collective"), but the outcome is problematic. The mythology of the hip hop scene has become the cornerstone of academic studies, which have adopted hip hop discourses rather than examining them: Havana hip hop as a movement, as a black space, as built on Afro-Cuban music; underground and commercial as distinct and opposing faces of hip hop culture; and reggaetón as worthy of little comment, if any. I would suggest that scholars would do better to treat these myths as stories that may or may not be true and as ideologies that motivate artists in their cultural production or bolster their claims on external support rather than to regard them (and promote them) as incontrovertible fact. The urge to describe the world and to change it is compatible with scholarship, but it needs to be handled with great care if the desire for change is not to distort the description.

Given the timing of my arrival in the Havana hip hop scene, not being an insider was useful. I caught the Cuban hip hop bug in 2003 when I went to my first concert at La Madriguera and saw the Buena Vista rap duo Los Paisanos.[25] Had my research taken place five years earlier, this would have been a very different book because, as many people told me, I had missed the best bit. Everyone has a slightly different take on when that was, but most agree that I missed it. To make matters worse, my arrival coincided with the boom of reggaetón, which was (I was told repeatedly) unoriginal, simplistic, banal, repetitive, and coarse, the worst thing to happen to Cuban music in living memory. It was everywhere, and it seemed to be the reverse of everything that Cuban rap had stood for: morally, politically, and intellectually empty, committed only to ass shaking and money making. Reggaetón was seemingly crushing conscious rap under its fashionably shod heel, and rappers were starting to think about getting out, tempted by the chance to find fame and fortune at last through music via the new style, or to start a new life overseas. I had definitely missed the boat.

Los Paisanos on the steps of the Buena Vista Social Club. Photo by Alex Lloyd.

Except that people were talking about music a lot. As the euphoria of the last few years evaporated from the rap scene, the discussion switched back and forth from the past to the future: how had this come about, and what were they going to do about it? I had clearly arrived at something of a turning point—a turning for the worse, in the eyes of many, but far from boring. Hip hop insiders, with their investment in the idea of message rap, have been reluctant to address the shift from hip hop to reggaetón, but it did not bother me that I did not like reggaetón. When the Havana hip hop scene was turned inside out, it was easier not being on the inside.

This book reflects my experience as someone who may have missed the best part but who saw a lot of changes and debates. It presents a critical view of urban popular music in Havana: critical because I believe scholarship (like conscious hip hop) should challenge, disturb, and ask difficult questions, but also critical because that was the atmosphere in which I carried out my research. The Havana hip hop scene has, in some senses, been going through an extended crisis ever since I began to observe it. I witnessed and participated in many moments of joy, pleasure, and excitement, but I also saw a lot of disappointment, disillusionment, and defections. I am not writing to criticize or defend either of the genres that I discuss; however, the fact that Cuban hip hop has had most of the good press and reggaetón most of the bad leads me occasionally to question the cheerleading and the disrespecting. The Cuban hip hop studies canon is based primarily on research undertaken during the heyday of Cuban rap—roughly 1997–2003—during which time scholars took an optimistic view of rap's potential as a social force in Cuba. Much of their research predated or drew a veil over the genre's rapid eclipse by reggaetón and other significant developments, such as the divisive effects of the ACR, the disappearance of the annual rap festival, and the exodus of many rappers. Hip hop's subsequent dramatic decline and reggaetón's encroachment on its cultural space have rapidly dated earlier studies, demanding a revisionist analysis. Cuban hip hop studies are more than a decade old, and while they have produced much material of interest, there has been a marked lack of debate within the field. I aim to take a critical look at some of the fundamental assumptions on which these studies are built and question some of their central tropes and conclusions.

By taking a critical line, I also aim to take the baton from Ian Maxwell

(2002; 2003) and provoke further debate about academic research on global hip hop. In Havana, at least, the roles of reporter and advocate are already well filled by journalists, filmmakers, activists, and above all, hip hoppers themselves. Ethnographers may usefully occupy these roles in certain contexts, above all when giving a voice to those who do not have one; but when dealing with an area in which voices and opinions and explanations circulate widely and openly, then the authorial role is surely different. I would argue that, especially in a heavily documented field such as Cuban hip hop, academics' contribution should be more than to describe, flesh out, and give a scholarly stamp of approval to local hip hop discourses; the distinctive slant we may provide is to take a further step and subject those discourses to critical scrutiny. U.S. hip hop studies is a sophisticated field in which intellectuals recognize that taking hip hop seriously is not necessarily synonymous with striking an advocate's pose. Scholarship on global hip hop has sometimes fallen short by comparison.

Much of my critical analysis centers around language and text: in many ways, I see language as more important than music, not just in the obvious sense that Cuban hip hop's lyrics have had more impact than its musical developments, but in the sense that language has mediated the extraordinary success of Cuban hip hop, both domestically and internationally.[26] Like many other socialist countries (Verdery 1991), Cuba is a land where language plays a striking role; however, Cubans have a particular capacity for transforming words that might seem forced or artificial in the mouths of others into natural, everyday speech (Guillermoprieto 2005, 37–38). In the case of hip hop, this capacity enabled crucial discursive connections between cultural production and national ideology to be forged, and I focus on the vital role of a shared language in negotiations between Havana hip hoppers, state institutions, and international activists, and the resulting generation of policies and projects that shaped the course of the local scene. More recently, linguistic negotiation has turned increasingly to contestation: disputes over the meaning and ownership of key terms employed by the Cuban state—revolutionary, communism, counterrevolutionary, *gusano* (literally "worm," used to mean dissident or traitor)—have formed the ideological core of Los Aldeanos' hugely popular critical discourse.[27]

Nevertheless, as a card-carrying musicologist, I must give music at least a supporting role in my discussion. My focus will be not detailed musical analysis but broader debates over the politics of style within and around the rap and reggaetón scenes, as I analyze the ideological motiva- tions behind dominant discourses and their disconnect with realities on the ground. Many of those who have commented on Cuban hip hop have stressed musical indigenization. This has become a commonplace, re-peated sometimes unthinkingly and sometimes strategically. It was very important for gaining a space for hip hop on the local and international levels, and it reflected what many people wanted to hear, but that does not make it an accurate reflection of what was taking place, or of the views of most hip hoppers. The academic study of popular music is often driven by a search for and valorization of difference, which can lead to the dismissal of sameness. My focus is primarily on the broad features of the period 2004–10, in which the musical direction of the Havana hip hop scene was away from indigenization. It may be debated whether Cuban hip hop has gone forward, backward, or sideways in recent years, but however one views it, the evolutionary narrative has been thrown into doubt. Havana reggaetón, similarly, displays more complexity than a sim-ple adoption-adaptation model will allow. I will examine the widespread disinterest in Cubanized versions of global musical styles, shedding light on Cuban cultural politics and broader debates about localization and globalization.

Although my focus is firmly on Havana's urban music scenes, this is not a history of Havana hip hop or reggaetón; there are many people who know more about those subjects than I do. Where I hope to throw in my grain of sand, as the Cubans say, is in the field of cultural politics, since I have had access to a broad range of oral, recorded, and written sources, pro-duced both in Cuba and overseas, that provide insights into the represen-tation of and debates around hip hop and reggaetón. I will focus on the ways that the raw materials of these scenes have been transmuted into discourses, documents, and documentaries.

A question that I kept asking myself is: What makes Cuban hip hop distinctive? For me, the answer is not the genre's popularity in Cuba or its effect on national culture; a lack of media and music industry space has limited its spread and impact on the island, and in this respect Cuba cannot be compared to "big" hip hop nations like France or Brazil.[28] Rather, it is the relationship between hip hop and the Cuban state that I find unique and particularly compelling, as well as the distinctive New York–Havana relationship and international influence of the Havana scene. The issue of hip hop and the state has been addressed by scholars but insufficiently understood; it will therefore be the focus of chapter 1. I will move on to pay sustained attention in chapter 2 to reggaetón, the elephant in the corner of Cuban hip hop studies, which has at moments threatened to squash the life out of the Havana rap scene (though not the academic studies that thrive on it). Race has been a favored topic; space, on the other hand, has been pushed aside. Since hip hop is space music as well as race music (Forman 2002), I will recenter this question in chapter 3. Finally, in chapter 4 I will broaden the scope of my investigation from the local to the transnational, exploring the role of foreigners—particularly North Americans—in cementing and representing hip hop in Havana, and examining the relationship between global and local in the sphere of urban music.

I hope to reach beyond the sphere of Cuban urban music to readers with broader interests in Cuban culture and society and global hip hop. While this book may be seen as another step in mapping the global spread of hip hop culture (e.g., Mitchell 2001b), I hope it is more than that. Derek Pardue (2008, 10) notes that North Americans often regard hip hop outside the United States as derivative and therefore trivial. This is not the case with Cuban hip hop, even though Havana's actively participating hip hoppers numbered a tiny fraction of the 200,000 that Pardue estimates for São Paulo (ibid., 2). The importance of Cuban hip hop lies not in its size but in its disproportionate influence on transnational hip hop culture, activism, filmmaking, journalism, and scholarship. Noteworthy local versions of hip hop exist around the world, but Havana has the distinction of being a place where hip hop has been declared by North Americans themselves to be more authentic than in the United States—a root of hip hop as well as a branch, a source as well as a reflection—and thus a place to draw inspiration.

The idea of hip hop as Caribbean-derived culture is hardly new, and the role of Jamaica and Puerto Rico is recognized by most scholars and many fans. However, Cuba, the third country in the Caribbean trinity of hip hop, is rarely mentioned, even though the island's political ideologies and musical traditions have left their mark on hip hop at crucial moments. One of my aims in these pages is nothing less than a redefinition of hip hop as a cultural form that has been both shaped and reshaped by Cuban influences.

1

¡HIP HOP, REVOLUCIÓN!

Nationalizing Rap in Cuba

Hip hop is the inverse of capitalism,
Hip hop is the reverse of colonialism.
—GREG TATE

Ideas are our weapons.—BILLBOARD IN HAVANA

In "the village," waging my own Battle of Ideas.
—EL ALDEANO (the villager), "Noches perdidas"

In August 2004, shortly before the opening date of the Tenth Havana Hip Hop Festival, I spoke to Alpidio Alonso, president of the Asociación Hermanos Saíz (AHS), the cultural wing of the Union of Young Communists and the organization behind the festival. Alonso recounted the association's efforts to promote rap and enthused about the dialogue between rappers and their audiences, the "authenticity of their discourse," and the international importance of their concerns. Rap originated in the United States, he said, as a form of resistance to the dominant culture, conveying

"Ideas are our weapons." Photo by author.

a revolutionary social message. Similarly, at an earlier press conference he had described the aim of the festival as "to project a revolutionary message from Cuba, a commitment to the cause of the downtrodden in the world." Rap in Cuba, he told me, embodied a struggle to change the world through ideas and music, and since the island was a global figurehead in the sphere of critical debate, "it's very symbolic that this event takes place in Cuba, with rappers who come mainly from Latin America, from countries that are subject to this imperialist pseudo-cultural invasion."

As Alonso, a middle-aged bureaucrat from provincial Cuba, sat in his office talking up hip hop, an urban youth cultural form, I was struck by his use of language. His comments shed light on the question of how a musical form imported from Cuba's ideological archenemy, and usually characterized as either a celebration of individualism and materialism or protest music, was not only assimilated into national culture but, within a few years, came to be actively promoted by the Cuban Revolution. The state not only organized and financed the annual hip hop festival from 1997 to 2005, but it also supports two institutions which promote rap, the AHS and the Agencia Cubana de Rap (ACR). My intention here is to

examine how and why the state has become so quickly and deeply involved with rap music, to an apparently unique degree among governments. The time that elapsed between rap's first "official" appearance
(the 1995 festival) and the creation of the ACR was just seven years; rock
musicians, who had been fighting for cultural space since the 1960s, did
not receive their own agency until 2007, even though key officials like
Minister of Culture Abel Prieto and Vice Minister of Culture Fernando
Rojas—formerly president of the AHS—are if anything more sympathetic
to rock than rap.[1] I will focus in particular on the discursive strategies of
leading figures in the hip hop scene and officials like Alonso. The terrain
of language will be central to my discussion; it is here that crucial steps
were taken and key distinctions between rap and other musical forms lie.

The importance of examining discourses about music for understanding how musical styles are incorporated into constructions of national
culture and identity is underlined by Peter Wade (2000, 238) in his study
of Colombian popular music: "the success of Costeño [coastal] music lay in
great part in its multivocality, which meant it could be talked about productively by different people in many different ways. . . . When I say
productively, I mean that the music could be harnessed effectively to the
constitution of identity." In Cuba, I was frequently struck by the productive ways that people talked about rap, though it was the similarity between discourses that caught my attention. When I attended public events
like the rap festival colloquium—a lengthy annual event which illustrated
the importance of talking about rap in Cuba—I noticed a marked consistency in discussions of the relationship of hip hop to national culture and
ideology. Leading officials, spokespeople, commentators, and artists had
adopted a shared public position, and I was drawn to explore what lay
behind this "party line" on Cuban rap.

I aim to investigate the place that hip hop has gained in Cuban national
culture, to enquire into the institutionalization and nationalization of
rap, and to analyze the discourse of *rap cubano* articulated by rappers and
politicians alike.[2] Views on the institutionalization of Cuban rap are
widespread and diverse; discussions continue because the motivations
behind state policies are impossible to prove conclusively. Nevertheless,
the question that lies behind them—how and why the culture of the
enemy quickly came to form a part of national culture—is a vital one, and
the answers illuminate recent Cuban cultural policy.[3]

Scholars of Cuban hip hop have addressed the relationship between rappers and the state. Alan West-Durán (2004, 8) writes of Cuban rap in terms of "a politicization and mobilization that is not tied to the state or party ideology, even if many Cubans share the ideals expressed by these two official institutions. Cuban rappers are functioning as a countervailing voice and the government knows this, which is why since 1999 it has 'recognized' and tried to co-opt their activities and concerts." This analysis fails to account for the ideological connections between hip hop and the revolution, and it is symptomatic of a widespread view of rap as a resistant musical form and a target for co-optation by state institutions.

Sujatha Fernandes (2006, 118–19) contends that "the Cuban state . . . realizes that it can harness the energy of these rappers as a way of bolstering the image of Cuba as a mixed race nation with African roots" and that "the state has harnessed various sectors of the movement as a way of recapturing popular support in the special period." This interpretation is also problematic, not least because no evidence is provided to support it. At the time that the state began its involvement with rap in 1997, there were still widespread reservations about the validity of this "American music," so it is scarcely credible that any "attempt to reconstruct national unity" at a time when official anti-U.S. sentiment was high would have focused on such an ambiguous cultural symbol. Furthermore, given the Cuban government's "fear of a black nation," as Fernandes glosses it, it is unlikely that rap's nonconformist racial discourses, which challenged rather than bolstered the myth of racial democracy, held much appeal.

The idea that "the Cuban state realizes" anything, meanwhile, suggests a unity of purpose that has been distinctly lacking and glosses over the key question of precisely who was supposedly realizing, harnessing, and so on. The Cuban state cannot be regarded as a monolithic entity (Kapcia 2000; Askew 2002): it incorporates divergent ideological tendencies, and this lack of uniformity is reflected in its cultural policies, including those relating to rap. Fault lines in cultural politics have been exposed by the differing policies pursued simultaneously by the AHS and ACR, as well as contradictory resistance from the state-run media. Processes of cultural nationalization are carried out by human agents, not some kind of actorless hegemony, and much supposed appropriation or harnessing is carried out not by elite groups but by ordinary musicians and low- or medium-level intermediaries (Wade 2000, 11), resulting in nuances and inconsistencies.

Magia López, a rapper, is currently director of the ACR, and leading hip hoppers have worked within the AHS, the ACR, radio and television, and the print media—in other words, within the state.

A binary rappers versus the state model thus needs to be questioned, and along with it the notions of control, co-optation, appropriation, and harnessing that tend to dominate discussions of state–hip hop relations. There are three fundamental problems with this dichotomy. First, it implies a false ideological distinction. Hip hop and the Cuban state do not just share extensive ideological terrain but are, in a deep sense, coming from the same ideological place, as this chapter will explore. Second, it employs a singular noun—"state"—rather than the plural noun used in Cuba—"institutions." The latter usage reveals that the state is experienced as differentiated and multifaceted; each government institution has its own modus operandi. Third, it ignores the role of cultural intermediaries who are neither government functionaries nor hip hoppers—or, in some cases, both government functionaries and hip hoppers—in rap's assimilation into national culture. *Pace* West-Durán, the rap scene *has* been tied to state ideology through these intermediaries, whose aim has been to promote rap, not co-opt it.

The Intermediaries

The process of rapprochement between rappers and state representatives was initiated by articulate leaders of the hip hop scene, who underlined the history of Cuban assimilation of foreign culture and parallels between conscious rap and Cuban national ideology to shape a discourse that appealed to government officials, Cuban rappers, and foreign observers alike. Their motivation was to avoid the problems that had plagued rock for decades, and to open the door to state support. While hip hop has had a number of spokespersons and allies, three figures are widely viewed as having played the most significant part in negotiating a space for rap within Cuban national culture: Rodolfo Rensoli, Pablo Herrera, and Ariel Fernández.

Rodolfo Rensoli, the founder of Grupo Uno, took the first steps in the institutionalization of rap when he began organizing the annual hip hop festival in 1995. Two years later, he approached Roberto Zurbano—a writer and scholar who was then vice-president of the AHS—and proposed that the AHS collaborate in organizing the event. Rensoli already had experience of promoting alternative music in East Havana, an interest he shared with the AHS's president, Fernando Rojas, who was trying to create a space for rock at this time. Rojas and Zurbano looked into the idea but got a cold response from the Instituto Cubano de la Música and other institutions, so they decided to take it on themselves; they saw the AHS's role as working with sectors seen as problematic by other institutions (Zurbano 2009, 144). As Zurbano (n.d.a, 7) recalls, he and Rojas began "working in parallel, questioning, in different fields, solidified concepts of nation, national culture and cultural politics"; they mediated between artists, the upper levels of state bureaucracy, concert producers, and the press—explaining, pleading, even insulting, "glimpsing a utopian horizon, believing in the construction of a new culture." There are three key points here: first, the leading figure in the nascent rap scene approached a state organization for help, rather than the other way around; second, this first institutional step depended on a shared predisposition toward alternative, foreign culture (rather than a desire to contain it); and third, Zurbano and Rojas had to struggle against the preconceptions of less forward-thinking branches of the state apparatus. From the outset, then, notions of state co-optation of rap—or unified policy—need rethinking.[4]

Pablo Herrera (who now lives in the United Kingdom) is Cuba's most distinguished hip hop producer. As a poet and language teacher at the University of Havana, he first encountered Cuban rap via his student Joel Pando, director of the rap group Amenaza. Herrera went on to become Amenaza's manager and mentor; they parted ways when members of Amenaza departed for France and formed Orishas. Herrera devoted himself to making hip hop instrumentals and became Havana's rap producer of choice from 1999 to 2005. In the pivotal year of 1997, Herrera had called the AHS and suggested a meeting between rappers and visiting U.S. hip hop legend Fab 5 Freddy, illustrating the proactive role of intermediaries in the hip hop–state relationship (Zurbano 2009, 144). As a professional translator, Herrera was perfectly equipped for his role as a mediator within this transnational cultural sphere.

Ariel Fernández (now based in New York) is a DJ and journalist who became national hip hop promoter for the AHS. The pivotal figure in the hip hop scene of the early 2000s, he presented a weekly half-hour rap show, *La Esquina del Rap*, on Havana's Radio Metropolitana and created and hosted the national rap show *Microfonazo* in a slot provided by the AHS on Radio Progreso. He was also the founding editor of *Movimiento* magazine.

At La Madriguera, the headquarters of the Havana branch of the AHS, Fernández and his successors, Williams Figueredo and Jorge Enrique Rodríguez, bona fide members of the hip hop scene yet also state employees, contributed to hip hop's development from 2000 onward as rap promoters. Figueredo, who had a tendency to break into verse while I was interviewing him, would try to persuade the presenters of radio shows to announce forthcoming concerts, play a song, and perhaps interview a group. His open preference for critical, underground rap could be seen in the spaces he provided for some of the most challenging groups, like Explosión Suprema, Los Paisanos, Hermanos de Causa, and Los Aldeanos. As AHS rap promoter from 2002 to 2005 and subsequently a presenter on the radio show *La Esquina de Rap*, he has been a key point of contact

Rodolfo Rensoli. Photo by author.

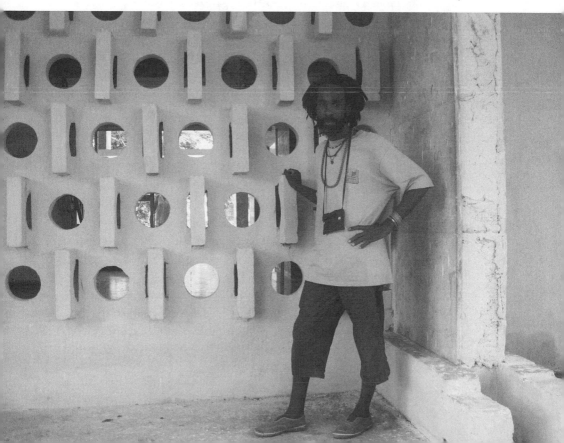

between the state and the rap scene, working within both spheres simultaneously. His successor, Rodríguez, moved on from promoting rap concerts at La Madriguera to working at the AHS national headquarters. Most recently, Rodríguez has been a key figure in negotiating the rehabilitation of Los Aldeanos under the auspices of the AHS after the duo was blacklisted by performance venues in 2009. The liminal, intermediary role of such AHS promoters is revealed in the following comments that one of them made to Laura García Freyre: "We deal more with the artists and the underground audience . . . sometimes we're the ones who discover talent in the street. I'm always involved in a series of independent, underground projects, in the street, apart from the institution of La Madriguera."[5]

The ambiguous roles of La Madriguera and the AHS will be a recurrent theme in these pages (see Baker 2011 for further discussion). Through the AHS, the state has provided free concert space, lighting, audio, and limited publicity for rap groups. If the development of Cuban rap has outstripped that of other countries in the region, the state must be given some credit. Many rappers see the AHS's involvement at least partially in positive terms and look back on the AHS-organized rap festivals as golden moments in the history of Cuban hip hop. The AHS has also helped rappers with the paperwork and institutional approval required for independent projects, such as the open-air rap peñas at 19 y 10 in Vedado. Its organization and promotion of performances by the outcast duo Los Aldeanos in 2010 is emblematic of its support for the hip hop scene at key moments. This support has been uneven, often full of contradictions and conflicts as personnel has changed, yet just as often, it has been a vital constituent part of the scene's greatest successes. The state–hip hop relationship cannot be understood without proper consideration of the role of the AHS, which might be regarded as an "intermediary institution," that is, part of the state, yet employing leading hip hop figures and being responsible for mediating between the hip hop scene and other government branches—at times creating spaces where none were to be found.

Several of these intermediaries have also taken an intellectual interest in hip hop. Fernández's (2000) article "Rap cubano: ¿Poesía urbana? O la nueva trova de los noventa" (Cuban rap: urban poetry? Or the *nueva trova* of the nineties) was a landmark attempt to promote hip hop among intellectual and government circles as a significant cultural phenomenon that could not be ignored by the state, while Herrera and Zurbano have contributed to academic debates on Cuban rap (e.g., Herrera and Selier 2003; Zurbano 2009). Herrera and Fernández, who played fundamental roles in mediating between the expectations of the state, rappers, and foreign observers, are both highly articulate and confident figures who forged links with senior figures in the AHS and the Ministry of Culture, worked with the ACR, and used their knowledge of Cuban cultural politics and global hip hop to shape a discourse which upheld both the aims of the Cuban Revolution and core values of underground hip hop. Crucially, they tried to legitimize rap cubano in the eyes of state institutions. Such proactive intermediaries have aimed to increase the space for Cuban hip hop by making it intelligible to cultural officials, and they have been prepared to argue hard when necessary; many outside Cuba—and even inside—are unaware just how fierce debates over culture may become behind closed institutional doors. A focus on these figures and processes reveals the limited relevance of the idea of state co-optation, and if there was any harnessing taking place, it was primarily by these intermediaries, who brought hip hop and the state together and fed Alonso the lines about hip hop and revolution that he recited in August 2004.

Havana: The New (Old?) South Bronx

Much of the work done by these intermediaries was discursive: it centered on framing hip hop in productive ways. Two potential stumbling blocks to the acceptance of rap in Cuba were the ostentatious commercialism and materialism of much U.S. hip hop and its very North American-ness. With respect to the former, rap's spokespeople drew on the reactions of foreign observers to characterize the Havana scene as an old-school, underground movement harking back to hip hop's origins in the South Bronx of New York City. They explicitly distanced Cuban rap from the material impulses so dominant in its contemporary U.S. counterpart: both Herrera and Fernández claimed that Cuban rappers would rather forgo commercial success than sell out (Foehr 2001, 21, 41)—views that were somewhat undermined by subsequent events. Certain features of the Havana rap scene that could have been regarded negatively, such as a paucity of commercial opportunities and material resources, were thus redefined as indicators of authenticity, an old-school vibe, and indeed of the moral superiority of the Cuban offspring to its degenerate North American parent. The discursive construction of the Havana scene as the new (or old) South Bronx—stressing, rather than downplaying, the New York connection—paradoxically facilitated the nationalization of rap; by linking Cuban rappers to hip hop's past rather than its present, intermediaries removed the stigma of commercialism and materialism and conferred a hyperauthenticity that appealed to both Cuban officials and foreign visitors.

Ariel Fernández has played a pivotal role in underlining connections between old-school U.S. and Cuban rap, steering the Havana scene by educating artists, listeners, and readers about the roots of hip hop via his work as a DJ, radio presenter, journalist, and editor of *Movimiento*. Four of the first five editions of *Movimiento* begin with articles about the history of rap in the United States, focusing on the birth of the genre in the 1970s and its politicization in the 1980s; conspicuously lacking are any references to the 1990s, when rap became a huge commercial success, or to mainstream U.S. hip hop in the 2000s. Other articles concentrate on old-school or conscious U.S. rappers like KRS-One, The Roots, and dead prez. A number of Cuban commentators have followed Fernández's line and concluded that Cuba's hip hop scene is not merely authentic but—as the guardian of the original spirit of hip hop which U.S. rappers have largely abandoned (e.g., del Río 2002)—more authentic than the original.[15] This allows a simultaneous connection with U.S. hip hop, the ultimate benchmark, yet also distancing from it, necessary for insertion into nationalist cultural politics.

In order for this imagined reversal to take on full legitimacy, another important element was necessary: the consent of informed U.S. observers to the characterization of Havana as the new home of old-school hip hop. This consent was achieved in considerable measure due to the efforts of Nehanda Abiodun, a U.S. citizen and former black liberation fighter living in exile in Havana. Abiodun, often described as a godmother to the Havana scene, mediated with government officials, using her authority as a revolutionary exile to argue the case for rap as a tool in the service of the revolution. She also forged vital transnational links: in 1998, the Black August Hip Hop Collective was formed out of conversations between Abiodun and hip hop journalists and activists in New York. Thanks to their efforts, leading U.S. conscious rappers were invited to perform at the Havana hip hop festival, and these artists and activists enthusiastically endorsed the local scene. Thus the development of Cuba's old-school, revolutionary rap discourse was cemented by a dialogue be

Nehanda Abiodun speaking at the Hip Hop Symposium in 2008. Photo by author.

tween Havana spokespeople and an exiled American, a New York–based collective, and visiting U.S. rappers: the central role of both Cuban and American intermediaries reveals a much more complex process than state appropriation.

The extraordinary interest provoked by the Havana scene raised Cubans' sense of pride in local hip hop. A meeting in 2002 between leading Havana hip hoppers and a visiting delegation—including the activists and actors Harry Belafonte and Danny Glover—is highly illuminating for the praise showered on Cuban hip hop by these distinguished American guests and the intense pride of their local hosts ("Encuentro entre amigos" n.d.). Ariel Fernández suggests that the Cuban rap movement is "one of the most critical in the world, perhaps, because of the influence of the social and political system that it has developed" (ibid., 22). Sekou of Anónimo Consejo claims that "many people overseas think that our rap is the kind of rap which the U.S. needs, since it has been overcommercialized there" (ibid., 20). He goes on: "What is happening in the U.S. is what we don't want to happen here." Kokino (Anónimo Consejo) thanks the American visitors for their support, adding: "It gives us strength to know that we're not alone in this struggle and that there are other people in the world who are as committed as we are" (ibid.)—an extraordinary statement about a recently imported culture.

Elsewhere, Kokino speaks of the high level of Cuban lyrics in comparison with those of other Latin American countries, claiming that "nobody can compare with us." He goes on: "Cuba is one of the Spanish-speaking countries with the highest cultural level and the richest language. Many Latin American rappers are just copying the Americans, with their lyrics about drugs, violence, material things. You've really got to search to find a positive lyric in Latin American hip hop. I think that, because Cuba is a country of revolution and struggle, you can see positive messages reflected in our lyrics. It's because of that that many people see us as the roots of hip hop that have been lost in the United States" (quoted in A. Fernández n.d., 9). This sense of pride and even superiority has been voiced by other rappers, Cuban journalists, and cultural spokespeople (e.g., Henríquez Lagarde 2002; Zamora Céspedes n.d.). Throughout the interviews in the first five editions of *Movimiento*, one finds this view that Cuban rap is a model for the rest of Latin America to follow.

In this respect, it is fascinating to compare the Havana rap scene with others, such as those in Tokyo, Sydney, or London (Condry 2006; Maxwell 2003; Hesmondhalgh and Melville 2001). While hip hop has flourished around the world, there are few if any places other than Cuba where the adopting country sees itself as the true inheritor and guardian and as the savior of U.S. rap from itself. Global rappers have struggled against perceptions that they are pale imitations of their U.S. counterparts, and their contortions to authenticate local hip hop practices contrast with the proudly projected hyperauthenticity of Cuban rap. This transformation of rap into a productive symbol of Cuban identity and cultural life is particularly remarkable considering the famously antagonistic relationship between the music's country of origin and its new context.

As far as the issue of North American roots is concerned, there are two main discursive strategies, both employed by Ariel Fernández. The first is to play down the American roots of rap in favor of the African (A. Fernández 2000, 5). The second places rap within the broader context of twentieth-century Cuban culture, underlining Cuba's historical capacity for incorporating and transforming North American cultural forms. In his editorial on the inside front cover of the first edition of *Movimiento*, Fernández describes transculturation as an inherently Cuban process: "The mestizo, emancipatory character which is at the root of Cuban culture and our position as an island mean that everything that reaches our shores ends up being appropriated, recreated, transculturated, as Fernando Ortíz would have wisely put it. This is what is happening right now, in Cuba, with hip hop culture. . . . It happened before with baseball, jazz and rock, and now it's the turn of hip hop." So the music may not be Cuban, but the way of processing it is. By presenting young Cubans' enthusiasm for hip hop as the latest stage in a century-long process of Cubanization of U.S. culture, Fernández played a key role in the discursive nationalization of rap.

Cuban Rap: The Nueva Trova of the 1990s

Aside from defining their relationship with U.S. culture, a contentious topic in Cuba, hip hoppers and their spokespeople also faced a more domestic problem: the need to justify the inclusion of protest music in Cuban culture and society. A key strategy was to highlight the theme of constructive criticism. This notion, crucial to acceptance by the state, dates back to Castro's statement in his 1961 *Words to the Intellectuals*: "Inside the revolution, everything; outside the revolution, nothing."[6] By emphasizing that rap works within the revolution, these intermediaries sought to find a space for critical rap that was nevertheless legitimated by the state. Herrera told Stephen Foehr (2001, 13–16): "Hip-hop artists are a major challenge to the social and cultural structures, so as to make them better. . . . What they are implementing is the evolution of the 1959 Revolution. It's almost the same ideological agenda as Castro's Revolution, but the next step. . . . we as black youth can participate constructively and positively in the development of our society and our nation, 'positively' and 'constructively' meaning that, if the Revolution is in place and has given us proof that it's valid and worthwhile, then we should devote ourselves to making it better, to making it greater. Not to make it die, but to make it flourish."

Herrera has made similar statements in many interviews (e.g., Pacini Hernandez and Garofalo 1999–2000, 38; Robinson 2004, 121), reinforcing the critical aspect of hip hop as popular participation in improving, not challenging, the revolutionary process. Fernández, meanwhile, told the journalist Eugene Robinson (2004, 118): "This is a cultural movement that focuses its message on improving the nation's social health. The rappers are not trying to escape from society's problems, they're trying to solve them."[7] This constructive line is echoed by other hip hoppers (Pacini Hernandez and Garofalo 1999–2000, 31–32); as Mano Armada proclaim in "Rap del bueno":

> My rap is conscious, constructive, radical,
> Rap with progressive aims, the objective is to revolutionize.

In "El juicio," Los Aldeanos claim of hip hop that

> Its mission is not to destroy but construct,
> To construct a better future.[8]

Gaining a space for rap, then, did not involve curbing its protest aspect. In her classic study, Tricia Rose (1994, 102) writes: "Rap music, more than any other contemporary form of black cultural expression, articulates the chasm between black urban lived experience and dominant, 'legitimate' (e.g., neoliberal) ideology." Cuban rappers, too, expose the gap between official discourses and lived experience: broadly speaking, this is acceptable as long as the gap is being criticized, rather than the discourses. Many interpret constructive criticism as the right to demand that state representatives strive to achieve the goals of the revolution, as praising its ideals but criticizing its practices.[9] With the radical upheavals that have affected Cuba since the early 1990s, there are plentiful opportunities to be critical, but this should not be confused with dissidence. As Ariel Fernández said in his talk at the Lehigh University El Proyecto event in 2008, the aim of Cuban hip hoppers was never to subvert the system, but to remind the government about living up to its promises and principles. The most radical and popular artists in Havana in the last few years, such as La Comisión Depuradora, display a kind of "revolutionary fundamentalism" in their attacks on inequalities, special privileges, materialism, and the decline in solidarity. As James Scott (1990, 105–6) notes in his study of the "arts of resistance," elites are vulnerable precisely in the areas in which they make the rules: an examination of the most hard-core Cuban rap groups illustrates his contention that "many radical attacks originate in critiques within the hegemony—in taking the values of ruling elites seriously, while claiming that they (the elites) do not." Castro's line "inside the revolution, everything; outside the revolution, nothing" therefore opens up more critical space than might at first appear.

Escuadrón Patriota and El Aldeano, in the introduction to "Resurrepción," state: "Freedom of expression, Article 53 of *your* Constitution. We have to say what we have to say," thus placing their scalding lyrics within the legal framework of the state.[10] In "Ya nos cansamos" (we're fed up now), Los Aldeanos ask: "So what's up, where's the equality?":

> We're always being told that we're equal
> That even generals get hit when a building collapses.
> Of course all the hospitals are free in Cuba
> But who do they treat better, me or the officials?

El B ("La ganga") takes this strategy of challenging the government on its own turf to extremes, pinpointing two areas that even the revolution's critics acknowledge as strengths: education and health. He raps:

> The minister of education was an asshole, people.
> Any trainee teacher could have told you that.
> I'm aware that no one is perfect, sure,
> But I can't accept being represented by a born idiot.

As a trainee teacher himself, El B's criticisms of the education system here and in "Niñito cubano" carry weight. The result of Cuba's much-vaunted education? "Every day the picture is the same / A country full of graduates pestering tourists." As for health:

> They always bang on about medical achievements, OK.
> Take a turn around the clinic on 26 Street,
> And you'll see quite the opposite.
> Your stay will be a short one because you'll be on your way to the
>   undertaker's.

Referring to Cuba's exchange programs with Venezuela, he raps:

> Free education and medical capacity, yes.
> We've got good doctors, but none of them are here.

Gaps between rhetoric and reality are a prime target for underground rappers. "Vamos bien" (we're going well) proclaim billboards across Havana; "we're going well . . . just backwards, like a crab," raps El Aldeano in "Veneno."

Critical rap may be seen as part of a recent "revival of moralism," a "back to basics" ethos recapturing the committed political rhetoric of the

1960s (Kapcia 2000, 241). Rappers do not simply criticize state representatives like the police, they also attack increasing individualism and materialism in the general population. El Aldeano's song "Miseria humana" blames his fellow habaneros for destroying civic culture by robbing, lying, and mistreating each other: "There are many people here in Havana infected with the virus of human misery." For him, "it's more a matter of the heart than of the government." Much recent rap can be viewed as efforts to correct the course of Cuban society and laments for the deterioration of its high ideals rather than attempts to undermine them; in "Honesto," El Aldeano portrays the rapper as the last bastion of honesty and morality in Cuban society. Like the political slogans on billboards across Havana, rappers exhort Cubans to stand firm at a time when the absolute truths of the revolution, its moral clarity and certainty, are under intense pressure from the forces of neoliberal globalization.

This critique of the revolution by focusing on its principles can also be seen in young people's revived interest in Che Guevara. Che is a hallowed, state-sanctioned figure, yet also a symbol of an early, idealistic stage of the revolution, untarnished by the difficulties of the Special Period; identifying with Che's image or words is a means of articulating both commitment and dissent, a kind of "safe radicalism" (Kapcia 2000, 212). This clearly overlaps with the constructive criticism of rappers; indeed, the figure of Che is ubiquitous in the rap scene, worn on T-shirts and praised in the lyrics of even the most confrontational rappers. Papá Humbertico ("Vivencias") declares:

> On the wall of my room hangs a picture of Che Guevara.
> His image is also in my wallet; he's not God but his ideals protect me.

Los Paisanos incorporate Che's slogan "Hasta la victoria siempre" in the chorus of their song "Hace tiempo ya"; a poster of Che with the word *guerrillero* (guerrilla) was prominently displayed on stage at a concert at La Madriguera; and both members of the leading group Anónimo Consejo have Che tattoos. Aldo's Che tattoo provides a striking reinterpretation of this core revolutionary symbol: Che is shown vomiting Cuba, literally unable to stomach the direction that his adopted country took after his death. Other earlier heroes are also held up as role models. Aldo claims in "Aldito el guzanito" that Camilo Cienfuegos (not Castro) is his commander in chief, while in "Los Aldeanos," he imagines going to heaven, where:

I'll ask after Camilo and Martí,
And I'll tell them about all the injustices I've seen here.[11]

Indeed, there are more than a few parallels between the way that rappers perceive themselves and Che's *hombre nuevo* (new man).[12] Explicit and positive references to the hombre nuevo can be heard in "Fuego" (El Aldeano and Escuadrón Patriota) and "Interlude" (Los Aldeanos). Rappers might be seen as a kind of *hombre nuevísimo* for the new millennium.[13] By aligning themselves with Che and describing Cuban rap in terms of constructive radicalism, rappers and intermediaries succeed in framing their music simultaneously within the paradigms of state ideology, youthful dissent, and conscious hip hop.

As any criticism which can be presented as aiming to improve the revolution is theoretically acceptable, a distinction cannot be made between those who criticize and those who support the state and its policies: publicly, at least, most rappers do both. As Alpidio Alonso revealed: "The preoccupations that the rappers demonstrate are in line with the sense of justice of the Revolution. The Revolution was born to eliminate racial discrimination and it's important that the rappers are concerned about these kinds of prejudices which still continue. . . . The Revolution provides this kind of space [for expression]" (Henríquez Lagarde 2002). Rather than ruling out criticism, Alonso inscribes the act of criticism itself within the revolutionary project, a theme echoed by Ariel Fernández (*East of Havana* n.d., 53): "it is known that here in Cuba we have a history of rebellion. Of combating things that are wrong. Of criticizing negative things." He neatly positions rebelliousness and critique within a nationalist frame. El Enano ("Que sería") asks simply: "What would revolution be without rebelliousness?" Thinking of Wade's "multivocality," words like "rebellion" and "revolution" are particularly malleable within the context of the Cuban Revolution, since they embrace both the status quo and challenges to it.[14] El B ends "La ganga" with a monologue: "don't have a go at me, I'm still here, I didn't leave when I had the chance, rather than getting out and talking shit about my country I'd rather carry on here being the voice of the silence of the lambs. Motherland or death! We will overcome!" In a neat twist, El B presents his trenchant criticism as an act of patriotism, ending with Fidel's signature finale (*¡Patria o muerte! ¡Venceremos!*).

If criticism is a revolutionary act, rappers may therefore be seen as a vanguard of the revolutionary process rather than dissidents. When Los Aldeanos were blacklisted in mid-2009 amid allegations that they had crossed the line between criticism and opposition, they responded by releasing two albums, Aldo's *Nos Achicharraron* and El B's *Viva Cuba Libre* in which they faced these accusations head-on and threw them back at their accusers. In "Aldito el guzanito," Aldo responds to the idea that he is a *gusano* (literally a worm, meaning a dissident or traitor) by constructing a song around the phrase "I would be a gusano if I . . .". He begins:

> I would be a gusano if I took advantage
> Of a supposed position and robbed my people,
> If I repressed and silenced a whole generation
> And cut off at their base the wings of their imagination.

He turns the tables on the government, suggesting that treachery lies in the actions of state officials rather than the words of critical artists. He ends with "you're the gusano, my brother, so stop disrespecting me."

This strategy of contesting accusations by seizing the revolutionary high ground is taken even further in songs from El B's album. The intro is recorded in a muffled, faraway sound that evokes historical recordings of Fidel's early speeches. Between claiming that Camilo Cienfuegos is his commander-in-chief and invoking the memory of Maceo and Martí, he states that "this goes out for the revolutionary consciousness that has died out" and "the revolution begins now." The key track, however, is "Contrarevolucionario" (counterrevolutionary), in which El B echoes Aldo in taking an accusation and throwing it back in the face of the government, claiming to be the true heir of the 1959 revolution. The rapper stresses his revolutionary lineage: "I'm not a problem, I'm the result of your experiment," and "I defend my ideals, does that surprise you? / I act according to reality, like you more than fifty years ago." He concludes: "I haven't broken any laws or violated any regulations / You're the counterrevolutionaries along with all your lies."

This kind of dispute over the meaning of key revolutionary terms and the power to assign labels is typical of Los Aldeanos' work. In "El chico pillo," El Aldeano asks:

> I want to know what's the basis of communism:
> Is it equality or keeping the best for tourists?

Similarly, in "Tiranosaurio" he raps:

> I want to know what solidarity means:
> I think it's sharing a little bit with someone who needs it,
> Not taking with one hand to give with the other
> Or putting up foreigners in hotels and locals in temporary
> accommodation.

El B states in "Aclaración" that his aim is "to awake a revolutionary consciousness that is held back and repressed by false doctrines and obsolete methods," and he claims "there is a big contradiction between what revolution is said to be and what it really means." The rapper sets himself up as a higher authority on the subject of revolution. One of his most daring moves is to appropriate Fidel's iconic slogans. In "Viva Cuba Libre," he borrows "revolution is to change everything that needs to be changed." In "Declaración," he signs off with

> Long live free Cuba! I don't have a reverse gear.
> Condemn me. It doesn't matter. History will absolve me.

This last line is a quotation from Castro's 1953 speech in court after he had led an attack on the Moncada barracks. Since Fidel used his speech to criticize the dictatorship of Fulgencio Batista, El B, by putting himself in Castro's shoes is thus implicitly putting Castro in Batista's. To appropriate such a foundational moment of Cuban revolutionary history is a bold move indeed.

Los Aldeanos' work depends on the distinction, whether implicit or explicit, between criticism and opposition; and their repeated rejection of the latter label rests in turn on a discourse that is hyper-revolutionary rather than counterrevolutionary. They consistently seize the revolutionary initiative rather than contesting its ideological basis; they challenge their listeners not to overturn the revolution but to revitalize it by taking it back to first principles. The constructive criticism or hyper-revolution lines, while sometimes shifting rappers offside, open up space for a surprising degree of outspokenness in Cuban hip hop.

In forging a space for protest music in the 1990s, hip hoppers were able to draw on lessons learned nearly three decades earlier by the musicians of the Cuban nueva trova movement. Initially there was considerable official suspicion toward this music, a local manifestation of the Latin American *nueva canción* (new song) which started out as an underground movement in the late 1960s (just like rap in the early 1990s), and musicians had to thrash out the relationship between protest song and the revolution (R. Moore 2003). The turning point came when nueva trova received the backing of the Union of Young Communists (UJC), which recognized its appeal to youth and invested in equipment and organized festivals (Foehr 2001, 48–50). There are clear parallels with the role of the UJC-backed AHS in the institutionalization of rap a quarter-century later; indeed, the Movimiento de la Nueva Trova was incorporated into the newly founded AHS in 1986. Herrera comments: "The hip-hop generation could be the second wave of the Revolution that was started rolling by the *nueva trova* movement in the early 1970s," while Fernández claimed that the founders of nueva trova "showed the direction for how to make revolution with the music" (quoted in ibid., 22, 35). This parallel was the bedrock of Fernández's groundbreaking article in 2000, which was in fact prophetic: a few years later, Silvito "El Libre"—son of none other than the greatest *nuevo trovador* of them all, Silvio Rodríguez—would emerge as one of the leading voices in La Comisión Depuradora. El Libre's first demo, titled *Conceptos y principios* (ideas and principles), is a perfect illustration of the intensely moralistic line that many underground Cuban rappers have taken, with its insistence on honesty and honor, and its biting critiques of a society in which "ethics and values have shattered into tiny pieces" ("Mi sociedad"). The rap–nueva trova parallel is repeatedly articulated by rappers in interviews and songs: this analogy clearly provides a useful tool for clearing a space for rap in national culture. By emphasizing continuities with the musical developments and cultural politics of the revolution, hip hoppers claim a legitimate place for their art while defending their right to voice criticisms.

"¡Hip Hop, Revolución!"

If the efforts of key intermediaries to attract support from the state revolved around framing hip hop within established notions of national culture and ideology, it was equally important to ground the idea of rap as a positive force for change and as revolutionary culture among rappers

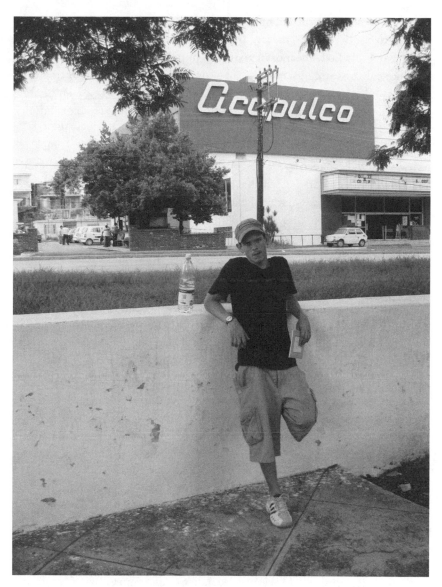

Silvito "El Libre" Rodríguez. Photo by author.

themselves. Cuban rap did not start out as a beacon of conscious rap, as it came to be portrayed in the late 1990s, much less as a hyper-revolutionary discourse à la Los Aldeanos in 2010: hip hop in Cuba began primarily as a dance culture, and observers recall early rappers slavishly imitating the lyrics and style of U.S. gangsta rap—down to the heavy coats and hats, even in the tropical summer. Fernández frequently refers to an evolution from this early "mimetic" period to an "authentically Cuban rap" (e.g., A. Fernández 2002), yet the Havana rap scene did not so much evolve as it was actively shaped by figures, both Cuban and American, who believed in conscious hip hop and felt that it held the key to more peaceful coexistence with the state: nationalization was something that they worked toward, using their knowledge of hip hop and the language of Cuban cultural politics.

Alongside Fernández, who used his position as the leading DJ, promoter, and hip hop writer to raise consciousness, Pablo Herrera, as Cuba's foremost rap producer, was in a prime position to bring his influence to bear on the local scene. With his background in teaching at the University of Havana, mentoring came naturally to him, and he had been reading about hip hop for some years. He started working with artists, "trying to push them to higher levels, telling them, 'You need to read this book about this and write songs about it'" (Smith n.d.). He worked with around twenty groups, many of them favorites in the Havana scene such as Anónimo Consejo, Hermanos de Causa, Explosión Suprema, Las Krudas, and 100% Original. He helped them tailor their style, worked on their flow, made beats with them, told them what to listen to and what to avoid. These informal workshops were practical but also philosophical: Herrera encouraged rappers to think about music with a social goal, and their responsibilities to their audiences.

Anónimo Consejo acknowledged this influence. They said of Herrera: "He advises us on everything from production to how we should express ourselves onstage. He gives us ideas for lyrics, and he also writes the choruses if necessary" (A. Fernández n.d., 9). Anónimo Consejo's philosophy, summed up by their slogan "¡Hip hop, revolución!," shows the influence of Herrera's blend of conscious hip hop and revolutionary thought (ibid.). The journalist Annalise Wunderlich (2001) paints a revealing picture of Herrera working with the duo: "In a T-shirt with the words 'God is a DJ,' Herrera shuffles through a stack of CDs and smokes a cigarette while Yosmel and Kokino sit on his couch, intently studying every page of an old Vibe magazine. 'Yo, check this out,' Herrera finds what he's looking for. 'En la revolución, cada quien hace su parte.' In the Revolution, everyone must do his part. Fidel's unmistakable voice loops back and repeats the phrase again and again over a hard-driving beat. Herrera nods to Yosmel, who takes his cue: 'The solution is not leaving / New days will be here soon / We deserve and want to always go forward / Solving problems is important work.'"

Another characteristic Anónimo Consejo chorus drives home the revolutionary message:[16]

Wake up, people, *revolution, my friend*,
It's time for justice, *revolution, my friend*,
Anónimo Consejo, *revolution, my friend*,
Hip hop revolution, *revolution, my friend*.

The slogan "¡Hip hop, revolución!" in many ways encapsulates a formula for success within Cuban hip hop, appealing equally to government officials (Anónimo Consejo joined the ACR) and foreign hip hop aficionados (the duo feature prominently in most filmed and written accounts of the genre in Cuba). This rhetorical strategy, subsequently adopted by a number of Cuban groups, has provoked occasional skepticism precisely because of its success. One leading figure privately described this kind of revolutionary rap as a tactic for accruing benefits such as overseas travel, and Los Aldeanos made the following acerbic observations in a song performed during the 2004 festival:

Here it's not all "¡Hip hop, revolution!" like it seems
With MCs who think they're tough but are limper than SBS.[17]

. . . .

There are many who for no reason cry "revolution"
In every song, but they don't know their true profession.

Fernández and Anónimo Consejo discussed how other groups had jumped on the bandwagon of "revolutionary rap" (A. Fernández n.d., 6). Fernández claimed that "we have seen opportunists . . . who use it to gain a space for themselves, so as not to remain outside of what's going on." Kokino replied that "many of them today keep saying 'Hip hop, revolution!' yet they can't read a book by Che or Malcolm X" (quoted in ibid.)

Nevertheless, this skepticism must be balanced by recognition that the idea of revolution is central to the discourses of U.S. rap groups admired by Cuban fans, such as Public Enemy and dead prez: this revolutionary rhetoric cannot simply be dismissed as a diplomatic line. Rap prospered in Cuba because it could be talked about productively. Thus whether or not all artists employed, or believed in, certain rhetorical strategies is less important than the fact that a sufficient number did, and that these strategies were sufficiently credible and appealing—not just to state officials but also to hip hoppers, both foreign and local. Legitimating "¡Hip hop, revolución!" entailed portraying revolutionary Cuban hip hop as a revival of the genre's original spirit. Otherwise, revolutionary rap might well have gone down the same path as official rock groups in the Soviet bloc and lost credibility as it gained state support. Instead, intermediaries such as Herrera and Fernández positioned Cuban hip hop—a genre that had started out as oriented toward dance and commercial U.S. rap—as reflective, constructive, revolutionary, and authentic, as well as the evolution of nueva trova and superior to its U.S. counterpart. They helped to create a public discourse and artistic philosophy around rap that, despite the multiplicity of artistic responses and beliefs that they covered (or covered up), were successful in creating spaces for hip hop on both local and international stages.[18]

Hip Hop and the Cuban Revolution: Ideological Convergences

The efforts of cultural intermediaries to create a space for hip hop in Cuba were aided by the fact that it shares a number of discursive tropes and moral positions with the Cuban Revolution, so rap could be presented to cultural officials in familiar terms. As Fernández has said, "hip hop is a completely revolutionary culture, in the broadest possible meaning of the word" (Robinson 2004, 120). Cultural intermediaries interpreted rap as the global protest music of all those marginalized by U.S. power, a vision that was adopted by functionaries like Alonso since it fits easily with the ideology of a revolutionary "protest state" at loggerheads with the United States. The critical stance of The Roots or dead prez is music to the ears of Cuban officials. Cuban rap is lauded for rejecting materialism, providing a voice for the marginalized, and criticizing impe-

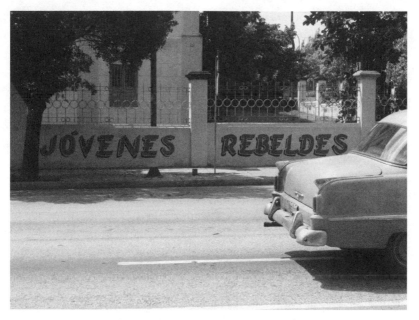

"Young rebels." Photo by author.

rialism and globalization. These are all perceived as reflecting the original essence of hip hop, yet they also underpin Cuban state ideology.

One of the clearest examples of this coincidence between elite and popular constructions of identity appears in the regular borrowing of state labels and slogans as names for rap groups, albums, or songs. The phrase "young rebels" is one example, referring to the leaders of the revolution (Fidel, Che, Camilo Cienfuegos) but also used as the name of a rap group and incorporated into EPG&B's song "We Were Young Rebels." The phrase "injustice trembles," found on an anti-American poster outside the U.S. Interests Section in Havana, was taken as the title of an award-winning demo by Explosión Suprema in 2006. The rap collective La Comisión Depuradora took its name from a military court headed by Che in the early days of the revolution: the object of purification may here be urban musicians rather than Batista supporters, but the original iden-tification with Che is not ironic. Rappers thus show a playful intertextual-ity in their recycling of state rhetoric, yet because they focus on tropes that are widely credible among young people, especially hip hop fans, they do not subvert the intended meaning but rather expand it.

There are many others ways that hip hoppers' discourses mirror those of the state. Anónimo Consejo and Papo Record both wrote songs ("Ley 5566" and "Asignatura") in the form of "ten commandments of hip hop." Anónimo Consejo's moral exhortations, such as "put truth first," "uphold the cry of 'to die for the motherland is to live,'" and "put your ideals above everything else, without fearing the risks," echo the revolutionary billboards all across Havana with their slogans "never lie," "always stick to your ethical principles," and so on. Thanks to all these billboards, driving through Havana from the airport is like entering a hip hop theme park. There is a powerful militaristic streak alongside the pseudoreligion: Clan Completo subtitled their project "the troops advance"; El Enano produced a track called "Armed Forces"; Hermanos de Causa and Los Aldeanos, in their defiant statement that hip hop is not yet dead in Havana ("Hasta donde sé"), rap "while there's still one soldier standing, the war isn't over"; Los Aldeanos and Mano Armada's slogan "rap is war" gave rise to a song, a video, and prominent tattoos; and the rapper Magyori is depicted as a child in military uniform, saying "I loved to dress like a *rebelde* . . . I'm the first guerrilla girl" (*East of Havana* n.d., 34). These and endless other examples of hip hop militarism are suggestive in a country whose leader, Fidel Castro, came to power through armed rebellion and is famous for wearing military fatigues. He might well approve of the militaristic streak in today's young rebels and their critical view of his old foe, the United States. In "América," El B excoriates a nation that "has a history written in pain, fear, hate, and blood" and concludes that "America is a stain of shit and blood on the map." This song has been played on Cuban radio, illustrating how the ultracritical vision of Los Aldeanos can still find an officially-sanctioned space.

Dreaming is another characteristic Cuban activity. As he unveiled a statue of John Lennon in a Havana park, Fidel Castro echoed the song "Imagine": "I am a dreamer who has seen some of his dreams become reality" ("Castro the 'Lennonist'" 2000). In our interview, Alpidio Alonso characterized Cubans' capacity to dream as one of their great virtues, and the political historian Antoni Kapcia (2000) has fittingly dubbed Cuba the "island of dreams." Los Aldeanos launched themselves onto the scene in 2003 by winning a competition with their song "A veces sueño" (sometimes I dream), and in 2008 El Aldeano's collaboration with Papá Humbertico, "Es un sueño," proclaimed: "It's a dream—hard to achieve, but that doesn't mean we're going to stop fighting for it"—words that could come straight from the lips of Fidel. Yet both the revolution and hip hop often dream in reverse, with a nostalgic focus on past triumphs.

The Battle of Ideas

The editorial by Ariel Fernández on the inside front cover of the first edition of *Movimiento* is subtitled "moving ideas," while the group Los Paisanos claim that hip hop "is a religion without god, but it's real / We don't worship images, we worship ideas" ("El hueco"). Fernando Rojas described to me his first impressions of going to hear rap in Alamar in the late 1990s: what caught his attention was seeing the audience standing in silence, listening. He perceived hip hop to be a movement of thinkers, which led him to characterize it as "the latest authentic countercultural movement of the Cuban Revolution." Rojas was president of the AHS at the time, so his perception was crucial to subsequent state support for the genre. While ideas are central to conscious hip hop, they also have a particular prominence in socialist culture and society (R. Moore 2006, 7–9). The notion of hip hop as an arena for debate in which Cuba has superseded the United States dovetails with the political vision of Cuba as trumping America primarily on an ideological level. A Havana billboard quotes Fidel: "Ideas are more powerful than weapons," a message echoed by a sign outside the U.S. Interests Section on the Malecón proclaiming: "Battle of ideas, a struggle for our times."[19]

The upheavals of the Special Period put great pressure on Cuban value systems and morality; Castro acknowledged in 1993 that compromises were required since the "pure, ideal, perfect socialism of which we dream" was no longer possible (Pérez 2006, 298–305). These compromises in the realm of policy and practice were, however, countered by attempts at ideological mobilization. A key moment occurred in March 1996, when Raúl Castro announced that the Communist Party would wage a "Battle of Ideas" in order to explain the measures of the Special Period and ensure that the people did not lose their belief in socialism or become swayed by consumerism (LeoGrande 2004, 193). Finally launched in 1999, the Battle of Ideas, Fidel Castro's last major political initiative (Anderson 2006), was a sweeping campaign to safeguard the revolution by revitalizing the ideological commitment of Cubans, especially the young, "seeking to fortify ideological resolve against the pressure from individualization and social division, and against the corrosive effects of the dollar and tourism" (Kapcia 2005b, 181–82). Kapcia (2005a) describes its aims as reinforcing ideology and morality and reinvigorating youth. There was a particular focus on education, which emphasized "the need to strengthen notions of a threatened equality and a resistance to the insidious penetration of dollarization, privatization and individualism," a "communitarian" morality, and a belief in solidarity, participation, and honesty (ibid., 410). A Cuban website describes the Battle of Ideas' urgent tasks as including "stopping and reversing the tendency toward the growth in social inequalities," "blocking prejudices and discriminatory racial attitudes," and "blocking attempts to banalize culture for commercial ends" ("La Batalla de Ideas" 2007).

The ideological overlap between these aims and the underground hip hop scene in Havana is remarkable. Both seek to combat the depoliticization of Cuban youth (Lueiro n.d., 2) and the decline in morality and solidarity. Kapcia's (2005a) study points toward an internal struggle in Cuba between policy (guided by realpolitik) and ideology (guided by idealism), and underground hip hop falls clearly on the side of the latter. While I am not implying a formal connection between hip hop and the Battle of Ideas, it is worth noting that both were institutionalized in the late 1990s, and that both the Battle of Ideas and the AHS (hip hop's parent organization) came under the umbrella of the UJC. State support for hip hop was thus coordinated by cultural officials at the AHS who were immersed in the ideologies and politics of the Battle of Ideas and attracted to hip hop, as Rojas told me, precisely as a thinking culture. The Battle of Ideas is thus an important frame for understanding hip hop. The terms of the debate are by and large the same: promoting culture and education among young people; combating inequality, discrimination, and commercialization; and reinforcing solidarity, raising ethical standards, promoting justice, encouraging participation and responsibility, and pushing for change. Los Aldeanos have repeatedly appropriated this label for their critical hip hop (e.g., "Los Aldeanos"), with El Aldeano ("Noches perdidas") describing himself as "waging my own Battle of Ideas," and El B describing his song "Contrarevolucionario" as "a Battle of Ideas against a defamatory campaign." If hip hop is a revolution within the revolution, it is also a battle within the battle.[20]

The Language of Revolution

"The mind and its creative capacity have transcendent powers in the face of dire streets. A love affair with thought and language offers salvation," writes the hip hop scholar Imani Perry (2004, 45). If language plays a central role in hip hop, Katherine Verdery (1991, 90) underlines the special place accorded to language by socialist governments. She paints a picture of contests for control of language in socialist Romania, one echoed in Szemere's (2001, 35) study of music in Hungary, where, "as in any authoritarian system, officials treated the polysemy inherent in any cultural text as a potential threat to the status quo." Yet Cuban hip hop reveals quite the opposite: language as a field of negotiation and a shared space of opportunity, largely because—as I will explore below—the common discursive ground was based on ideological and historical foundations.

What is striking about the language of so many hip hop lyrics and statements is their contiguity with the rhetoric of the state and, above all, the ambiguous relationship between the two. Marc Perry (2004, 225) recounts a discussion with Anónimo Consejo: "Yosmel and Kokino explained to me . . . that their invocations of 'revolution' were not necessarily in reference to *the* Cuban Revolution, at least not directly so." The key words here are "necessarily" and "directly": polysemy and ambiguity allow the rappers to position themselves simultaneously within and apart from the state. This is why the slogan "¡Hip hop, revolución!" was so effective: it sits perfectly with state discourse, yet the confrontational meaning of the word "revolution" can be evoked to provide distance.

In another interview, Anónimo Consejo claim that "revolution means defining yourself and being consistent with your principles in every situation. It's a way of life that you have to face up to and take on board" (A. Fernández n.d., 6). Again, the virtue of the term "revolution" is its flexibility: each individual can define it for himself or herself, while remaining "inside the revolution," as Castro insisted. This play around the word "revolution" is found frequently: as Magyori says in the documentary *East of Havana*, "I feel quite revolutionary—in my own way, but quite revolutionary." Adding in the words "in my own way" allows her to play both angles at once. Anónimo Consejo's criticism of "double morality" (ibid., 7) is similarly ambiguous: are they referring to the state itself or to the kinds of immoral individuals that undermine the state? The strength of this discourse is that the question is left open, so the statements retain both their supportive and critical meanings.

The words that hip hoppers use to describe their culture—revolution, rebellion, struggle, battle, resistance—have all been central to state discourse in Cuba since 1959, yet their meaning suggests confrontation. Even the most militaristic imagery in the most subversive rap lyrics and performances—hip hop as music of war, rappers as soldiers taking aim and firing at their enemies—circulates in a (battle)field staked out by the revolution. A performance by the collective Clan Completo, among the most hard-line rappers in Havana, began with a sample of a famous speech by Fidel: "Revolution is a sense of the historical moment; it is to change everything that needs to be changed; it is full equality and freedom; it is to be treated and to treat others as human beings." Is this ironic? Is there an implied critique? How is the audience supposed to understand it? These questions are all left open. Of course, it was not hard to read a critical intent into this moment, given the reputation of the group on stage, yet nothing was said to give the game away: they simply played a snatch of Fidel's speech without comment. What could be wrong with that? In private conversations, rappers would often tell me that hip hop "is *our* revolution," but when they stood up on stage and rapped, they spoke to revolutionaries of all stripes. Many lines by Mano Armada, one of Havana's most respected underground groups, merge seamlessly with official discourse: "Rebelliousness, strength, discipline, youth" ("Rap del bueno"); "Never, never will we sell out our ideals" (ibid.); "We must fight without thinking about failure / An ideal has more power than a hundred thousand bullets" ("Revolución dentro de la revolución").

The language of revolution allows space for criticism, since the idea of change is inherent in it; it is always possible to present change as continuity, and continuity as change. In contrast to the picture painted by Verdery and Szemere, within the realm of Cuban hip hop, language is a space of opportunity rather than struggle. The veteran rapper Yordis (Grandes Ligas) told me that freedom was located in metaphor: in other words, double meaning and wordplay are sources of liberation. Rappers are rebellious youths in a country with an official newspaper called *Juventud Rebelde* (rebellious youth) and a leader who says he has been a rebel all his life (Castro and Ramonet 2008, 82). It is the inclusiveness of the common discourse that is striking, and hard to imagine with any other musical genre. At the colloquia that formed part of the hip hop festival, state officials, intellectuals, and hip hoppers came together and spoke the same language—whether or not they meant the same thing.

There is an extraordinary passage in the song "Los Aldeanos" in which the eponymous duo starts by proclaiming its artistic independence from institutions and the music industry, and then continues:

> I'm everyone, I'm the 'hood, I'm the people,
> I'm the street, I'm the white, I'm the black,
> I'm my law, I'm my constitution,
> My Battle of Ideas, I'm *my* revolution.
> I'm Cuba, I'm peace, I'm war,
> I'm my struggle, I'm blood, I'm earth,
> I'm my government, I'm Cuban hip hop,
> I'm my *comandante*—we're Los Aldeanos.

The declaration of artistic independence morphs into a political one, the postulation of an imaginary alternative state, with rappers as the commanding officers at the head of their own revolution. This song, released in 2009, symbolizes a recent change from ambiguity to more open confrontation, mirrored by a shift on the part of leading hip hop figures from the conviction that negotiation with state institutions was the way forward to a more independent, even oppositional, stance—and yet the ideological framework of Cuban society is retained. The alternative state mirrors the existing one, with laws, a constitution, a Battle of Ideas, a revolution, a government, even a comandante (the word typically used to refer to Fidel Castro), but all of them constituted by Los Aldeanos.[21]

Hip Hop and Cuban National Ideology

In considering the parallels between conscious hip hop and revolutionary ideology, it is illuminating to examine the "codes" which Kapcia (2000, 85–91 and 237–43) regards as underpinning Cuban national ideology throughout the twentieth century and having received a renewed boost in the 1990s. Six of Kapcia's seven codes—collectivism, moralism, activism, culturalism, revolutionism, and internationalism—have clear links with the philosophies of conscious hip hop groups.[22] It is instructive to examine first the Black August Hip Hop Collective's "Statement of Pur-

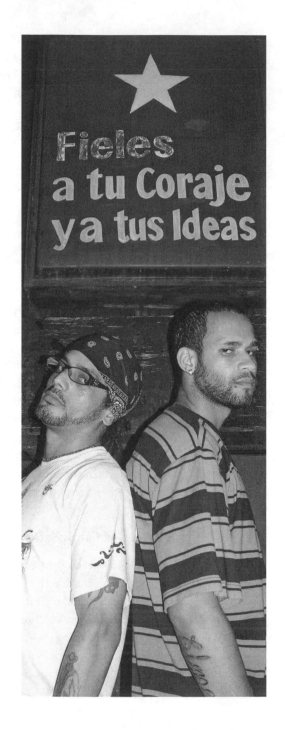

Los Aldeanos: "Faithful to your courage and to your ideas." Photo courtesy of M. Rivière, Emetrece Productions.

pose," given the decisive influence that this organization has had on Cuban hip hop ideology:

The Black August Hip Hop Collective strives to support the global development of hip hop culture by facilitating exchanges between international communities where hip hop is a vital part of youth culture, and by promoting awareness about the social and political issues that effect [sic] these youth communities. Our goal is to bring culture and politics together and to allow them to naturally evolve into a unique hip hop consciousness that informs our collective struggle for a more just, equitable and human world. ... Through an effective merging of hip hop culture and political information, The Black August Hip Hop Collective promotes our own hip hop aesthetic, which emphasizes sincere self-expression, creativity, and community responsibility.[23]

The parallels between this expression of hip hop ideology, the Havana scene, and Kapcia's codes are numerous and striking:

Collectivism is evident in the very title, The Black August Hip Hop Collective, as well as in the rhetoric of collective struggle, equality and community responsibility, and the ubiquitous references to rap as a movement.

Moralism underpins conscious hip hop: Black August envisions "a more just, equitable and human world," and much underground Cuban rap is based on moral judgments about abuses of authority by policemen and party officials, the perceived moral laxity of young women, rising materialism and individualism, the decline of honesty and deterioration of friendship, and above all the omnipresence in Cuban society of a double morality—saying one thing and doing another.

Activism is a core part of the philosophy of the Black August Collective and of conscious hip hop more generally, dedicated to "collective struggle" against oppression; the word "struggle" also permeates the rhetoric of Cuban rappers.

Culturalism, or faith in education, culture, and the intellectual's political role, is evident in Cuban rappers' promotion of reflection and reactions against mindlessness, materialism, and frivolity. La FabriK combines culture and education in its community projects with children and prisoners (Borges-Triana n.d., 8–9), while Ariel Fernández, in his editorial to the first edition of *Movimiento*, twice refers to hip hop as an "artistic and intellectual" movement that creates space for critical dialogue.[24] Hip hoppers' negative feelings about reggaetón center on a perceived distinction between rap as a serious activity and stimulus for reflection and reggaetón as mere entertainment.

Revolutionism underpins U.S. and Cuban underground rap as well as Cuban state ideology, as perfectly expressed in Anónimo Consejo's "¡Hip hop, revolución!" and a Black August press release: "Black August holds these elements—hip-hop, U.S. political prisoners, and Cuba—together with the common theme of revolution: Hip-hop was and is a revolutionary cultural art form. Cuba, with all its faults and attributes, is defined by its revolutionary history. And U.S. political prisoners and exiles, many of whom have been given asylum in Cuba, are products of revolutionary movements within the United States."[25]

Internationalism has historically informed Cuban efforts toward Latin American solidarity. As Alpidio Alonso told me, the hip hop festival represented a chance to bring together Latin American rappers in condemnation of U.S. imperialism, and it stimulated many transnational connections. Black August is a transnational organization, its aims including "facilitating exchanges between international communities." Latin American–centered internationalism is expressed clearly throughout the fourth issue of *Movimiento* and is articulated by Hermanos de Causa in "Latinoamérica," a collaboration with the Argentinean rapper Malena:

Onward, Latino, bring down dictatorship,
America is your home, you are one race,
Cuba summons you, raise your heads,
Our strength lies in unity.

The fact that the central pillars of Cuban national ideology are also cornerstones of hip hop goes a long way toward explaining the rapid acceptance of rap as part of national culture. This ideological overlap has been vital for hip hoppers and intermediaries who have sought to negotiate with state representatives for greater openings, but it has also at times served the political purposes of state institutions. Although I am arguing against a simple model of appropriation by the state, this process has not been entirely absent.

During the preparations for the 2004 Havana Hip Hop Festival, the AHS created a website (no longer available) whose address reappropriated Anónimo Consejo's slogan "¡Hip hop, revolución!" Intended as an Internet discussion forum on hip hop, it introduced nine themes for debate:

1) Hip hop is a universal sociocultural phenomenon that embodies struggle and resistance against the fascist, belligerent, and marginalizing politics of imperialism.

2) Hip hop is a cultural manifestation of rebellion by minorities who are oppressed and excluded by the political and economic power centers of capitalism.

3) Rap has arisen in Cuba as the new voice of an island that is besieged and assailed by the U.S. empire. It is also the sound of the revolution, expressing the problems and hopes of young rappers.

4) An avant-garde, belligerent, critical rap can be an alternative to the pseudocultural products of the musical market.

5) How can the Latin American hip hop movement unite further and create new spaces for cultural and ethical exchange and debate?

6) Can rap now be considered a genre or a style?

7) Hip hop, with its special characteristics, can be considered part of the national culture of a country. Is that happening in the various scenes where hip hop is developing today?

8) Latinos have played a very important part in hip hop since its birth. Very few of the books that supposedly relate the history of this culture refer to this. What is your opinion of this?

9) Rap is considered a belligerent response to the phenomena of social exclusion and marginalization, and an opportunity for expression on the part of the oppressed masses. Should its cultivators focus on the transnational music market? Should they change this perspective and pursue other avenues of promotion and commercialization without abandoning the aesthetic and ethical premises of the movement? Is there an alternative which responds to these particular promotional needs?

The language and themes of these questions for discussion provide a fascinating insight into the meanings and uses of rap to the AHS, encapsulating many of the points made so far. Rap is interpreted as the resistance of the marginalized against their oppression and exclusion by the forces of capitalism and imperialism as embodied by the United States, an interpretation which is close to classic analyses of U.S. rap (e.g., Rose 1994). More specifically, Cuban rap is perceived as a voice of resistance to the pressure exerted on the island by its powerful neighbor. Whereas writers on global rap have tended to de-essentialize the genre in order to legitimate local scenes (e.g., Mitchell 2001c, 1–12), the AHS discourse stresses the perceived essence or origins of rap in order to keep the focus of critique on the U.S. government and its policies, rather than on the Cuban state. At the same time, however, there is no mention of the United States as the originator of the genre: instead, rap is described as a universal phenomenon, the role of Latinos in its gestation is underlined, and thus the use of this critical tool in Cuban hands is validated. Interestingly, although Latinos are mentioned, the roots of rap in the African diaspora are not; the question of race is largely elided by that of class ("the oppressed masses"), in classic Marxist style.

From this list of questions, it can be seen that hip hop has provided an appropriate discursive framework within which to restate long-standing ideological positions of the Cuban state, such as critiques of U.S. power, the defense of the oppressed, Latin American unity, and hostility toward capitalism. It is particularly worth noting the internationalism of the AHS vision of hip hop: Alonso told me that the rap festival provided an opportunity "to project a revolutionary message from Cuba," its focus firmly on broadcasting messages from Cuba to the rest of Latin America and the United States. Global recognition of Cuban rap is also useful to the government, as praise from foreign observers is seen as reflecting positively on the revolutionary social project. Cuban commentators and officials such as Alonso seize on international validation of Cuban rap as evidence of the virtues of the political system in which it thrives (e.g., Henríquez Lagarde 2002). Foreign perceptions of Cuba as a key node in a global conscious rap movement, even deposing the United States as its leading force, have considerable appeal to government officials (as well as to rappers), hence Alonso's description of the festival as a "symbolic" event. The possibilities for expressing national ideologies and for reflecting positive judgments onto the nation go some way toward explaining the state's promotion of rap.

A Revolution within the Revolution

So is this close correlation between the ideologies of the Cuban state and conscious hip hop a coincidence? Is it a convenient but fictitious concordance, the result of ingenious discursive manipulation on the part of hip hop intermediaries or institutional officials? I would argue not, for all that such figures may have made the most of this overlap for various ends. There is in fact a deep connection between the Cuban Revolution and hip hop; they are like two branches of the same tree, their shared roots making the question of appropriation or co-optation philosophically redundant. The common ground of hip hop and the revolution is the result of historical connections between Cuba and the United States that date back to the nineteenth century and were revitalized in the 1960s and 1970s.

Political connections between African Americans and Cubans can be traced back at least as far as the expressions of solidarity by Frederick Douglass and other African American leaders with the Cuban Ten Years' War (1868–78); indeed, "no country in the nineteenth century, other than Haiti, so stirred the African American imagination as Cuba did" (Brock 1998, 8–9). José Martí, the spiritual father of the Cuban Revolution, spent a significant portion of his adult life in the United States and was closely connected to African American abolitionists like Douglass and Henry Highland Garnet, who headed the Cuban Anti-Slavery Society, founded in New York in 1872. Moving into the twentieth century, Cuban and African American intellectuals, artists, and trade unionists kept in close contact, and—in the context of the U.S. neocolonization of Cuba in the first half of the century—political movements in both countries were highly critical of the dominant U.S. model of political democracy (Marable 2000, 93–96). The black Marxism that took root in 1920s America, above all in New York, was influenced by flows of Caribbean immigrants and Caribbean political thought (Dawson 2001). Indeed, black Caribbean immigrants played a significant role in shaping African American identity and politics in New York from the Harlem Renaissance right through to the black power era (Matory 1999), and throughout this period "Cuba's geographical proximity to the United States gave the 'Negro in Cuba' particular significance and familiarity for North American persons of African descent" (Guridy 2003, 20). From the 1860s onward, then, African

American and Cuban radical politics were closely entwined, not least because of their linkage in New York City.

The Cuban Revolution thus drew on a transnational political sphere that was nearly a century old, and black American radicals of the 1960s and 1970s, in turn, found inspiration in the Cuban Revolution. It is worth recalling an incident from the revolution's earliest days, when Castro was visiting New York in 1960. Unhappy with his treatment at his midtown hotel, he was invited by Malcolm X to stay at the Hotel Theresa in Harlem. Castro decided to accept, regarding Harlem as the place where his "best friends" were (R. Young 2003, 31). His meeting with Malcolm X marked the beginning of a half-century of solidarity with African American political causes (he revisited Harlem in 1995 and 2000 to speak before largely appreciative audiences). Castro also met Harry Belafonte during his Hotel Theresa stay, and these meetings laid important foundations for the institutionalization of Cuban hip hop some forty years later, in which Belafonte was to play a catalytic role.

1960 also saw a visit to Cuba by Robert Williams, LeRoi Jones, and Harold Cruse (C. Young 2006, 18), launching a period of intensive transnational exchange. Black American leaders expressed support for Castro and the Cuban Revolution from the start, and Fidel responded by offering opportunities for state visits or asylum. Stokely Carmichael and Angela Davis made high-profile trips to Cuba, while the Black Panthers Huey Newton and Eldridge Cleaver spent longer periods in Havana. This contact between black American radicals and the Cuban Revolution in the 1960s and 1970s had a major impact on the U.S. black political sphere: during this period, as Cynthia Young (ibid., 50) notes, "black American identity was not forged in isolation; it did not emerge solely within the U.S. political context. Rather, it resulted from a transnational consciousness, one that drew on anticolonial critiques for its political analysis and international legitimacy." The Revolutionary Action Movement, which made an important contribution to black radicalism of the 1960s and 1970s, was closely aligned with Third World anticolonial liberation movements and "saw Afro-America as a de facto member of the nonaligned nations" (Kelley 2002, 81). Not only were the Black Panthers Marxists, but Huey Newton regarded the Cuban and Chinese revolutions as their ideological wellspring (ibid., 94), ensuring that the revolutionary politics of Cuba and black America, which had been linked for a century, were closely entwined in this period.

The environment in which hip hop was born in the early 1970s was thus significantly marked by revolutionary ideologies and, specifically, by the inspirational image of the Cuban Revolution. In New York, political groups like the Black Panthers looked to revolutionary struggles overseas, in particular in Cuba, and Puerto Rican–dominated organizations like the Young Lords and the Ghetto Brothers brought a new wave of Caribbean-style socialism to the city, specifically to the South Bronx at the start of the 1970s (Chang 2005). Hip hop emerged from a revolutionary generation in which the Caribbean influence was strong: the three original titans of hip hop (DJ Kool Herc, Grandmaster Flash, and Afrika Bambaataa) were all of Caribbean descent, and many pioneering figures, including Bambaataa and Fab 5 Freddy, grew up surrounded by black Marxist ideologies (ibid.). As Grandmaster Caz of the Cold Crush Brothers said in *From Mambo to Hip Hop*, "we were either going to start hip hop or start a revolution." At first this ideological bent remained latent (it was *either* hip hop *or* a revolution), and it was more evident in hip hop's years of gestation than in its infancy. But this ideology surfaced in the mid-1980s, finally exploding into America's (and the world's) consciousness in the music of Public Enemy toward the end of that decade. Public Enemy embraced the black Marxism of the previous generation—the group became known as the "Black Panthers of rap"—and Chuck D proclaimed himself a communist (Chang 2005, 253–54). Message rap drew on the legacies of Malcolm X, black power, and the Black Panthers, whose images fill Public Enemy's video "Shut 'Em Down" from *Apocalypse '91* (Perkins 1996, 22; Allen 1996, 164). Twenty seconds in, the words "Where are the revolutionaries?" flash up on the screen.

The revolutionaries were, of course, in Cuba, where Public Enemy's music soon caught on with young fans of música americana: in his song "Como fue," Alexey Rodríguez recalls that the first cassette he owned was by the group. Public Enemy rapped about Fidel's friend Malcolm X, Havana's allies the Black Panthers, and Assata Shakur, the American exile in Cuba; the imprint of the Cuban Revolution on the group's ideology was unmistakable—and unsurprising, given its formative influence on the previous generation of black American radicals—and their music found a home on the island. Two key players in the development of politicized hip hop in Havana in the late 1990s, Nehanda Abiodun and Fab 5 Freddy, were Americans who had grown up in New York around black Marxist ideologies, and their discovery of the Havana hip hop scene in 1997 was crucial to reconnecting the two branches of revolution that had been running in parallel in America and Cuba since the 1960s. This was not an alien cultural invasion: the revolution that Public Enemy rapped about and the revolution that Fidel instigated were two branches of the same tree, planted in nineteenth-century New York and revived by Castro's meeting with Malcolm X in Harlem.

Perhaps the most symbolically and practically important moment in the nationalization of rap in Cuba was the visit of the American singer, actor, and social activist Harry Belafonte in the pivotal year of 1999.[26] Belafonte, who has a long-standing interest in hip hop as a force for social change, met with members of the rap scene and then went straight on to see Fidel Castro. Belafonte relates that this "quickie lunch" turned into an eleven-hour meeting with the Cuban leader, as Castro showed great interest in learning about hip hop around the globe. According to Belafonte, Fidel "was *really* focused on this" and "took it *very* seriously," and the two spent the entire day discussing hip hop. While Abel Prieto had spoken positively about rap earlier that year, Belafonte's intervention at this important juncture appears to have consolidated the government's involvement. As Magia López (Obsesion) reported in 2002: "After that meeting there were some very positive changes for us. And many others came out of that meeting that Harry had with Fidel. We know that and it will go down in the history of Cuban hip hop" ("Encuentro entre amigos" n.d.). Certainly, Fidel seems to have taken particular interest in hip hop around this time: he organized personal meetings with rappers, including Orishas and Los Reyes de la Calle (the latter were treated to a banquet), and he discussed hip hop with Yrak Saenz at an AHS congress, putting forward the idea (that he had gleaned from Belafonte) that Cuba could be a place where hip hop provided a space for reflection, potentially serving as an example to Latin America and even to the United States. He also told Osmell Francis (Cubanos en la Red) about the forthcoming creation of the ACR, again at the AHS congress (Castillo Martiatu n.d.a, 20).

It is not hard to see why Castro would have taken Belafonte's views on hip hop to heart. Belafonte was a leading figure in the U.S. civil rights movement, a cause with which Castro has been closely associated, and he was one of a number of influential black Americans whose sympathy for Cuba led him to visit the island in the 1970s. He is the same age as Castro

and had been talking to him for thirty years, and he represents an era and   73
a political movement that Castro understands well. When Belafonte met
Castro in 1999 and declared that hip hop was a global movement that
could be a force for good, and that Cuba potentially had much to contrib-
ute, this clearly triggered something in Castro, who would not let Belafonte go until midnight. Castro's meeting with Malcolm X in 1960 symbolized his early alliance with and ideological proximity to radical black
politics in the United States in the pre–hip hop years. It also sowed the
seed of Cuban state involvement with radical hip hop nearly four decades
later. All that was needed was a catalyst to spark the connection in Castro's mind between the young rebels of the 1950s and those of the 1990s,
and that catalyst was Harry Belafonte.

Therefore all the discussion of the relationship of hip hop to the revolution (whether it is co-optation, appropriation, control, strategy, or articulation) has missed a key point: the two are built on the same bedrock of
New York–Caribbean Marxist principles, and thus their relationship is
not a marriage of convenience but rather one of kinship. Kapcia's codes
and hip hop ideology are so close because they have their sources in the
same political ideas that had been circulating since the 1870s, and there
was renewed and intensified cross-fertilization in the 1960s, precisely in
the years that hip hop was gestating. The political destinies of the United
States and Cuba may have split dramatically in 1959, but their revolutionary movements continued to run in parallel throughout the 1960s in
constant dialogue, and hip hop emerged from the tail end of a black
movement that had close ties to Havana. For all the surface politicking,
for all the strategizing, it is not ultimately a question of the state's controlling and co-opting hip hop, nor of hip hoppers' adopting the discourse
of the state. You cannot appropriate or adopt something that is already
yours. When hip hoppers likened Cuban hip hop to a "revolution within
the revolution," they hit the nail on the head.

In the otherwise problematic documentary *Guerrilla Radio*, discussed in
chapter 4, the director has one flash of insight: "Had Fidel been born 50
years later, he might have used hip hop as a means to power. . . . His
speeches read like rap lyrics, and they apply as much to today's rappers as
they did to his own rebels back in 1959." Alpidio Alonso makes a similar
observation in *A Short Radiography of Cuban Hip Hop*: "I believe that rap
and the views it expresses are in the same vein that Fidel voices . . . and

this speaks to how revolutionary this movement is." While the latter may sound like pure propaganda, it is a view that is shared by even the most critical rappers: Los Aldeanos claimed that "what is happening now with us is very similar to what happened with them fifty years ago. The only difference is that they made armed revolution. The same thing is happening now, it's just that we are doing it with music."[27] Castro's speeches and rap lyrics voice the same principles, because they spring from the same historical sources.

Buena Vista to the Bronx and Back

If hip hop's politics were marked by Cuban influences, the same can be said for its music. Observers have long pointed out that the absorption of hip hop in Cuba is the latest in a long line of musical and cultural exchanges between the island and the United States. Accordingly, African American and Afro-Cuban music are not two separate strands that influence each other but are in fact inseparable (Acosta 2005). Hip hop did not simply arrive in Cuba as something from "out there" that made its way ashore "here" in Cuba; the Cuban musical context was already indissolubly American, and the incoming music was already indissolubly Cuban.

When hip hop emerged from the South Bronx in the early 1970s, the ethnic makeup of the area was majority Latino, with large groups of Caribbean descent. As Chang (2005, 17) writes of the formative places and years of hip hop, "most of New York City north of 110th Street was reimagined as a new kind of 'South,' a global south just a subway ride away." In some ways, the Caribbean-flavored South Bronx had more in common with Havana than with downtown Manhattan, and one of the dominant musical influences on the New York Latin music scene of the 1960s and 1970s was Afro-Cuban music.

Robert Farris Thompson (1996) provides fascinating details of the Caribbean ethnic and cultural environment of early hip hop. While several scholars have made significant efforts to rescue the obscured history of Puerto Rican and Nuyorican participation in the early days of hip hop (e.g., Flores 1996; Rivera 2003), far fewer have noticed the Cuban influence. Thompson, however, notes that "thousands of blacks from Cuba live in the Bronx. The smell of Cuban coffee and the sound of Cuban mambos enliven the streets. . . . It was only natural for Afro-Cuban conga drums to become one of the favored percussive springboards for early

breakdance improvisation" (1996, 214). He quotes a Bronx resident who proclaims: "Afro-Cuban bongos gave power to our dance." The music of hip hop began with the idea of the "percussion break": in the words of the pioneer Afrika Bambaataa, "break music is that certain part of the record that you just be waiting for to come up and when that certain part comes, that percussion part with all those drums, congas, it makes you dance real wild" (ibid., 215). Hip hop started with DJ Kool Herc's extensions of conga, bongo, or timbales solos on Latin funk records (Toop 2000, 60), and thus break-beat music, while also incorporating trap-kit solos, is profoundly marked by New York Latin-Caribbean, but also specifically Afro-Cuban, musical influences.[28] Thompson (1996, 215–17) underlines that the "dance performance break" is found in Cuban *rumba abierta*, and he illustrates this with a nineteenth-century Cuban engraving that shows "a black dancer, bare chested and with a belt of bells, spinning on his left palm in the streets of Havana on Epiphany, the Day of the Kings. His pose is like a stop frame from a film of today's New York breaking step, the four corners." It is little wonder that break dancing was the first element of hip hop to take off in Cuba.

African American and Cuban musics were thus intimately connected during hip hop's years of gestation, just like their politics. Indeed, Cuban musicians and musical genres had a formative influence on most of the major popular musics to emerge from New York in the twentieth century (Roberto 1979), including mambo and salsa, the dominant styles in the South Bronx before hip hop emerged.[29] The epitome of Cuba's foundational role in both hip hop's music and its politics is the New York group the Last Poets, considered by many to be one of the godfathers of hip hop, and specifically of message rap (e.g., Perkins 1996; Toop 2000). On their eponymous 1970 album, they include the proto-raps "Niggers Are Scared of Revolution" and "When the Revolution Comes" over the beat of a conga drum. These godfathers of rap told the filmmaker Luciano Larobina that they were heavily influenced by the Cuban Revolution; of Fidel and Che, they said simply, "they were our heroes" (pers. comm.). The Last Poets mixed Cuban instruments and Cuban politics as they created the immediate precursor of rap in New York, linking the civil rights and hip hop generations. Emir García Meralla (2007, 3) describes how Cuban socialism differs from its European counterpart thus: "It was created to a conga rhythm. It was rhythmic socialism." It is hard to think of a pithier or more evocative description of political hip hop, of Public Enemy, and above all of the Last Poets than "rhythmic socialism," a phrase that sums up the relationship between hip hop and revolution.

There is a line, therefore, that can be drawn from the barrios of Havana like Buena Vista to the South Bronx, from the *son montuno* to mambo to salsa, exemplified by the trajectory of the great sonero Arsenio Rodríguez (García 2006). There are other lines, too, that lead from Havana to New York: the Afro-Cuban drums which fed into the Latin break-beats that spurred on early hip hop dancers, and the revolutionary rhetoric of Fidel and Che that inspired the Last Poets and the Black Panthers. Both musical and ideological connections testify to a century of cultural and political synergy between Cubans and African Americans. When hip hop made its way to Cuba, it was in some ways making its way back, completing the circle by returning to the Havana barrios. Hip hop was already Cuban and already socialist when it arrived in Cuba; its dance with the revolution was an old one.

Hip Hop and the Fractured State

Given that hip hop might be considered the epitome of revolutionary culture, that its fit with Cuban state ideology is perfect, that influential figures like Abel Prieto, Fernando Rojas, and even Fidel Castro have pronounced in its favor, why is it that hip hoppers frequently complain that institutional barriers have stunted the growth of their scene? Why is the government more commonly regarded as a hindrance than a help? For all that hip hoppers and the Cuban state share a common language, there have been many inconsistencies within state policy which undermine the relatively harmonious picture painted so far. The very term "state policy" must be questioned, given the wide range of state employees who have regularly made (often contradictory) decisions relating to rap; singular nouns like "state" and "regime" deny the debates, fractures, and internal contradictions that the typically Cuban term "institutions" captures.

William LeoGrande (2004, 191–92) discusses the struggles between hard-liners and reformers at the highest level of government in the days before the 1991 Fourth Congress of the Cuban Communist Party. While the former won by a narrow margin, reformers were still prominent in the new leadership, including Abel Prieto, the head of the Union of Cuban Writers and Artists (UNEAC), who joined the Political Bureau as minister of culture, and Roberto Robaina, who became the first secretary of the UJC. The reformers argued for more political space for "dissenting views that were not manifestly counterrevolutionary" (ibid.). The Cuban state is thus not monolithic, and different leaders have different ideas about how much room to allow for debate. In the context of the rise of hip hop, it is significant that both the Ministry of Culture and the UJC (the parent organization of the AHS) were led by reformers. As a result, the arts became the sphere of greatest freedom in 1990s Cuba; hard-liners controlled the political sphere, but reformers had a grip on culture. The openings for hip hop were therefore connected to particular individuals and organizations rather than to the state as a whole, and the differentiation, fragmentation, and personalization of politics in Cuba explains some of the inconsistencies in the nationalization of rap.

Internal variations within the state have long been exploited by those with a more experimental or progressive artistic agenda. Silvio Rodríguez underlines the importance of the Casa de Las Américas in promoting nueva trova, under the patronage of Haydée Santamaría, adding: "We were fortunate that Casa de las Américas had such a strong ethical position toward culture, definitely based upon ideological concerns, since at that time there were no other cultural institutions that did anything like this" (quoted in Kirk and Fuentes 2001, 6). Similarly, the Grupo Experimentación Sonora del ICAIC was created by Alfredo Guevara and Leo Brouwer in 1969 as a safe haven within the state-run film institute, the ICAIC (the Instituto Cubano de Arte e Industria Cinematográficos, that is, the Cuban Institute of Cinematographic Art and Industry), for young musicians who sought to push the boundaries of creativity and contestation (Pacini Hernandez and Garofalo 2004, 55–56). The hip hop scene initially found a home within the AHS, which "had the steadfast goal to work with sectors . . . often seen as problematic by other official institutions" (Zurbano 2009, 144). Cuban musicians thus have decades of experience of seeking out spaces of relative freedom under the umbrella of more progressive state institutions. Hip hop has also been associated with the Consejo Nacional de Casas de la Cultura, the Instituto Cubano de Música (ICM), and the Ministry of Culture. This multiplicity of points of contact has created opportunities—but also bureaucratic hurdles, contradictions, and frustrations, especially when hip hoppers have tried to expand beyond these havens.

Some of these internal contradictions within the sphere of cultural policy were externalized in 2002, a crossroads year in the history of Cuban rap, with the formation of the ACR. An elite group of professional rappers was taken on by this state-backed music agency, under the aegis of the ICM, thereby dividing the scene into amateur members of the AHS and professional members of the ACR.[30] A strong, flexible discourse had been constructed around the idea of Cuban rap as harking back to the days when hip hop was about changing the world, not making money, yet some of the best-known rap groups were incorporated into a state agency with an explicitly commercial agenda, and several even began trading in conscious rap for shake-your-booty reggaetón. In 1999, a New Afrikan exile said at the hip hop festival colloquium: "For one thing, the revolution ain't gonna have no 'Squeeze yo titties if you love hip-hop'" (quoted in Hoch 1999). Just three years later, the state employed its first reggaetón artists via the ACR. By 2004, there were signs of serious dissent, not just among AHS rap groups who felt excluded, but among figures of authority and cultural commentators close to the hip hop scene who were disillusioned with or dismissive of the ACR, and even from hip hoppers who worked for the agency.

Not only was a gulf emerging between Cuban rap's underground rhetoric and the commercially oriented practices of some of its leading exponents, but these two state-funded organizations simultaneously began pursuing diverging policies in relation to rap, resulting in tensions between the two. The ACR is committed to making its groups commercially successful, whereas the AHS exists to promote alternative music, particularly that which prioritizes the aesthetic over the commercial or which reflects on problems in Cuban society—such as rising commercialism. In 2001, Abel Prieto, the minister of culture, praised leading rap groups for "the seriousness and rigor with which they take on real problems, at the same time rejecting commercialism" (Fernandes 2006, 119). Yet within a year, the Ministry of Culture had incorporated the same groups into the ACR, the aims of which, according to publicity material on the inside back cover of the first issue of *Movimiento*, include "to commercialize the groups in its catalogue."

It is thus hard to generalize about cultural policy with regard to hip hop. Different branches of the state have been involved with hip hop since the creation of spaces for dance events in the early 1990s. Since the AHS became more actively involved with rap in Havana in 1997, its relationship with the genre has gone through several phases: the initial progressive stage under the leadership of Fernando Rojas and Roberto Zurbano, during which rap grew exponentially; the stewardship of Alpidio Alonso from 2001 to 2006, which saw some of the highest and lowest points of the history of Cuban rap (from the continued growth of the hip hop festival to its eventual suspension); and the most recent phase, since 2006, under Luis Morlote, during which the national AHS was less involved in rap until 2010, when it supported Los Aldeanos' comeback and the Puños Arriba awards. Not only is talking about "the state" problematic, but even individual institutions are more variable than many accounts allow.

A senior figure in the AHS in the late 1990s agreed that this organization had been both the hero and villain of the piece. At first, he said, hip hop appealed to AHS leaders as a new cultural force, and the organization sought (and achieved) funding, spaces, and visibility for it. The AHS created new cultural policies, such as providing scholarships for rappers, because it recognized that the existing ones were not working for young artists.[31] However, after Alonso took over in 2001, the new AHS directorship began to move backward; earlier efforts were dismantled, and the field of negotiation with rappers was reduced. As my informant told me, the AHS had been an "umbrella" for rappers in the late 1990s, but in the early 2000s that umbrella closed and became a trap—the ACR—with a small group of rappers caught inside and the rest left out in the rain. While the AHS's decision to discontinue the hip hop festival in 2005 dismayed many, a more independent project, the Hip Hop Symposium, was launched by La FabriK in the same year, with the assistance of Fernando Rojas, who had become president of the Consejo Nacional de Casas de la Cultura. Rojas had watched the festival decline since his departure from the AHS, and he supported the symposium as a way of rescuing what he saw as its essence; as the AHS let go of hip hop, its ex-president took up the slack. The fact that La FabriK decided to rekindle its relationship with Rojas rather than with his former institution illustrates the personalized nature of Cuban cultural politics.

There were marked differences not only between the Rojas and Alonso years but also between the national headquarters of the AHS, in the Pabel-lón Cuba on La Rampa, and the Havana city branch of the association, half a mile away at La Madriguera in the Quinta de los Molinos. While the national organization's support for hip hop had been in decline since the suspension of the festival in 2005, the rap promoters at the city headquarters were doing everything in their power to keep the culture alive. Even within this single institution, then, it is hard to talk about a coherent policy toward hip hop at any given moment, much less over time, because promoters at La Madriguera felt and acted as though they were relatively independent of the national body.[32] This inconsistency was manifested in a dramatic week for Los Aldeanos in April 2009, when their long-running weekly peña was shut down, and their performance at the Puños Arriba hip hop awards was prevented by the event's curtailment, allegedly on the orders of AHS president Luis Morlote. Yet the following day, they performed a "secret" gig at La Madriguera, which would have been impossible without the support of the venue's employees.

From this point onward until January 2010, Los Aldeanos were effectively banned from performing since no venues would touch them after a series of controversies. The complex nature of Cuban cultural politics was evident during the duo's rehabilitation in the first half of 2010, during which period the importance of internal negotiations within the state became clear. The AHS debated Los Aldeanos, who were members of the association, and decided to back the group, apparently convinced by the argument that Los Aldeanos' discourse is critical but not counterrevolutionary, indeed that it is highly revolutionary; but they then had to convince other branches of the state to play ball since the duo was beyond the pale for performance venues and other cultural institutions. Jorge Rodríguez told me about the complex, fraught, multilevel negotiations (including with state security) that followed in order to enable Los Aldeanos to perform at an event at La Madriguera in January 2010. Together with Melisa Rivière, Los Aldeanos' international representative, Rodríguez succeeded in reopening the door for Los Aldeanos, another illustration of how opportunities have been created through the combined efforts of foreign activists and local hip hop supporters working within state organizations.

One day, when I walked into his office, Rodríguez was on the phone to the Acapulco Theater, trying to confirm Los Aldeanos' comeback concert in late April. When he put the phone down, he said that the concert had been given all the necessary official authorization by the AHS and the Ministry of Culture but that the Provincial Directorate of Culture kept putting obstacles in the way. He also said that lower-level figures (such as venue staff) often caused problems even when decisions were authorized higher up, perhaps because of a personal dislike of rap. As a result, he had to keep confirming and reconfirming with the theater to ensure that nothing went wrong. He underlined the divisions between institutions and the poor flow of information between them. This lack of communication resulted in the need to explain and argue from scratch to each different organization. After the event, he told me that the two days leading up to the concert were very tense because the Acapulco staff kept raising problems. This evidence of institutions working independently or even at odds with each other provides a snapshot of why the nationalization of rap has been incomplete and frustrating, despite the numerous openings that have been created.

It is worth pausing for a moment to consider further Los Aldeanos' rehabilitation because it provides a valuable glimpse of the detailed workings of the institutionalization of rap and of the AHS's capacity to overcome political obstacles and to act with a certain degree of independence. When the AHS decided to back Los Aldeanos, Rodríguez began working in a mediating capacity between artists and venues, negotiating Los Aldeanos' comeback performances and also the Puños Arriba awards ceremony, which found itself without a venue at the last minute after the Acapulco withdrew its support. The AHS was thus functioning as an intermediary organization: Rodríguez put forward proposals to other branches of the state, persisted in the face of institutional or personal resistance, and ultimately succeeded in gaining permission for three of the most important hip hop events of the year.

Aside from his belief in critical hip hop, Rodríguez also felt that backing Los Aldeanos was a good strategic move for the AHS, given the duo's extraordinary popularity at the time: institutions often come in for criticism from music fans, so by aligning itself with Los Aldeanos, the AHS was boosting its own profile as well as helping the group. The AHS decided that it was better to be with Los Aldeanos than against them. Afterward, Rodríguez told me that the Acapulco concert was one of the AHS's greatest achievements in its twenty-four years of existence. Los

Aldeanos thus went from blacklist to driver's seat in a short space of time. Despite all its conflicts with institutions, the duo managed to bend cultural politics in its favor through its sheer popularity. In the light of such complex and localized negotiations, with different institutions pulling in different directions and a hip hop fan playing a pivotal role, it is hard to generalize about cultural policy or to sustain an argument that the process of nationalizing rap can be reduced to a simple term like co-optation or harnessing by the state.[33]

The issue of state policy becomes even more complicated when we consider the role of the media. TV and radio program directors have their own cultural and political agendas, and complaints have been rife for years that they failed to support rap, even as political leaders opened up to it. This inconsistency in attitudes to new music has been apparent since the early 1970s and the rise of nueva trova: "Each different cultural institution or area of culture had its own cultural line and logic. The radio and television, and each program director, had their own ideas about culture. One radio station might play a song and another station would ban it" (Foehr 2001, 50). Even when conditions improved for the *trovadores*, media resistance persisted (R. Moore 2003, 20), revealing radio and especially TV to be some of the most conservative branches of the state apparatus. This gulf in attitudes was illustrated vividly to me when I accompanied the group Los Paisanos and Williams Figueredo, the AHS promoter, to a radio broadcast to promote a forthcoming AHS concert. The group played their track—"Negro," a song about race relations—and although they performed it regularly in concerts at La Madriguera, the program director was furious about the lyrics and ejected the artists from the building, telling them not to come back. The relationship between the AHS and the media, both in effect arms of the state, had to be carefully negotiated, and in this case the negotiations failed spectacularly.

Sekou of Anónimo Consejo, a group which epitomizes politically correct rap and is employed by the ACR, expressed his bewilderment at the gulf between the state's supportive rhetoric and the limited promotion of conscious rap in the media: "It's difficult to understand how in Cuba, a country that is synonymous with revolution in every sense, we don't hear Anónimo Consejo or Hermanos de Causa, yet on every radio station we hear Eminem, an American rapper who is obscene, foul-mouthed and one of the most violent examples of this culture" (quoted in A. Fernández n.d., 8). Doble Filo underlined the disjunction between the market-driven music industry and socialist cultural policy, claiming that "when the record labels work in tandem with the cultural politics of our country, . . . that's when you'll hear our CDs in Cuban homes" (quoted in Torna 2007).

Nor is it just members of the rap scene who criticize the media for its musical content: a journalist writing in the newspaper *Juventud Rebelde* referred to "the poor quality of some programs in the media" as he condemned the pervasive influence of reggaetón (Castro Medel 2005a). In our interview, Alpidio Alonso drew a clear distinction between the AHS and the media, suggesting that the former promoted serious, revolutionary culture while the latter inclined more to banal, commercial offerings. He put these criticisms in print in 2007, writing of "the vulgarity and stupidity (in two words, great irresponsibility) of some of our leading radio and TV programs" (Alonso 2007). Another AHS official, Natacha Cabrera Cepero (2007, 18), was equally scathing, opening her article with the question: "Why do the media seem to be working to promote music without paying any attention to the cultural policies of the nation?"

Once again, rather than homogenizing "the media," we must be alert to its inconsistencies. My interviews with radio and TV presenters revealed that individual directors have considerable room to maneuver. While I heard rumors of directives "from above" concerning the amount of reggaetón on the radio, almost everyone I spoke to laid primary responsibility for programming choices with presenters and directors. The radio presenter Guille Vilar told me that some are more daring while others are more conservative, likening directors to artists who had their own tastes and exercised their discrimination. A stronger view came from a hip hop intermediary who also worked in the media, who claimed that most directors of radio shows were narrow-minded and conservative: they were risk averse at best and ignorant racists at worst, and many just said a blanket "no" when the subject of rap came up. A radio presenter who played rap and other alternative musics on his show told me about his regular conflicts with his bosses, who carefully scrutinized his invitees. He described the irony of a socialist country with conservative state media and claimed that those who ran the media were suspicious of black culture and afraid of genuinely revolutionary discourse, hence their widespread distaste for rap. A hip hop figure who worked in TV told me of the old-fashioned, archaic, nationalist mentality among TV directors; he described them as mainly older, white people who listened to son and salsa and distrusted what they perceived as black youth culture. Like many, he regarded TV as the most conservative cultural institution in Cuba. To be sure, the existence of the hip hop radio shows *La Esquina de Rap* and *Microfonazo* and the spaces for rappers on more general-interest shows like *A Propósito* and the TV program *Cuerda Viva* illustrate that the system is sufficiently flexible to allow a handful of sympathetic program directors and presenters to provide Cuban hip hoppers with limited airtime. Nevertheless, the policies pursued by progressive institutions such as the AHS have clearly met with considerable resistance from the conservative state-run media.

The degree of independence of the media is surprising. A senior journalist told me of the separation between media institutions and the Ministry of Culture; within each, key individuals have their own fiefdoms. According to one leading rapper who met him, Castro said that there were things that even he could not do, above all dictate to the media. However one may regard this comment—which the rapper himself had taken seriously—there is ample evidence that the articulation between the media and other branches of the state is not straightforward, and that this had a decisive impact on rap. The digital revolution did not take hold fully in Havana until after rap's popularity had started to subside in favor of reggaetón; the lack of mass media exposure thus seriously limited the music's spread beyond live performances, especially in the absence of Internet access by the vast majority of the population.

The nationalization of rap could be summed up thus: it happened to a degree, mainly within specific cultural institutions, because of hip hop's alignment with revolutionary ideology; but it has been partially blocked because, as an in-your-face, foreign-derived youth culture generally perceived as black, it faces resistance from the mainly older, whiter Cubans who dominate the media and who run many cultural organizations and performance venues. The discursive process of nationalization, which allowed figures like Abel Prieto and Alpidio Alonso to talk fluently and enthusiastically about hip hop, contrasts with the practical obstacles that rappers have faced in securing performance and media spaces. Roberto Zurbano (n.d.b) observed that, twelve years after his groundbreaking meeting with Rodolfo Rensoli, institutions still did not deal with hip hop properly; indeed, thanks to the declining support from the AHS, hip hop had almost gone into reverse. But rap was nonetheless nationalized to a remarkable degree. Understanding its trajectory—the openings and the closed doors, the spaces and the barriers—requires delving into the relevant institutions to observe the individuals who, in often contradictory ways, guided this process.

The Cuban Rap Agency

The creation of the ACR may be seen as a moment which brought the tensions and inconsistencies within state policies toward hip hop out into the open; many also see it as one of the triggers of hip hop's decline in Havana. Was the agency, as many believe, created to launch a new, more controlling phase in the nationalization of rap, to divide and conquer the rap scene in the wake of the denuncia social incident at the 2002 festival? Was this the moment when the government decided to try to co-opt hip hop once and for all? Definitive answers to these questions are unknowable at present, since decisions were taken at least at the level of the minister of culture, Abel Prieto, and indeed it seems that Castro himself was involved (Castillo Martiatu n.d.a, 20), and the motivations of these leaders are impossible to ascertain; but there is plenty of circumstantial evidence to take into account.

The idea of the agency grew out of discussions between rappers, the AHS, and officials at the Ministry of Culture. In other words, leading rap groups played a key role in negotiations: they first fought for inclusion in existing artistic agencies, and then, frustrated, pushed for their own dedicated agency (E. González 2007). As the founder of Primera Base, Rubén Marín, put it: "The Agency was something that we, the rappers, always wanted, a dream come true" (quoted in Cordero n.d., 23). It is important to bear in mind that for all the skepticism surrounding the rap and rock agencies as supposed instruments of state control, leading groups were clamoring to be included in both because they wanted increased promotion and a steady income from music. The dream soon soured, however; the ACR rapidly became unpopular outside (and even within) the small circle who benefited from it, and a much more negative view of institutionalization developed in the wake of its inception. Nevertheless, for all the grumbling, most concrete accusations laid at its door have concerned not specific cases of control or manipulation, but rather a failure to live up to expectations in terms of organization, promotion, and democracy in the selection process, and above all the division of a previously cohesive rap scene. The creation of the ACR was in many ways the most dramatic and controversial moment in the nationalization of rap in Cuba; however, I do not see it in terms of control so much as the willing insertion of leading rappers into the heart of Cuba's highly bureaucratized professional music system, with all the problems that entailed, echoing Peter Wade's argument that much supposed appropriation is carried out by ordinary musicians and low- or medium-level intermediaries.

Although a case of ACR censorship is presented in chapter 4, this appears to have been the exception rather than the rule. Instead, agency rappers have been tied up with the excessive red tape that accompanies the music profession in Cuba. Yrak Saenz told me that ACR groups constantly criticize the stifling bureaucracy that has been created around an originally rebellious, antibureaucratic cultural movement. He cannot arrange a concert without reams of papers and authorizations; he noted the irony that it is easier for a subversive underground group to perform live than it is for his professional group, Doble Filo, since the former can deal directly (if illegally) with a concert venue without any paperwork. Control is less an active intervention than a passive burden (the dead hand of bureaucracy).

A lot of the problems come back to the creation of a self-financing, commercial rap agency under the auspices of the ICM, rather than a subsidized hip hop center. In order to pay the bills, the agency rappers are sent on regular ICM-organized tours to the provinces as support acts for timba orchestras. As Zurbano told me, the response to rappers' demands was ill thought out, an administrative rather than conceptual solution that squeezed hip hop into an existing professional structure rather than creating a new space for it. As a result, there was no room for those who pursued the nonmusical, noncommercial elements of hip hop (graffiti and break dance), and even DJs—vital players in hip hop culture—were included on the agency's books only as sound technicians, not artists. Through its insertion into the ICM, rap has been removed from its context, considered not one of the four elements of hip hop culture but rather a style of music, like salsa or reggaetón, which can be used to generate money and can just as well be paired with any other style. Leading artists are regarded less as social or cultural activists than as rap musicians, and the nature of the provincial tours puts considerable pressure on rappers to entertain rather than educate. Performing to an inebriated crowd at 2:00 a.m. after a salsa show is frequently a depressing experience for conscious rappers, who often face an audience with no interest in hearing music for reflection rather than for dancing; even when not pushed by the agency itself, the temptation to switch to reggaetón is strong. The ICM tours that provide their daily bread also shift the focus of their work from Havana to the provinces; they perform less often in the capital and have lost a significant portion of their Havana fan base. It is impossible to know if this was the aim, but it was the outcome.

The veteran ACR rapper Rubén Marín told me candidly about the pressures on agency rappers to give audiences what they want in order to make enough money for their own and the agency's economic survival: "When you go professional, you have to respond to governmental interests. If you're not economically viable, you'll be removed from the agency. And if I go back on the street, I'll give up rap, because at my age I've got to support myself." It is worth noting that "responding to governmental interests" is conceived of in economic, not political, terms, and that Marín moved into reggaetón as a result. Rappers were forced to think about the bottom line, to make a return for the ACR, otherwise—as Marín saw it—the agency would disappear, and rappers would risk losing their hard-won professional status, which turned out to be a bind as much as a blessing. Today, fear of losing this status impinges on rappers' artistic choices, pressuring them to think and behave like professional musicians rather than cultural activists.[34]

Thus the creation of the ACR imposed unanticipated norms on rappers, norms that were not so much political as economic and bureaucratic. Rappers wanted to be treated as equal to other professional musicians, but achieving this led to considerable disillusionment. Nationalization has created an institutional space for rap (though much less so for hip hop culture), symbolized by the ACR's large office on the ground floor of the ICM, but at times this has felt like an institutional straitjacket since it obliges senior rappers to play by national rules.

Those who see the ACR as an instrument of control emphasize that its first director, Susana García, was a writer with no prior knowledge of the hip hop scene. Yet it is an open secret that this imposition of an outsider was the result of an unresolved power struggle for the position between two leaders of the scene, suggesting that hip hoppers themselves were partly to blame. After five years of disappointments, Magia López of the ACR group Obsesion was made director, but the fact that little changed in the first three years of her directorship revealed that the problems were systemic. Rappers' complaints that an outsider was running the ACR gave way to accusations that an insider in charge equated to a conflict of interest, implying that the problem was fundamentally one of a poor fit between the agency and the hip hop scene rather than one of government control. Furthermore, the issue of self-censorship reared its head. In authoritarian cultural climates, artists who have worked hard to negotiate a space for themselves are often reluctant to see that space eroded by what they see as the irresponsible actions of others. The combination of internal and external pressures—self-control and the rigid professional music system—has left the ACR little room to maneuver.[35]

"We Have Allies and Enemies at the Controls"

In his celebrated study of the state and the arts under communism, *The Velvet Prison*, Miklós Haraszti (1988, 78–79) writes: "In our eyes the state represents not a monolithic body of rules but rather a live network of lobbies. We play with it, we know how to use it, and we have allies and enemies at the controls." The fractured nature of Cuban state institutions and policies and the personalization of cultural politics has turned the ability to negotiate with state representatives into an essential skill for hip hoppers, something that members of La FabriK have articulated frequently. Many of the achievements of the hip hop scene have come as the result of such negotiations with allies at the controls.

At a public forum at the Casa de la Amistad in July 2008 (discussed in chapter 4), Alexey Rodríguez responded to a complaint about the lack of support for hip hop with a spiel about artists' responsibility to seek out institutions and their resources, rather than wait for institutions to come to them—he stressed the importance of *learning the language* of institutions to access their benefits. His colleague Roberto Rossell added that one had to learn to present projects in a way that gave institutions no room to say no. If leading hip hoppers played a proactive role in the institutionalization of rap during its boom years, then they must also take responsibility for the genre's subsequent decline. Rodríguez regularly blames hip hop's recent travails on the fact that hip hoppers have forgotten how to negotiate, and he refused simply to hold the AHS responsible for the disappearance of the festival. In the past, he said, all the rappers would put their heads together, then go to the institutions and make demands. Today, he feels that rappers are not willing to push for what they want; they have become used to institutional support, and when it does not appear, they complain. Magia López, too, spoke of the new generation's failure to knock on institutional doors: she has had to insist and demand during her whole career, she said, and her current job as director of the ACR is no different. According to these figures, the decline of hip hop is not the result of increased state control but rather a story of paternalism, dependence, and apathy.

Yelandi Playa (El Yela), who spent three years working as a producer with Obsesion and La FabriK, emphasized the collective's personal relationship with Fernando Rojas, the president of the AHS who moved on to the Consejo Nacional de Casas de la Cultura, the institution that supports the Hip Hop Symposium. "Fernando Rojas always supported rap groups 100 percent from the AHS," he told me, so launching the symposium was straightforward. Cuba functions on a personal level, he continued: on the one hand, there are institutions, with their norms; on the other hand, there are relatives, friends, and neighbors, with whom more informal bonds of solidarity prevail. Playa emphasized that the personalization of cultural politics meant that negotiation was absolutely key. Many people criticize institutions or make accusations of censorship, he said, yet they assume in advance that institutions will not support them rather than knocking on doors, presenting their projects, debating, and contesting any rejections. The members of La FabriK focus on the importance of individual responsibility; they believe it is for artists to present ideas to state bodies, not the other way round. When Yrak Saenz met Castro at an AHS congress, he argued that the Cuban musical sphere needed to provide more space for reflection and self-expression, rather than focusing so much on dance and entertainment.

Many other leading figures in this story—such as Rodolfo Rensoli, Ariel Fernández, and Roberto Zurbano—underlined the importance of negotiation. Rensoli attributed the growth of the festival from 1995 to 2000 to his understanding of this art. His brothers are party militants; "since I was a kid, I've known the margins within which you can move," he told me. Fernández felt that the only way to get anything done was to get inside institutions and push constantly, and while he was often frustrated in his attempts, he also won victories, and he admitted to me that "to be quite honest, I enjoyed the fight." The picture that emerges is one of considerable agency on the part of hip hoppers—while regularly frustrated, they do not see themselves as powerless, nor do they act that way. Recently, as the role of the AHS and Almendares Vivo has diminished, direct negotiations between hip hoppers and the administrators of small commercial clubs have become increasingly important to the health of the hip hop scene.[36] Arguably, the managers of Barbarám, Karachi, and Atelier have played a larger role in the creation of spaces for hip hop in recent years than have the president of the AHS or the minister of culture; the organization of regular peñas in these venues, which formed the mainstay of the scene between 2007–10, had more to do with hip hoppers' personal contacts with club administrators than with any abstract notion of state cultural policy or assimilation.

While some would like to see fearful artists under the thumb of the state, the reality is often far different. The documentary *Young Rebels* captures a scene in a public debate during the 2003 festival in which Soandres del Río (Hermanos de Causa) puts Alpidio Alonso on the spot in front of a room full of people and video cameras. Del Río was not afraid to embarrass or debate with Alonso in a public meeting, and I saw similarly heated public discussions in 2004 in which rappers were openly critical of the ACR's director, the Cuban media, the handling of the cancellation of the 2004 festival, and so on. The rapper Edgar González criticized the ACR in a published interview, claiming it was excessively commercial and conventional (Torna 2007); indeed, he subsequently published a similarly critical article in the UJC magazine *El Caimán Barbudo* (González 2007, 15), in which he argued that the ACR risked "killing the spirit of our culture in order to integrate us into that voracious market which negates all magic." Far from bringing consequences for its outspoken author, this article was soon followed by the departure of the ACR's director. The same magazine encouraged Ariel Fernández to publish two articles in defense of hip hop in the late 1990s, inviting him to respond in the second to criticisms of the first made by an AHS official. Vigorous debate and the public criticism of officials are part of the cultural scene in Cuba, and some of it is actively encouraged by organs of the state.

My concern in this chapter has been to complicate simplistic notions of the relationship between the state and hip hoppers as one of control, co-optation, harnessing, and so on, by stressing some of the ways rappers and their spokespeople took the destiny of the scene into their own hands, and by underlining the uneven institutional field in which they operated. However, for all that hip hoppers have been proactive in the nationalization of rap, the imbalance of power between their scene and the state is very real. This imbalance tends to be less overt at the lower levels of the state hierarchy, in spaces such as cultural centers and small clubs, where interactions between sympathetic officials and strong-willed hip hoppers can sometimes blur the power dynamics considerably: La Madriguera promoter Jorge Rodríguez described working on a "creator to creator" level in order to include "risky artists" like Los Aldeanos (Fuller 2008). But one area in which hip hoppers are forced to come into contact with higher reaches of the state bureaucracy, and in which the limits of their agency are often painfully revealed, is that of foreign travel. Most leading rap groups have been invited to perform overseas, and although some have gone, most have at some point been refused permission to leave the country, sometimes repeatedly.[37] These negotiations are probably the most unequal of those to which rappers are exposed, and a number have found the experience of being denied permission to take up opportunities overseas particularly dispiriting, contributing to their urge to emigrate altogether. One of the most egregious cases has been that of Bián Rodríguez (El B) of Los Aldeanos, who won the Cuban Red Bull improvisation contest—La Batalla de los Gallos (cockfight)—in 2007 and 2008, but who was denied permission to leave the island to participate in the Latin American grand final in both years.[38] Such cases are a firm reminder of who, ultimately, holds the reins of power.

Two broad issues must therefore be taken into account in understanding the state–hip hop relationship, relating to the gap between official and operative ideologies (Pekacz 1994). Officially, rap is supported by the Ministry of Culture, the ACR, the AHS, and other cultural institutions, and has been publicly embraced by the minister of culture and Castro himself. On the operative level, however, initiatives to support rap have often been hampered by media exclusion and a lack of performance options; a lot of power lies at lower levels of the state hierarchy, in the hands of individual program directors and venue administrators, whose preferences and prejudices are crucial. There have also been occasional repressive measures toward individual artists. Los Aldeanos were banned from the Almendares venue in 2005: they turned up to perform one day and were told to leave because they were on a state security blacklist. The same happened at every peña they went to for a while. Yet—and this is the second issue to consider—nothing more serious occurred, and after a while the venues began to relax their restrictions, the duo started to appear again, and they went on to become the most regularly performing rappers in Havana, without making amends or softening their line. Those responsible for their exclusion apparently had short memories or were not paying close attention. The case of Los Aldeanos illustrates perfectly the incomplete and contradictory process of nationalizing rap in Cuba: having earlier been banned, the duo won the 2008 *Cuerda Viva* TV award for best rap demo and the major concert opportunity at the Pabellón Cuba that went with it; they presented the following year's award in person to Doble Filo at a huge, filmed event at PabExpo; their songs are played regularly on the radio show *La Esquina de Rap*; and they appeared at a huge 2008 concert at the Tribuna Antiimperialista, Havana's largest concert stage, as guests of the legendary trovador Pablo Milanés. Blacklisted again in 2009, they performed sellout shows at La Madriguera and the Acapulco Theater in early 2010 with the backing of the AHS.

Thus if there is a gap between official and operative ideologies on the level of state support, the same is true with regard to state control. The contradictory policies of different branches of the state have led to disillusionment and dispersal within the rap scene, but also to surprising spaces for distinctly confrontational artists. Creating and exploiting such opportunities is often a question of having allies like Jorge Rodríguez, the AHS employee who facilitated Los Aldeanos' comeback, at the controls.

Nationalizing Rap, Internationalizing the Word

Any global explanation of how and why rap became nationalized in Cuba will be inherently flawed, in that it will depend on imputing agency to "the state" or "the Cuban leadership" rather than the wide array of state, nonstate, and intermediary actors who have taken often contradictory decisions and actions over a period of many years. Nationalization has been a gradual process, with different individuals and branches of the state coming on board at different times and to different degrees. Casas de la Cultura (houses of culture) became involved in the early 1990s, the AHS in stages through the decade, and higher-level political leaders in 1999: there was no unified strategy. Nevertheless, the question is still worth asking.

To begin with some of the answers that have already been proposed, the core of Sujatha Fernandes's theory of "artistic public spheres" is that "the Cuban leadership . . . sought to create spaces for critical discussion within the arts" (2006, 40–41). This, however, attributes too much agency to the top of the cultural hierarchy rather than to the bottom, where movement began. Fernandes alternates between the expressions "the Cuban leadership" and "the state" in her discussions of cultural policy, suggesting a distinctly top-down vision. In the case of hip hop, however, the spaces for critical discussion were forged between artists, promoters, and lower-level functionaries at the Casas de la Cultura and the AHS; significant involvement from higher-level institutions and the Cuban leadership did not arrive until several years later, after early disinterest. Fernandes's theory has its virtues, but it needs qualification, for it reflects only a limited, middle period of the history of Havana hip hop. The critical spaces that opened up during the initial period were beneath the radar of the Cuban leadership, and more recently the spread of digital technology has notably reduced government control over cultural production, leading to a marked downturn in the collaboration and incorporation on which Fernandes's model rests and eroding the arts-media dichotomy she posits.[39] Controversial artists like Elvis Manuel, El Micha, and Los Aldeanos rose to fame on the margins of the institutional sphere, their homemade recordings passed from hand to hand, their burgeoning careers illustrating the creation of a mass-mediated "artistic public sphere" that is increasingly detached from the state-run media and government policy. Live performances by underground artists often take place illicitly, evidence of a growing underground music economy and declining official management of culture (Baker 2011).

The question of why state involvement moved up a notch in 1999 is an intriguing one, not least because in that year both Abel Prieto and Fidel Castro became personally and publicly involved with hip hop. It is demonstrable that the major policy decisions with regard to hip hop in the period 1999–2002 were taken on at least the ministerial level, and it seems almost certain that Castro himself had a hand, since his interest in hip hop and willingness to meet with rappers around this time is a matter of record. Fernandes (2006, 85) proposes that Cuban leaders "harness[ed] rappers' creative energy as a way of rebuilding popular support in a time of growing racial divisions." Popularity never seems to have been high on the list of priorities for the Cuban leadership, however, which has tended to be more concerned with revolutionary internationalism than domestic bread and circuses. The AHS, on the other hand, does seem to have been thinking about its own popularity when it decided to back Los Aldeanos in 2010. But there is a crucial difference with Fernandes's view: the state as a whole had reduced Los Aldeanos' space to nothing, but the AHS decided to row against the current, illustrating policy formation and popularity seeking at the institutional (rather than leadership) level.

Ariana Hernandez-Reguant (2006, 253), meanwhile, suggests that "spheres of critique were facilitated, to some extent and temporarily, by the state itself . . . and were justified as both revenue generating and controlled outlets for leisurely discontent." This strategic view of cultural policy is defensible with respect to timba, the genre that Hernandez-Reguant discusses, but it is at best only partially applicable to the predominantly amateur rap scene, which has never generated much income. A safety-valve theory of hip hop places too much agency at the top of the state hierarchy and omits the important issue of ideological congruency, which suggests that there were also less cynical motivations at play.

I would argue that the key lies instead in the Black August exchanges of 1998 to 2000 and Belafonte's meeting with Castro in 1999. The former saw the focus of attention shift from Havana to New York: the American visitors were less interested in hearing or articulating criticism about Castro or socialism than expressing their excitement about being in Cuba and fixing their sights on the U.S. government and its capitalist system. These were eminently palatable messages for the Cuban government, and the increased investment in the festival in 1999 implies that the Ministry of Culture decided to give the visitors a bigger platform, having seen the previous year's trial run go off without problems. The internationalization of the focus of Havana hip hop was capped by Belafonte's meeting with Castro, when the idea of rap as a global revolutionary culture reached the pinnacle of the state hierarchy.

The combination of blackness and internationalist radicalism within hip hop at the end of the 1990s invites comparison with the 1960s. As numerous scholars have shown, Castro embraced black American Marxists in the earlier decade—but he did so despite, not because of, their blackness. It was their Marxism he was interested in, and the fiercely anti-U.S.-establishment views and actions that went with it. Although his policies have brought notable gains for Africans and their descendants on both domestic and international levels, Castro is widely recognized to have little interest in blackness and black culture per se; he has, however, been drawn to the internationalist revolutionary views displayed by numerous black leaders around the world. As Katrin Hansing (2002, 144) notes, the Cuban government supported the black power movement because it was aimed against the U.S. government, and although African American figures were welcomed in Havana as anti-imperialist heroes, their ideas about race and blackness were brushed over. Cuban leaders portrayed the race aspect of black power as a reaction to specific American circumstances, not as a stimulus for internal reflection. Castro's eyes were fixed firmly on the international stage. Carlos Moore (1988, 256) relates: "Fidel Castro had always gone beyond the limit to attract black Americans, their movements, and their leaders. [He was] keenly aware that winning and maintaining Afro-American support had practical value for any country in conflict with the U.S." Mark Sawyer (2006) uses the term "inclusionary discrimination" to characterize the Cuban government's policies on race, concluding that Castro used a racial agenda to advance his anti-imperialist and anticapitalist politics overseas while dismissing the issue of race at home. Sawyer observes: "Cuban internationalism served Cuban racial ideology: Internationalism allowed the Cuban Revolution to externalize racial problems and the battle against racism. The regime's ideological battle against racism was about combating U.S. imperialism and capitalism more than it was about any real domestic agenda" (ibid., 62–63).

In this light, Fernandes's (2006, 119) suggestion that Cuba's political leaders realized "that they can harness the energy of these rappers to bolster the image of Cuba as a mixed-race nation with African roots" and to recapture popular support rings false. Castro may have pursued antiracist policies and begun describing Cuba as an "Afro-Latin" nation in the context of Cuba's anti-imperialist adventures in Africa in the 1970s, but "while encouraging the violent aspects of Black Power activism, the Cu-

ban authorities looked upon its cultural manifestations as being negative," and they clamped down on African American hairstyles, clothing,
and music (C. Moore 1988, 259–60) and closed down "the flourishing,
alternative black public space" (Sawyer 2006, 68). To be sure, the cultural
climate in the late 1990s was more open, but it is hard to believe that
Castro underwent a conversion forty years into the revolution and decided to promote the culture of the African diaspora for its racial messages. Rather, Belafonte apparently convinced Castro that the pros of
supporting contemporary African American radicalism outweighed the
cons of opening up more space for outspoken black culture in Cuba.
Castro chose to support a transnational genre because he was interested
in its transnational impact, absorbing Belafonte's lessons about the Black
Panthers of rap for the same reason that he had embraced the Black
Panthers themselves.

What appealed to Castro in the 1960s, and again in 1999, was the
political radicalism of black Americans, not their blackness. He listened
so attentively because Belafonte described rap as a form of revolutionary
culture, and Belafonte himself linked the 1990s to the era that was clos-
est to Castro's heart, the 1950s and 1960s. Perhaps control was also a
motivation. But if Castro were interested only in controlling hip hop, why
spend an entire day debating it with Belafonte, an old friend and ally?
This was more than a question of power—it was also an intellectual and
political connection.

The record of Belafonte's meeting with Castro is illuminating: Belafonte
explained hip hop as an international movement that serves as a voice for
the oppressed around the globe and "Fidel expressed great interest *from a
global perspective*" ("Encuentro entre amigos" n.d., 19, emphasis added). In
our interview, Belafonte confirmed that he had described hip hop to Castro as "a platform on which to find international identity" and "a comfort
zone in what was going on globally." He went on: "I told Fidel Castro that I
thought that young Cuban people becoming part of an international hip
hop movement could be a wonderful exchange. . . . they could bring a lot of
ideas to the table, and tell young people that they would meet in America
or Germany or wherever they would go. . . . I told Fidel, it's all over the
world. And as he heard all of this—I don't know that anyone had ever told
it to him this way—he saw this [as] universal." A few years later Alonso told
me that the aim of the festival was "to project a revolutionary message

from Cuba"; and in a published interview after the 2002 festival, he alternated between disdain for the "manipulative" reactions of the foreign press and pride at the amazement expressed by North American rappers at the level of institutional support in Cuba (Henríquez Lagarde 2002). Alonso explicitly told Ariel Fernández that the festival's importance lay in its international appeal, and in our conversation, Fernández was in no doubt that the state's support for the festival was motivated by the opportunity to spread the message of the Cuban Revolution overseas. If the world's eyes were on Cuba during the festival, the eyes of Cuban leaders were on the world.[40]

Sawyer's term "inclusionary discrimination" is a good way to describe state attitudes toward Cuban rap: the combination of support and restriction, of discursive enthusiasm and practical obstacles, of funding and expanding an international festival and largely excluding hip hop from the domestic media. The hip hop festival itself around 2000 might be characterized by this phrase, given the event's international character and all-star line-up yet heavy and intrusive police presence. State support for a large international festival undermines the idea of simple control as motivation: if that were the case, why provide confrontational groups with a platform? Yet to suggest that this was simply a case of currying popularity or providing a safety valve misses the ideological and political motivations at play. As Jorge Domínguez (2008, 203) notes, one international strategy pursued during the Special Period was the exercise of "soft" power, "promoting internationally the attractive qualities of Cuban society in order to develop a constituency abroad, especially in the U.S., friendly to Cuba and its people." The other face of this soft power, visible in the hip hop festivals, was using culture to promote Cuban political goals overseas. As with the government's support of black power in the 1960s, hip hop served as a stick with which to beat the United States while raising Cuba's profile overseas. It is no coincidence that the largest investment made by the state was in the international hip hop festival. As Sawyer suggests, the motivation behind this internationalism was "externalizing"—addressing an international audience and tackling international issues. The roots of these developments should be sought in Cuba's foreign policy rather than in its domestic agenda.

Far from promoting an image of Cuba as "a mixed-race nation with African roots," official constructions of Cuban hip hop usually elide the question of race altogether, as in the online forum for the 2004 festival.[41] One of the problems with academic constructions of Cuban hip hop is that the race lens is frequently adopted a priori, and thus scholars see the hip hop scene as made up of *black* youths. But blackness is not the only frame for the social, cultural, or political movements of the African diaspora, as the conflicted history of African American Marxist politics of the 1960s and 1970s shows. What Rojas saw, as he told me, was *thinking* youths, and what Castro saw (thanks to Belafonte) was *revolutionary* youths who might take their place on the global stage.

Conclusions

Cuban rap was transformed from a street subculture to an official, sponsored part of national culture in the space of a few years, and an examination of this development reveals the extent to which the formation of national culture is negotiated on a variety of levels by practitioners, key cultural intermediaries, and state officials rather than imposed from above (Wade 2000; Askew 2002). For all that the aim of nationalizing rap was articulated by the minister of culture in 1999, this process has not simply been one of state co-optation, or any other such abstraction that denies the active participation of non-elite actors who had ensured that it was already well underway by this time. Rather than seeing nationalization as a process of alienation, based on an oppositional relationship between hip hop and the state, we should note that hip hoppers were protagonists, keen to see their culture occupy a place within national culture.

Leading hip hoppers feel that they are responsible for many aspects of the nationalization of rap, both good and bad. The abandonment of conscious rap by a number of leading groups since 2002 has been a response to the commercial possibilities opened up by the boom of reggaetón, and to the increasing economic exigencies of daily life in contemporary Cuba, rather than to any political pressure, which echoes Wade's contention that the commercialization of popular music is often led largely by musicians themselves. Most accounts put the state largely in the driver's seat, yet in reality it has generally been reactive rather than proactive. The rapid nationalization of rap reflects how quickly a fruitful conversation was established by hip hop intermediaries, a group that included North American participants. Somewhat paradoxically, non-Cubans played a significant part, both practical and discursive, in the nationalization of rap: there was a palpable sense of self-confidence about the Havana rap scene in its heyday which came as much from interventions and approval by foreign observers as it did from acceptance by the state or popularity with local audiences.

It is important to uncover the complex, fragmented, negotiated nature of the incorporation of rap into national culture in order to form a considered response to the central issue of state involvement, one of the defining features of Cuban hip hop. When I went to a screening of the documentary *Inventos* in London, I was struck that the audience laughed when Pablo Herrera mentioned Abel Prieto's statement in 1999 that it was time to nationalize rap. This brought home to me that people outside Cuba tend to assume that nationalization and popular music make incongruous bedfellows. However, I suspect that many Cubans would not have found this remark strange; after all, it was the leading rap groups who clamored for their own agency, and many AHS artists, aware that they lack the resources to put on their own concerts, would like to see more involvement from this state organization.[42] Most culture is nationalized in Cuba, and nationalization was vital to hip hop's expansion and visibility in the 1990s, before the digital revolution changed the rules of the game. Herrera and Fernández saw engagement with state institutions as the only way forward. Unlike their nueva trova predecessors, they could look back on thirty-five years of the institutionalization of culture and see that this process, if not always problem free, had opened up significant local spaces and global popularity for artists such as Pablo Milanés, Silvio Rodríguez, and Carlos Varela; they could also see how rockers, for whom such engagement was much more ideologically problematic, had struggled. I am not suggesting that nationalization is perceived as trouble free, but rather that it should not be characterized as a Stalinist fist closing in on an unwilling cultural movement.

Accounts of the nationalization of rap thus depend on their ideological starting point. Those who take a negative view of state intervention see a process of co-optation or control; one Cuban exile claimed that the state has two methods—censorship or assimilation (quoted in R. Moore 2003, 24). However, having seen Los Aldeanos perform at the opening concert of the postponed rap festival in November 2004 and criticize the AHS president Alpidio Alonso and the ACR director Susana García, both of whom were present, by name, concluding that the postponement of the festival was evidence that "the institutions are full of shit," I would suggest that such a polarized view is untenable in relation to contemporary Cuban rap. Certainly both censorship and assimilation continue, and there are many artists active in the rap scene who are vocal in their criticism of state institutions; however, the fact that such criticism is voiced openly in meetings and live concerts points to a third way.[43]

I also heard positive views about the AHS expressed on a regular basis. Edgar González (2007, 15), one of Cuba's best-known rappers, gives the AHS much of the credit for creating a hip hop "movement," arguing that the AHS "taught us and integrated us into the Cuban cultural panorama, including us among the creative people of this country." The AHS, far from co-opting rap, was cast in the role of protecting it from the market forces, above all the boom in reggaetón, that threatened to swamp it. While Alonso was criticizing reggaetón in public, his opposite number at the ACR was overseeing eight groups, five of which were in fact busy churning out this rival genre. In fact, if—as several scholars have recently suggested (e.g., Cloonan 2003; Akpan 2006)—the market is an important form of music censorship, then the Cuban state (via the AHS) may be seen in part as protecting socially engaged hip hop from the restrictive effects of the global music industry, which may not operate directly in Cuba but whose products circulate freely in digital form.

As Robin Moore (2003, 33) has argued, a starkly negative characterization of the institutionalization of popular music—of the kind generally found in studies of the Soviet Union and Eastern Europe—is inappropriate in the case of Cuban nueva trova, and I would extend this argument to rap. Studies of music in socialist countries tend to paint a polarized picture, drawing a sharp distinction between official and unofficial rock groups (e.g., Ramet 1994). Soviet and Eastern European musicians who received substantial state backing usually made significant artistic compromises and were not taken seriously by dedicated rock fans. However, the generalized anti-authoritarianism of rock, which makes its assimilation by state organizations problematic, cannot be mapped directly onto rap, which tends to articulate protest against marginalization and inequality rather than against authority per se. Given that the progressive philosophy of conscious hip hop shares ideological roots and a discursive framework with the Cuban Revolution, a considerable degree of accommodation between state institutions and rap artists has been possible without seriously affecting perceptions of artistic integrity.

The involvement of the state lends a distinctive character to the case of Cuban rap. By providing the majority of spaces and opportunities for professional and amateur rappers alike, the state has contributed to the development of Cuban hip hop and has aided the longevity of many leading groups in the face of difficult conditions (such as the lack of a domestic recording market and the limited commercial appeal of rap in the era of reggaetón). The nationalization of rap in Cuba has been a process mediated by the state, rather than by the music industry or media, as has generally been the case with the nationalization of foreign musics such as funk, reggae, and rap in other parts of Latin America (e.g., Pacini Hernandez 2003, 27–28; Sansone 2001; Giovannetti 2003; dos Santos Godi 2001). The establishment of rap relied on live performance and therefore government support, which in turn depended not on the commercial viability of rap but the extent to which it could be incorporated into dominant visions of national identity. In many other Latin American contexts, arguments over the relationship between African American musics and national identity, though commonplace, have tended to be conducted somewhat on the sidelines, since commercial imperatives have dominated. But as Cuban rap relied on state involvement, a greater degree of political negotiation was necessary, meaning that questions of national identity have been foregrounded. As the official announcement of the 2005 rap festival stated, "the central objective of the competition will be the search for a national identity for the movement."[44]

Of course, state involvement has not always been positive. Robinson (2004, 114) talks of a "constant, low-level struggle" between rappers and the authorities throughout the 1990s, and there is plenty of evidence that, for all the recent history of state support, this struggle continues. In the aftermath of the cancellation of the rap festival in August 2004 due to hurricane damage, a concert by ACR groups was also canceled—so late that the audience had already arrived—but this time without any explanation being given to the audience or the artists, who are of course state employees. Hastily organized replacement concerts in the patio of the Teatro Mella in Vedado were interrupted on several occasions when the venue director pulled the plug on the sound system with rappers in midsentence. Yet when the festival was finally put on in November, Los Aldeanos, arguably the most radical group in Havana, was allowed to perform a full, uncensored set at the giant La Tropical venue. Contradictions between policy and practice abound, usually being met with the typical shrug and "that's Cuba."

Since the state must be given some credit for the successes of Cuban rap as well as some blame for its failures, an examination of Cuban hip hop is therefore an opportunity to question the characterization of rap as oppositional or resistant music, something of an orthodoxy in studies of global hip hop (e.g., Martinez 1997; Mitchell 2001b; Whiteley, Bennett, and Hawkins 2004).[45] Looking at the complex engagement between artists, intermediaries, and state institutions, we can see at different times appropriation, support, conflict, and the coexistence of genuine shared beliefs. Our case demonstrates that resistant identity and state ideology are not necessarily at opposite poles in an ideologically progressive society. Rappers can reinforce the ideological positions of the state, while the state can provide spaces that rappers use to criticize government institutions and representatives, a notable example of "entanglements of power" (Sharp et al. 2000). In Cuba, the nationalization of protest music has not entailed the purging of resistant elements, but instead the highlighting of facets that correlate to the ideology of what may be considered a protest state, since Cuba has institutionalized the notion of resistance. I am brought back again to Peter Wade's remark that the success of coastal music in Colombia depended on its "multivocality." Cuban rap has been talked and written about extensively by Cubans and non-Cubans, and incorporated into constructions of identity at local, national, and global levels. Rap flourished in Cuba due to the crystallization of a revolutionary discourse which facilitated the constitution of collective identity among local and foreign hip hoppers ("the movement") while simultaneously reinforcing prominent features of national identity, drawing on a shared rhetoric of revolution and resistance to U.S. hegemony that brings a transnational dimension to hip hop's oppositionality.

This is not to deny altogether the validity of the characterization of rap as a music of resistance, but rather to ask the crucial question: resistance to what? Whereas political rappers in the United States tend to criticize dominant ideologies, in Cuba they often focus on the failure to live up to them. While rappers may strike oppositional poses, their targets are often the same as those of the state. Indeed, the very notion of resistance lies at the heart of (revolutionary) national ideology: if one aim of hip hop is "to generate an appropriate, autonomous discourse that recovers the symbols of resistance of the Cuban nation" (Lueiro n.d., 3), then resistance links hip hop to the state as much as it separates the two.

In his article on recent educational reforms in Cuba, Kapcia (2005a, 411) argues that the new schools could be interpreted as "a fascinating experiment in renewal, using two fundamental ideological codes—education and moralism—as the principal weapons for resistance, recreation and community." Aside from the fact that this statement about schools could apply equally well to underground hip hop, it is notable for the use of the word "resistance" as an attribute of the revolutionary state. While this parallels my earlier discussion of the language of revolution, it also ties in with the fractured state: educational reforms might be seen as evidence of the state's resistance to its own policies (such as opening up the country to tourism and the U.S. dollar, allowing private enterprise, and so on). While rappers reaffirm key tenets of state ideology, the state resists itself.

In November 2005, Castro declared all-out war on corruption and theft and on the Special Period inequalities and the ethical decline that underpinned them: "We are involved in a battle against vices, against the diversion of resources, against certain widespread habits" (Castro and Ramonet 2008, 596). Thousands of social workers were brought in as a kind of anti-corruption task force (ibid., 602–3). These are the very same concerns that run through underground rap lyrics that teem with fakes, frauds, corrupt officials, and morally bankrupt citizens, summed up by the "virus of human misery in the streets of Havana" (El Aldeano, "Miseria humana").

Another sense in which resistance links hip hop and the state is that it may be considered a constitutive part of state power, as theorists such as Michel Foucault and Slavoj Žižek have argued (Loomba 1998, 50; Žižek 2007). While many of the resistant discourses of hip hop may be aligned with state ideology, others go beyond it to strike more discordant notes— yet this may be no threat to the state, if "resistance is surrender," as Žižek argues (ibid.). "Those in power often prefer even a 'critical' participation, a dialogue, to silence," he suggests ("Democracy" 2007), and hip hop fits this bill precisely. Rather than co-opting hip hop, state officials may simply have preferred confrontational interaction to being ignored (as is occurring with reggaetón). It is notable that only in extreme cases are critical voices in hip hop actually silenced, illustrating Žižek's (2007) "strange symbiotic relationship" between power and resistance.

Another way to view the special relationship between hip hop and the socialist state in Cuba is to compare rap to timba or rock. Many timba musicians embraced a conspicuous materialism and hedonism that ran counter to official socialist ideologies and often set them at odds with the Cuban authorities (Perna 2005); if they have continued to flourish, it is because of their importance in generating revenue for the state and also a marked toning down of their act since the late 1990s to fight for a larger share of the market. Rock has provoked official disapproval for a variety of reasons, including its lack of any clear artistic philosophy, and for the first twenty-five years of the revolution it was variously censored or denied institutional support as it was considered "the mouthpiece of global imperialism" (Manduley López 1997, 137). Rap, however, does not carry the same association with U.S. cultural imperialism as rock because of its African American origins (Pacini Hernandez 2003, 27), and message rap presents a relatively coherent vision of progressive social action, making it more comprehensible to Cuban officials. In "Manifiesto," Mano Armada claim that "Our hip hop is more than contracts, record companies, and money / Our hip hop is a cause, a religion, our life," a sentiment unlikely to be echoed by many timba or rock musicians. To take one example of this contrast, Gorki Aguilar of the punk-rock group Porno Para Ricardo proclaims in the documentary *Cuba Rebelión*, "enough of the Battle of Ideas and all that shit, you've got to feed the people," whereas El Aldeano ends his song "Noches perdidas" by describing himself as "waging my own Battle of Ideas." If Aguilar rejects the ideological frame, El Aldeano appropriates it; rappers do believe in such notions, but in their own way.

Given the alignment between rap and socialist ideology, it is perhaps unsurprising that rap has found particular acceptance in countries with current or recent histories of socialist politics. In East Germany, the state increasingly tolerated rap from the mid-1980s on, allowing hip hop artists to use spaces and equipment in youth centers and clubs: "Arguing that hip-hop supported the state's proclaimed internationalism and solidarity with the struggle of the black urban working class in the U.S., state

officials tried partly to incorporate hip-hop culture into their system of
funding and promotion" (Hoyler and Mager 2005, 247). Italian hip hop
of the early 1990s was based in the *centri sociali*, a network of underground social centers that "developed indirectly from the Italian Communist Party's *case di lavoro*, or community centers, and functioned as more
than simply music venues, providing nurturing places for the development of indigenous Italian rap styles and 'posses'" (Mitchell 2001a, 197).
There are parallels between both these cases, in which socialist community centers provided a crucible for rap, and that of the Cuban Casas de la
Cultura, most famously in Alamar but also in Plaza, 10 de Octubre, Habana Vieja, and other Havana municipalities, which have sheltered hip
hoppers irregularly for nearly two decades.

Tanzania offers another point of comparison. Alex Perullo (2005, 96)
writes that "Tanzania's socialist past also affects contemporary rap music. Although socialism officially ended in the 1980s, it remains an important influence on local cultural and educational practices. Many musicians view their role in society as educators of the public—a conception
that was greatly strengthened during the socialist period." Sidney Lemelle (2006) also underlines the links between hip hop and *ujamaa* (African socialism); at a time when neoliberal economics and the International
Monetary Fund came to rule the roost in Tanzania, rappers harked back
to an earlier kind of politics. Their nostalgia for ujamaa of the late 1960s
and 1970s has close parallels in the revolutionary fundamentalism of
underground Cuban hip hop. In other societies that have remained politically socialist yet moved toward a more capitalist economic model, hip
hop plays a role in articulating critiques of capitalist practices and mentalities; this is the case not only in Cuba but also in China (Wang 2009),
another country where hip hop is being reclaimed as a socialist cultural
form that laments the loss of ideals in a society increasingly fixated on
money.

In socialist systems, then, the resistance of hip hop needs to be re-
thought: there are still oppositional discourses, but the deep ideological
alignment between rappers and state in such contexts warns against
regarding hip hop as an oppositional template that can be used with
minor recalibration pretty much anywhere in the world. In Venezuela and
Bolivia, for example, Hugo Chávez's and Evo Morales's bitter ideological
struggles with their country's entrenched elites place many rappers on

the side of the government and the resisters firmly on the side of the president. The Venezuelan case is not identical to the Cuban, however; along with the parallels, there are also crucial differences in the ways that hip hoppers relate to the state in various left-wing contexts. The degree of interpenetration of hip hop and formal politics in Cuba, Brazil, and Venezuela, for example, is actually quite different. Many hip hoppers whom I saw perform at the Tiuna el Fuerte cultural center in Caracas explicitly and vocally supported Hugo Chávez; Fidel Castro, on the other hand, is almost never mentioned by name at hip hop concerts. Cuban rappers opt instead for the long-dead Che or Camilo Cienfuegos. They share an ideological and discursive field with the state, but unlike their counterparts in Venezuela and Brazil, most are keen to disassociate themselves from governing politicians.

Brian George (2007, 101) discusses whether rap might be seen as "one of the consummate cultural products of late capitalism." In the light of the numerous socialist contexts in which rap has flourished, this position should perhaps be refined. Although message rap emerged out of a hyper-capitalist context, it was informed by black Marxist ideologies: it both fed off and critiqued Reagan-era New York City. In its most politicized manifestations, it articulated many socialist principles, even as the practices (and music industry) that underpinned it presented a much more capitalist aspect. Perhaps, then, message rap was one of the consummate cultural products of the late cold war: a dialectical cultural form (I. Perry 2004) that encapsulated a tension between socialism and capitalism and emerged as a global force in the mid-to-late 1980s, counterbalancing the decline of socialist ideologies in the sphere of formal politics at precisely this time. Rap's emergence in Cuba, one of the few places in which this war is still being waged, is then particularly resonant.

Hip hop has taken root in a variety of forms around the world, and while it is easy to see its global spread as a manifestation of Americanization in its guise as capitalism, individualism, and the glorification of guns and money, its reception in Cuba and other socialist contexts is a reminder of hip hop's roots in Marxist political thought and thus evidence of another side to America and Americanization. The trajectory of hip hop in Havana, from official rejection to incorporation into national culture, was enabled by a shift in emphasis from one face of Americanization to the other, as gangsta rapper outfits gave way to black power salutes. For all that I have labeled this process nationalization, it was significantly influenced by North American artists, activists, and ideologies, underlining the historical interconnectedness of Cuban and African American politics and culture and the appeal of U.S. black radicalism both to Cuba's youth and to its revolutionary government.

2

THE REVOLUTION OF THE BODY

Reggaetón and the Politics of Dancing

I know that when I sing the ladies are happy,
There's a huge line and loads of people outside,
I'm the number one and I don't get into beefs
And the whole of Cuba knows it.
—GENTE DE ZONA, "El animal"

Distribution of assets, reggaetón for shaking your ass,
Or rap for maturing the mind of the immature.
—EL ALDEANO, featuring Danay, "Andate che"

Alexánder Delgado rolled up in a shiny black 4x4, very late. He had just
come from the Cuban Music Institute, where he had been given a tongue-
lashing by his bosses. They had got wind of a video of the concert that his
group, Gente de Zona, had performed at the Casa de la Música. One of the
group's invitees, Insurrecto, had made lewd gestures on stage, and this
seemed to be the final straw as far as the Ministry of Culture was concerned. Still, Delgado didn't seem too bothered: there was talk that he

Alexánder Delgado of Gente de Zona (right) with the hip hop producer Pablo Herrera.
Photo by author.

might not be allowed to travel to his next overseas engagement, but he laughed it off. "I've got all of Havana dancing with me," he said, implying that nothing too bad was going to happen as a result. As we pulled into the parking lot at the Karl Marx Theater, he was stopped by the represen tative of a foreign clothing brand, who wanted to give him some new gear. They swapped phone numbers. Delgado, Pablo Herrera, and I headed inside the theater to the bar, all heads swiveling as we passed. As we sat down to talk, a young boy came up and started singing Gente de Zona's latest hit, "El animal": Delgado sang along, clicking the *clave cubana* on his fingers—"that's rumba," he said, laughing.[1] Indeed, there was something of the *rumbero* about him: the dapper look, the streetwise bearing; but sitting there with his iPhone, talking about how he had hustled his way to the top, he was also the personification of Havana's twenty-first-century music economy.

In 2003 my attention was on hip hop. True, it took a little seeking out; when I first asked around, people pointed me to the dancehall-like sounds of Candyman and Cubanito 20.02 that were all the rage. This was not what

I was looking for, and I did not pay much attention to it at first. However, once I began my research in earnest the following year, I realized that I could not ignore reggaetón: it was a constant and growing presence, blasting out of houses and cars everywhere, inserting itself into almost every conversation I had about music. Indeed, I saw a sign of what was to come on my first day in Havana in 2004, when I bumped into Cubanito 20.02 in the Pabellón Cuba. We chatted briefly and then headed outside into the street. Suddenly they were besieged by (mainly young, female) fans—shrieking, touching and kissing them, and asking for their autographs. This was a far cry from the underground hip hop scene from which they had emerged.

The formation of Cubanito 20.02 by ex-members of the rap group Primera Base in 2002 was a pivotal moment in the emergence of reggaetón in the capital, and also a watershed in Cuban rap. In the wake of this successful bid for a higher commercial profile, most rappers have followed one of two paths: dancing with the enemy and embracing reggaetón, or vociferously resisting the new genre. The resisters deride reggaetón for promoting mindless entertainment and dancing over social commitment and reflection: El Aldeano and Danay's song "Andate che," which begins with a parody of Cubanito 20.02's hit "Mátame," is one of many caricatures and barbed critiques that have circulated within rap circles since 2004. The relationship between rap and reggaetón has been one of the most common (and contentious) topics of conversation within hip hop in recent years. Despite resistance from across the musical spectrum, however, reguetoneros (reggaetón artists) have emerged as clear winners. As reggaetón has rapidly become the dominant form of popular music in Cuba, its verbal, musical, and performative styles have posed major challenges to dominant conceptions of Cuban national culture. The resulting debates illuminate both recent developments in Cuban cultural politics and also, more broadly, the contradictory and conflicted relationships between socialism and capitalism, ideology and pleasure, that are characteristic of Havana in the new millennium.

Reggaetón in Print

Many articles critical of reggaetón have been published in the Cuban press since 2005, in particular in *Juventud Rebelde*, the newspaper of the Union of Young Communists (UJC). One of the first and most notable, titled "¿Prohibido el reguetón?" (Castro Medel 2005a), criticized the genre's repetitive beats, suggestive lyrics, and licentious dance moves not just as "banal, corny, trashy," but also as potentially inciting vulgarity, lust, vice, and drug abuse. While not actually proposing prohibition, the article suggested that something needed to be done. The author's follow-up article (2005b) questioned the critical faculties of those who promoted music in the media and alluded to "backward steps" in behavior, "vain and absurd lyrics," and the alarm that reggaetón was causing among "people of vision." Even a more balanced analysis by Alberto Faya Montano (2005) centered on a lengthy critique of reggaetón's supposed corruption by commercialism. These written accounts reflect wider attitudes. Alpidio Alonso, president of the AHS, warned the Eighth Congress of the UJC in 2005 about "so much terrible reggaetón, with so many second- and third-rate groups" (quoted in Castro Medel 2005a). Many professional musicians see reggaetón as damaging to Cuban popular music, eroding interest in traditional genres and betraying their high professional standards with amateurish, yet addictive, creations; one distinguished musician claimed that reggaetón had set the country back by fifty years in musical terms (Castro Medel 2005a and 2005b; CIDMUC 2005).

After the initial culture shock, the furor over reggaetón has not so much abated—Carlos Alfonso, the director of the rock group Síntesis, apparently likened it to a form of terrorism (Caballero 2007a)—as it has shifted its emphasis. Both enemies and defenders have increasingly noted that the criticisms of reggaetón have multiple and illustrious historical precedents—one need think only of the scandals surrounding timba in the 1990s (Neustadt 2002; Perna 2005), or those provoked by son and rumba in the early twentieth century (R. Moore 1997) and by popular urban genres such as tango, merengue, and *cumbia* in other parts of the Americas around the same time. Of course, all these supposedly scandalous musical styles went on to become hallowed symbols of national identity. Horrified reactions to African-influenced popular music and dance styles in the New World can be traced back to the sixteenth century and the emergence of the *chacona* (chaconne) and *zarabanda* (sarabande). Criticism of licentious dance moves and crude lyrics is therefore par for the course when a new genre of Caribbean popular music appears. What is distinctive about today's commentators is that they are often quite aware of these historical precedents and the risks they are running in echoing earlier generations of critics, who were made to look hidebound or even foolish by subsequent events. This has led some of the more perceptive critics to write about their internal struggles and contradictory urges to defend and attack reggaetón.[2] There has also been a shift away from alarmist reactions to reggaetón itself toward a concern over the broader social and cultural connotations of Cuban youth's infatuation with it. What does reggaetón's popularity say about Havana today? Or, in the words of Rufo Caballero (2008), "where did we go wrong?"

The aura of negativity around reggaetón has rarely been countered by academic interventions. Recent years have seen a plethora of studies of Cuban rap, but these predate, ignore, or dismiss the boom of reggaetón. Alan West-Durán (2004, 36) relegates reggaetón to a single footnote, as "often a bad equivalent of what might be considered Jamaican dancehall at its most frivolous." Marc Perry (2004) devotes one paragraph to reggaetón in his doctoral thesis; Sujatha Fernandes (2006) does not mention it at all in her book. Despite achieving a far greater level of popularity than rap, Cuban reggaetón rarely appears in dissertations or scholarly conferences. Reggaetón is something of an inconvenient truth for Cuban hip hop studies: since the first exponents of reggaetón in Havana came from the ranks of the rap scene, their defection raised tricky questions for those who had identified with underground hip hop and perceived reggaetón as its opposite pole. Advocating one form of music over another is nothing new among those who study popular music, often in the context of championing a supposedly resistant form over more commercialized genres. Rap has often been the beneficiary of such an approach in countries where message rap has been taken as a template for local production, whereas commercialized, dance-oriented genres like reggaetón have tended to lose out within academic circles.[3]

More recently, there have been serious attempts to analyze reggaetón in Havana (Fairley 2006; Valdés 2007; Zurbano n.d.b), though the broadside against such efforts by Leonardo Acosta (2008), one of Cuba's most eminent musicologists, suggests that the topic's contentiousness has not subsided.[4] The first study, however, was an unpublished report produced by researchers from the Centro de Investigación y Desarrollo de la Música Cubana (CIDMUC 2005). This report employed a wide range of analytical tools and was an important milestone in the investigation of the genre. But despite the researchers' efforts to remain evenhanded, their backgrounds in research on rap and timba surface in concerns over reggaetón's supposed deficiencies in comparison with its longer-established cousins: the negative perceptions include a poverty of ideas (in relation to rap) and discontinuity with Cuban popular traditions and artistic standards (in relation to timba). While eager to point out the positive aspects of reggaetón, the researchers struggle to find many, regarding most of it as mediocre or worse in terms of both musical and lyrical content, and describing the genre in terms such as "lexical violence," "impoverishment," and "loss of the most basic aesthetic standards"; the "simplistic" results "may retard the individual listener in the evolution of his/her aesthetic personality" (CIDMUC 2005, 19, 34). This report is a genuine and valuable attempt to understand reggaetón, but it also reveals the depth of reggaetón's challenge to Cuban cultural and intellectual traditions.

Whereas intellectual treatments of rap have historicized the genre, charting the brief history of reggaetón is a challenge. Reggaetón has had no influential, articulate cheerleaders in Havana, no Rodolfo Rensoli or Ariel Fernández or Pablo Herrera; there have been no festivals, no high-profile foreign visitors, no colloquia, no important speeches defending the genre. The minister of culture has never announced plans to nationalize reggaetón, nor has he spoken approvingly of its artists. Because it has had a more fractious relationship with institutions and intellectuals, reggaetón's history in Havana appears shapeless; it is certainly yet to be written. Although the Panamanians Nando Boom and El General had been known for years, reggaetón's explosion began when it swept into the capital around 2002 on a wave of pirated CDs. While reguetoneros have forced their way into the consciousness of state officials and seized cultural and institutional spaces, they have not been welcomed with open arms. This is not to say that reggaetón has been officially shunned: for example, a number of groups have been incorporated into official artistic agencies including the ACR, which produced a large reggaetón concert at La Tropical as part of the Cubadisco trade fair in 2004. But the generalized high-level suspicion of reggaetón has ensured that, despite its artists' overwhelming popularity, it is rarely featured in large-scale public performances like those put on during carnival or on public holidays. The genre's invasion of Havana was at first by stealth and more recently by overwhelming force, and it is still regarded as an occupier by most Cuban cultural gatekeepers.

If rap has had more official and scholarly acceptance, reggaetón has been the people's choice since 2003. The reggaetón revolution represents the paradigm shift in Cuban culture that rap promised but never delivered, so much more study is required—not least because the negative responses to reggaetón across artistic, critical, and institutional spheres suggest that some important issues are at stake. Susan McClary's (1994) discussion of the politics of music making is highly relevant: urging greater attention to body-centered genres (of which reggaetón is a prime example), rather than those which focus on politicized lyrics (e.g., rap), she claims that "the musical power of the disenfranchised . . . more often resides in their ability to articulate different ways of construing the body, ways that bring along in their wake the potential for different experiential worlds. And the anxious reactions that so often greet new musics from such groups indicate that something crucially political is at issue" (ibid., 34). I will take this as a call to move beyond the widespread dismissal of reggaetón as simply music "for shaking your ass," as not only rappers but many scholars and critics would have it, and ask: is reggaetón's appeal to the body stimulating "different experiential worlds" among Havana's youth, and if so, what is their significance? Why has reggaetón provoked such anxieties? And what social and political issues are at stake?

Linguistic Violence

Even reggaetón's critics have sometimes admitted the seductiveness of its beat, but its words are another matter: Castro Medel (2005a) sums up the genre as "a very rhythmic music, but one with rather poor lyrics." Critiques center on the banality of the ideas expressed—which tend to focus on girls, sex, dancing, and the singer himself, in various combinations—but also the language in which these "non-ideas" are articulated.[5] Locally produced reggaetón is not contentious in the same way as versions in some other countries are; references to weapons or drug use, for example, are infrequent or coded. Oneilys Hevora of the Havana group Los 3 Gatos claimed, with some justification: "I don't move anyone to violence with my music" (quoted in Ravsberg 2005). The authors of the CIDMUC report disagree, though they locate the aggression at the level of language, using terms like "lexical violence." Indeed, they highlight a perceived flow of slang from reggaetón lyrics to everyday popular speech, suggesting that their concern centers on the "violence" the genre does to established conceptions of national linguistic culture.

There are three broad strands of locally produced reggaetón in Havana: music produced by officially sanctioned, professional reguetoneros (e.g., Cubanito 20.02, Eddy-K [now known variously as Los Intocables, Los Salvajes, and Los Cuatro], and Gente de Zona); reggaetón produced by "underground" artists, which circulates primarily via the gray economy (e.g., Los 3 Gatos, Elvis Manuel, and El Micha); and the reggaetón-timba fusions created by leading timba groups, often featuring invited reggaetón artists, to maintain their popularity in the face of this new wave.[6] The CIDMUC authors are careful to distinguish between three registers of language, corresponding broadly to the three strands of local reggaetón: the only one that they regard as seemly, however, is that used by professional timba groups in their fusions. The researchers characterize the texts of official reggaetón groups as banal and mediocre, while describing those of underground groups as vulgar, obscene, or even pornographic. The authors reveal a sense of regret that the Cuban popular linguistic tradition of *picardía* (puns, double meanings, and euphemisms) has given way to blunt, obvious signification (CIDMUC 2005, 16–17).[7] There is certainly some justification for this, but it is also worth considering that these texts—with their directness, simplicity, and hedonistic focus—offer a particular challenge to a national culture framed by Marxist ideology, in which respect for elaborated ideas is so fundamental (R. Moore 2006, 7–9). The Battle of Ideas is waged from large, prominent billboards across Havana. Language, too, is prized; Gabriel García Márquez's (2006) recent portrait of Fidel Castro began: "His devotion is to the word." In reggaetón, however, there appears to be a widespread refusal to engage at the level of sophisticated ideas or lyrical discourse, coupled with a transgression of linguistic norms.

The aim of most Havana-based reggaetón artists that I met was *pegarse*: to "stick" easily with dancing and drinking audiences through simple, easy-to-repeat phrases. As one reggaetón producer privately told me, anything too complicated simply does not get through to the public, which just wants something easy to digest "en su borrachera y jodedera" (while getting drunk and fooling around). Another way to stick is to shock. The linguistic violence perpetrated by underground Cuban reguetoneros, most famously by Elvis Manuel in songs like "La tuba," is above all sexualized. This is not an isolated phenomenon: the novels of Pedro Juan Gutiérrez, too, expose "lives of sexual abandon [and] moral depravity" (Whitfield 2008, 98). The X-rated lyrics of underground reggaetón artists may shock the sensibilities of many (especially older) habaneros, but they are very much a sign of the times, reflecting the intense sexualization of Havana since the Special Period as bodies became one of the few freely available sites of pleasure and an important locus of profit and social mobility.

This verbal challenge marks a clear departure from most Cuban rap, which was accepted as part of a national culture conceived of in terms of linguistic and intellectual excellence: rappers made a name for themselves both at home and abroad because of the elaboration and commitment of their lyrics, which meshed with the state's ideology, but reggaetón artists tend to stand outside socialist principles altogether, sharing little or no discursive space with the state.[8] El Micha spoke for many reguetoneros when he said: "My lyrics speak about what young people are living, without getting involved in politics or anything like that, because that's got nothing to do with me" (quoted in Israel 2009). This almost dismissively depoliticized view is a notable statement in a revolutionary society. Reguetoneros' perceived banality or vulgarity, coupled with their extreme popularity among Cuban youth, raises thornier issues about national culture and identity than rap did, explaining the bewilderment or hostility of cultural commentators who had come around to the idea of rap cubano.

Lest this dismissal of reggaetón lyrics should go unchallenged, it is worth mentioning Alexánder Delgado's response when I put this question of lyrical content to him. He described his song "El animal" as "a story of the barrio" and "Tremenda pena" as a "social chronicle," though one focused on personal experience (the latter recounts the story of a friend's girlfriend who falls for the singer). The debates between rappers and reguetoneros recall earlier ones over *salsa dura* and *salsa romántica*. Lise Waxer (2002, 142–43) defends the latter genre from its detractors, arguing that lyrics about personal relationships do not betray salsa or its social relevance but rather shift its emphasis from social processes to the effects of those processes on individuals and their personal lives. This may shed some light on the transition from the broad social consciousness of rappers to the more individualized views of reguetoneros.

It is also interesting to note the opinion of Roberto Zurbano, whose critical perspective centers on his view that "reggaetón discourse does not try to go deeper into reality, but just to describe it, often reproducing alienated forms of culture that become aspirations for the music's young consumers" (n.d.b, 10). Thus his criticism is based on the idea that reggaetón is *too faithful* to social reality, lacking the transformative urge found in conscious rap. Reggaetón lyrics may often be as banal and vulgar as their critics contend, but it would be hard to argue that they are disconnected from personal or social realities.

Globalized Sounds and the Problem of National Culture

Anxieties in musical and intellectual circles over the relationship of reggaetón to a national culture that has traditionally focused on linguistic dexterity were exacerbated by the musical aspects of reggaetón in Havana, which was dominated by Puerto Rican models during its first few years. In contrast to more established Cuban dance musics like timba, a reliance on digital technologies rather than live musicians led to a predominance of electronic sounds and a scarcity of characteristic Cuban elements such as instrumental timbres and rhythmic or melodic virtuosity. In 2009, the general view, even from within the reggaetón scene, was still that the majority of Cuban reggaetón was mimetic and overly similar to that of Puerto Rico. For most critics, a process of indigenization needs to occur before reggaetón can be considered an authentic manifestation of national culture. The problem of musical nonadaptation has been a common theme in critical responses: Castro Medel (2005b) refers to the genre in terms of "a possible aggression against national culture." Even though the musical root of reggaetón is essentially the habanera, the rhythm that left Cuba in the nineteenth century bearing the capital city's name has not been welcomed back by cultural critics in the twenty-first century.

While Cuba has long absorbed external influences, a compromise between international musics and nationalist intellectual traditions has typically been brokered through a discourse of Cubanization—an adoption-adaptation model which stresses the transformative power of Cuban culture. This discourse eventually opened the gates of national culture to include rap cubano; rap groups such as Anónimo Consejo and Obsesion, by occasionally incorporating traditional Cuban musical elements such as African-derived drums and Yoruba chants, have been widely accepted as representing an "organic" development of Cuban musical traditions (even if this argument has been overstated by rap advocates and scholars). Reggaetón, however, has proved more resistant to such indigenization, hence its greater challenge. Not only are the musical backgrounds (instrumentals) perceived as relying excessively on foreign models, but there is little sense as yet of a distinctive Cuban reggaetón vocal flow. The CIDMUC report includes a critical description of a popular reggaetón song that imitates Puerto Rican slang and vocal intonation, while Cubanito 20.02 told me they felt a strong affinity with Jamaican *ragga*.

The issue of indigenization is a complex one, not least because the genre is young in Havana, and the terrain is constantly shifting: by the time these words are printed, the picture may well have changed. Nevertheless, during the earlier part of my research period (2003–7), audience demand seemed to be working against indigenization. Consumers of reggaetón in Havana lapped up Puerto Rican reggaetón and its local imitations, and enthusiasm for Cubanized reggaetón by critics and foreign record companies was not always matched by that of young habaneros. Some regarded this attraction to foreign reggaetón as simply reflecting the higher quality of overseas musical production, stemming from superior technological resources—though it could also be argued that the attraction of reggaetón for young Cubans, few of whom have left the island or have access to the Internet, may be related to its international character. Reggaetón speaks to the current obsession among young people in Havana with *lo traído*—imported goods, above all foreign-label clothes, accessories, and cellphones.

The self-taught status of many reggaetón producers has apparently fed back into the sound of Cuban reggaetón. My conversations with urban music producers made it clear that they had not simply inherited Cuban musical knowledge; it was something that had to be studied, and most of them had not had that opportunity. Experimenting with fusions with Cuban music is a tricky path for producers without formal training in Cuban musical traditions, as local audiences are discerning in their judgment of familiar styles. The nonadaptation of much local reggaetón production may be linked to the greater difficulties that such adaptation poses. For many, it is both more feasible and commercially viable to imitate Puerto Rican backgrounds and adopt a more overtly electronic sound. The prominence of techno elements and synthesized sounds might also be understood in the context of the technological boom of recent years, the democratization and fetishization of digital technology, and an urge to sound hypermodern rather than to hark back to Cuban traditions.

Furthermore, a combination of the recent expansion of computer ownership and a relatively liberal cultural climate has resulted in reguetoneros' becoming the first stratum of popular music producers in socialist Cuba to be more or less immune from the political pressure to fit in with dominant cultural norms. Reggaetón may dismay cultural critics and government officials for sounding too Puerto Rican, but this has little impact on its producers, because reggaetón—to a greater extent than any previous genre since 1959—functions primarily in a commercial space where the yardstick is audience appeal rather than government approval. In the 1990s, the emergent hip hop scene had little commercial support, and it was thus obliged to gain a space in the institutional cultural sphere by engaging in a dialogue with cultural gatekeepers, entailing a move (discursive as much as musical) away from a mimetic approach and toward Cubanization. Today's reggaetón producers have their own equipment and commercial networks, and they are much more independent of the state. The wider availability of technological resources, the growth of a parallel, gray, or underground music economy (Baker 2011), and, above all, the sway of commercial imperatives in Havana's night life, have freed up these musicians to make their own aesthetic rules.

Puerto Rican reggaetón thus had a major influence on local production: the most audible artist in the streets of Havana in 2007 was Elvis Manuel, whose underground productions combined *perreo* (Puerto Rican–style) musical backgrounds with hard-core lyrics. However, Manuel's death while traveling illegally by boat to the United States and the emergence of Gente de Zona as the biggest player in Cuban reggaetón changed the musical landscape considerably, and in 2008 Cubanized reggaetón seemed finally to be emerging from the shadow of its Puerto Rican elder sibling. On the one hand, this might lead one to conclude that indigenization is simply a matter of time: most accounts of Cuban rap stress an initial mimetic phase followed by adaptation and assimilation, and the recent growth of timba-reggaetón fusions by groups such as Charanga Habanera and Bamboleo suggests a move toward a certain kind of nationalization.[9] On the other hand, this process was more complicated in the case of rap than has been recognized, since many groups resisted the second, Cubanizing phase, which they regarded as selling out rather than evidence of greater authenticity. Arguing for the musical indigenization of rap has involved a considerable degree of cherry picking. Similarly, while some of

Gente de Zona's songs may be held up as examples of Cubanized reggaetón, others show strong Puerto Rican and Dominican leanings, and leading artists such as Baby Lores and Insurrecto, Eddy-K/Los Cuatro, and El Micha have pursued more international aesthetic lines, as have most second-tier and underground artists.

The simultaneous exploration of a variety of musical paths and the continued rarity of Cubanized sounds beyond Gente de Zona and timba groups suggest that in the digital age, musical localization is not simply a matter of time or inevitability after all. The spread of digital technologies has led to a democratization of musical production; with the creative process no longer concentrated in the hands of Cuban music specialists, this democratization is audible in the widespread lack of local musical characteristics in Havana reggaetón (the same is true in the case of recent hip hop). Digitalization has undermined the primacy of local musical materials. By 2009, there were effectively two broad strands of reggaetón in Havana, "pure" reggaetón and timba-reggaetón, and barring Gente de Zona, most of the new hits that I heard that year (e.g., Junior & De Calle, featuring Jota B, "Échale un palo"; Pipey & El Micha, "Gerente"; Kola Loka, "La estafa del babalao"; and Los Confidenciales, "Aceite y agua") fell into the former category, showing minimal signs of musical Cubanization. In sum, while explicitly localized reggaetón is certainly in evidence eight years after the genre became a significant presence in Havana, international-style reggaetón is still sufficiently popular to preoccupy most gatekeepers of Cuban culture; for all Gente de Zona's success, it is still rare to hear a musical authority proclaim reggaetón as an authentic or fully assimilated Cuban genre.

The idea of Cubanization as choice rather than inevitability came clearly into view when I began visiting reggaetón producers in their studios. When I raised this question, they would say "sure, I can do that" and play me a track fusing reggaetón with timba or son or conga or rumba. But then they would play me a whole range of other tracks, mixing reggaetón with *bachata*, merengue, samba, cumbia, reggae, techno, and so on; their fusions were more often imitations of those created in other parts of the Caribbean (such as bachata-reggaetón). They saw Cuban musical traditions as one option among many of equal value and validity, and they saw themselves as musicians of the world, not standard-bearers for national culture.

To the producers I interviewed, hybridization and indigenization were quite different—they were all committed to the former but much more lukewarm about the latter, which they viewed differently than most scholars and cultural critics. The standard opinion, that any musician worth his or her salt will filter an incoming global genre through a local musical lens, underestimates the combined effects of a widespread lack of formal musical training among music producers, formative years immersed in international styles, powerful computer programs, and commercial imperatives. A new generation of Cuban music producers has emerged with no specialist skill in or knowledge of Cuban genres, nor a pronounced nationalist cultural streak, and when they get their hands on digital technology and start to produce music, they experiment and fuse with anything they can. There is neither a hierarchy which places Cuba at the top, except possibly a commercial one, nor a layer of Cuban musicians and musical traditions through which new ideas have to pass. The democratization of musical production has led to greater hybridity—available at the press of a button—but less localization, which depends on greater musical knowledge or access to musicians.

Producers could see the value of having some Cubanized reggaetón up their sleeve, but they did not see this as somehow more natural or authentic than any other kind. When I went to see the leading Cuban reggaetón group Triángulo Oscuro perform live in Havana, I was struck by the musical mixture: the rappers threw in dancehall delivery and hip hop freestyle, covers of Bob Marley's "No Woman No Cry" and Sergio Mendes's "Mas que nada." If this was an expression of identity through music, it was a hemispheric identity, not a national one. Since the eclecticism that I saw in the studio was expanded even further in performance, this attitude to creativity among reggaetón producers calls for an expanded notion of local adaptation. As producers' horizons have broadened with globalization and technological change, musical creation has become much more than a case of filtering a global music through a local lens to produce a local-global hybrid. Instead, one globalized sound (reggaetón) is mixed with other globalized sounds (such as bachata), some of which (such as timba) contain Cuban elements.

Reggaetón or Cubatón?
Cubanía, Imitation, and Difference

There are two principal reasons behind the disjuncture between the expectations of cultural critics and the aims of reggaetón producers: differing attitudes first to sameness and second to commercial strategizing. At the root of reggaetón is Jamaican dancehall, a musical genre based on the "riddim." Jamaican DJs often string together many versions of the same riddim, and repetitiveness is not perceived negatively in dancehall (Stolzoff 2000, 203). Reggaetón is a genre built on versions of the "dem bow" riddim, and as Wayne Marshall (2009, 42–45) reveals, it drew from U.S. hip hop as well as dancehall, and thus sampling, copying, borrowing, and "versioning" were fundamental to its early manifestations in Puerto Rico. Reggaetón was marked from early on as a hyperderivative musical form, and its repetitiveness may be understood as continuity with Caribbean musical traditions. Jorge Hernández, one of Cuba's top regguetoneros, was untroubled by accusations that he copied Puerto Rican reggaetón: for him, music was either good or bad, whether it sounded similar to something else was unimportant. Indeed, he insisted that imitating required talent and that copying was an art. "Take Pavarotti," he told me, "go ahead and try to copy him." Nevertheless, reggaetón's aesthetics have clashed with expectations of originality in culturally nationalist Cuba, where it has caused consternation among critics and intellectuals.

Decisions by reggaetón producers about sameness and difference are often based on commercial rather than musical criteria. They value eclecticism and experimentation, but they ultimately explain their artistic decisions in terms of strategies to appeal to audiences. Gente de Zona now have a high-profile international career, which means that they need some obviously Cuban music to play to foreign audiences; unlike less successful groups, they can now afford to hire musicians. Hernández's Los Cuatro, however, were pursuing a more house-oriented route in 2008–9, because they felt that was where music was going in Puerto Rico, and they did not want to be left behind. Hernández told me that he wanted to be part of the commercial mainstream. He acknowledged that there were certain pressures to Cubanize his music, but he portrayed them as coming from outside (from commentators and critics) rather than as a natural consequence of his Cubanness. He embraced sameness because, to him, it represented being up to date and at the forefront of global musical currents. His unashamed adherence to Puerto Rican norms is amply illustrated in the title of a song by Los Cuatro (featuring Jacob Forever of Gente de Zona and El Micha) that addresses the criticism directed at reggaetón—"Conmigo no, con Puerto Rico," or "don't blame me, blame Puerto Rico."

I was interested to note, therefore, that Los Cuatro had started to take a more Cubanized route by the time I returned in 2010. I heard a significant change in their sound (for example, in their song "Fresa y chocolate"), which had been markedly international and electronic just a year earlier. In the light of my interview with Hernández in 2008, it was clear that this was not a simple case of gradual or natural indigenization over time since he had explicitly rejected this notion and stated that he was motivated by examples of commercial success. Although I did not have the chance to talk to him again, I suspect that his Cubanizing turn was motivated by the popularity of Gente de Zona's timba-reggaetón and by the urge to put on a more impressive stage show with live musicians rather than just rappers and a DJ.

Similarly, the steady growth of timba-reggaetón fusions by established timba groups should be seen not simply as a natural assimilation of reggaetón into Cuban culture but rather as a commercial marriage of convenience. To bring together the two most popular forms of Cuban music is a no-brainer: the reguetoneros benefit from the timberos' music industry experience and contacts, while the timberos access the reguetoneros' cachet and audiences. But it is no secret that relations between the two camps are often strained. Many timberos simultaneously look down on reguetoneros for their lack of formal musical training and envy them for their rapid and overwhelming success, while many reguetoneros are well aware of these sentiments and take a certain pride in having caused an upheaval in the timba world.[10] On the whole, then, this alliance is no natural meeting of musical minds but rather a strategy to maximize audiences so as to get ahead in the music business.

Carlos, the producer at TC Records in Centro Habana, contrasted music for musicians with music for the general public. He had tried making both, and while he enjoyed making more experimental music, it was mainly appreciated by other musicians and left the public cold. *Facilismo* (taking the easy option) was the order of the day, and since he was trying to make a living, he had decided to provide people with simple entertainment. Nevertheless, he had a mixed repertoire: he played me a cha-cha-cha fusion titled "Cuba" that worked in more upscale venues where musicians and foreigners went, though ordinary Cuban audiences did not like it so much. El Tosco of NG La Banda had complimented him on the song and urged him to continue down this line, but he said that if he followed the famous timbero's advice, he would end up with great music and no audience. He also played me the video for "Máximo respeto," a song by a reggaetón-timba "super-group" called Cuba Sound Forever that included many top Cuban reguetoneros. The sound was distinctly Cubanized, and Cuban percussion instruments appeared in the video. The song was aimed at projecting Cuban reggaetón to the world, especially to Europe, he said; it was more for an external than an internal public, as it would be too difficult to perform this song in concert in Cuba, with all the live musicians required.

Carlos thus raised an issue that came up over and over again in my discussions with producers of both hip hop and reggaetón: *cubanía* as a product for export. Since Cubanness also appeals to nationalist cultural officials and critics, the priorities of capitalism and socialism, or the market and the state, coincide in the field of national branding. Cubanía in contemporary, digitally produced urban music is an example of Roland Robertson's (1990, 50) "universalization of particularism" and Richard Wilk's (1995, 118) "structures of common difference": a response to globalization and powerful interests both inside and outside Cuba rather than one that springs naturally from either local producers or consumers. The Cuban reggaetón groups that have produced most-localized versions of the music are those that work most regularly overseas: Cubanito 20.02 and Triángulo Oscuro, who travel to Europe as part of their contracts to promote Havana Club rum, and Gente de Zona. The members of Cubanito were encouraged by their European record label, Lusafrica, to aim for more of a foreign world-music audience for their second album: they even included a remix of the opening track, "Miente a lo cubano," in French with the title "Mensonge." However, the softening of the beats and introduction of live instruments rather than samples did not work in Cuba, where audiences apparently wanted a harder, more Puerto Rican sound, and the group's popularity at home nose-dived. Triángulo Oscuro's producer, Rubén Estévez, told me that his variety of fusions was vital for the international market: if the group goes to Mexico City or London, au-

diences do not respond to straight reggaetón but love the mixes with
more traditional Caribbean rhythms. The venue where I saw them in
Havana, El Diablo Tun Tun, was filled primarily by tourists. Alexánder
Delgado told me that when he travels to overseas festivals, audiences may
not understand a word he says, so they must identify him as Cuban via
the music. It is on stage in Paris or Rome—or in the tourist venues of
Havana—that Cubanized reggaetón comes into its own.

While examples of Cubanized reggaetón exist, then, they tend to be
created with an eye on the global market. Eddy-K and Gente de Zona
combined on "Ya llegaron los cubanos" (the Cubans have arrived), exhort-
ing the listener to "ask around if you've got any doubts / Head down the
Caribbean and ask Cuba," and the song seems aimed, metaphorically at
least, at foreigners. Its clichéd reference points—salsa-reggaetón, the Malecón, rumba, fiestas with rum and girls—illustrate a crude form of post-
card nationalism. The underground star El Micha, in contrast, tells his
listeners at the start of his first demo: "Don't play the foreigner / I've got
Havana in a spin with my homemade reggaetón." He implicitly acknowledges that his "homemade" (i.e., Puerto Rican–style) reggaetón may not
grab overseas listeners but it speaks to people on the streets of Havana.

It is indicative that the attempt to localize reggaetón discursively by
giving it a new name, "Cubatón," was promoted by Michel Miglis, the
president of a Swedish production company. This marketing label was
pushed by a foreign music producer with an interest in creating a distinctive Cuban brand for the international market. It is occasionally seen in
Havana but never really caught on locally: it tends to be used to promote
products and events aimed at international audiences, such as compilations by Miglis's label Topaz Records, Gente de Zona's album *Lo mejor que
suena ahora* (released in Italy), and the concert at the 2004 Cubadisco
international music fair. Localization is thus, to a significant degree, a
sign of the marketing strategies of local artists and international record
companies rather than of the vitality of local traditions. It is not a counter to the cultural imperialism thesis, but instead evidence of the expanding empire of the ideology of cultural difference.

A more nuanced vision of sameness and difference is thus called for. On
the one hand, there is a tendency within cultural criticism and musicology to look at a form like reggaetón and immediately search for evidence
of localization and national variants. But perhaps what is interesting

Poster for a Cubatón concert at the 2004 Cuba-disco international music fair. Photo by author.

about Havana reggaetón is precisely the relative lack of localization—the emergence of a "bling-bling" club scene that would not look out of place in many cities across Latin America and the Caribbean. There are moments when you could be in Miami or San Juan, which is surely the point. The emulation of the musical and visual codes of Puerto Rican reggaetón sends a clear message about Havana's relationship to the rest of the hemisphere: Jorge Hernández revealed that being local is less important to him than being up to date and part of the mainstream. While less experienced groups may imitate because they do not know any better, Hernández is a key player who has been at the top of the urban music game for a long time, making calculations and choices about musical style that until very recently did not prioritize the kind of musical localization prized by scholars and critics. He made no bones about the fact that reggaetón's models came from outside and that he was trying to keep up with them; he had recorded songs with more Cuban influences but argued in 2008 that to continue down that road would be to swim against the tide. The mimetic aspect of reggaetón is a statement that, for all Cuba's political exceptionalism and cultural exclusion, Havana is no musical backwater but is rather in the fashionable Latin loop.[11]

There are two recurring ideas in critical responses to Cuban reggaetón. The first is that reggaetón is an authentic Caribbean musical genre that has been corrupted by the hypercommercialism of the global music industry and by a lack of discernment on the part of the Cuban media, rather than an inherently problematic cultural form.[12] The second is that the threat of commercialized, globalized reggaetón could be readily reduced by a greater effort toward local adaptation, and that such Cubanization would be the result of natural evolution. Both of these ideas, perpetuated even by perceptive cultural critics like Faya Montano (2005) and Zurbano (n.d.b), are suspect. As Marshall (2009) shows, early Puerto Rican reggaetón borrowed heavily from Jamaican dancehall and U.S. hip hop—both genres decried for their commercialism. Reggaetón thus has its roots firmly planted in the sampling and versioning of commercial music. Also, the Caribbeanization or "tropicalization" of Puerto Rican reggaetón was the outcome of efforts toward commercial success and the seeking of a mainstream, pan-Latin audience (ibid., 36). In a Cuban context, too, the work of artists like Cubanito and Gente de Zona is evidence that commercialization and localization are two sides of the same coin.

Reggaetón, Timba, and Rumba

Despite the widespread ideology of sameness, Cuba's most prominent reggaetón group, Gente de Zona, takes the opposing line, suggesting that Cubanized reggaetón's hour may have finally come. However, it is worth taking a closer look at this group's music, because the picture is not quite as clear-cut as a first hearing of "El animal" would suggest. To begin with, Gente de Zona's music is very eclectic. In some songs, it seems to be a straightforward Cuban–Puerto Rican mix—in other words, Cubanized reggaetón—since the minor percussion (*tumbadoras*, *campana*, etc.) are Cuban and the major percussion (bass drum, snare) is taken from Puerto Rican reggaetón. Other Cuban elements that the producer Nando Pro

Nando Pro in his studio. Photo by author.

regularly uses are the rumba clave and piano *tumbaos* from timba that he himself plays (unusually for an urban music producer, he is a trained musician, having studied piano at the Escuela Nacional de Arte). However, he also mixes in elements from salsa, merengue, cumbia, bachata, techno, and so on, creating more of a Caribbean or pan-Latin melting pot—much more than reggaetón passed through a Cuban filter.

One of the most notable issues is that Nando Pro uses preset, prepackaged computer percussion tracks in his music. Rather than building up the percussion in the backgrounds instrument by instrument, he selects a ready-made ensemble from a list of choices on the Látigo program. The idea of localization implies that local musical skills, instruments, or aesthetics act as a filter on globally circulating sounds, but when it is just as easy to hit the "cumbia" button as the "salsa" one, a more pick'n'mix, postmodern approach emerges. The issue of localization in the digital age was brought home to me as I talked to Nando Pro in his studio. He explained that one Cuban element of his music was *bomba*. This is a complex word with many musical meanings, so I asked him to elaborate. He described bomba as a climactic moment in a timba track; he turned to the computer, hit the bomba button, and said "like this." How-

ever, the bomba on the Látigo percussion program—the percussion back-
ing that Nando Pro used most often, which he considered to be adding a Cuban touch to his instrumentals—is actually the characteristic Puerto Rican genre of the same name. This is a snapshot of how complex the idea of Cubanization is in the age of computerized music making, when even a skilled, formally trained, and highly successful producer may regard using digitized Puerto Rican percussion as adding a Cuban feel to his music.

If apparently Cubanized music may be less localized than it seems at first, there may also be local elements in unexpected or hidden places. What precisely are we looking for as evidence of indigenization? Would we necessarily know it when we hear it? For that matter, does it have to be audible to count? The producer Rebeld' Malcoms, who makes predomi-nantly commercial hip hop and slightly left-field reggaetón, and who ex-pressed the same take-it-or-leave-it attitude to musical cubanía as other producers I interviewed, told me that he sometimes includes a Cuban element in a song, but when all the parts are mixed together it is inaudible. His song "El Cubaneo" has a Cuban bass line, but it is camouflaged as techno, he told me, so it is virtually impossible to pick out of the mix. Once again, digital music production has changed the rules of the game.

While the bomba example suggests that apparently localized timba-reggaetón is a bit less Cuban than it appears, there is also a counterargu-ment that suggests that indigenization is more prevalent than most pro-fessional critics have noticed. As noted above, Alexánder Delgado referred to the chorus of "El animal" as rumba, and he clicked the rumba clave as he sang it to me. Elvis Manuel also performed rumba, and El Micha told me that he had grown up singing rumba and rap, claiming that he could take any of his reggaetón choruses and transfer them straight to rumba—something that I was able to observe repeatedly in 2009 when his collab-oration with Los Cuatro, "Si se va a formar que se forme," was a popular choice for cover versions by rumba groups. When I went to a peña of the famous rumba group Los Papines that summer, I heard both an original song, which they described as *rumbatón*, and a cover of Gente de Zona's "El animal." I witnessed similar rumba-reggaetón fusions at two peñas of the rumba group Yoruba Andabo and at the Sábado de la Rumba at El Palen-que, and I spent a memorable half-hour on a Havana bus with a group of child rumberos who sang a whole string of reggaetón hits to the accom-paniment of live rumba percussion.

While "El animal" is a song with a distinct Cuban flavor in the instrumental, thanks to Nando Pro's piano tumbaos, most of El Micha's backgrounds do not *seem* to contain any such musical Cubanization: his is the kind of Puerto Rican–derived reggaetón that drives critics and trained musicians up the wall. Like Elvis Manuel, he makes reggaetón that is supposedly mimetic, and thus evidence—according to most critics—of discontinuity with Cuban traditions. However, his early affinity for rumba and the easy, frequent incorporation of his songs by rumba musicians and audiences confirm the link of which he and Delgado spoke: it is not a theoretical connection, but one that I witnessed on multiple occasions. Rumba is the thread, the source of continuity, which goes beyond the musical style of the song's background and centers on the chorus. El Micha's supposedly mimetic songs are incorporated in rumba settings just as easily and regularly as Gente de Zona's fusions, implying that the difference between these two opposing strands of reggaetón, obvious to a music critic, are less clear to a rumbero. It seems that Cuban audiences are hearing even apparently nonlocalized reggaetón as distinctly Cuban, and it is among rumba musicians and audiences, in the processes of reception and recycling, that Cuban reggaetón's local connections may be observed. The fit between genres may be less audible in recorded songs, but it becomes clearer in performance.

The idea that rumba lies at the heart of Cuban music is a commonplace one. My argument is thus perfectly in line with Cuban musicological tradition and musical discourse, yet I have never heard it applied by music scholars or critics to reggaetón, which is treated as an alien invasion and a threat to Cuban music. The CIDMUC report expresses concern over the rupture of Cuban musical traditions and sees the solution in a closer relationship with timba. But it is in the choruses and their relationship to rumba—rather than the instrumentals, which may or may not imitate Puerto Rican reggaetón—where we may find the evidence of continuity. Although this has apparently passed most critics by, it seems to be evident to artists (who view themselves as twenty-first-century rumberos) and audiences (who hear them this way); perhaps, then, what is needed may be not more indigenization, but rather a different form of listening and a redefinition of what it means to sound Cuban.

The dependence on Puerto Rican models within Havana reggaetón is tied to the transgression of hegemonic notions of national culture in more ways than one: not just the dominance of foreign styles, but also the irruption of amateur producers and performers, often with no formal training, into the professionalized, highly skilled sphere of Cuban popular music. Since the habanera has been described as the most important rhythm to come out of Afro-America (Thompson 2005), the rupture of reggaetón is as much to do with class and education as it is with musical tradition; criticism is often implicitly or explicitly a reaction against untrained barrio youths' making music on computers and disturbing the hegemony of virtuosic graduates of Havana's impressive music schools. In other countries, there has been much more of a do-it-yourself attitude to popular music, and it is quite common for musicians to have had little or no formal training. Cuban popular music, however, has long been distinguished by the state's rigorous education programs and the quality control imposed by the professional music agencies; leading artists are therefore often highly trained musicians. Rap and reggaetón, however, have moved the goalposts over the last decade; knowledge of and access to computers and music technology have become more important than traditional musical training, posing a major challenge to the music profession, the institutions that regulate it, and established definitions of what constitutes a musician or musical skills.

In Cuba, the word *músico* typically means a musician with either years of formal training in the state system or a similarly thorough apprenticeship in traditional music—for example, as a result of growing up in a well-known musical family. Access to the music profession is tightly regulated by state-run music agencies that have traditionally tested the musical skills of aspiring members. Since the boom in rap and reggaetón over the last decade, however, cultural institutions and officials have been forced to respond to the (painful) fact that many of the island's most popular musical performers are not músicos. As only professional musicians can legally be paid to perform in Cuba, cultural institutions have been faced with two somewhat unpalatable choices: allow non-músicos to join professional music agencies, or deny them membership and thereby feed the booming underground music economy. The idea of "music without musicians" is troubling to many: Leonardo Acosta (2008) denied electronic dance music, reggaetón, and most rap the status of music on this basis. The formal categories of "musician" and "music" have thus been destabilized in unprecedented ways by the spread of digital technologies and the rise of urban music stars who honed their skills in the street.

These newer genres have opened a door for those without formalized musical training—a democratizing step, but one that has caused anxiety among many professional musicians and cultural observers. Such observers fear that amateur reguetoneros are lowering the high professional standards that made Cuban popular music a productive symbol of national identity during the twentieth century; practicing musicians in other genres are also clearly concerned that the rise of reggaetón threatens their position in Havana's musical marketplace. Indeed, there is widespread resentment among musicians that reguetoneros have moved to the top of the heap so quickly and with so little formal training. The idea of paying one's dues is firmly entrenched in the timba scene, so the sight of reggaetón singers becoming stars just a few years after starting out has grated on many. As Delgado acknowledged in our interview: "In just three years, three people appear who are street artists, who haven't studied music, who don't have musical training as such, and our music is listened to more at the moment than the music of the greatest musicians of our country, and I think that those musicians get annoyed sometimes."

Reggaetón thus provides a marked contrast to the timba world, which has a rigid hierarchy that makes professional mobility slow and laborious. With reggaetón, however, a clever producer and a mixture of good strategy, persistence, and luck can provide an inexperienced singer and rapper combo with a shortcut to the top. Even artists who were shunned by the state-run music agencies and media, like Elvis Manuel and El Micha, catapulted themselves to fame through the viral spread of digital recordings and unsanctioned live performances. That these untrained artists were being paid good (if illicit) money to perform to large audiences might have been unremarkable in other countries, but in Cuba it was a shock to the long-established system.

Nevertheless, institutional resistance continues to weigh on artists. It is very hard for amateur musicians to break into the professional ranks and thereby legitimize their position and increase their earnings, and even professional reguetoneros feel hampered by the antiquated agency system and the lack of opportunities at the largest public events in the capital. Two of Cuba's most famous reggaetón artists, Eduardo Mora (Eddy-K) and Elvis Manuel, both defected to Miami in 2008 (though the latter died in the attempt). Both felt that there was a glass ceiling for reggaetón artists, particularly for amateurs. Even though Elvis Manuel and El Micha had achieved fame (or at least notoriety), many doors were still closed to them, and moving to the next level of commercial success was a challenge.

The amateur-professional divide runs throughout the CIDMUC report, in which many of the perceived negative characteristics of the genre, such as musical and lexical poverty, are attributed primarily to amateur producers, and the future transcendence of the genre is seen to depend on its greater adoption by professional musicians, particularly timba groups. This notion of "transcendence"—the idea that a new music emerges as a kind of rough diamond which can then be polished—is characteristically Cuban, for it encompasses not just the incorporation of foreign elements into national culture, but also the unique structure of the music profession in Cuba and the equally distinctive idea of *superación*, or self-improvement. Transcendence in the case of Cuban popular music is not just a question of local adaptation: it specifically implies the elaboration by professionally trained musicians of musical styles developed by amateurs, or the professionalization of the amateurs themselves through a structured, formalized process of superación.[13]

Some rappers have taken steps down this path, participating in *cursos de superación* at the Ignacio Cervantes "professional improvement school" in La Víbora (R. Moore 2006, 89), which allowed them to deepen their formal music skills and knowledge of Cuban musical traditions, as well as facilitating their incorporation into hegemonic constructions of national culture. The mere act of engaging with the process of superación suggests a certain assimilation of traditional ideals. Thus while rap, too, was critiqued in the 1990s for its lack of professionalism, this view has been tempered as leading groups have taken state-sponsored music courses and gained the kudos associated with belonging to a music agency, the ACR. If rap today is regarded by most cultural observers as having "transcended" to the level of national culture, most reggaetón production currently stands outside this formalized, distinctively Cuban process; its home-produced feel, preference for globalized electronic sounds and often scant regard for Cuban musical traditions, and its insistence on provoking pleasure without necessarily adhering to traditionally defined notions of quality (based on criteria such as rhythmic, melodic, and timbral virtuosity and variety) all suggest a lack of engagement with the striving and serious intent behind superación.[14]

Reggaetón has shaken up Cuban popular culture in significant ways. It has challenged the indirect, playful linguistic traditions of Cuban popular music with often vulgar straight talking and has invaded Cuba's professionalized musical world with the computer-generated creations of amateurs who have generally learned their skills through experimentation rather than extended, state-supported education, and whose music often resists incorporation within the canons of national culture via the discourse of Cubanization. The disturbance of the rigid hierarchies of Cuban popular music has been seen as much more transgressive and threatening in the case of reggaetón than in that of rap, not least because rappers never received the level of exposure of leading reguetoneros today. While rap was initially perceived as a threat because of its U.S. origins, those associated with the nascent scene perceived a way toward state acceptance via the social commitment of message rap and claims of musical indigenization. Reggaetón, however, currently offers no comparable route to ideological compatibility. With both music and texts attracting censure, it poses a more intractable problem for the guardians of Cuban culture.

The Politics of Dancing

The challenges of reggaetón are not to be found solely in the fields of musical and lyrical production, but also in audience reception. Reggaetón entails a focus on dancing; indeed, it is based on a rhythm labeled the "call of the dance" in its earlier manifestation as the habanera (Thompson 2005, 115). This has provoked the scorn of underground rappers who espouse the strict dichotomy—music for listening (positive) versus music for dancing (negative)—articulated by El Aldeano and Danay; but this hierarchical mind-body division is also constructed much more broadly within Cuban intellectual and cultural spheres. As Robin Moore (2006, 15) notes, Cuban socialist thought prefers music that contains an ideological element and a politicized message, and the same could also be said of many who discuss and write about music, both in Cuba and around the world. Where rappers, intellectuals, and state officials may characterize body-centered music simply as an ideological vacuum and the negative opposite of "music for the mind," it is also possible, following McClary (1994), to discern something more positive and challenging. It has been suggested by more than one writer on timba that dance music and its attendant pleasures and physicality may be an oppositional space in Cuba; in a highly politicized context, being apolitical may be an effective form of political statement. Vincenzo Perna (2005) claims that dance music has been at odds with officialdom for much of the Cuban Revolution. The white elite preferred serious styles like *canción* and nueva trova, which focused on individual performers, were meant for listening and not for dancing, and lacked the carnivalesque nature of Cuban dance music. Cuban underground rap has numerous parallels with nueva trova (see chapter 1), but a shared distrust of dancing is one similarity that is mentioned less often. Robin Moore (2006), meanwhile, has talked about the resurgence of timba in terms of an antisocialist aesthetic of hedonism and materialism. He discusses the opposition between pleasure and thinking in official ideology, with the former seen as working against efforts to persuade people to elevate themselves: as a result, politicians and cultural officials have tended to promote serious music with political or socially conscious lyrics. In a similar vein, the recent espousal of reggaetón and its ethos of personal gratification by Cuban youth might be interpreted as a certain rejection both of such politicized music and, more generally, of the state's enthusiasm for thought-provoking culture.

Moore regards timba's emphasis on pleasure and avoidance of seriousness and political correctness as a form of liberation from cultural norms. Reggaetón may be seen to take a further step in this direction: the idea of dance as liberation was evoked by many interviewees cited in the CIDMUC (2005, 21) report, who perceived reggaetón dancing in terms of freedom from the social and choreographic conventions of Cuban couple dances (including timba). Delgado echoed this, describing reggaetón to me not as a *baile dirigido* (led dance) but one, like house or techno, which allowed the dancer to let go and be free. He contrasted foreign and local attitudes: tourists like to go to dance schools, learn fixed steps (like salsa), and then go out dancing to demonstrate their knowledge; but young Cubans are now more attracted to the easier, freestyle dances of reggaetón. Given that there was also a marked rise in the popularity of house and techno music during my research period, there was evidence that the globalization of dance styles was working in two directions: foreigners were going to Cuba to learn bailes dirigidos, while young Cubans were turning to freer international dances like reggaetón and house.

As with the *despelote*—the solo style of timba dancing performed by women that emerged in the 1990s and came to overshadow the couple-dancing style known as *casino*—the traditional physical dominance of the male partner in Latin music has been reversed in reggaetón: men play a subsidiary role, while women are the main focus of attention and the principal driving force. Unlike in couple dances, in the despelote and reggaetón the woman does not need a partner and does not need to be "led"; during live shows, female dancers are often prominently placed on the stage, and in the audience, female dancers usually dance alone or in front of their partners, on whom they have their backs turned, with the man's role reduced from leader to follower or even observer. Reggaetón dancing is not only female-centered but also transgressive in its open sexuality. Perna has argued that, in the case of timba, this reflects changing gender dynamics linked to the social and economic upheavals in Havana since the early 1990s, and these new dance styles may thus be seen as participating in renegotiations over gender roles and liberation from social conventions.[15]

Reggaetón is a music of pleasure par excellence, and dancing and bodily pleasure can provide temporary freedom from hardships and pervasive ideologies, whether Marxist or capitalist. Cubans often consider sexuality to be an important aspect of life that lies outside government control, and the body may thus be perceived as a site of freedom and self-expression. Yet it is also a site of contestation, for the phenomenon of *jineterismo* (literally "jockeying," covering a range of activities from mild hustling to prostitution), which has assumed a major role in Havana's social imaginary and informal economy, is periodically the target of efforts at state control. Since the early 1990s, with the explosion of jineterismo and attempts to police it, the bodies of young habaneros have been a nexus of struggle with the state for access to the benefits of tourism: hard currency, material goods, foreign travel, and so on. Bearing in mind McClary's (1994, 34) argument quoted above, that "the musical power of the disenfranchised . . . more often resides in their ability to articulate different ways of construing the body, ways that bring along in their wake the potential for different experiential worlds," the rise of an exhibitionist pleasure-centeredness in dance may be interpreted as resistance to the reduction of the body to a productive machine for the benefit of others (see Fraser Delgado and Muñoz 1997).

In the context of the profound crisis in Cuban society since the Special Period, during which the body emerged in Havana as a prime asset and an important source of social and economic capital, fought over by the state, tourist industry, and young Cubans themselves, the fact that reggaetón refers constantly to the body and sex in both lyrics and movements cannot be produced—as it is often is by observers—as evidence of its inconsequentiality. Although not literally rebellious, it can be read as a statement of liberation from social, political, and even economic constraints, as constructing a "different experiential world" and reinventing the body as a site of pleasure, personal gain, and social mobility rather than productive, collective labor. It is also a refusal to engage with the state on the state's preferred terms of official ideology and articulated discourse, though this does not make it empty: as Simon Frith (1998, 224) puts it, "dance is an ideological way of listening." The government is able to exercise some control over the field of verbal discourse, for example through censorship and restrictions on media content, but dancing bodies are much harder to reign in. The body might be perceived as a prime articulator of free "speech" in public contexts where verbal expression is subject to regulation by the state. "Ideas are our weapons," proclaims a political sign in Havana, but "bodies are our weapons" might be closer to the truth for many young habaneros today.[16]

On the one hand, every African-influenced popular dance style to emerge in Cuba over the last two centuries has at first been considered transgressively sexualized, so in one sense there is nothing new with reggaetón. On the other hand, the fact that the classic dance move of reggaetón, the perreo, is named after (and imitates) a sexual position suggests a heightened degree of sexualization: this is not just in the mind of the strait-laced observer. Reggaetón's eager adoption in Havana is suggestive in the context of the commodification of sex in the city over the previous decade. Sex has become something of Havana's trademark, and reggaetón is the music of young people who have grown up with this reality. There is a significant presence of *jineteras* in many of the prime venues where reggaetón is performed live, such as Las Cañitas at the Hotel Habana Libre and the Cabaret Nacional. Just as Perna found with timba, reggaetón performances provide opportunities for young women to show off their wares, pointing to a dynamic relationship between music, sex, and tourism. Reggaetón's highly sexualized movements and lyrics thus need to be understood in the context of a city where dancing and sex provide both metaphorical and literal routes of escape, enabling spheres of experience beyond state ideology and Special Period hardship, but also potentially constituting a commodity in the gray economy, a way forward in life, and a way out of the country.

The body may thus be perceived as a creator of complex meanings rather than, as many rappers and critics would have it, the absence of mind. This perspective can be brought to bear on the issue of reggaetón's problematic relationship to national culture. The dominance of Puerto Rican reggaetón aesthetics in Havana has caused anxieties for intellectuals whose prime model for analyzing the interaction of global and local is one of adoption and adaptation at the level of production. Yet it appears to be primarily in the sphere of reception—of dancers' bodies—that local and global, traditional and modern, are mediated, as evidenced by the incorporation of reggaetón in rumba peñas. Local reggaetón dance styles have evolved from the Puerto Rican perreo to a more indigenous blend of reggaetón and break-dance moves with those derived from timba (the *tembleque*), rumba, and various other Cuban dances of African descent, giving rise to distinctive movements known as *el reloj*, *el tranque*, *la onda retro*, and so on (CIDMUC 2005, 20). For all that reggaetón dance holds the power to liberate participants from dominant social norms, it seems to be in the sphere of bodily movement that Cubanization is most in evidence. Reggaetón dance both reflects and constructs the specific, sexualized environment of twenty-first-century Havana, but as a transgressive, African-derived dance over the habanera rhythm, this "revolution of the body" displays clear echoes of Cuba's cultural history.[17]

Havana Goes Bling

To continue in the realm of the physical and the visual, I was struck by Alexánder Delgado's appearance and accessories when we met: particularly the 4x4, but also the iPhone and the Dolce & Gabbana clothes. They are hardly unusual for a successful popular musician in other countries, but they stood out in socialist Havana. And they are supposed to stand out. Susan Eckstein (2007, 186–87) has focused not just on the widening gap between rich and poor in Havana but also on the "new materialism": the recent embrace of consumer lifestyles and mimicking of Miami mores. As Rory Carroll and Andrés Schipani (2009) note, "it used to be taboo to show that you were living better than others"; now the flaunting of material wealth is commonplace, almost de rigueur. The limited reforms introduced by Raúl Castro in 2008, which revolved primarily around widening access to electronic consumer goods, "have underlined that split by giving the privileged minority more opportunities to consume. You see them snapping up Sony wide-screen televisions, Paco Rabanne perfume and Adidas trainers in shopping centres like La Puntilla, out of bounds to most but with a poster of Fidel's revolutionary exhortations at the entrance" (ibid.). The cellphone became a particular status symbol: it was portable, prominent, and (even after its legalization) far too expensive for anyone on a state salary to afford, so sporting one was evidence of access to hard currency. It was a highly symbolic object in 2007–8, an emblem of Havana's burgeoning materialism but also the surreal nature of the local economy. That reggaetón groups Los Cuatro and Clan 537 wrote odes to the cellphone speaks volumes, and that the former's song is named after a specific brand—"Motorola"—illustrates the encroaching of international marketing on late socialist Havana, in part through urban music (Red Bull and Havana Club have also benefited from rap or reggaetón tie-ins).

The cellphone is a symbol of recent changes in political, social, economic, and musical fields: permitted at last by the government, embraced by reguetoneros, and scorned by rappers precisely because it embodies consumerism and inequality. It appears regularly in rap lyrics as a stand-in for Havana's slipping society. In "El periodista," El B raps derisively that "dim-witted youths put all their efforts into cellphones, cars, fashions, sex, and three-peso fiestas"—precisely the goods and activities that reggaetón celebrates—while El Aldeano ("Nos achicharraron") exclaims ironically, "a cellphone at your waist and bingo! You're the star of the show." In reggaetón, however, appearances are everything. An aspiring reguetonero on the edge of the big time told me that reggaetón artists need to maintain their image—gold chains, designer clothes, cellphone, minders, a car if possible. The appearance of success was the route to success, which meant investing in one's image.

With its emphasis on foreign fashions, jewelry, and the fetishized cellphone, reggaetón embodies Havana's new conspicuous consumption. In Perna's (2005, 154) study, the expression "to show off their merchandise" appears as a metaphor for one of the functions of the despelote dance move in timba; reggaetón dancing combines this metaphorical sense with the more literal one, blending the overt sexuality and materialism that are central to youth culture in Havana today. Reggaetón's natural habitat is the *discoteca* (nightclub), where clothes, accessories, and behavior are on display (see, for example, the video for Gente de Zona's "Mami yo te enseñé," or any live Gente de Zona footage on YouTube). The music acts as a catalyst for the creation of a new kind of urban subject after fifty years of revolution. Reggaetón in Havana is about wearing money, spending money, and dreaming of money—aspirations that have been bottled up for half a century are now being projected onto this imported musical form. The cover of Gente de Zona's first album shows the artists sporting designer clothes and sunglasses and thick gold chains, and the music feeds the image, providing the perfect soundtrack for the new materialist Havana. As Marshall (2009, 56) notes, around 2003 the leading Puerto Rican reggaetón producers Luny Tunes introduced synthesizers, techno influences, and pop production, creating "sleek, shiny tracks which seemed to embody in sonic form the flashy style of *blin-blineo* (or 'bling-bling')."

Unsurprisingly, the ostentatious materialism of reggaetón stars, aspiring stars, and their better-off fans has attracted less than admiring responses from journalists. The title of Rufo Caballero's (2008) article in *Juventud Rebelde* was simply "Dinero" (money). After analyzing a live reggaetón performance that dismayed him, he continued: "However, there was no excess that bothered me as much as this one: several of the singers, when they addressed the audience, referred to money as a sacred value, with questions like 'who has more money—women or men?' This was one of the constants of the event: the showing off on the basis of the need for money, of the desire and the possession of money. Money as ideal, as paradigm, as model." What makes this article particularly notable, much more than a knee-jerk reaction, is that its author had criticized a "crusade" against reggaetón and made benevolent remarks about the genre only three months earlier in the same newspaper (Caballero 2007b). What had changed? His initial praise was founded on a recorded song by Eddy-K, while his subsequent disapproval centered on his experience of live performance. This underlines my argument that a considerable part of

the cultural meaning (and culture shock) of reggaetón lies in the performative and visual realms. Most leading reggaetón artists, carefully protecting their territory, do not generally seek to outrage dominant sensibilities in their recorded music; but what takes place live onstage and in
the auditorium is another matter, as illustrated by Delgado's brush with
the authorities just before I met him. Indeed, much of the meaning is
generated outside the realms of music and lyrics, for example in commentary, improvisations, and actions between songs. During a gig at the Salón
Rojo in 2009, Delgado twice accepted drinks from members of the audience between songs: the first was Red Bull, the second champagne from
the bottle—both absurdly expensive in Havana. In *Animals of Cuban Music*,
Delgado is filmed being given cash (euros) and an expensive-looking watch
by audience members halfway through performing a song. The messages
that reggaetón artists and audiences project through their appearance and
such performative behavior are predominantly economic at heart.

One of the most notable aspects of reggaetón in Havana is the way that
it has crossed over from the lowest sectors of society into the ranks of the
nouveau riche. When Gente de Zona play the Salón Rojo of the Hotel
Capri, the venue is filled to the rafters with Havana's dressed-up, mon-
eyed crowd, ready to pay 35 CUC (Cuban convertible pesos—the equivalent of two months' salary at a state job) for an evening of music (45
CUC if they want a chair). Only five years earlier, reggaetón had been the
music of bicycle-taxi drivers and poor immigrants from eastern Cuba. Its
leading names soon made their fortune in the rapidly commercializing
night-time economy, and they now represent and appeal to the opposite
social pole as well. They began to target the *farándula*—the young, fashionable, upwardly mobile, predominantly female crowd—and now going
to reggaetón concerts in posh venues, wearing designer clothes and laden
with jewelry, is one of the ultimate markers of economic distinction in
Havana.[18] Nevertheless, the most marginal sectors of society continue to
identify with reggaetón, and this capacity to attract fans from both ends
of the social spectrum in Havana has been key to its overwhelming success. The combination of humble origins and brash, arriviste materialism
has converted reggaetón into a symbol of Havana's new rich and of the
aspirations of many thousands of poor urban youths.

While attending a reggaetón concert in a top club is a route to social
distinction, the frequently mimetic character of Havana reggaetón on a

musical level reveals a desire for equality, though in the international sphere. Young Cubans want to feel up to date, connected, in the global loop: they carefully monitor international fashions and music. Consumption is a means of approaching international parity: " 'We like to buy good stuff, nice stuff, like you do in your countries,' said Miguel, 20, clutching a mobile and queuing at an Adidas store in Neptuno Street" (Carroll and Schipani 2008). In a perceptive article, the journalist Rory Carroll (2009) writes: "In recent years British and other tourists have flocked to Cuba to see what it is like 'before Castro goes.' . . . But Cuba seems already poised for change. . . . The result will be an island that looks more like everywhere else. For some outsiders that may be cause for regret. So be it. Cuba is not their island and they do not live there. If Cubans want to be more like the rest of the world, warts and all, who has the right to stop them?" Carroll contrasts foreigners' desire for difference with Cubans' desire for sameness, and reggaetón (like other contemporary music trends such as electronic dance music, emo, and heavy metal) speaks to the latter, appealing to young people straining not to be left behind by global trends.[19]

"This Is Business": Reggaetón Economics

Reguetoneros' transgressions of the hierarchies of the music profession and of the economic morality of the revolution come together in their ways of doing business. Most reggaetón artists bypass some aspects of the formal music industry; while some engage in an underground economy that borders on or crosses over into illegality, even top groups adopt strategies that are legal but surprising for some of Cuba's most successful musicians. Since there is virtually no market for original CDs in Cuba, leading groups bypass the formal song or record release altogether and deal directly with pirated CD producers and consumers. Jorge Hernández told me that his group's main means of promotion is to take new music straight to the *quemadores* (burners), who create compilations and sell them through informal stalls on the streets: "here it works back-to-front—the quemadores are our record label." He makes no money from recordings, just from live performances, so he passes recorded music directly into the gray economy to create the necessary buzz. Delgado relied on even more direct methods in 2008: "The street promotes me." He gave his music to DJs and people in the street: "I get into a taxi and I give them my CD—'hey, listen to this.' . . . I didn't have a record company—my record company was me . . . and my distributors are me, my cousin, my mother, my uncle."[20] El Micha said he simply did not know how his music had become popular: he claimed never to have sold or promoted his CDs, which were just passed from hand to hand and made their way into the prime reggaetón distribution networks—bicycle- and motor-taxis and pirated CD stalls. He told the journalist Esteban Israel (2009): "in Cuba, reggaetón moves thanks to piracy." Thus the leading artists in 2008 depended on the same underground distribution networks that had propelled Cuba's first reggaetón star, Candyman, to fame in 2002–3.

Delgado, one of Cuba's most successful musicians by 2008, was upfront about the ways that he had created an extraordinary level of fame despite resistance from cultural institutions, the media, the music industry, and the music profession. Bypassing more official channels, he went straight to the small commercial clubs, which were interested only in pulling in audiences. He made a big effort to watch the fashionable faranduleros— where they went, what they were wearing, what they were dancing to— and to make personal contacts with key players like DJs. If he was now a wealthy star, it was because he had attracted those who had (or aspired to have) money to identify with his group. His success was considerably boosted by his association with P.M.M. (*por un mundo mejor*, or "for a better world"), a group of DJs, promoters, and party organizers who became leading players in Havana's nightlife scene.[21] As with so many other aspects of reggaetón, what is notable is not so much Delgado's rapid rise to stardom via a mixture of hard work, hustle, and networking (which would be perfectly unremarkable in many cities around the world) as its relationship to the socialist context and rigid professional world of Havana, in which such strategies are an edgy novelty.

One step down the pecking order, the leading amateur reggaetón artists perform in small commercial clubs, for illegal fees if they are a sufficient audience draw. Performances are not officially advertised but rather promoted by word of mouth, text messages, unofficial fliers, and announcements. The careers of underground reggaetón artists provide a window onto the booming gray economy of Havana, since they rely on unofficial payments and informal distribution networks. The possibility of creating an alternative entertainment economy is still very new in

Cuba, and it is one that is being explored primarily by reguetoneros, whose popularity (and therefore economic potential) outweighs their acceptance by official institutions. Reggaetón in Havana thus straddles the formal and informal economies. Leading groups are part of artist agencies, perform in official venues, and make marketing deals with companies like Havana Club. Yet most artists also have one foot in the gray economy of bedroom music studios, pirated CD distributors, under-the-table performance fees, payola, kickbacks, and so on. Reggaetón carries more than a whiff of *el bisnes*, the wheeling and dealing so characteristic of twenty-first-century life in Cuba's capital (Hernandez-Reguant 2009c): as one of Triángulo Oscuro's singers said to me as we sat in the studio, "this is business." For those who have stuck with the shrinking hip hop scene in Havana, this whiff is more of a stench, since in their eyes, the conversion of many leading rappers to reggaetón was a question of the wallet winning out over the heart. More than any other musical genre of the previous fifty years, reggaetón places business and money at the forefront, and in so doing it encapsulates one of the core features of Special Period cultural production (Whitfield 2008; Hernandez-Reguant 2009a). The seat of this business-like musical scene is the night-time economy and nocturnal establishments, most of which (according to several of my informants) have their "irregularities," illustrating the opportunism and rule-bending emblematic of life in "a nation of hustlers and micro-capitalists" (Carroll 2009).

Broadening out to a transnational frame, if real and imagined connections between Havana and New York underpinned the boom years of Cuban hip hop, it is the Havana-Miami axis that has subsequently taken over with the rise of reggaetón. The late 1990s New York connection was primarily political and ideological, while the Miami connection a decade later is commercial at heart, as Florida money (or the promise thereof) has entered the Havana reggaetón scene. The Black August collective saw Cuban hip hop as a spur for social change in the United States (and, to a degree, in Cuba itself), whereas Havana reguetoneros like Eduardo Mora and Elvis Manuel were tempted by dreams and promises of making it big in Miami, and Miami entrepreneurs see investment opportunities in the success of top island-based reggaetón artists like El Micha. If hip hop once articulated race-based, political connections to African Americans in New York, reggaetón speaks to ethnic links to the rest of the Caribbean

and to the Cuban community in Miami, and above all to the hope of   145
economic betterment that Miami represents.

THE REVOLUTION OF THE BODY

Time and Nostalgia

As the economic fortunes of the top reggaetón stars have gone through the roof, the critical reactions of a range of observers—intellectuals, cultural officials, rappers—have focused on their ostentatious materialism. The discursive resistance of Havana hip hoppers to cultural commodification, the rise of the market, and the play of surface appearances, and reguetoneros' embrace of these phenomena, provide fuel for the argument that hip hop displays characteristic aspects of twentieth-century modernism while reggaetón embodies postmodern cultural traits. This argument is bolstered by the differing attitudes toward time that they evoke in listeners. If hip hop is already "incredibly nostalgic music" (I. Perry 2004, 54), Cuban hip hop lies at its most nostalgic edge. The idea that authenticity is located in the "old school" and "back in the day" (in the South Bronx of the 1970s) is evidence of a modernist worldview: as Peter Wade (2004, 276) notes, "modernist views of time rely on the idea of rupture from tradition to modernity, a break which provides the possibility of nostalgia and a hankering after authenticity." Postmodernity, on the other hand, may be conceived in part as a collapsing of the past and future into the present and thus a loss of history. In a musical sense, Cuban reggaetón illustrates this with its infrequent references to national traditions and also in its minimal sense of musical evolution over time: there is little evidence of a reggaetón canon in Havana, since older hits are rarely played, and no narrative history of Cuban reggaetón has been written.

It is instructive to read recent critical reactions to reggaetón in Havana through a temporal lens. This is the theme of an article by the renowned Cuban novelist and cultural critic Leonardo Padura Fuentes. Not one to be drawn into a simplistic dismissal of reggaetón, he offers a more subtle, reflective, wistful critique: "I am 50 and I am a 'rememberer' who lives from his memory and memories, and when I feel the urge to reject the aggressive rhythm of reggaetón, I make myself remember that thirty-five years ago, I and my contemporaries were criticized and accused of being 'penetrated by the ideologies of imperialism' and other such fine things, because we liked dancing to the songs of The Beatles, The Rolling Stones, Led Zeppelin" (Padura Fuentes 2006, 51). He is well aware that generations always come into conflict over shifting tastes, but "what pains me about reggaetón and its lyrics is not so much what they provoke now among their consumers as, above all, what kind of cultural, sensorial, affective sediment they will leave in these consumers, what kind of sustenance for remembering when today becomes yesterday" (ibid., 52). Padura describes putting on a cassette of Rubén Blades and Willie Colón's salsa classic *Siembra* and the memories it brings forth. For him, the value of the music of his youth is not necessarily inherent in the music itself but rather in its capacity for "productive" nostalgia. In contrast, "I have no choice but to feel a little sorry for the reggaetón generation, which has access to so much information, including cultural, but which is creating its future nostalgias with songs by Daddy Yankee and Don Omar" (ibid.).

Padura's reflections are worth taking into account because of his eminence as a writer and thinker, but also because of the light that they shed on reggaetón as the music of the moment. This issue of time and nostalgia—of whether to live in the present or in the past and future—recurs in music criticism, especially in the pages of *Juventud Rebelde*. Critics struggle to imagine their children in the future remembering their past, and they are torn between two opposing visions: one, that future generations will remember reggaetón, but only with shame; the other, that reggaetón will leave a black hole of memory. For these writers, popular music's value lies as much as anything in its capacity to evoke nostalgia; reggaetón, however, seems to spell the end of (musicalized) history.

Echoes of Padura can be found in Antonio López Sánchez's (2005) regretful characterization of reggaetón as ephemeral music, and in Luis Raúl Vázquez Muñoz's article "The oblivion of reggaetón" (2006), concerned with how history will judge reggaetón and how today's youth will look back on it. Julio Martínez Molina (2007b) sympathizes with a fellow journalist who voiced his concern for his children's generation: "In a distant future, historians will search through the remains of our era and ask: what kind of society produced this?" Caballero (2008) remarks snidely that "in two years' time those who shout today will not remember the name of their idol." The musician Amaury Pérez quotes Billy Joel's alleged line that "if the future of rock is rap and reggaetón, rock has no future" (quoted in Caballero 2007a), while Danay Galletti Hernández and Adianez Fernández

Izquierdo (2007) implicate reggaetón in the loss of childhood innocence: with reggaetón permeating the island, the ages of man seem to collapse into one as children talk, dress, and act like adult consumers. Childhood is lost twice—once in the living, and again in the forgetting.

Reggaetón is thus charged with either obliterating time, history, and memory, or creating debased memories of which today's youth will only be ashamed. At play is the construction (or not) of musical history, the relative merits of living for the moment or creating memories for future consumption. Not for the first time, it seems as though responses to reggaetón tap into deeper social questions: in this case, they suggest a generation gap, with middle-aged critics holding on to their modernist nostalgia, (hi)storytelling, and sense of loss, and young reggaetón fans letting go of time in a postmodern embrace of the moment. This is suggestive in the context of the Cuban Revolution, the epitome of a twentieth-century modernist project that is limping, with much less fanfare than expected, across the fifty-year mark as I write. Fidel Castro's famous 1953 line "history will absolve me" is emblematic of the revolution's strong historical sense, and since the Special Period, much of the revolution's continued legitimacy rests on its historical achievements; yet the reggaetón generation, as viewed by cultural commentators, desires nothing more than to live in the now, oblivious to the past and to its legacy for the future. The rise of a generation with less historical consciousness than their parents may be significant in the context of a political project that is buttressed by its history.

"¿Prohibido el regueton?"

In Book IV of *The Republic*, Plato famously argued that authorities "must beware of changing to a new kind of music, for the change always involves far-reaching danger. Any alteration in the modes of music is always followed by alteration in the most fundamental laws of the state" (1992, 103). In the face of reggaetón's widespread and multilayered transgression—linguistic, musical, corporeal, economic, and temporal—how has the state responded? Reggaetón in Cuba has been described variously within official and intellectual circles as a problem that needs solving, an infection that needs curing, an invasion to be resisted, and a flood threatening to drown the island. A student leader memorably compared reggaetón to pork: "It's not very nutritious, but it's tasty. If you eat too much it can be bad for you, though you don't care about that while you're consuming it" (Castro Medel 2005a). He proposed various solutions as "the best medicine" for this problem.

The issue of cultural policy with regard to reggaetón is complex and contradictory: reggaetón's supporters say that the government has waged a campaign against it, while its detractors claim that the state promotes it. Both are partly right. Particularly in hip hop circles, the ubiquity of reggaetón and its dominance over rap are taken as evidence of government design: the leadership allegedly prefers people to shake their booty than to think and organize. However, while reggaetón does seem to be omnipresent in Havana, whether this is evidence of government intent is another matter. It may suggest, as I have argued in chapter 1, that the state is fragmented and the government does not have total control over the cultural sphere.

While hard facts about government measures are scarce, there is plenty of anecdotal evidence of control and restriction. All the reguetoneros I spoke to were adamant that they had faced significant institutional hurdles at one time or another: exclusion from cultural organizations or artistic agencies, marginalization in the media, interference by cultural officials, and rejection by venue managers. Their relationship with state institutions and representatives is thus frequently tense. Jorge Hernández claimed that reggaetón had triumphed despite all the restrictions: if local artists had more opportunities to perform at mainstream venues like the Casas de la Música, he said, reggaetón would be even more popular than it is now. Eduardo Mora, Jorge's former partner in Eddy-K, complained after his defection to the United States that reggaetón was not well regarded by the authorities in Cuba, and he claimed that his attempts to put on concerts (at his own expense) at open-air spaces like La Piragua were repeatedly thwarted.[22] One reggaetón DJ told me in 2008 that the music agencies had been instructed to close their doors to any new reggaetón groups, and another pointed out in 2009 that the top two reggaetón groups in the country could not perform at the Casas de la Música and were never on TV. Although reggaetón could sometimes be heard on the small screen, the groups that performed were usually little known. Several journalists confirmed to me this generalized low-level antipathy within institutions and mentioned directives aimed at limiting the quantity of reggaetón in the media. One, Alcides García, spoke of a "national crusade against reggaetón" (Ravsberg 2005). Nevertheless, these restrictions are all partial at most: reggaetón groups have been included in music agencies and can still be heard daily in the media and at prime music venues.

There are two logical conclusions: first, that some branches of the state promote reggaetón while others restrict it; and second, that in the age of globalization and digitization, there is only so much the government can do to control the circulation of music. These conclusions were bolstered by my interview with Fernando Rojas, the vice-minister of culture, in 2008. Rojas had been involved with the hip hop scene for over a decade, and he repeatedly contrasted rap and reggaetón, to the detriment of the latter. He described hip hop as an authentic movement of thinkers; reggaetón was just hollow spectacle. He lamented the commercial turn of the ACR and the demise of the hip hop festival, both of which he blamed on the fact that so many rappers had "switched codes" to reggaetón. Comparing a hip hop concert at Alamar with a reggaetón concert at the Casa de la Música, he claimed that the rappers worked constructively with limited resources, whereas the reguetoneros had everything available to them yet used these opportunities destructively. Since the reguetoneros had all the advantages and the rappers none, he wanted to even up the playing field. He dismissed the idea of banning reggaetón but also rejected the position (adopted by some of his colleagues) that the market should be allowed to take its course, that reggaetón should be tolerated as long as it brought money into the artistic agencies. He wanted to tighten up the agencies' regulations and implement them more strictly.[23]

Despite his negative characterization of reggaetón, Rojas portrayed himself as having limited power against the market and globalization. He argued that the situation had become markedly more complex over his ten years of involvement with urban music. Back in 1997, when the AHS became involved with hip hop, his agenda had been very simple, but the ground had shifted under him (and under Cuban institutions in general) over subsequent years, resulting in the disappointments of the ACR and the suspended rap festival. It seems hard to disagree that the rapid spread of digital technologies and the hemispheric boom of reggaetón took a considerable amount of power out of the hands of state institutions, and that many of the changes within the sphere of urban popular music were led by the shifting tastes of artists and audiences and by developments overseas. Rojas believed that government intervention was necessary, but also that such intervention would necessarily be limited in scope; as I talked to Rojas, it seemed clear that reggaetón preoccupied him, but that doing something about it was not straightforward. He evidently did not like the genre, and a senior journalist told me the same about Abel Prieto, Rojas's superior. Julián González, president of the National Council for the Scenic Arts, stated that "in the cultural world there is concern about the excessive popularity of reggaetón" (Israel 2009). There is good reason, then, to believe that in the corridors of the Ministry of Culture, at least, there is no campaign to pacify the Cuban people with trashy music. Indeed, it is hard to believe that Cuba's top leaders approve of the image of the country projected by reggaetón, since it contradicts almost everything that the revolution stands for.

It is therefore illuminating to read Roberto Zurbano's (n.d.b) argument that reggaetón is concentrated in centers of fashion and consumption like hard-currency clubs and fast-food joints, urban spaces where Havana's new materialism is performed: "In such spaces, as may be imagined, it is very difficult to apply the rules associated with the country's cultural institutions and, as a result, to apply a cultural policy, since in Cuba such a policy is only applicable in those spaces that are under the jurisdiction of the Ministry of Culture; also excluded are the mass media—radio, television, press—where cultural policy has little strength or space to operate." Zurbano's picture of a range of institutions and spaces functioning under different jurisdictions provides a perfect illustration of the fragmentation of the state, and it suggests that the ubiquity of reggaetón is not the result of government design but, on the contrary, of the music's flourishing in spaces out of range of coordinated cultural policy.

It is worth underlining the divide between cultural institutions, where socialist cultural policy largely holds sway, and centers of consumption, where the market—and reggaetón—dominates. In the 1990s, hip hop grew in locales like the Casas de la Cultura and La Madriguera, branches of socialist cultural institutions that are subsidized by the state. Reggaetón rarely appears in such venues in Havana: its home is the nightclub, a commercial venue which charges a higher entrance fee and functions as a business. Many people, especially critics of the Cuban government, speak as though cultural policy in Cuba were uniform and inflexible—a singular vision related to the idea of an autocratic regime. Yet, as Zurbano reveals, there are divisions and contradictions between different branches of the state, and the Ministry of Culture has more power over the cultural institutions where rap blossomed than over the media and the commercial spaces where reggaetón is flourishing. The boom of reggaetón has revealed contradictions within national cultural policy, illuminating fractures between cultural institutions, the media, and commercial clubs.

Even a view that pits the media against the Ministry of Culture is overly simplistic, since there is ample evidence that the media have not embraced reggaetón with open arms. According to the CIDMUC report, reggaetón had little presence in the media in 2003–4, but the fact that young people claimed that they listened to reggaetón primarily in informal spaces and via pirate CDs suggested that this limitation was having little effect on listening habits. Even a stern critic like Acosta (2008, 18) admits that the media are reticent about reggaetón; he argues that this has only added to its power, by giving it the cachet of the underground, and he muses that more exposure in the media might actually weaken the genre's hold. So the idea that media exposure is responsible for reggaetón's success is questionable. My discussions with artists and media employees suggested that reggaetón was underrepresented on TV and the radio in comparison with its popularity in the street. Certainly, immensely popular songs with stronger lyrics by artists like Elvis Manuel and El Micha have been kept off the air, so media discretion is undeniable (see Martínez Molina 2007a).

Reggaetón has received much more exposure than rap, which annoys hip hoppers and fuels the "bread and circuses" explanation. However, whether that exposure is a cause or effect of reggaetón's popularity is harder to determine: the CIDMUC statistical survey suggests the latter, though it is now quite out of date. As Jorge Hernández (a rapper turned reguetonero) saw it, rap and reggaetón have the same problems in the media, facing similar resistance, but reggaetón's greater popularity has forced the doors wider open. It is clear that reggaetón has not been given unlimited exposure nor been left simply to the market and popular demand; had that been the case, it would be headlining at Havana's carnival, in the Casas de la Música, and on TV on an almost daily basis. The more commercially oriented branches of the state embrace reggaetón as a source of revenue, but restrictions in other spheres undermine the view that the government is flooding the country with reggaetón to stop people from thinking. Rather, reguetoneros have used their popularity and economic clout to carve out spaces where state cultural policy is weak.

Many discussions around reggaetón and rap simplify a range of institutions and venues to a monolithic state and their variegated policies to either support or control. The reality is much more complex. Each governmental institution has its own policy, subject to regular and unexplained changes. State employees at times work against each other—Alpidio Alonso fulminated against reggaetón while the ACR promoted it, and Osmell Francis (Cubanos en la Red) claims that a group of important journalists led by Pedro de la Hoz went to the ACR to tell its artists to stop producing reggaetón (Castillo Martiatu n.d.b, 19). Furthermore, there is a large gray area between support and restriction. Many of the spaces to which reggaetón has gained access exist on the edges of legitimacy, carved out using the underground strategies of the informal economy, or are public spaces that can be temporarily commandeered (Acosta 2008, 18; Martínez Molina 2007a). Much of the criticism of reggaetón in print revolves around the question of public noise and contests over urban space; but while critics lament the impossibility of escaping the sound of reggaetón, they regard its grip on the streets as equally beyond control.

Rather than talking about "state policy" toward reggaetón, then, we would be better to think of Ministry of Culture policy, which seems to be a "middle way" of containment and regulation rather than active promotion or total censorship. Cuban journalists revealed to a Reuters correspondent that Prieto had rejected the prohibition of reggaetón but had requested the promotion of the best examples in the media and recommended that the phenomenon be studied carefully (CIDMUC 2005, 84). Prieto told a communist youth meeting in October 2006 that reggaetón "shouldn't be banned, but rather pushed away, distanced."[24] Although a DJ told the BBC that the state was limiting the diffusion of Cuban reggaetón in educational and cultural centers such as the community Casas de la Cultura because of the genre's bad language (Ravsberg 2005), in mid-2006 the Casa de la Cultura of Centro Habana had a weekly showcase for rap and reggaetón groups, suggesting a policy of selectivity, education, and surveillance. In this light, it is notable that the CIDMUC report, an academic investigation, makes much of the need to define the positive and negative aspects of reggaetón before taking remedial action, and it concludes with a series of policy recommendations (CIDMUC 2005, 39–40). These include:

—Selecting the best examples for diffusion in the media.

—Ensuring compliance with current regulations with regard to the music played in recreational, commercial, and dining centers and at public events run by state organizations.

—Increasing the number of spaces for live dance music, emphasizing variety and quality in order to attract the public.

—Providing more state-sponsored dance venues as an alternative to street parties, which tend to be uncontrolled and to generate social conflicts.

The preferred "solution," as proposed by the report, seems to be to provide the Cuban public with more official spaces; a healthier, more varied musical diet; and better music education, focusing on the promotion of Cuban traditions, rather than the more heavy-handed tactics that some feared in the wake of Castro Medel's (2005a) article "¿Prohibido el reguetón?" Given the impossibility of controlling the diffusion of reggaetón in the digital age, the government has decided to take a different approach to the hard-line measures prompted by rock in the 1960s. Indeed, the CIDMUC report itself might be seen as part of this attempt by the government to study and understand reggaetón rather than simply crack down on it.[25] It is clear that reggaetón policy is up for debate. Even those critics of reggaetón who favor intervention (e.g., Martínez Molina 2007a) recognize the impossibility of a unified approach or total ban; they simply ask that socialist cultural institutions like the Casas de la Cultura do not promote reggaetón. The limits of the state's control are taken for granted.

Bonches, or street parties, the scene of the most "problematic" reggaetón, are considered a consequence of the decline in affordable live-music venues and thus a trend which could potentially be reversed by the state. Similarly, the promotion of supposedly healthier alternatives to reggaetón has been led by the state, as exemplified by a TV editorial aired on 14 May 2009, which suggested that schools and families should promote traditional cultural values and forms like son, and showed a group of children singing Daddy Yankee covers as an example of the consequences of failure.[26] However, some of the possible solutions are seen to lie partially or wholly outside the state's purview. One implication of the CIDMUC report is that good, live timba may be an important ally in the fight against bad, recorded reggaetón. The report's authors argue that more variety of styles and greater exposure to live dance music will lead to more catholic tastes among Cuban youth. They also urge professional musicians to create new fusions with local genres, though the authors note that "*unfortunately* this type of reggaetón is not currently the most widespread among the Cuban population" (CIDMUC 2005, 9; my emphasis). The solution to the supposed problem is thus seen to lie in the hands of timberos rather than reguetoneros, who enjoy greater popularity. Cubanization and transcendence of reggaetón are still seen as achievable, but through its adoption by professional musicians who perform established Cuban styles rather than through the efforts of its own specialist practitioners. The current prevailing attitude to foreign culture is therefore not that it should be banned but that it can and should be nationalized, as Robin Moore (2006, 13) contends—a process that is seen to lie in the hands of artists as well as state functionaries.

"¡Hip hop, Revolución!" to "Mueve la cintura": A Crisis of Faith?

The boom of reggaetón in Havana brought about a crisis in the rap scene, and this dual development is worth examining in detail, for it tells us much about both musical genres, the culture and society of which they are a feature, and representations of recent urban music. Controversy has been stoked by the perceived gulf between the ideologies behind rap and reggaetón and by the polarization of institutions and groups connected to urban music. There is a sense in which certain key rap artists, by switching styles, undermined a unique and surprisingly productive pact between institutions, musicians, critics, and overseas activists, one which had led to considerable investment in rap by the Cuban state since the late 1990s. For at least the five years preceding 2002, Cuban rap had been presented as a socially committed, critical yet constructive movement that exemplified the richness of Cuban culture in comparison with the poverty of most rap in the United States. A range of parties, both Cuban and foreign, had found in committed rap a shared language and set of concerns, and local rappers had gained international recognition—if little economic benefit—for their conscious stance.

Therefore, the sudden boom of hedonistic reggaetón, and above all its adoption by a number of leading figures in the rap scene, was a great disappointment to the many observers who had championed Cuban rappers as figureheads of social commitment. Rap legends of the mid-1990s to early 2000s such as Amenaza, Alto Voltaje, Papo Record, and Primera Base—whose dedication to revolutionizing Cuban society from within had been trumpeted not only by the artists themselves but by many admirers of socially conscious music—underwent an apparent conversion. The first three groups left the island and ended up performing predominantly reggaetón in Europe—Norlan of Alto Voltaje was reincarnated in Finland as "the missionary of reggaetón"—while the fourth split into Cubanito 20.02 and Primera Base Megatón. Groups that had been singing until recently about Malcolm X and Nelson Mandela were now to be found urging their audience to move their waists (*mueve la cintura*) and shake their booty. This seemed like a rather abrupt shift, considering that, in contrast to the evolution of rap in the United States, Cuban rap became increasingly socially conscious during the 1990s, and the Havana hip hop festival of 2002 is widely considered to have marked a new high in the political commitment and outspokenness of the scene. Where had the engagement with black radicalism gone? How might we interpret this apparently seismic shift in the scene? Hip hop is often likened to a religion—did the switch to reggaetón indicate a crisis of faith?

What is clear is that the arrival of reggaetón foregrounded a significant clash between ideological rectitude and economic pragmatism. An underground (anti-commercial) stance was often closely related to a relative lack of economic necessity; as Ariel Fernández put it in a speech at Lehigh University (see chapter 4), "we were young, black people trying to do something positive with our lives, trying to occupy our time, because we didn't have to pay bills in Cuba." By the early 2000s, however, most leading rappers had been in the game for five to ten years; some were no longer so young, while others were under increasing pressure to pay bills, yet few had seen their cultural capital transformed into economic benefit. The underground orientation of the scene had opened institutional doors at home and attracted many fans from overseas, but it had restricted the development of a sound economic base. Many rappers spoke of the pressures that they felt from their families as they continued to live at home and had little or nothing material to show from their years of dedication to rap. So when necessity appeared—in the form of responsibility for family or children or as a result of emigration to Europe or North America—many rappers saw a shift to a more financially viable style of music as a logical, even inevitable, step. Reggaetón presented them for the first time with the opportunity to earn a living from music; for the older rappers, whose domestic responsibilities were mounting, it was almost a question of reggaetón or bust. Thus while it is easy to criticize artists for "selling out," it was less a question of getting rich than escaping from poverty, meeting their responsibilities, and continuing to make music by any means necessary.

As Rubén Marín reveals, however, the weakness of hip hop was not simply economic (Matienzo Puerto n.d., 15). While money was a motivation behind his change of tack, he claimed that the biggest factor was his disillusionment with the gap between the politicized, racialized, onstage claims of his fellow rappers and their offstage behavior. In our interview, he was adamant that, despite the current tendency to blame reggaetón, the rap scene had already been showing cracks by the early 2000s. Ariel Fernández, meanwhile, told me that "the view that the world has of Cuban hip hop is a wrong view," since rappers were less politically conscious and much more money-oriented than most commentators allow. The idea of reggaetón creating a rupture in hip hop depends on the notion of a radical change in values initiated by the former, yet Marín and Fernández, two pillars of Cuban hip hop, suggest that the underground credentials of the pre-reggaetón hip hop scene were overplayed by rappers and foreign observers. If the faith was less deeply held than some realize, then the emergence of reggaetón seems less like a rupture than the surfacing of tendencies latent within the hip hop scene.

The discursive construction of Havana hip hop, both from within and from without, involved a degree of selective vision, and the rise of reggaetón is evidence not just of a cultural shift but also of the flourishing of the side of the hip hop story that usually went untold, since it accorded with neither national, transnational, nor academic imperatives. In essence, the hip hop scene began to turn itself into a niche culture in the late 1990s, as leading figures rejected commercial hip hop and embraced underground ideologies and aesthetics. This growing fundamentalism led in turn to criticism of artists who pursued a more commercial aesthetic line and exaggerated reactions against those who allegedly sold out. This highly dichotomized view of underground and commercial, which ill fitted the complex local realities, was reinforced by foreign visitors. The great majority of those who came to support or document the scene from overseas fell in love with the underground, and this preference made its way into most writings and films about Cuban hip hop. Everyone wanted to interview Anónimo Consejo; no one was interested in Eddy-K (soon to become one of Cuba's top urban music groups). The arrival of reggaetón was thus judged from this polarized perspective, according to which Havana hip hop was an underground movement and reggaetón was its opposite.

Yet while artists who crossed over from rap to reggaetón were portrayed as traitors by their fundamentalist former colleagues, most had in fact shown some commercial tendencies all along. Sujatha Fernandes (2006, 108–9) constructs the underground pole of her underground-commercial dichotomy around Primera Base, yet the group's CD *Igual que tú* reveals an eclectic range of underground and commercial beats and lyrics, and their director, Rubén Marín, has long expressed his attraction to commercial rap in public pronouncements, stating baldly in the documentary *Havana Hip Hop Underground* that "we do commercial songs." Perhaps it is little surprise, then, that all the members of the original group went on to become reguetoneros. Gente de Zona emerged from Alamar, the spiritual home of Cuban rap; initially, their commercial (i.e., dance) orientation kept them on the sidelines of the scene, but reggaetón opened up a path for them, and they became the island's most popular artists within a few years. Papo Record was accused of being a turncoat, yet he had released rap songs titled "I will prosper" and "I don't criticize those who are commercial." The crisis in the hip hop scene had as much to do with the splintering of the narratives created around it in the late 1990s as with musical or ideological changes.[27]

The rise of reggaetón has posed some difficult questions about the intellectual framing of politicized music. There may be a lesson here about the risks of rushing to embrace ideologically charged music and overstating its social and political significance. Rap appeared to be a powerful social force when it was fashionable, but almost as soon as reggaetón appeared on the scene, rap began to fade quickly from view. It could be argued that the features of Cuban rap that were so attractive to intellectuals and foreign observers actually contributed to its decline. The serious, committed, anticommercial strand of the rap scene was a joy to behold for cultural critics, but the hegemony of this underground fundamentalism led to a gulf between truly popular culture and conscious culture, leaving the rap scene wide open to the invasion of good-time reggaetón. Both rappers who had converted to reggaetón and those who remained wedded to the underground told me that conscious rap risked overloading people with information and "burning them out"; it has a strong appeal to the politically minded, especially those who live in consumerist societies, but in a highly politicized society like Cuba, it may simply be too much like more of the same. Its rejection of dance as a distraction from its political message, meanwhile, alienated some potential audiences. The social commentary of reggaetón, limited though it may be, is more tongue-in-cheek and ambivalent, less lecturing or hectoring; with its humorous, risqué approach, reggaetón contrasts strongly with official rhetoric and speaks to more young people in contemporary Havana than does rap, with its echoes of the serious, committed music traditionally promoted by the state.

The ACR versus the AHS: The Institutionalization of Urban Popular Music

As rap boomed in Havana in the late 1990s, the leading groups started pushing the government for greater promotion and commercial opportunities, leading eventually to the creation of the ACR in 2002, the same year that reggaetón took off in the capital. The ACR's initial roster included two reggaetón groups: Cubanito 20.02 and Cubanos en la Red, though the former, who signed up with the French label Lusafrica, did not remain in the ACR for long. By 2004, the total number of groups represented by the ACR had dropped from ten to eight, but four of the original rap groups (Eddy-K, Alto Voltaje, Primera Base, and Papo Record) were turning increasingly to reggaetón, leaving reguetoneros in the majority within the rap agency. The lineup of the agency continued to change, as some groups left the country or switched agencies, but most of their replacements (Gente de Zona, Eminencia Clásica, La Fres_k) were drawn from the ranks of reguetoneros, and thus the dominance of reggaetón in the ACR was perpetuated.

The creation of the ACR was already a controversial move, consolidating the division of the scene into professionals (ACR) and amateurs (AHS). But the adoption of reggaetón by the majority of ACR groups within two years of its creation was the final straw for many supporters of rap, who saw an unparalleled opportunity to boost the profile of hip hop

dissolve before their eyes, and the gap between the two institutions that
supported rap became a chasm. The rapper Edgar González (2007, 15)
asked in print whether the AHS "had planned to lose track of" the ACR. It
was not only among rappers and reguetoneros that the battle lines were
drawn. While spokespeople for the newer ACR were carefully diplomatic,
many employees of the AHS were as scornful of reggaetón as the amateur
rappers whom they represented: it was the president of the AHS, Alpidio
Alonso, who publicly criticized reggaetón at the Eighth Congress of the
UJC in 2005. It is important to note also that *Juventud Rebelde*, the
source of Alonso's comments as well as most of the critical articles about
reggaetón cited above, is the official mouthpiece of the UJC, the parent
organization of the AHS; the regular bad-mouthing of reggaetón in the
pages of this paper appears to be part of a general shift against the genre
within the ranks of the UJC.

The antagonistic relationship between rap and reggaetón was thus
underpinned by an institutional division. The AHS—the main institutional support for amateur rappers—is an old-fashioned socialist cultural
organization, which was founded in 1986 and which aims to support
culture that prioritizes the aesthetic over the commercial; when I began
my research in mid-2004, it was promoting hip hop (and not reggaetón)
concerts at La Madriguera and had reputedly expelled rappers who had
switched to reggaetón. The ACR, however, is a more recent creation with
an explicitly commercial agenda, and it has provided a home for many of
the professional reguetoneros; at the Cubadisco music industry fair in
2004, it promoted its reggaetón groups exclusively, organizing a "Cubatón" concert at La Tropical. Of course, this institutional dichotomy is
artificially neat: there are many underground reggaetón producers not
attached to any organization, while a core of three professional ACR
groups has remained focused on conscious rap. Nevertheless, debates in
Havana revolve around such polarizations, for they represent two distinct and competing visions of Cuban culture and society in the new
millennium, and the division of the institutional support for urban popular musicians and the fundamentally distinct philosophies of the two
organizations encouraged such a dichotomized view.

Given the ideological division that developed between the two institutions, it is worth recalling that the ACR was in fact a creation of the AHS.
Fernando Rojas defended the idea of the ACR to me, but he said that the

reality had been much more problematic. In his eyes, the agency had been "contaminated" by the market; he lamented this turn toward commercialization and pinned the blame on the artists themselves. Rojas claimed that the split, already evident just a year and a half after the agency's creation, was the result of broad and uncontrollable changes in Havana's cultural scene provoked by globalization, digitization, and the international boom of reggaetón. While this may be part of the story, what is interesting about the ACR is not so much its day-to-day workings but rather the fact that this kind of professional, commercial agency was created in socialist Cuba and emerged out of a rap scene that was regarded primarily as underground, had been supported by the amateur, noncommercial AHS from 1997 to 2002, and had been praised for rejecting commercialism by the minister of culture (Fernandes 2006, 119).

The core difference between the organizations is that the AHS is subsidized while the ACR is self-financing; they thus illustrate pre- and post-1990 institutional models. As a result, the rap agency, unlike its parent institution, is not insulated from the market. The "contamination" by the market that Rojas laments was an almost inevitable consequence of creating an institution that depended on taking a 24 percent cut of its artists' fees in order to survive.[28] When the rapper Magia López took over the directorship of the ACR in 2007, there was hope among hip hoppers that the dominant influence wielded by reguetoneros would finally be reversed. However, López was in a bind: while she was adamant that reggaetón did not need any help from the agency, there was no chance that reggaetón artists would be moved out to create space for more rappers. Reggaetón was vital to the self-financing of the agency: since reguetoneros received much larger fees than rappers, they provided the lion's share of the ACR's income. Ironically, the ACR conscious rap artists, who had no sympathy for reggaetón, needed their commercial counterparts in order to keep in business. The AHS could reject commercial culture because it was subsidized, but the self-financing ACR could afford no such luxury. As a result, the directors of the agency have found themselves caught between a rock and a hard place, criticized by rappers for betraying the agency's original purpose (as captured by its name) and by reguetoneros for failing to get fully behind the groups that made the ACR viable, causing several to leave (Castillo Martiatu n.d.b, 20).

The divisions that emerged between the AHS and ACR were thus indicative of recent shifts in cultural policy and economics, as well as fractures in the Cuban state, and they dramatized the tensions between socialist and capitalist ideologies and practices that have grown in Havana since the Special Period. There are useful parallels to be drawn here with Thomas Cushman's study of rock music in the last years of the Soviet Union and the early post-Soviet period, which argues that, instead of seeing free-market economics as the major driving force of cultural freedom, "the replacement of political control of culture by the commodification of culture represents the substitution of one form of constraint on human expression for another" (1993, 27). Cultural perestroika (the restructuring of key organizations, in particular the state music company Melodiya) led to a new commercial focus in Soviet cultural production, which contributed to "an emerging division in the rock community between those musicians who saw in music a viable means for the voicing of protest and opposition and those who considered music primarily as an aesthetic experience and form of entertainment" (ibid., 52). Significantly, this division was not just a question of personal ideology: the restructuring of cultural production, designed to ensure the economic viability of companies like Melodiya, placed musicians under institutional economic constraints rather than the political ones they had previously faced.

Cuba went through its own perestroika in the 1990s—the Special Period —as a direct result of the collapse of the Soviet Union; as the economy underwent wholesale transformations, the music scene became considerably more commercialized, with marketability and sales assuming an unprecedented importance (R. Moore 2006, 241). Across the spectrum of cultural production, there was a shift from state subsidies to a self-financing model (though the AHS was an important exception). Some senior rappers, now responsible for keeping not just themselves but also their agency afloat, switched to reggaetón; by embracing music "as an aesthetic cultural commodity rather than an aesthetic means for the expression of dissent," as Soviet rockers had done (Cushman 1993, 58), they contributed to the fragmentation of the rap scene.

Despite its skirmishes with state censorship and incomprehension in the 1990s, rap's greatest enemy turned out to be not government control but the hemispheric boom of reggaetón in the following decade. The rise of reggaetón and decline of rap was not just a question of shifting tastes, however, since reggaetón's emergence in Havana in 2002 coincided with a change in the institutional organization of urban music. If the rap scene lost some of its idealism and political force in the five years after the creation of the ACR, as with Soviet rock, it was not state control so much as the incursion of the market into Cuban cultural production that was primarily responsible. To the extent that control has been a feature of the ACR, it has been less political than economic—in Cushman's words, "the substitution of one form of constraint on human expression for another." The shift from rap to reggaetón is thus a little more interesting than a standard narrative of popular musicians' selling out or losing faith— commercialism had always been present in Havana hip hop, and it became more prominent because the underground scene lacked a viable economic foundation and because new institutional pressures appeared.

Crisis or Postcrisis? Music and Social Change

What does the rise of reggaetón tell us about society in Havana today? Cuban researchers have analyzed reggaetón in terms of a "pendulum swing" away from timba, a simple response to the excessive complexity of timba music and dance (CIDMUC 2005, 33, 36).[29] It might also be instructive to consider the rise of reggaetón as a swing away from underground rap, one linked not only to changes in the economics of cultural production but also to broader shifts in Cuban society since the 1990s.

The relationship between the emergence of new body-centered musics and social upheavals has been recognized since the time of Plato (McClary 1994, 29). Closer to the modern day, Angela Impey's analysis of *kwaito* is of particular interest, for she relates the rise of this music—a commercially oriented South African dance genre which has numerous parallels with reggaetón—to a major moment of political change. According to Impey (2001, 45), "*kwaito's* tendencies are towards materialistic, hedonistic, and flighty preoccupations, and groups such as Boom Shaka appeared to unleash amongst young black consumers an explosive desire to disengage from the long years of oppression and political protest of the apartheid era." She continues: "*Kwaito* represents the music, style and attitude of post-apartheid black urban youth; it represents a sub-cultural practice which liberates black urban youth from the culture of protest of the '80s" (ibid., 49). Also on the subject of kwaito, David Coplan (2005, 20) writes of South African urban youth's demand for a society that fulfils their material aspirations and "accepts their pleasure principle as a valid replacement for the now painfully passé politicized ideology of social sacrifice." To these writers, then, the emergence of body-centered kwaito is indicative of a wave of materialism, hedonism, individualism, and political disengagement in a postpolitical moment.

Other commercialized dance genres that have been widely criticized for their hedonism and overt sexuality (sometimes called slackness) have also been partially rehabilitated by perceptive scholars for their resistance to hegemonic ideologies. If kwaito may be reclaimed from its critics as an expression of liberation from the relentless political focus of popular culture of the apartheid years, *funk carioca*, a distinctive musical style which emerged in Rio de Janeiro in the mid-1980s, might also be considered a reaction against the elaborately discursive, politicized music of the long years of military rule (1964–85). George Yúdice's (1994) analysis of Rio funk reveals many parallels with reggaetón, in particular a resistance to engaging with established ideologies and identities and an emphasis on individual freedom expressed through dance and pleasure, rather than adherence to notions of collective identity and action. Carolyn Cooper (1993, 141), meanwhile, in her study of female slackness in Jamaican dancehall, claims that "it can be seen to represent in part a radical, underground confrontation with the patriarchal gender ideology and the pious morality of fundamentalist Jamaican society. In its invariant coupling with Culture, Slackness is potentially a politics of subversion. For Slackness is not mere sexual looseness—though it certainly is that. Slackness is a metaphorical revolt against law and order; an undermining of consensual standards of decency. It is the antithesis of Culture." Cooper's remarks reveal much about the potential political connotations of commercial dance music.[30]

Given the close relationship between reggaetón and dancehall, Norman Stolzoff's (2000, 99–103) analysis of the transition from roots reggae to dancehall in the early 1980s may illuminate the similar emergence of reggaetón and decline of political rap in Havana. Stolzoff places the rise of dancehall, with its celebration of consumerism and sexuality, in the context of the 1980 Jamaican elections, which marked a political turn from democratic socialism to free-market neoliberalism. Popular disenchantment with the socialist government that had ruled the country in the 1970s led to the election of a neoliberal prime minister, and the rejection of

1970s politics was accompanied by a move away from the Rasta ideologies of roots reggae and toward the embrace of consumer capitalism and dancehall music. The conservative Rastas failed to move with the times; they had also lost some of their oppositional power because of their ties to the socialist government. Dancehall embodied and expressed the new ethic of instant gratification and was a sign that, "after years of frustration, it became increasingly difficult for the masses to sacrifice their worldly desires to the high ideals of Rastafari and socialism" (ibid., 103).

While there has been no political change in Cuba to match the end of South African apartheid, Brazilian military rule, or Jamaican socialism, the collapse of the Soviet Union and the resulting crisis of the Special Period shook the island to its foundations. The 1990s was a decade of transformation and transition from a socialist to a sociocapitalist economy based on tourism, joint ventures with foreign companies, and limited private enterprise. By the beginning of the new millennium, the worst of the Special Period was over (in material terms, at least). Both state and individuals had to learn new ways of getting by, and as the years passed, burgeoning alliances with the Venezuelan president, Hugo Chávez, and with China lent greater stability to the Cuban economy and political establishment. Esther Whitfield (2008, 2) dates the Special Period from 1990 to 2005—a time frame that fits closely with the rise and fall of hip hop in Havana. If the start of this period saw the emergence of the first rappers, the end marked the lowest point of hip hop in the capital (symbolized by the suspension of the festival) and the time when reggaetón fully emerged as the dominant form of popular music. Perna (2005) claims that timba was the "sound of the Cuban crisis"; I would suggest that this label is just as appropriate to rap, given that it both rose and fell with the Special Period, and that reggaetón may be considered the postcrisis, post–Special Period sound. I would argue that the shift in Cuba from protest music (rap) to postprotest music (reggaetón) relates to a broader swing in the new millennium away from a politicized national culture of socialist ideology, collectivity, and self-sacrifice and toward one increasingly centered on pleasure, the reassertion of individuality, and self-fulfillment.

Cubanito 20.02 explicitly linked their abandonment of Primera Base and switch to reggaetón with social and economic changes: they claimed that the moment for underground rap had passed with worst of the Special

Period. Reggaetón seems to be linked to a new phase in which political ideologies play a much-reduced role in people's thinking, above all among young people. As Damián Fernández (2008, 99) notes, "Cubans, tired of politics and mobilization, are retreating to the private, trying to avoid politics." Day-to-day survival has become a greater priority, and reggaetón reflects this prioritization of the economic over the political, the immediate over the historical. Reggaetón's core audience is youths in their teens and early twenties, who are too young to remember Cuba before the Special Period; they have grown up with the contradictory realities of post-1990 Cuba and have never witnessed socialism properly in action. It is not surprising that many are apolitical—they are the first late-socialist generation, which has known neither the purer socialism of their parents' childhood nor the divisive capitalism of their grandparents' formative years. Tourism and foreign investment have brought huge changes to Havana: principles and ideas have given up much of their hold to images and display. When the state has abandoned key ideological tenets, in practice if not discursively, and capitalist wealth is visible daily on the streets of the city, then it may be unsurprising that many individual citizens, particularly the young, feel little connection to the politicized ideologies that inspired earlier generations.

The shift from rap to reggaetón reveals both an ideological split and a generational one. María Isabel Dominguez (2007, 297–98) writes that young people's age during the Special Period was crucial and that a new generation emerged at this time. She analyzes a fracturing that took place during the 1990s that saw greater integration among members of this generation but less identification across generations. Such intergenerational misunderstanding comes out strongly in the reggaetón criticism discussed above, but it is also evident in the rap-reggaetón division. Dominguez notes that even those aged just twenty-five to thirty see younger people as lacking culture, education, and moral and political values. This is precisely the age group that my informants in 2008 identified as the core of the hip hop generation, since younger people were more interested in reggaetón and most of those over thirty had moved away from hip hop as family and work responsibilities took over.

The hip hop generation, entering its teens during the depths of the Special Period, was able to analyze, compare, and speak out. Rap was music for those who were old enough to react to drastic socioeconomic changes with analysis and words.[31] The members of reggaetón's core audience—whose first memories are of material scarcity, self-preservation, and the commodification of female bodies—were too young to reason during the early 1990s. Reggaetón is the music of those who grew up with barely enough to eat, watching their parents hustle to survive, those who grew up with one foot in the official world and one in the gray economy. If the rap generation questioned the huge changes that it saw in society, the reggaetón generation knew only the harsh new world. Reggaetón is a crude, raw music that emerged from a crude, raw reality. It is the music of the marginalized class that expanded due to the economic crisis, the mass of young people in poor barrios who do not see themselves represented on TV, on the radio, or in the newspapers and for whom appearances may provide an economic lifeline and niceties often take a back seat to necessities. Today their voices boom from speakers across the city, broadcasting the issues of the street in the language of the street, and other members of the reggaetón generation answer this call on the dance floor.

This generation gap may also be observed in the differing attitudes to time discussed above. The rap generation has a strong sense of history: many recall the years before the fall of the Soviet Union and the major changes that this event brought to Cuba, and they have questioned the relationship between the present and the past. Most have a clear awareness of the history of hip hop, of its origins in New York in the 1970s and its more recent trajectory in Cuba, and they frequently mention important figures in Cuban and American history such as Antonio Maceo, Che Guevara, Camilo Cienfuegos, Malcolm X, and Mumia Abu-Jamal. Havana's reguetoneros are much less concerned with Cuba's revolutionary history and are more focused on contemporary hemispheric developments in music and fashion. If the popularity of reggaetón really is a sign of a new generation without the same historical consciousness as older Cubans, this points to social changes with implications for the future of the revolutionary project.

The boom of reggaetón as the Special Period was waning may be seen as revealing a subsequent ideological crisis, subtler than, yet just as pervasive as, the earlier economic one. For those who adhere to longstanding socialist ideologies, the crisis is in full swing. Unsurprisingly, underground rappers are among those who see reggaetón's ascendancy as evidence of a state of psychological emergency. El Aldeano and Escuadrón Patriota rap in "Fuego" that "the mental Special Period has never ended," while in "Crisis de fe" (Crisis of faith), Los Aldeanos proclaim: "We need psychological help / The crisis is more about faith than economics." Yrak Saenz told me: "Reggaetón has taken up so much space in Cuba because there is a crisis in Cuban society—that's real. When black people are thinking that they're inferior, when women are thinking that they're objects, when men think that money is the best, when the youth thinks that some guy who's got more money, who's got a car, who's got a pad, who's got God knows what else, is an idol, a model to follow, then there's a lack of values, a lack of so many things, and reggaetón isn't doing anything to help, it's just reflecting the emptiness that we're living though." In an article on reggaetón, Caballero (2008) notes widespread concerns over "the possible discontinuity and breaking of the spiritual legacy of Cuban society," further suggesting that this musical genre is linked to a wider moral panic.

The rise of reggaetón might then be seen as coinciding with the end of the official, economic Special Period and marking the beginning of a new phase in which materialist desires among younger habaneros are placing socialist ideologies (and underground hip hop) in crisis. It is worth recalling Stolzoff's argument that the rise of dancehall was linked to the declining appeal of socialism in Jamaica. The parallels between reggaetón and dancehall point to popular disenchantment, frustration, and desire for change rumbling beneath the surface of political continuity and an attraction to consumer capitalism beneath the socialist exterior. The examples of dancehall, kwaito, and funk carioca, all of which link the emergence of a major new commercial dance genre (and its partial eclipse of socially committed music) with a significant ideological shift, above all among young people, shed light on recent developments in Havana.

Debates over commercialization take place in popular music scenes around the world, but they take on particular urgency in a society at an economic turning point, at which commercialism is considered by the state to be ideologically suspect but a necessary evil, and at which dabbling in el bisnes to acquire *fulas* (hard currency) to buy consumer goods is a prime activity. Reggaetón swept into Havana as the Special Period was fading; of course, it was booming in many parts of the hemisphere at the same time, though it took hold to differing degrees in different regions of the Americas, but in Havana it came to symbolize the new economic realities and dilemmas.

The debates that have accompanied the high-profile emergence of reggaetón have tapped into broad questions over the relationship between art and commerce and the place of globalized, commercialized culture in this rapidly changing socialist society. They reflect a city increasingly exposed to capitalist forces, which some resist and others, especially among the young, embrace with relish. While reguetoneros have seized their commercial opportunities, underground rappers criticize this growing materialism and the commercialization of cultural and social life (at least in their lyrics—see chapter 3 and Baker 2012). It is significant that a number of reguetoneros were formerly struggling, if admired, rappers: their success led to the characterization of reggaetón within the rap scene as a "temptation." "Staying firm" with rap was a sign of strength and morality, while adopting reggaetón was portrayed as weakness in the face of the seduction of commerce.

Within artistic and intellectual circles, then, reggaetón is a symbol of the commercialization of Havana's culture and society, and one's position on rap and reggaetón is, arguably, a position on this process and on the contradictory realities of late socialism itself. A negative view of commercialization is a prominent feature of artistic and intellectual responses to reggaetón in Havana, and the blame for the genre's supposed corruption is laid firmly at the door of the media and the international music industry, which are portrayed as guilty of promoting only the most shallow, vulgar examples of the music (CIDMUC 2005, 12; Faya Montano 2005; Martínez Molina 2007b). Cuban rap, on the other hand, is seen as ideologically progressive and largely untainted by commerce. Discussions of rap and reggaetón are entwined with judgments about the uneasy marriage of socialism and capitalism in contemporary Havana—hence their tendency to polarization. An argument can be made that rap and reggaetón have shared roots in Jamaican music and are thus two branches of the same musical stream rather than separate currents. Nevertheless, Cuban reggaetón filled the gap of the Other against which anticommercial artists and critics defined themselves, and it became a symbolic pole in urban music debates. The "rap versus reggaetón" argument epitomizes a city at a crossroad: idealism, moralism, and socialist ideology is the path it has just traveled, while pragmatism, consumerism, and commerce is the road that beckons.

Reggaetón, Rap, and the Battle of Ideas

In the face of disenchantment, shifting values, and creeping materialism, the state has not abandoned its ideological efforts. On the contrary, as discussed in chapter 1, in 1999 it launched the Battle of Ideas, the commanders of which were a group of loyalists drawn from the UJC. The fact that the UJC is (via the AHS) the parent organization of the hip hop scene reveals a kinship between rap and the Battle of Ideas. Conversely, the UJC has been behind much of the negative press directed at reggaetón; one might conclude that it has taken a stand because the new musical style is seen as antithetical to the central aim of the Battle of Ideas, which is to re-engage Cubans with the ideals of the revolution. While there is no formal connection, hip hop might be characterized as a popular face of the Battle of Ideas—independent, iconoclastic, but pursuing quite similar aims, in very similar language, and sharing its distaste for reggaetón. The most committed underground rappers react against the moral decline that reggaetón symbolizes, and their positions line up closely with those of the UJC. The adversarial relationship between hip hop and reggaetón might be seen as a microcosm of the Battle of Ideas: a struggle between moralism and slackness, between mobilization and depoliticization.

The enthusiastic adoption of reggaetón by Cuban youth may therefore reveal much about the progress of the Battle of Ideas among young residents of the capital. Listening and dancing habits may speak eloquently about realities and attitudes that are not officially admissible. Even though consumerism and capitalist practices are rampant in Havana, even within branches of the state, it is still not politically correct to embrace such urges explicitly. Reggaetón eloquently expresses such emergent desires, as Jamaican dancehall did two decades earlier. Perhaps bodily performance is the best way to speak truth to power in Cuba. Reggaetón seems to encapsulate a rejection of the discipline, blurring of individuality, and abnegation of self under socialism; its focus on self-indulgence and pleasure (often sexual) is implicitly a form of liberation from the official, politicized national culture, and the embrace of fashions and consumer goods speaks to materialist urges. To draw a parallel with Cooper's analysis of Jamaican dancehall, in Cuban reggaetón it is arguably the moralizing, paternalistic discourses of socialism that are being rejected through slackness. For all the state's recent efforts, then, reggaetón's popularity suggests the existence of a postpolitical Special Period generation which has remained largely immune to the consciousness-raising of the Battle of Ideas. Any attempt to understand the significance of reggaetón in Havana must take into account the fact that this generation is both the key target of the government's political campaign and the prime consumers of this defiantly apolitical musical genre.

The appeal of rap to intellectuals and the state in Havana was that its producers, although hailing from marginal barrios, were actually producing a sophisticated critical discourse that seemed to illustrate that social, economic, or geographical marginality in Cuba did not imply a parallel ideological stance. Rappers from tough neighborhoods could be seen as participating on some level in the regeneration of the revolution's ideas. Reggaetón, though, poses deeper problems: its vulgar and banal language seems to reveal a marginality of the mind and to suggest that social commitment and ideological resolve do not spread evenly across Cuban society after all. As Fernando Rojas saw it, rap revealed the best of the barrios, reggaetón the worst. Cuban critics are troubled by the question of why reggaetón's crude lyrics are so popular among Cuban youth, despite the island's much-vaunted education system, and so far they do not seem to have found many reassuring answers (CIDMUC 2005, 5).

Reggaetón from Havana has remained resolutely one-dimensional with regard to lyrical topics, avoiding broad social or political themes. The lack of variety in Havana is striking: despite emerging from a globally admired conscious hip hop scene, Havana reggaetón has produced no Tego Calderón, no Calle 13. No leading artists have tried to merge hip hop's socially engaged lyrics with reggaetón's seductive beat. In Jamaica, dancehall may have overshadowed roots reggae from 1980 onward, but it has included artists and songs with more conscious leanings. There is no inevitability about the limited range of topics and avoidance of broad social questions in Havana reggaetón; it must therefore be a response to local conditions and priorities. Contrary to the earlier evidence of rap, it seems that the Battle of Ideas is being lost on the urban margins after all—many young habaneros are too busy dancing to fight.

Rap was a music of the transitional period of the 1990s, expressing the pain and bewilderment of the shift from socialism to sociocapitalism, but today, to many listeners, it sounds like the music of a former era, just as "music with a message" in South Africa came to sound dated after the end of apartheid (Stephens 2000), and roots reggae in Jamaica reeked of the old socialist order at a time when neoliberal change was in the air. Reggaetón's insistence on pleasure has made rap's politicized ideology, with its rhetorical overlap with the Battle of Ideas, look slightly old-fashioned in Havana. This depoliticization of culture is not limited to rap and reggaetón: timba, too, has seen a marked decline in the controversy of its lyrical topics since the late 1990s. It seems that rap, with its socially committed lyrics, fell out of step with the times once the worst of the Special Period was over. After the turn of the millennium, irreverence and independence became the hot tickets, and the conservatism of underground rap at a time of rapid changes made it quickly redundant to large sections of the younger population. This conservatism was manifested in resistance to the breakdown of values since the Special Period; reggaetón, however, celebrated this breakdown with bluntness and insistent repetition.[32] In an echo of the fate of roots reggae in Jamaica, or the increasing obsolescence of Soviet rock under glasnost (Cushman 1995, 231), hip hop's partial incorporation into the socialist politics of the state gave it space and respectability but also yoked it to an increasingly dated ideology, and rap's messages declined in appeal to young people entranced by the new materialism. Today, "¡hip hop, revolución!" simply does not raise pulses in the same way as Los Confidenciales' cry "¡aceite . . . agua!" or Junior & De Calle featuring Jota B's suggestion "échale un palo." Reggaetón's consolidation of the pleasure principle and its eclipse of conscious rap suggest that, to echo Coplan on kwaito, politicized ideologies such as the Battle of Ideas are now dismissed as "painfully passé" by the majority of the capital's youth.[33]

"De Donde Son Los Cantantes"

The story of reggaetón's rise in Havana at the expense of hip hop is underpinned by issues of geography and race. On one level, it is sometimes characterized as the triumph of Caribbean music (filtered through Santiago de Cuba) over African American music (filtered through Havana).[34] It thus raises issues of regional identity and rivalry, and their place in constructions of national identity. Havana is a western city that tends to look north to the United States and Mexico; Santiago, in contrast, looks south to the Caribbean. Reggaetón spread from Santiago across the island, as son had done nearly a century earlier, and it pushed U.S.-derived hip hop into the background in the capital. If hip hop drew upon and revived the historical connections between Afro-Cubans in Havana and African Americans in New York, reggaetón reactivated the historical empathy between Cuba and Puerto Rico, often described through the symbol of a bird with two wings. Reggaetón also emphasizes connections with other Caribbean nations (such as Jamaica and the Dominican Republic) and with the Cuban diaspora in Miami, bringing different geographical and ethnic imaginaries into play.[35]

Santiago's musical triumph has been equivocal, however, in a number of ways. To begin with, immigration from Santiago to Havana is viewed ambivalently: while "de donde son los cantantes" (where the singers are from), a line from Trio Matamoros's "Son de la loma," evokes the musical authenticity attributed to eastern Cuba, it is also the title of a 1967 novel by Severo Sarduy in which immigration from the east is associated with the decay of Havana in the revolutionary period (Álvarez-Tabío Albo 2000, 368–69). In the case of reggaetón, the musical innovation of eastern Cuba is viewed as both powerful yet potentially corrupting, hence the linguistic turns of Havana-based journalists, who described reggaetón as an invasion, avalanche, or epidemic. Furthermore, after Candyman burst on the scene around 2002, no more artists from Santiago triumphed in Havana until Kola Loka hit the city in 2009 with "La estafa del babalao": some Santiago reguetoneros have gone on to have successful careers, but the dominant figures in Havana (and therefore in the media and overseas) emerged from the Havana rap scene, not from Santiago. The creation of the ACR in 2002 turned out to be crucial, because it ensured that the first reggaetón artists to have an institutional base from which to launch their careers were Havana-based former rappers. Santiago's reguetoneros may have sparked off the Havana boom, but since none of them were included in the ACR, they did not benefit from it.

The issue of geography is closely tied to that of race. Santiago is generally perceived to be a more Afro-Cuban city than Havana, and the first reggaetón to become popular in Havana was notably black in image: both Candyman and Cubanito were clearly influenced by Jamaican dancehall and the ragga vocal style (even though neither Candyman nor two of the three members of Cubanito would be identified as black in traditional Cuban terms). However, as Marshall (2009) has shown, international reggaetón was undergoing a steady shift from "black music" to "Latin music" around the beginning of the millennium, and this "tropicalization" soon had an effect in Cuba. The blacker aesthetic of Santiago reggaetón was left behind as artists in the capital latched onto the Latin aesthetic emerging from Puerto Rico. In Havana, the stylistic "lightening" of reggaetón soon came to coincide with the social desires (including whiteness) of post–Special Period new materialism. As reggaetón's stars became figureheads of the nouveau riche, the social and economic aspirations of producers and consumers were crystallized in videos that showed artists wearing designer clothes and jewelry, driving flashy cars, and—crucially—consorting with light-skinned models, for example in Gente de Zona's videos for "Tremenda pena" and "Mami yo te enseñé."

Due to global trends and local socioeconomic changes, questions of blackness soon dropped off the radar in Havana reggaetón after an initial flowering. Many of the artists are dark-skinned and emerged from a hip hop scene in which discourses of negritude had become prominent, but race is barely addressed as a lyrical topic, and the musical and visual codes have become increasingly Latin or European rather than African.[36] This whitening has also taken place to a certain degree in timba and hip hop, though for different reasons. The message from the sphere of urban popular music is thus quite distinct from the academic field, where scholars continue to argue for the growth of black cultural movements. This is not to suggest that such cultural movements do not exist, but rather that their impact on Cuban society may have been exaggerated by a certain academic tendency to ignore the most widespread, commercially successful cultural manifestations in favor of niche phenomena. As Escuadrón Patriota, one of Havana's most radically pro-black rappers, told me ruefully, bringing two hundred people together for a hip hop concert means nothing in an island of 12 million; most people don't know that Cuban rap exists. Scholars regularly turn to rap to support a broader race argument, ignoring the declining salience of race in the hip hop scene in recent years, the diminishing influence of hip hop more broadly in Cuba (with the exception of the white-coded Los Aldeanos), and the steady whitening of the most popular form of music on the island today.

Finally, the tropicalization of reggaetón might be read in the context of an economy focused on tourism. Reggaetón is connected to the international marketing of Cuba as a Latin-Caribbean paradise island; Cubanito

20.02 and Triángulo Oscuro have marketing contracts with Havana Club rum and Havana Holdings, and their travels to Europe are promotional exercises that depend on and bolster the popularity of the Cuba "brand." The first stop on tour for reggaetón stars like Gente de Zona and Eddy-K is usually Italy, one of the main sources of tourists to Cuba, where there is a large potential audience of Italians who have visited Cuba and Cubans who have married Italian tourists. The musical repositioning of Cuba both feeds into and feeds on the tourism boom, providing economic benefit for the artists, for the Cuban tourist industry, and for the transnational companies that profit from Cuba's global cachet.

Conclusions

Much can be learned from exploring how discussions of rap and reggaetón mirror and participate in wider debates about the direction of Cuban society in the twenty-first century. In Havana, what might be regarded as a local spat between two rival styles of popular music sheds light on broader questions of national ideology and identity, and hegemonic academic and political discourses. Debates about reggaetón have provided a vehicle for discussing issues of fundamental importance in contemporary Cuban society, and much censure of reggaetón (and praise of rap) relates to attempts to defend established notions of national culture and identity in the face of the challenges posed by globalized, commercialized culture. The dismissal of reggaetón as almost beneath consideration is prescriptive as well as descriptive, for there is a widespread perception that "something needs to be done" about it.

Preferences for rap reveal both political and academic agendas: Cuban rap may be viewed as both resistant to and participating in national discourses, and it can therefore be talked about productively by artists, state officials, and Cuban and foreign critics, whereas reggaetón—despite its overwhelmingly greater popularity—is generally regarded as too debased by intellectuals and the state to be the focus of much more than dismissal or "solutions." A problematic source of pleasure, it is disciplined as deviant in language that recalls many moral panics over Latin American popular music through the centuries. Unlike rap, reggaetón cannot be framed by Cuban observers in terms of constructive criticism, and the internationalism that it expresses is the "wrong" kind, painting Cuba

predominantly as the passive recipient of secondhand commercialized
culture from overseas rather than a country that has usurped the United
States in a "serious" field of music.

The negative reactions to reggaetón by intellectuals and counterculture
advocates, both local and foreign, recall the similar condemnation of
Jamaican dancehall in the 1980s (Stolzoff 2000, 100). Those who had
been inspired by roots reggae tended to view its local eclipse by dancehall
as evidence of poor taste, unoriginality, and greed, rather than trying to
understand the appeal of the new style and its relation to its social
context. Furthermore, the greater popularity of Bob Marley's music than
of dancehall overseas from the 1980s onward illustrates the disjunction
between the tastes of local fans and international audiences, something
that has consequences in the realm of academic research. The intellectual
preoccupation with Cuban rap today is out of kilter with its minor role on
the island, while the hugely popular reggaetón is widely dismissed, like
dancehall before it. There is nothing wrong with the academic attention
paid to hip hop, though the shunning of reggaetón is more problematic;
both interest and disinterest are noteworthy cultural phenomena in and
of themselves. But it must be recognized that at times, Cuban hip hop
scholarship is no more representative of urban popular music in Havana
today than the plethora of books on Bob Marley is of the contemporary
Jamaican reggae scene.

While I am not writing to defend reggaetón, it is worth at least opening
up the idea that the genre might have cultural value and interest, rather
than reproducing dichotomies and prejudices heard in hip hop and intellectual circles. As a point of comparison, Davarian Baldwin (2004) provides a thought-provoking critique of the usual intellectual biases that
favor conscious hip hop over gangsta rap, arguing that the former's politics are notably conservative while the latter can be conceived of as a
productive space for a politics of social engagement, personal liberation
and reinvention, and playful performance. It is also worth recalling Carolyn Cooper's characterization of slackness in dancehall as "a radical, underground confrontation with. . . . the pious morality of fundamentalist
Jamaican society." The words radical and underground are much more
commonly associated with the moralistic and fundamentalist hip hop
scene, but these terms might be more appropriate to Elvis Manuel, the ultimate Havana musical outsider of recent years, than to rappers whose dis-

course merged with that of the revolution and who ended up employed by a state institution. Imani Perry (2004), meanwhile, suggests that it is the dialectical aspect of hip hop—the tension between opposing elements—that gives it its strength. Reggaetón in Havana has often been treated by rappers and intellectuals not as the other term in a dialectic with hip hop but as the enemy, creating a polarization rather than a productive tension and ultimately, I would argue, contributing to the weakening of hip hop as reggaetón boomed. Intellectual attitudes have colored hip hop's public realm, and not necessarily in a positive way.

Robin Moore's (2006, 263) enlightening book on music and the Cuban Revolution ends with the observation that "now more than ever, the arts represent a quasi-independent realm of commentary in dialogue with the state. These creations, representing varied reactions to a unique environment, help provide an insightful and nuanced view of the revolutionary experience." While this comment provides an illuminating summary of the forty-odd years of musical production that he analyzes, it sits somewhat uncomfortably with the subsequent arrival of reggaetón. Clearly, an analysis of reggaetón may shed light on the relationship between the state and the arts, and on young Cubans' experiences of the revolution. But most regguetoneros seem uninterested in any sort of dialogue with the state, as evidenced by El Micha's apparently innocuous statement "I don't get involved in politics or anything like that, because that's got nothing to do with me," and even the genre's most ardent fans are unlikely to argue that their idols' views are either "insightful" or "nuanced." That Vice-Minister Fernando Rojas was visibly more uncomfortable with reggaetón than with rap, despite hip hoppers' more explicit rebelliousness, illustrates Žižek's (2007) notion that silence and withdrawal test the state more than resistance does. In its lack of dialogue, reggaetón offers an unprecedented challenge to Cuban revolutionary culture.

Reggaetón in Havana has amply illustrated Plato's contention that "the modes of music are never disturbed without unsettling of the most fundamental political and social conventions" (quoted by McClary 1994, 29). The question remains whether the rise of reggaetón will turn out to be, as Plato would have it, "a hazard of all our fortunes" (ibid.). Jacques Attali (1985, 11) claims that music is a form of prophecy and a "herald of the future": "Its styles and economic organization are ahead of the rest of society because it explores, much faster than material reality can, the entire range of possibilities in a given code. It makes audible the new world that will gradually become visible, that will impose itself and regulate the order of things." Reggaetón has indeed brought in new styles and pushed the boundaries of economic organization. Can we read Havana's future in the figure of Alexánder Delgado?

3

THE HAVANA YOU DON'T KNOW

Urban Music and the Late Socialist City

This is the real Havana by night and I'm part of it,
As you're asleep I'll have to tell you about it.
—PAPÁ HUMBERTICO, "La Habana que no conoces"

San Cristóbal de La Habana is much more than rumba,
Much more than cathedral, rum, cigars, and partying.
—HERMANOS DE CAUSA, "San Cristóbal de La Habana"

It was dark when my friend Miguel and I got off the bus at the bridge over
the Almendares River on the western edge of Vedado, a central neighborhood of Havana. To the left lay El Chévere, a club for tourists and wealthy
Cubans, with its drinks priced in dollars and conspicuous jineteras. We
turned right and took the footpath down into the Parque Almendares,
the gloomy tree-filled gorge that spreads out below the bridge. We weaved
our way through the trees and came to a small, open-air amphitheater; we
paid our five pesos (twenty cents) each and made our way inside. After
the usual hugging and handshaking with friends, we sat down on one of

the concrete benches. The DJ Alexis D'Boys was on stage, playing U.S. rap on two portable CD players hooked up to a PA, but most people were too busy meeting and greeting to pay much attention. Someone had snuck in a plastic bottle of rum which was making the rounds. More people trickled inside, most of them rappers or DJs, or their partners and friends; some had small children with them. It wasn't a big crowd—maybe a hundred people, most dressed in U.S.-style hip hop gear.

Eventually two rappers took the stage: a backing track came up on the PA, and they launched into their routine. The beats were underground—hard and spare—and the voices animated and intense. People didn't dance; they sat or stood still and listened, mostly in silence, nodding intently, and sometimes mouthing the words to a chorus. After a couple of songs, two more rappers made their way onto the stage from the audience, and the evening continued with groups coming and going, sometimes performing a track together then rejoining the audience. This wasn't party music, this was serious stuff. Los Aldeanos spat out their lyrics with particular venom, almost haranguing the audience. Their songs "Ya nos cansamos" (we're fed up now) and "Mi país" (my country) had the audience whooping and whistling, spurring on the rappers as they pushed the limits of the sayable and laid bare the ills of Cuban society. When Los Aldeanos left the stage to whistles and applause, they wandered into the audience, where Aldo picked up his baby son. After the live music had finished, the DJ came back on stage: the rum had been flowing, and the audience was soon up and dancing to recorded U.S. hip hop. But Almendares is not a commercial club, so before long it was time to get everyone out and shut up for the night.

The crowd wandered slowly out of the amphitheater and up the hill to the bridge. What was everyone doing next? It was only 11:00; the night was young. Someone said that one of Havana's top DJs, El Piz, was playing at a house party in the distant neighborhood of 10 de Octubre; after brief deliberations, a group of us ran after a bus that was crossing the bridge and jumped on. The bus was packed, so we spread out among the passengers. One of the rappers from the concert, Wilder 01, turned and made a quip to another, Reynor (aka Mahoma, of Explosión Suprema), who was standing further back. Reynor answered back, rhyming his response with Wilder's remark, and what had started as a casual comment quickly escalated into joking banter and then a no-holds-barred rap battle, a rapid-fire exchange of improvised rhymes. At first the pas-

Redman, a young hip hop fan, at the Almendares amphitheater. Photo by author.

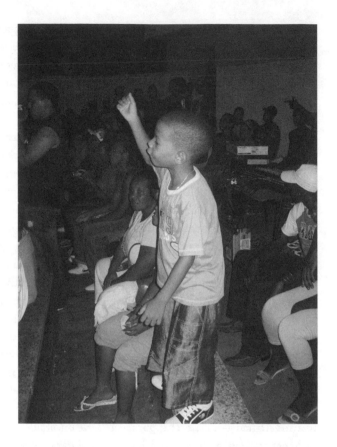

sengers pretended not to notice, but after a couple of minutes there were sniggers at some of the funnier lines, encouraging the participants in this battle of wits. Soon half the bus was in stitches as each rapper outdid the other with his rhyming puns. Suddenly someone shouted "let's go": we had arrived at 10 de Octubre.

We squeezed our way off the bus and headed down a dark street where dim streetlights illuminated dilapidated buildings. The crowd in the street was visible from a distance, perhaps fifty people milling around in the semidarkness. We got to the door and pushed our way into a small house. Inside it was even darker, and all I could see was a mass of dancers and, at the back, the DJ hunched over his equipment. There was no furniture in the house: just dancing bodies and music, mainly U.S. hip hop. There was something distinctly underground about this house party.

It wasn't anything to do with words or sounds—after all, the recorded music was commercial and in English—but rather with the transformation of the house, as well as a certain charge in the air, perhaps because such a large, loud party could easily attract unwelcome attention. After a while, Miguel and I left, caught a lift in a passing truck, and arrived back in Vedado shortly before dawn.

As I reflected on that evening, I was struck by the places we had been. Members of the hip hop scene, drawn across Havana by their affinity for rap, had made these spaces theirs, claiming and redefining them through their words and actions, pushing the limits of what might be considered appropriate behavior and forms of expression. Furthermore, the rappers' lyrics addressed the problems of their urban environment and in particular the sociospatial inequalities of a tourism-driven city where, according to Los Aldeanos, "an apartment block takes years to build but a hotel goes up in months"; where tourists pay ten dollars to go to El Chévere, while across the way locals pay twenty cents at the Almendares amphitheater, where, as Hermanos de Causa put it with apocalyptic simplicity, "la calle está en candela" (things are bad on the street).

"It's a Street Thing"

Charlie Chase, the DJ for the rap pioneers Cold Crush Brothers, confronted African American rappers at the New Music Seminar in 1990: "I went off on these guys because they were like 'Black this, and Black music,' and I said 'Hold it!' I jumped up and I said, 'Hold up, man. What are you talking about, a Black thing, man? . . . It's a street thing. I liked it because it came from the street and I'm from the street. I'm a product of the environment. . . . It ain't no Black, White or nothing thing, man" (quoted in Flores 2004, 78). El Tosco—José Luis Cortés, director of NG La Banda and one of Havana's best-known popular musicians—described rap as "the sweat and blood of the barrio. You've got to live in a barrio to know, to be able to understand what rap is. It's the street, the philosophy of the street" (Cortés n.d.). Over the past dozen years, music scholars have begun to pay increasing attention to issues of space and place (e.g., Leyshon, Matless, and Revill 1998; Whiteley, Bennett, and Hawkins 2004), particularly to the role of music in struggles to appropriate and rework urban spaces (e.g., A. Bennett 2000; Krims 2007). Hip hop scholars have begun to explore the idea that hip hop is not (just) a "black thing" but (also) a "street thing"—space music as much as race music—since appropriations, transformations, and representations of urban spaces have been central to hip hop since its beginnings in New York City. Murray Forman's (2002) work stands out for its geographically informed approach: he places the city at the heart of his analysis of U.S. rap, underlining the centrality of spatial practices and discourses in rap and the broader hip hop culture of which it forms a part. It is worth inquiring, however, into the relevance of this to global manifestations of hip hop—does the urban focus of urban music survive its deterritorialization and reterritorialization (Lull 2000)? In global hip hop, does space still matter?

While analyses of rap outside the United States have often focused on issues of ethnic or racial identity, rap produced in two major hip hop markets—Brazil and France—shows evidence of the central, firmly rooted spatial awareness discussed by Forman. Derek Pardue (2004) notes that under the influence of the group Racionais MCs in the 1990s, Brazilian rappers began to focus increasingly on marginal urban spaces, in particular the *favela* (shanty town) and *periferia* (urban periphery). Race, he observes, took a back seat to sociogeographical realities as marginality came to be defined as much in spatial as in social terms, and he devotes further attention to the relationship between hip hop and urban change in his later book (2008). In France, meanwhile, the marginalized spaces of the *banlieue* (suburbs) and *cité* (housing project) are key sites in hip hop culture and the rap imaginary. Rappers have produced powerful critiques of dual cities like Paris, describing the landscape of decaying housing projects on the periphery of the city, a world apart from the urban core, and exposing what has been termed "postcolonial urban apartheid" (Silverstein and Tetreault 2006). Ministère Amer's "Un été à la cité," for example, may be based on the Lovin' Spoonful's "Summer in the City," but it is no paean to the joys of urban life.

Hip hop has been characterized by spatial practices as well as discourses (Rose 1994; Forman 2002). In his studies of Japanese rap, Ian Condry (2001, 2006) explores the social spaces of the Tokyo rap scene, investigating the world of hip hop clubs as sites which allow the creation of social networks, facilitating communication and interaction across a vast city. Some of his most useful insights concern his idea of *genba* (actual site) globalization and the role of performance—illustrated by a freestyle (improvised contest)—in simultaneously actualizing the local and the global.

There is good reason to suggest, therefore, that a focus on hip hop's spatial practices and discourses may be fruitful in considering the genre's global manifestations, yet space has taken a back seat to race in most academic studies of hip hop outside the United States, particularly in the growing body of work on Cuban rap, in which scholars have centered on textual analysis and explicit sociopolitical concerns, above all questions of blackness. The self-perception and self-presentation of Cuban rappers as artists with a message have shaped academic approaches, which tend to treat rap lyrics as transparent documents and pay less attention to hip hop's performance contexts, the lived realities of the scene, and implicit meanings transmitted through practices such as improvisation, dance, selling CDs, and hustling.[1] It is worth heeding Robin D. G. Kelley's (2004, 130–31) critique of social science approaches to hip hop that "reduce expressive culture to a political text to be read like a less sophisticated version of *The Nation* or *Radical America*" and his claim that "in most cases, the explicit meaning or intention of a particular cultural form is not the thing that makes it attractive." Paradoxically, then, focusing on Cuban rap's message may mean missing much of its point. Examining the contexts of rap performance and consumption is vital to understanding the pleasures, and thus the politics, of hip hop.

While Cuban rap lyrics have undeniably presented powerful new perspectives on race issues, I would argue that these perspectives are entwined with the shifting relation of habaneros to urban space. Discrimination and inequality are spatialized and countered on that level, for young Cubans have used hip hop in order to claim spaces and forge social networks that counteract their marginalization. Racial discourses are rooted in contests and negotiations over space, and it is thus necessary to investigate the places where hip hop is practiced and its meanings constructed through performance.

I will focus on hip hop in Havana as urban practice and urban knowledge, as a means of claiming and representing the environment in which young habaneros live, creating distinctive social and economic spaces and narratives of locality. Underlying my analysis is Setha Low's (1999b, 112) definition of the social construction of space as "the actual transformation of space—through people's social exchanges, memories, images, and daily use of the material setting—into scenes and actions that convey symbolic meaning." In the Cuban capital since the 1990s, as in the South Bronx in the 1970s, the urban environment has been a key constitutive element in hip hop's development; but this relationship has been di-alogic, and rappers have also participated in the social construction of late socialist Havana. I also draw on Andy Merrifield's (2002) concept of "dialectical urbanism." Merrifield understands the relationship between urbanization and urbanism, the process and the human experience it generates, as a productive tension or contradiction. I will argue that hip hop—the archetype of urban music—embodies this concept, exhibiting a similar dialectic at its core as it simultaneously feeds on and critiques urban change.

The Context: Havana since 1990

The collapse of the Soviet Union and the end of its preferential trade arrangements with Cuba led to the most profound upheavals in the is-land's economy and society since the 1959 revolution. In 1993, in the face of severe shortages and plummeting living standards, the Cuban govern-ment took radical measures to breathe life into the ailing economy, includ-ing legalizing the possession of dollars, permitting small-scale private enterprises, encouraging joint ventures with foreign companies, and, above all, promoting tourism as a vital source of foreign exchange. The connections between the crisis of the Special Period and musical forms such as rap and timba have been well documented (e.g., M. Perry 2004; Perna 2005; Fernandes 2006). However, while scholars of music have focused on the transformations of the economy and their effects on urban society, less attention has been paid to the physical transformation of the city and its repercussions on musical practices.

Two recent studies examining the evolution of Havana during the twen-tieth century shed light on the Special Period (Rutheiser 2000; Kapcia 2005b). After 1959, Havana was relatively neglected by the revolutionary government, which preferred to focus its resources on rural areas, and the city's infrastructure steadily deteriorated. The dilapidated colonial center, Habana Vieja (Old Havana), was named a UNESCO World Heritage Site in 1982, but it was only in the early 1990s that efforts to restore the city's architectural heritage took off, as the growing economic dependence on tourism led to a shift from earlier anti-urbanism toward the reinvention of Havana as a tourist attraction. In 1994 the City Historian's Office launched the "Plan Maestro para la Revitalización Integral de la Habana Vieja," which aimed to restore historical monuments in the former colonial center and invest money in its crumbling residential infrastructure. While Charles Rutheiser and Antoni Kapcia agree that the state has made efforts to improve living conditions for residents of Habana Vieja as well as for tourists, they differ in their assessment of the effectiveness of these measures. Kapcia (2005b, 2) is reasonably optimistic, suggesting that "with restoration under way, Habana Vieja is a beautiful city in the re-making." He conflates Habana Vieja with Havana, implying that the restoration of the old center is enough to rejuvenate the city as a whole. This view is not shared by all the capital's residents, many of whom would agree with Rutheiser's more pessimistic conclusion that the scale of the problem—the sheer dilapidation of the city's residential fabric—dwarfs the localized efforts to solve it.

If the state has made efforts to serve the interests of Habana Vieja's residents, investment by the joint ventures with foreign enterprises that have blossomed since the Special Period, focusing on the old city and the upmarket districts of Vedado and Miramar, has been aimed squarely at providing an infrastructure for foreigners and a small Cuban elite with hard currency to spend. This blending of socialism and capitalism in joint ventures—sometimes termed *sociocapitalismo*—has thus fed a spatial reordering of the city. As David Harvey has noted (quoted by Forman 2002, 6), uneven capital investment is a prime factor in the production of difference in space, and sociocapitalist ventures in Havana have caused "dramatic eruptions of unequal value in an otherwise uniform land-rent surface" (Rutheiser 2000, 234). Tourism and foreign investment have thus led to the emergence of a dual city, with the redevelopment of sections of Habana Vieja, Miramar, and Vedado intensifying the disparity between these districts and the areas of the city that lack architectural distinction or tourist appeal. The rapid development of Habana Vieja and of hotels, restaurants, and transportation for tourists saw inequality permeate the capital's infrastructure in just a few years (Whitfield 2008, 9).

The government's tourism strategies led to rising sociospatial segregation, creating both tourist enclaves set apart from the rest of the city and also a form of "tourist apartheid" within those enclaves (Rutheiser 2000, 233). Although policies were relaxed slightly in 2008, security guards ensured for years that many Cubans were unable to set foot in these new spaces; even if they could, the prices were beyond the reach of most of them. Local resentment over this double segregation is only increased by the high (and often intrusive) police presence in key areas to ensure both tourist safety and, in some cases, their separation from the local populace. Young, particularly darker-skinned Cubans are stopped for identification checks with depressing regularity in tourist areas; the high visibility of police underlines the emergence of such urban spaces as contested zones. The relationship between city residents and urban space in Havana has thus altered significantly since the early 1990s, with the emergence of marked differentiation in the built environment and sociospatial divisions—highly contentious in a socialist society—as well as increasing competition over public space in key areas. The contested environment of this city in flux will be the scene for the discussion of urban music that follows.

Hip Hop Social Club:
Urban Music and Alternative Social Spaces

Music and dance have long been fundamental in promoting sociability among Havana's population. From the start of the Special Period, however, many of Havana's music venues became "hard currency only" clubs aimed at tourists and a local elite. Timba groups shifted their emphasis toward playing for predominantly foreign audiences and economically successful Cubans in clubs and on overseas tours; though their music continued to be widely heard on recordings and the radio, affordable live performances became rarer. Emir García Meralla (2007, 4) notes that in the Special Period, "the consumption of music was perhaps the clearest expression of the new social division." The live-music circuit was reduced to the city center as it became more exclusive, and young people often ended up spending their evenings sitting on the Malecón (Havana's sea wall), watching the world go by.

Hip hop provided a precious opportunity for young habaneros of limited means to participate in a cultural and social scene. Venues for recorded hip hop or live rap (some of them private, others provided by the state) offered alternatives at a time when tourism was having a negative impact on civic sociability and young people's access to cultural spaces. As Ariel Fernández reveals, música americana parties acted as social "glue" for his generation during the tough years of the Special Period: "I liked this lifestyle, as did a lot of other people in my generation. We had a place every weekend to go to parties without problems and fights while people danced to this music"

(*East of Havana* n.d., 152). Regular house parties sprang up across the city; in some cases, such as the parties put on by DJ El Piz in 10 de Octubre or the street jams organized at 19 y 10 in Vedado, hip hoppers transformed private spaces into cultural hot spots. They also used more official venues—such as the amphitheater and a disused swimming pool in Alamar, the Casas de la Cultura in Habana Vieja and Plaza, and later the amphitheater at the Parque Almendares and La Madriguera in Centro Habana—to create alternative social spaces, claiming and adapting these locations through their music and associated practices. Entrance to most venues cost nothing or only a nominal fee in local currency. At a concert I attended at La Madriguera, the duo Los Paisanos set up the stage to look like a living room, with armchairs, a coffee table, a telephone, and other props. Their theme for the evening was to pretend that the audience was eavesdropping on a rehearsal in their house; various rappers "dropped by" to "rehearse" tracks with them for a "forthcoming" concert. The stage set and "visits" by guest artists stressed intimacy and community and domesticated the venue, transforming public space into private.

It should be emphasized that La Madriguera, like the Parque Almendares, is a complex, multiply inflected space: it is run by a quasi-state organization, the AHS, which provides the space and equipment at no charge, and the low entrance fees reflect the institution's noncommercial policy and state subsidy. While this fact colors any understanding of this space as "alternative," a group of young habaneros remade this venue through hip hop into "their" place—not simply a crumbling concrete shell in the depths of an urban park, but a key node in a vibrant social and cultural scene, a platform for alternative voices and social critique, albeit temporarily and with the approval of state employees.

There is a long history of accommodating certain kinds of critical voice within state institutions in revolutionary Cuba (R. Moore 2003). Since the early 1990s, the state's combination of socialist theory and capitalist practice has undermined any illusion of ideological coherence, and the alternative or oppositional stance adopted by rappers frequently entails siding with the theory (community, equality, activism, and moralism) against the practice (socioeconomic differentiation, the dual economy, and rising materialism and individualism). Many underground rappers share the government's ideological resistance to these Special Period socioeconomic trends, opposing not so much dominant ideologies as the failure to live up to them. It is to the problematic and paradoxical realities of late socialist urban life, then, that hip hoppers seek to provide an alternative.

The notion of an alternative space in a government-controlled venue is therefore not as contradictory as it might first appear, especially bearing in mind the discussion in chapter 1 of the fractures in state policy and the sometimes less-than-harmonious relationship between (even within) different institutions. The idea of an alternative space within the state is only contradictory if we regard the state as monolithic. The AHS provides opportunities for more idealistic or challenging young artists; it also has a firmly noncommercial stance and can therefore be seen as resisting the commercialization of Havana's cultural life by other state organizations (such as music venues, the media, and artistic agencies—including the other hip hop institution, the ACR). Furthermore, there have been divisions between the national AHS and the Havana city branch, La Madriguera, which was described to me by two of its rap promoters as an alternative space in that it pursued a different line to that of the national body, continuing to support hip hop at a time when the national AHS had withdrawn from its commitment to the annual festival. The fact that rap concerts were organized and overseen by AHS promoters who were also members of the hip hop scene allowed for an even greater sense of license, and rappers then regularly pushed the limits of what the promoters thought was acceptable. Control over performances at La Madriguera was somewhat tenuous during the time that I was in Havana because there was a conscious sense of distancing, or self-perception as alternative and independent, at every link in the chain of command from the UJC to national AHS to city AHS to promoter to artist.

An employee at La Madriguera provided fascinating insights into the curious status of this liminal space.[2] He revealed that the venue was in poor shape in 2008 because of a breakdown in the relationship between the city AHS, the national directorship, and the UJC (its funder). In 2006, the venue closed for a year because funds for renovation were diverted to other projects and then, after a burglary in which all the equipment was stolen, La Madriguera's parent institutions did nothing to help. Institutional differences led to the venue's neglect, and it only reopened thanks to the efforts of those who worked there, who sought help from outside Cuba and renovated the site themselves with material help from sympa-

Entrance to La Madriguera. Photo by author.

thizers. Although they finally managed to reopen La Madriguera, its upkeep was difficult without institutional support. Far from being a simple state venue, this employee said, La Madriguera had "become a no-man's-land."

There are thus two sides to the coin of La Madriguera: recently, it has been relatively free of state control on the one hand, but lacking support on the other, leaving it vulnerable when a new cloud arrived on the horizon. Eusebio Leal, the official city historian who is in charge of the "Plan Maestro" for urban renovation and who, as a friend of Fidel Castro, wields considerable political and economic clout, decided that he wanted to restore the Quinta de los Molinos (in which La Madriguera is located) along with its museum, once the residence of General Máximo Gómez. Leal thus began the process of removing the city branch of the AHS from La Madriguera. The promoters, however, had other ideas. This particular employee not only worked at La Madriguera, but he had been going to hear music there since his youth, so he felt a personal attachment to the place. He described the location as perfect: it is surrounded by a park, and thus musicians can make noise without disturbing neighbors—a great asset in Havana. It is both central and set apart from the city, easy to access yet secluded. "I don't think there's a better place and that's why we're fighting for it," he said, using the classic revolutionary word *luchar*. "We love this place, we have a sense of ownership, we're trying to fight for it because we know what it represents for the alternative movement in the city, since there are very, very few spaces." He and his colleagues decided to launch a "battle of ideas"—once again, adopting a good revolutionary phrase; they petitioned the minister of culture and sought support from overseas sympathizers, and Jorge Rodríguez, who was running the venue at the time, published an article arguing that La Madriguera played an important role in the revolution. At the time of the interview, the future was uncertain: the government had not made a decision, but it was not helping them economically either.[3]

La Madriguera is a fascinating space, particularly since it is so closely associated with alternative music in Havana. Its name means literally a burrow, and figuratively a hide-out; it is tucked away in the woods, providing a sanctuary for artists who were once known as "moles" because of their "underground" status. Its motto for many years has been "a hidden place for open ideas." It perfectly illustrates the fuzziness of state control over artistic activity at the margins: a place where state employees struggle against the state to create space for alternative music, in a building that the state owns but no longer wants to fund, leading its employees to wage a "battle of ideas" within (or against) the Battle of Ideas. The alternativeness of alternative music in Havana is thus closely bound up with the institutional spaces in which it sometimes thrives and sometimes struggles to survive.

This sheds light on the larger issue of the state and the arts in Cuba. Sujatha Fernandes's ambitious attempt to construct an overarching model of "artistic public spheres" linking film, visual art, and rap, founded on the idea that "the Cuban leadership . . . sought to create spaces for critical discussion within the arts" (2006, 40–41), fails to take sufficient account of the differences between the institutions and art forms involved. Castro is well known to have kept close tabs on the film institute (ICAIC), but not all cultural management is equally centralized; in other institutions, rules are also made up by low-level functionaries close to the artistic coalface. AHS music promoters have fought to carve out independent spaces for alternative artists. As Roberto Zurbano (2009, 143–44) reveals, the AHS's involvement with the rap festival took off at the behest of Rodolfo Rensoli, its organizer, and when Fernando Rojas, the AHS's director, sought approval from higher-level institutions such as the ICM, "their response was aloof and the effective lack of support convinced us to fully take charge of the rap festival ourselves." The AHS was not simply an extension of the Cuban leadership; in fact, it "had the steadfast goal to work with sectors, such as rock musicians, often seen as problematic by other official institutions." Rap's public sphere has thus been forged from the bottom up, in "hidden places for open ideas" like La Madriguera. The recent history of this venue, such an important place for hip hop and alternative music in general, shows a considerable lack of either support or control on the part of higher levels of the state; divisions and differences of opinion among the UJC, national AHS, and city AHS turned La Madriguera into a "no-man's-land," and this space for critical discussion only kept going because of the efforts of its low-level employees.

Furthermore, rap is a performative art, hip hop production is increasingly a cottage industry, and a lot of rap has never been recorded or even written down; unlike film, it could never be more than incompletely harnessed by the state. Many of the spaces for hip hop were not granted by the state but created by hip hoppers—in private houses, on buses, and even in government-owned venues—and this independent streak has intensified in recent years with the rise of digital technologies and increasing opportunities to exploit irregularities in the management of music venues. To place the Cuban leadership at the center is to underestimate the looseness of its grip over an art form realized through performance and improvisation in spaces partly or entirely outside the reach of the upper levels of the state.

Finally, the case of La Madriguera and Eusebio Leal reveals the struggles over urban space at the heart of Havana's urban music scenes. The city AHS was evicted from its original base, the Casa del Jóven Creador in Habana Vieja, to make way for a rum museum for tourists; in 2008, its new home, La Madriguera, was under threat, again by a tourism and heritage proposal. The battle over public space, in which urban tourism and urban music are often at loggerheads, could not be clearer. Alternative music is closely linked to the creation of social spaces that provide alternatives to tourist- and capitalist-driven urbanization. The dialectical relationship between urbanism and urbanization is not just a topic for musicians' lyrics; in concrete ways, it impacts the very existence of the alternative music scene.

An important aspect of such alternative social spaces is the community feel, evident in rap peñas in the sharing ethos (bottles of rum are passed round, rather than drinks being sold), the importance placed on greeting friends and acquaintances, and the presence of children: one prominent DJ would begin every announcement with the word "family," and his own toddler was often in the audience or even on his lap as he played. I was told repeatedly that rap concerts provided a healthy, safe environment, in contrast to salsa and reggaetón concerts, where troublemakers supposedly went and where fights were common. Given the reputation of rap concerts in some other countries, and the frequent, high-profile characterization of hip hop as opposed to so-called family values in the United States, it may be surprising that the rap scene in Cuba defined itself as a more wholesome environment than other musical alternatives.[4]

It could be argued, then, that despite being subsidized by the state, rap concerts contain elements of symbolic critique of the restrictions and deficiencies of life in Havana (Bennett 2000). They provide alternative social spaces for ordinary young Cubans who are largely excluded from Havana's nightlife, spaces they shape through the practices of hip hop as a positive, communal environment. This also illuminates the significance of the house party that ended my evening described above: the party counteracted the exclusion of its participants from mainstream nightlife. This kind of informal party, or bonche, played an important role in the early 1990s, as hip hop moved indoors from the street. As Bennett (2000, 68) suggests, house parties are a way for members of a scene to "celebrate a shared underground sensibility that is designed to challenge the perceived oppression and archaism of [the] official night-time economy." With Havana's official late-night music venues typically charging the equivalent of a Cuban monthly salary, there was incentive for participants in the rap scene to make their own underground arrangements. While this type of event was not explicitly political, it was a reaction by young Cubans against a nocturnal environment that marginalized them and a symbolic statement against the rampant dollarization and commodification of culture that engendered it.

This kind of implicit spatial critique becomes explicit in rap performances. Los Aldeanos underlined the spatial exclusions of Havana's nightlife in a particularly creative manner at the 2007 Hip Hop Symposium, where they performed their song "Mangos bajitos" (easy pickings), a blistering critique of the inequalities of tourism-driven Havana. They introduced the song by calling out: "Where are the people from France? And the people from Spain? And the people from Italy? And the people from Russia?" This is standard practice in tourist music venues, and a few people in the international audience, who did not know what was coming, shouted out or raised a hand; when Los Aldeanos finished the song with a repeat of this introduction, there was total silence.[5] Their ironic citation of a touristic practice laid bare the sociospatial polarization of Havana by night, contrasting their concert venue—the bare, sparsely lit yard of the Casa de la Cultura in Plaza—with glitzy, tourist-oriented clubs just a few blocks away, and serving to emphasize the role of hip hop in creating critical alternatives to mainstream music spaces.

Hip Hop and Urban Geography

One of the ironies and contradictions of the Special Period has been that urban popular music has boomed at the same time that venues for its performance have been squeezed by tourism-driven urbanization. In a poll in 2006, several internationally known musicians complained about the lack of spaces for less commercial music in Havana (Vizcaíno Serrat 2006). For them, the struggle over space was a direct consequence of rising music capitalism. Artists have thus been driven either to carve out new, alternative spaces, or to look outside the city altogether. While music like rap and reggaetón is "a street thing" and its producers are mainly city-based, the rise of tourism in Havana and conservative programming at many venues means that many of the performance opportunities for urban musicians have shifted to the suburbs or provinces. It is little wonder that rappers see tourism as the enemy.

Even commercially successful musicians feel squeezed in Havana. Jorge Hernández of reggaetón group Los Cuatro told me that it was hard to give big concerts in the capital, even though his group was one of the top few in the country. No reggaetón or rap groups were invited to participate in carnival in Havana in 2008, so they went to provincial cities instead. He found it bizarre that he could be paid large sums of money to perform in the provinces yet could not sing, even for free, in Havana's carnival. The professional rappers have also found themselves working mainly outside the city. The regular provincial tours organized by the ICM provided their groups (and the ACR) with an income but ended up de-urbanizing the main professional hip hop artists; as a result, they lost some of their audience in the capital, and their place was taken by younger, amateur groups like Los Aldeanos.

The amateur-professional division thus became significantly interrelated to the urban-provincial one; while professional groups performed more often in the provinces, amateur rappers were largely restricted to the city. For economic and political reasons, it was difficult for amateur musicians in Havana to travel outside the capital to areas where more openings could be found. While the AHS provided occasional opportunities, many amateur rappers who formed the core of the Havana scene were frustrated by their confinement, and the sense that hip hop had nowhere to go was particularly acute during my 2006 visit. Interestingly, an article in the hip hop magazine *Movimiento* describes 2006 as a great year for Cuban hip hop, yet all the examples are one-time events: foreign tours, the Hip Hop Symposium, an event at Almendares, and Rodolfo Rensoli's revived festival in East Havana (Sáez Rodríguez n.d.a, 10). When I was in the city that year, there were no hip hop peñas at any of the old venues. The only one took place in the basement of El Tropical, a club in Vedado so tiny that it feels packed if there are fifty people inside, and that it has no space for a stage—the rappers had to clear a circle in order to perform.

Far from being a great year, 2006 marked a nadir for hip hop in Havana, and rappers were glum; but another shift in the organization and geography of the rap scene led to a renaissance. When I began my research, La Madriguera and the Almendares amphitheater, both subsidized state venues, were the two main pillars of the scene: from the low point in 2006, however, the focus shifted to small, commercial clubs, designed to generate profits via higher entrance fees and drinks sold for hard currency.[6] By 2008, there were hardly any events at the old subsidized venues but, instead, three weekly events in clubs (Monday nights at Barbarám in Nuevo Vedado, Wednesday night DJ and freestyle sessions at Karachi in Vedado, and Friday nights at Atelier in the same neighborhood). The center of gravity of the scene has thus been shifting steadily over the years, from outlying Alamar in the 1990s, to the edges of Vedado when I began my research in 2003–4, to the heart of Vedado and Nuevo Vedado (two of Havana's more desirable neighborhoods) in 2008–9. This is not an insignificant detail: it is the equivalent of what happened to New

York hip hop in the early 1980s, when it shifted from the South Bronx to downtown Manhattan.

I heard two principal explanations for this change. The first was that in 2001, the AHS was taken over by provincial bureaucrats who did not understand Havana's multicentered urban geography and culture, did not "get" Alamar, and sought to centralize (in every sense of the word) the hip hop festival. As hip hop became more institutionalized, conferences and official meetings tended to take place in central venues like the Museum of Music, the Casa de las Américas, or UNEAC. Alamar may have been known as "rap city," but once hip hop became a focus of attention at the municipal, national, and international levels, Alamar's peripheral location left it out on a limb.

The second explanation was that as foreign consumers became the financial mainstay of the scene, Alamar rap groups sought to perform in central venues where they could attract more tourists, who would in turn buy their CDs. La Madriguera is within walking distance of the tourist thoroughfare of La Rampa, whereas Alamar is on the very edge of Havana. In recent years, the numbers of foreigners at performances has tailed off, and they have been replaced by youths from the areas around the clubs (particularly in the case of Barbarám). In 2008, the typical rap peña attracted a racially and economically diverse Cuban audience to a small but central commercial club; five years earlier, I was part of mixed Cuban and foreign audiences at La Madriguera and Almendares; five years before that, marginality (geographical, racial, and economic) was the order of the day in Alamar. Hip hoppers began by seeking out spaces on the urban periphery, but their culture has moved increasingly toward the urban center as an economy and institutional politics has grown up around rap.

This process has its critics. Rensoli sees the shift of significant parts of the hip hop festival from Alamar to the city center as cutting the festival off from its roots, and thus as a key reason for its decline and ultimate suspension in 2005.[7] Youth cultures and large parties were very common in East Havana beginning in the 1980s; a more relaxed environment on the city's margins, it was a place of relative freedom. Rensoli conceives of East Havana as young, radical, and popular, and thus closer to the original concepts of the revolution—a dynamic space on the urban periphery, away from the corrupting influences of the sociocapitalist city center.

Soandres del Río (Hermanos de Causa) saw the changes in location as affecting hip hop's audience. He told me that he doubted that the new hip hop fans in Vedado and Nuevo Vedado—a lighter-skinned, more "middle-class" crowd whom he described as a "new elite"—would come to an abandoned swimming pool in distant Alamar. For him, Nuevo Vedado leaves its mark on rap production: audiences want to hear something different there, and rappers respond. The geographical shifts have thus affected the style and content of Havana rap and have brought new class and race issues to the forefront; some older and/or darker-skinned rappers have little time for hip hop's "new elite" audience, though others see this development as progress and a broadening of the genre's appeal. In one way, however, the clock has turned back: hip hop has passed through a phase of blackness and is now more racially mixed, just as it was in the early days.

The movements of hip hop around Havana are undoubtedly significant. Alamar provided a community foundation for hip hop in a relatively relaxed (because peripheral) environment; the shift to more central locations with greater proximity to tourist dollars brought economic benefits to rappers but saw hip hop lose ground to reggaetón back in East Havana. It was something of a psychological blow for hip hoppers to see the Capital de la Moña become the capital of reggaetón, even though they were partly responsible. The more recent shift to commercial clubs in Vedado and Nuevo Vedado is interpreted by some as hip hop's losing touch with its roots, and these clubs are more restrictive environments than, for example, Almendares or La Madriguera, above all with regard to the age range of those who attend. At about a dollar, the entrance fees are more expensive, which sometimes prevents poorer hip hop fans from going, and some worry that younger teenagers who are not allowed to enter these clubs are being drawn to reggaetón instead: the core of the rap scene is now made up of twenty-somethings.

Nevertheless, a new kind of freedom emerged in these commercial venues, where economic considerations could sometimes trump political ones; this shift from institutional to commercial venues boosted the creation of alternative urban spaces.[8] The clubs operate on the same principles as others like them around the world: they need to get paying customers through the door and buying drinks. A rap group that can achieve this will have considerable leeway; one that cannot will not.

When I went to Havana in 2007, Obsesion and Anónimo Consejo were struggling to attract audiences to their peña at the Delirio Habanero; despite being members of the ACR and the two most politically correct rap groups in Cuba, they lost the gig soon afterward. In 2008, the hottest show was Los Aldeanos' peña on Mondays at Barbarám, which was often full to overflowing. Where the professional elders had failed, the controversial Young Turks were succeeding. As long as they continued to fill the venue on a traditionally quiet night, they had a guaranteed slot. The manager was happy because the money was coming in, so he seemed relatively relaxed about hosting some of the city's most contentious music. This alternative space did not depend, then, on like-minded cultural officials, as was the case at La Madriguera, but rather on the simple logic of the musical marketplace—something of a surprise in a (supposedly) centrally planned cultural economy. Los Aldeanos were the hottest hip hop act in Cuba, and therefore they had their own space; indeed, the manager of Atelier called them in the summer of 2008 and offered them a weekly peña on Fridays, which they accepted, giving them two weekly club nights to perform more or less whatever they pleased. The fact that they were the most controversial hip hop group in Cuba seemed of minor importance within this particular sector of the nighttime economy; three years earlier they had been on a state blacklist, but now that they had a large fan base, venues were calling them. As long as they brought their paying crowd with them, these were "their" spaces.[9]

These questions of urban space and geography were brought into sharp focus one Friday evening in August 2008. Since the departure to Canada of the promoter and DJ Alexis D'Boys, Almendares had dropped off the hip hop map, but the enterprising young DJ Vans organized a one-time event at the amphitheater, inviting most of the leading underground artists in Havana to perform. Although Almendares had been a key node in the hip hop network, it had always been more problematic than La Madriguera, for its director was a middle-aged white woman who did not have the same affinity for rap as the young black men who promoted hip hop at La Madriguera. I had seen problems at Almendares before: concerts were canceled at the last minute because of "technical issues"; controversial rappers were temporarily banned from performing there; a young Cuban researcher who recorded a concert that I attended had her tape confiscated. This "revival" concert in August 2008 had its dangers, then, ones that the eighteen-year-old promoter was perhaps too young to realize. He scheduled the less-established groups early in the program, leaving the better-known artists for the end, and the former tried to make their mark by going over the top, criticizing the government, swearing, refusing to leave the stage, and throwing down a microphone. Eventually the venue director came on stage and gave an admonishing speech, reminding the audience about all that the revolution had done for young Cubans, and said that only one more group would be allowed to perform—the headliners, Los Aldeanos. Aldo took the microphone and declared that those present at the concert were more revolutionary than the people who went to official marches in the Plaza de la Revolución. This was the final straw, and the director stopped the concert. However, as he was leaving the stage, Aldo grabbed the microphone again and shouted out: "Don't worry, I'll tell you a secret—Atelier."

It was a Friday, the night that Los Aldeanos held their regular peña at the Vedado club, and he had effectively said: "Don't worry, come back to my place." That he did so over the PA at a particularly tense juncture in a public event revealed his confidence and sense of ownership about the club. If anyone had had a lingering sense of a unified state policy with regard to hip hop, it would have been shattered at that moment; the biggest underground hip hop concert for some time had just been censored in midflow, the police were hovering by the stage (two organizers were subsequently arrested and briefly detained), yet Aldo announced publicly that the concert would continue—not in secret but in another "official" venue. A sizable portion of the audience followed Los Aldeanos on foot across Vedado to Atelier, and the rappers continued where they had left off, with no one trying to stop them: a state-owned venue was to be the refuge from state censorship. The emergence of a sociocapitalist music economy in Havana meant that, in contrast to earlier periods of the revolution, it was much harder for the government to silence or control groups. Barbarám, Atelier, and Karachi had, to a limited degree, become the rappers' fiefdoms, and the fact that Los Aldeanos could so confidently invite the audience to "their" peña revealed that they felt the place was "theirs" because, quite simply, they could fill it with their paying fans.[10]

Los Aldeanos started their peña at Atelier that night with a freestyle—an improvised exchange of rhymes over a backing track. This allowed them to reflect on the events that had taken place earlier at Almendares and more generally on their gripes about life in Havana, but also to relieve the tension, joke around, spar a little with each other. Rap concerts create spaces for public reflection and debate as well as social activity. An Afro-Cuban interviewed by Pedro Pérez Sarduy and Jean Stubbs (2000, 71) in the mid-1990s complained: "We have no places to meet where we can argue and discuss these problems [principally racism]. And there's no motivation to create a kind of center that is attractive to people and where serious topics can be discussed." The rap scene, however, has created exactly this kind of place for young people, and they do indeed discuss serious topics: racism, police harassment, and the negative effects of tourism, but also issues of more specific relevance to the hip hop scene, like the commercialization of rap, the meteoric rise of reggaetón, the relationship between artists and state cultural institutions, and—the prime topic that Friday—censorship. The very freedom of Los Aldeanos' freestyle at Atelier contrasted dramatically with the constraints on display at Almendares just an hour or so earlier.

Rap concerts provide a space for discussion and debate that includes but also goes beyond composed lyrics. To a greater extent than more-commercialized genres, rap performances have a significant hands-on aspect, allowing those present to participate in and create a "scene" rather than simply attend a concert. Most concerts are organized as peñas, which means that there is frequent coming and going onstage as groups join in and drop out; thus, a broad range of viewpoints is aired. This blurring of the distinction between performer and audience is increased by the freestyling that often occurs during or after performances, allowing invited guests and even unknowns to join in. Rappers talk to each other and to the audience between songs, during changeovers between groups, in freestyles onstage and off, and in conversations before, during, and after the performance. Rap concerts are thus places of extensive and multidirectional communication: it is precisely as places to discuss, rather than just to listen or dance, that rap concerts are distinctive. In its explicit, straight-talking focus on social questions, the interactivity of rap peñas goes a step further than the improvised commentary, both verbal and kinetic, that is a feature of Cuban musical traditions such as rumba, son, and timba. Emphasis is placed not only on showcasing finished products but also on a continuous process of critical exploration, evolution, and collective debate.

A focus on the interaction between rappers and audiences, in their banter between songs and their improvised freestyles, reveals a broader range of issues than the song lyrics alone and demonstrates that rap serves as a particularly appropriate vehicle not just for occupying space but also for constituting social relations within it. Musical performance may serve as a means of resolving conflict, negotiating disputes, and thus shaping social relations (Askew 2002), and a number of the Cuban rappers to whom I spoke saw their role almost explicitly in these terms. One of the best-known groups is called Anónimo Consejo (anonymous advice), while Papá Humbertico took his stage name from the idea of a father giving advice to his children. Social realignment also happens in a more contingent, unscripted sense in the gaps between songs at concerts, when rappers often contextualize their lyrics by discussing topical issues within the rap scene; and above all in freestyles, where disputes often come to the forefront, and flow and immediate relevance are paramount.

When I began my research, there were sometimes organized freestyle sessions at the end of concerts, in which established artists and members of the audience lined up to come onstage and improvise a few verses; these freestyles acted as a kind of counterpoint to the composed songs, offering a commentary on them or on the current state of the rap scene. These onstage freestyles were fairly serious and aired contentious topics: one leading rapper, Papo Record, was accused of "betraying the rap movement" by another, El Adversario, during such a freestyle session. Papo Record was one of the small number of artists who joined the ACR, enough in itself to arouse suspicion within the hip hop scene, but he had recently started performing reggaetón, which was beyond the pale for underground rap fans. Rappers are willing and able to wax eloquent to interviewers about their (composed) message, but live debates within the rap scene often focus on other, more immediate questions—who is selling out or causing trouble, who won a freestyle or stole the show.

In 2004, reggaetón and the ACR—both regarded as significant threats to the hip hop scene—dominated the agenda in these more-formalized freestyle sessions. Although these debates can, on the surface, seem somewhat superficial or parochial compared with song lyrics about problems facing wider Cuban society, they reveal important issues affecting young Cubans in general and artists in particular, forming a subset of more general questions about the commodification of culture since the Special Period, and the role of artists in society and the state in the arts. They also highlight the increasing materialism of Cuban society, contrasting underground rappers, who choose to "follow their line" despite its lack of commercial viability, with commercial rappers, who have changed tack to profit from the reggaetón boom. "Following your line" has deep resonances in Havana at a time when state ideology and practice are increasingly divergent, and ordinary Cubans see their government's rhetoric of equality undermined by its increasingly market-driven policies and preferential treatment of foreign tourists.

By 2008, freestyling had taken on a bigger role in the hip hop scene. A number of the rappers who formed part of La Comisión Depuradora, the collective behind the scene's 2007 renaissance, are skilled improvisers. Los Aldeanos made freestyling a central part of their Monday and Friday peñas, and the Wednesday night sessions at Karachi were devoted entirely to improvisation. The Karachi peñas served as the preliminary rounds of the annual Batalla de los Gallos freestyle competition, sponsored by Red Bull, which was widely regarded as the most important event in the hip hop calendar in Havana in 2008 and 2009. Participants were given topics on which to improvise, usually specific either to local sociopolitical concerns or to the rap scene: examples included freedom of expression, double morality, and the alternative social scene at Parque G in Vedado. Freestyling was therefore more than just a sideshow to performances of composed songs.

If onstage freestyles often broach serious issues, impromptu freestyles like the one that I saw on the bus tend to be more light-hearted, focusing on skillful rhyming and facetious boasting. They may be intensely competitive, but usually only in the sense of playful jousting—verbal dexterity, flow, and sound as semantic content take the lead roles (Maxwell 2003, 218–24). Of course, play and serious intent are not necessarily opposed. One particularly memorable freestyle that I witnessed in 2008 involved, once again, Los Aldeanos: Aldo would improvise a verse in made-up English (a language he does not speak) and El B would respond by "translating" it into Spanish. Although much more humorous in tone, it paralleled the introduction to "Mangos bajitos" in the ironic citation of a practice associated with a tourist entertainment venue, thus providing a critical reflection on spatial dualization and the sense of alienation of living in an environment increasingly driven by tourism. Given the regular appearance of foreign delegations and observers at more official hip hop events, such as those organized in conjunction with the ACR, the critique may have also been aimed closer to home.

In the hands of artists like Los Aldeanos, freestyling can be a way of circumventing the constraints put on rap by government institutions and officials. It can be instantly adjusted to the limits or freedoms of the moment; its location and timing are utterly malleable; and it leaves no trace. However, I found that overt politics, though present on occasion, were less common than humor, showing off, and settling scores. Participants reveal a sense of communality (freestyles often take place in a circle, with those who are not rapping providing a vocalized backing track, and anyone can take a turn) but also competition (the sharpest tongue wins). Rap performances are thus more than merely sites for reciting scripted denunciations of social ills: they are occasions for the construction of social spaces and identities, as rappers come together to know themselves and to recreate a community, even as they display their individual talent. I witnessed a freestyle at Karachi in 2008 which brought together the new school rappers Anderson, El Discípulo, and El Enano with the old school Sekou (Anónimo Consejo), who had become a little divorced from the club scene through his ACR commitments, and Miki Flow, formerly of Explosión Suprema, now living in the United States. The freestyle was noticeably more amiable and less competitive than the norm: there seemed to be an unspoken agreement that this was an opportunity for the recreation of a fractured community, a chance to bring together old and new generations, local and émigré figures. It was in large part the nonverbal aspects and what was *not* said—the choice of participants, the physical gestures, and the lack of aggression—that forged unity in the moment.

This location of meaning in the social practices of music making concords with Simon Frith's (1996, 111) suggestion that "making music isn't a way of expressing ideas; it is a way of living them." It may be argued that music making can enable a community to generate (rather than simply embody) a different social order and a distinct set of moral values (Stokes

1994, 12). The organizational principle of rap peñas—as communal, interactive, semi-improvised performances—challenges a social order in which opportunities to speak publicly about social issues are limited, such public utterances are usually carefully planned and controlled, and professional distinctions often separate musicians and audiences. The significance of freestyling is underlined by Edgar González, the master of ceremonies at the Red Bull final, who argues that "it's a good thing to compete, because paternalism coerces, controls, disguises, so you need to eliminate these things from yourself" (quoted in Castillo Martiatu n.d.c, 24). Freestyling is more than just a way to pass the time in González's eyes: it is a way for rappers to free themselves momentarily from the paternalism of Cuban society. Rap performances, then, do indeed produce a different social order, one based on spontaneity and free speech. As the Brazilian rapper MV Bill put it, "rap music isn't music, it's a form of free discussion" (quoted in Neate 2003, 191). Viewed in this way, hip hop has provided not only an outlet for self-expression but also a set of practices which have facilitated the production of communal values and knowledge; freestyles are thus of central importance, for it is here that a democratic community is created.

Communal events in the rap scene thus allow young Cubans to construct more congenial social spaces within the city, which also permit critical reflection on the difficulties of urban life. Because it requires no equipment—freestyles are often not amplified—rap spills over into the times and spaces surrounding formal concerts (most commonly out on the sidewalk after a peña or on the bus home), allowing performers and audiences to enter into conversations with each other, to shape ideas as well as listen to them. Many of the hip hop performances I attended exemplified Mark Mattern's (1998, 29) deliberative form of "acting in concert," in which music making serves as a "communicative forum."

There are strong echoes of the link between jazz improvisation, social practice, and alternative community formation discussed by Daniel Fischlin and Ajay Heble, in particular their claim that improvisation stimulates "envisionings of possibilities excluded from conventional systems of thought" (2004, 11). For these scholars, improvisation fosters solidarity while maintaining a questioning spirit: it is about "an ongoing process of community building, about reinvigorating public life with the spirit of dialogue and difference that improvisatory practices consistently gesture toward" (ibid., 11, 17). While Fischlin and Heble's utopian vision does not map neatly onto hip hop improvisation, in which aggressive "battling" plays an important part, the social aims and effects of freestyling are nevertheless as often constructive and dialogic as they are destructive and oppositional, at least in Havana.[11] The notion of improvisation as "reinvigorating public life with the spirit of dialogue and difference" is a highly suggestive one in the context of urban studies and, specifically, the work of scholars such as Richard Sennett (2000) who have pointed to the decline of the public realm in modern cities. If live music in general might be considered a counterbalance to the loss of the public realm, hip hop—with its emphasis on freestyling—could be seen as playing a very specific role in maintaining a space of debate. In the face of Havana's tourism boom and the progressive privatization of public space, freestyling is a small gesture of resistance to the consequent deterioration of the public realm. Scholars have underlined the importance of unpredictability, spontaneity, and performance in the maintenance of a rich public life (Bridge and Watson 2000a, 370); public hip hop improvisation is a small step in this direction.

Rap has attracted attention as a dynamic area of social commentary in contemporary Havana, yet performers' observations directed toward the rap scene itself tend to engage audiences' attention as much as externally directed social critiques. Much of the activity at live events focuses on more or less serious competition and disputes, and thus the renegotiation of social bonds. The most charged moments are often those centering on rivalries between individuals, institutions, and artistic ideologies, which sometimes make their way into composed lyrics but which are carried out just as often in the unscripted parts of peñas. The fact that, for example, many audience members at Los Aldeanos' peñas know their lyrics by heart suggests that communicating a message through composed songs is not necessarily the only or even the principal locus of meaning in live performance. Improvisations are often key moments, when tension peaks or is released through humor. Furthermore, Soandres del Río talks about rapping "so that people who felt like me and thought like me didn't feel so alone" (*East of Havana* n.d., 58). He was speaking to people who already thought like him: education was thus less significant than solidarity, and the message was in the social moment as much as the words.

Freestyling further underlines the limitations of lyrical analysis: as Ian

Soandres del Río.
Photo by Oscar Castillo.

Maxwell (2003, 228) explains, words may be less the bearers of meaning than elements of sound and badges of skill, and despite rappers' insistence on the centrality of their prepared messages—"it's all about the words"—freestyling may be "not simply about the words at all. It's about these moments, this flow, this flight from ego, the feeling of being led away by the energy of the rhyme. . . . The words here are the devices for getting there, to that state." In the hands of artists like Los Aldeanos or El Adversario, freestyling may be a way of inventing meaning out of nothingness; Anderson or Etián, however, often lead the audience away from meaning into a world of surreal sounds and associations. If rap performance evidences the freedom to speak, freestyling may also be a form of freedom from sense (ibid., 225), and thus a performative mode of liberation that has broader resonances in Cuban society, where elaborated ideas are given pride of place by the state. It is important to take into account the full range of rappers' verbal expressions—the conversations and debates, confrontations and reaffirmations, but also the "strings of nonsense" (ibid., 219)—if we are to understand the pleasures and challenges of live rap performances.

Rap Concerts as Economic Spaces

It is important to balance out lyrics with freestyles in order to restore the dialectic that is so central to hip hop (I. Perry 2004) yet so often overlooked in global hip hop scholarship. Improvisation is fundamental, not just in the musical realm but also the social and economic. In Havana, the dialectical relationship between the two forms of rap, composition and improvisation, is mirrored in the relationship between the moralism of most rappers' lyrics and the everyday strategies they (like most habaneros) adopt to get by. Verbal freestyling has a socioeconomic counterpart: "inventing."

As the reputation of Cuban hip hop grew internationally, small but significant numbers of foreigners sought out the Havana scene and were generally welcomed by local artists and audiences.[12] If rap concerts started out as an alternative for young habaneros to the dollars-only tourist venues, they also became an alternative to these same venues for foreign hip hop aficionados and adventurous overseas visitors looking beyond the more traditional, packaged, expensive musical experiences of Habana Vieja and the Casas de la Música. They became a hip, alternative tourist attraction. The overwhelmingly Cuban social spaces of hip hop in the 1990s thus expanded into more transnational social networks around the start of the new millennium—and with the foreigners came the hustle.

As most young Cubans have never left the island, they are often eager to make cross-cultural contacts out of pure curiosity. But as tourism has become a mainstay of both the formal and the informal urban economies, habaneros have also come to rely increasingly on foreigners in order to overcome everyday hardships and, in some cases, to realize larger dreams. Those who are fortunate enough to live in desirable parts of the city, own cars, or have skills, goods, or knowledge that foreigners seek to acquire have been able to accumulate hard currency by providing services to tourists, thereby raising themselves economically above the peso-earning majority of Havana's residents. At its most extreme, the quest for hard currency is evident in the dramatic increase in hustling and prostitution (jineterismo); yet many young habaneros, under pressure from material scarcity and limited career possibilities, see contact with foreigners as a way forward, which might entail anything from a free beer or a tip to something much more substantial, such as the gift of an iPod, camera, cellphone, or laptop, or even marriage and emigration.

Tourism and its perceived nefarious effects—prostitution, rising materialism, the increasing dominance of the dollar—are often criticized in rap lyrics. Fernandes (2006, 108) paints a picture of commercial rappers who justify hustling, but continues: "Most underground rappers, however, reject *jineterismo* as a way of surviving in the special period, suggesting instead that socialist values of honesty and work are important in efforts to raise oneself up. The criticism of *jineterismo* in underground rap music is a polemic against the consumerist mentality that has emerged with increased access to a market economy and a condemnation of the desire of young people to find an easy fix rather than work hard to achieve the goals of the revolution." This is an accurate description of many underground rap lyrics, but it clashes with the very real material needs of those who voice them and should therefore not necessarily be taken at face value. A glance at the rap scene in 2004 revealed laptops, DJ equipment, electronic goods, music, clothing, and other gifts donated by foreigners, as well as a marked enthusiasm for selling self-produced CDs to foreigners for hard currency at concerts. Fernandes's polarized perspective reflects rappers' lyrics but ignores the more complex realities of their lives, encapsulated in the very Cuban word *inventar*. Translated roughly as "to make something happen" or "to get by somehow," and including a large gray area of semilegal or illegal activities, "inventing" is an inherent part of daily life in a city where state salaries are generally considered too low to cover the cost of living; it has even been described as a "national sport" (Chávez 2005, 9). Archibald Ritter (2005, 27–28) states: "The nature of Cuba's planned economy itself has inadvertently promoted widespread entrepreneurial values, attitudes, behavior, and *savoir-faire* as citizens have had to buy and sell, hustle and 'network' in order to improvise solutions to their personal economic problems." An account of Cuban rap which describes a dichotomy of hard work and hustling fails to reflect a reality in which most habaneros, rappers included, have to invent to a degree in order to survive, and in which *la lucha*—the struggle of everyday life—encapsulates both hard work and the search for easy fixes.

A documentary aptly titled *Inventos* includes a scene in which the underground duo Anónimo Consejo, one of Fernandes's key examples, discuss the need to invent in order to survive, given the inability of the music industry to meet their needs. Most underground hip hoppers are similarly open about the need to invent and hustle to make ends meet; as Papá Humbertico raps ("Vivencias"), "sometimes, forced by scarcity, I do things I really don't want to," and he claims ("Lo que hace falta") that "a la zurda soy diestro" (I'm good at getting things done on the side). Many rappers do not work in the formal economy, and of those who do, few are very enthusiastic about it.

Foreigners who have spent time in Havana will know that attempts to invent will often center on them, as many have economic resources beyond the wildest dreams of most Cubans, and all have the most precious commodity of all—a foreign passport. More blatant forms of jineterismo are rare, though not unknown, in the rap scene, but foreigners receive plenty of attention. It is thus naive to imply that underground rappers subscribe in an uncomplicated manner to a belief in the "socialist values of honesty and work." As the foreigners who have sufficient linguistic skills and interest in hip hop to hunt down rap concerts are generally interested in underground rap, it is in fact underground hip hoppers, rather than those espousing a more commercial outlook, who have been best placed to make the most of such interactions. The regular "condemnation of the desire of young people to find an easy fix rather than work hard to achieve the goals of the revolution" looked a little different a few years later, by which time many leading hip hoppers had switched to reggaetón or emigrated (or both), often drawing on contacts made through the rap scene.

Involvement with rap can therefore open up an alternative kind of urban existence and the possibility of accumulating not just cultural capital but material benefits. *Pace* Fernandes, a rap lifestyle often involves, in practice, an active rejection of the dominant discourse about work and an engagement with the new economic realities characteristic of late socialist Havana—in other words, inventing. Rappers often said that it was not worth having a normal job, and many did not work in the conventional sense: they might earn ten dollars a month working in a state enterprise, yet they could earn the same amount of money selling one demo CD to a foreigner, so a number preferred to rely instead on occasional bursts of entrepreneurial activity centered on rap concerts.

Indeed, on some occasions I heard rappers describe their motivations for attending concerts primarily in terms of the need to raise money, and one well-known underground rapper said bluntly that the festival was just about selling CDs as far as he was concerned. Rap may thus provide an alternative to the dominant socialist work ethos and the peso salaries provided by state employment. If music producers and the more entre-preneurial underground hip hoppers might be considered examples of the burgeoning area of unofficial *cuentapropismo* (self-employment), their alignment with socialist values of honesty and work may be questioned, since, as Emma Phillips (2007, 317) argues, "the partial abstraction of cuentapropistas from the centralized state labor system . . . represents a fundamental challenge to the collectivist social pact underlying Cuban socialism."

Both Cuban and foreign observers have frequently constructed the Ha-vana rap scene as a manifestation of hip hop that harks back to the culture's South Bronx origins before it was corrupted by money. This perspective has been vital to its national and international success, but it overlooks not only the contradictory realities of the Cuban scene—Ariel Fernández told me that, contrary to academic opinion and widespread moralistic discourses, most Havana rappers were "really pro-capitalist people, people who want to make profit, money from this"—but also the extent to which the pursuit of financial gain has been integral to the history of hip hop since its inception (Forman 2002, 101–3). Hip hop emerged at a time of economic decline in New York City and provided minority youths with urgently needed economic opportunities as well as outlets for cultural expression. As Jeff Chang (2005, 316) notes, if blues was the music of hard work, hip hop was the soundtrack to diminishing opportunities for formal employment in 1970s New York; DJ Kool Herc's mythical first hip hop party in 1973 was a money-raising event. Indeed, as Mark Anthony Neal (2004b) argues, black music in New York was under-pinned throughout the twentieth century by the urgent need for survival tactics in the face of inadequate resources. He focuses on the rapper Biggie Smalls, whose "narratives suggest an intimate relationship between suc-cessful social flow and credible lyrical flow—and they suggest a direct correlation between his social improvisation and his lyrical improvisa-tion" (ibid., 213). In other words, Biggie's "street flow" was both an artistic and a socioeconomic practice. In general terms, then, "hip-hop provides powerful evidence of the ability of black youth to use their improvisatory musical practice(s) to also create and improvise opportunities in their social, political, and cultural lives" (220). If hip hop is a street thing, scholars cannot afford to ignore street practices and street flow.

The glorification of cash in much U.S. hip hop is hardly surprising given the straitened circumstances in which it evolved, and it has found widespread acceptance not least because of its mirroring of the American dream. Overt materialism is more dangerous in socialist Havana, however, not least within the rap scene itself, in which the label underground is valorized and commercial is viewed askance. Cuban rappers have to tread a far narrower line between economic necessity and rhetorical orthodoxy than their American counterparts, something that should be borne in mind when their public pronouncements are considered. Nevertheless, there is one parallel between the South Bronx in the 1970s and Havana in the 1990s that is rarely noted: these were both periods in which many youths were forced to survive by turning to the informal economy and seeking new ways of making money. The hip hop economy in Havana, like the broader Cuban economy of which it forms a part, has both formal and informal sides, and the Manichaean moralism of underground rap lyrics thus needs to be balanced by observation of what takes place on the street. The rigid moral code is just one half of a dialectic with inventing. Hip hop is also about improvisation—a way of claiming spaces, stimulating dialogue, and reconstituting social relations, but also of creating economic breathing space in challenging times.

By focusing on the social and economic aspects of the hip hop scene, I am underlining the fact that while rap may be a form of political music, its meanings are not limited to this; nor, indeed, are its politics to be found solely in its lyrics. Maxwell (2001, 266) warns against a tendency to simplify and overstate these political dimensions, suggesting that his status as a researcher "frequently elicited highbrow explanations for a given person's involvement or engagement with hip-hop. Virtually everyone I met could, to one extent or another, talk the talk: hip-hop was 'the voice of the streets'; it was 'giving a voice to people who don't have one'; it was, simply, 'political.' I am not denying that this is, to an extent, the case. It is not, however, the whole story, and it is the other side of the story that does not get written about enough."

Maxwell locates "the other side of the story" in "the groove of it," an observation that resonates in Havana. When reggaetón took Havana by storm in 2002–3, rap artists and fans started to jump ship, revealing an unexpected allegiance to "groove," a renewed interest in the car-women-cash triad, and a less-than-wholehearted espousal of rap's explicit politics. If this should introduce a note of caution into the celebration of Cuban rap's overt messages, I would also argue that the appeal—and the politics—of hip hop should not be characterized so narrowly, since hip hop culture also includes the distinctive spaces that have been carved out by its practitioners. There may in fact be another side to the story in Havana, which is not written about enough: not just groove but also street flow. By proposing that the unwritten story of hip hop in Havana encompasses the social and economic possibilities opened up by young Cubans, the pleasures as well as the politics of rap, I am thus expanding, rather than undermining, hip hop's political significance. To understand the politics of hip hop, we need to grasp both the fixed and the fluid, the composed and the improvised. This is a point that Paul Gilroy (1993, 38) argues persuasively in his analysis of the dialectical nature of black musics: "The politics of fulfillment is mostly content to play occidental rationality at its own game. It necessitates a hermeneutic orientation that can assimilate the semiotic, verbal, and textual. The politics of transfiguration strives in pursuit of the sublime, struggling to repeat the unrepeatable, to present the unpresentable. Its rather different hermeneutic focus pushes towards the mimetic, dramatic, and performative." Hip hop's politics are enacted in performances as well as lyrics, in the drama of freestyles as well as rational texts, and, to echo Kelley, its surface meaning as message music is not necessarily where its appeal primarily lies.

Ariel Fernández described the hip hop scene in the worst years of the Special Period as "an alternative space for the youth at the time that was very necessary. There was a lot of frustration, and this place meant that you belonged to something, that you weren't alone" (East of Havana n.d., 150). He has regularly talked about involvement with hip hop as a way of keeping busy in disorienting times. Cuban hip hop later grabbed the attention of the Hip Hop Nation for its lyrical messages, but were their invigorating effects felt primarily outside the scene rather than inside it? As Edgar González told me, Cuban hip hoppers thought that what they were doing was pretty ordinary, but for visiting Americans it was something special. It was Gilroy's "politics of fulfillment" that caught foreign imaginations. But perhaps hip hop's meaning on a local level had as much to do with opportunities for young Cubans to create for themselves pockets of air, both social and economic, as the weight of the Special Period seemed about to asphyxiate them. Was this where much of the politics of Cuban hip hop lay—in the fleeting social moments, in the economic lifelines, in the implicit, performative "politics of transfiguration," rather than in the explicit, formal realm that is so much easier for outsiders to grasp because it can be recorded, transcribed, and quoted?

The Movement of the Movement: Taking on the City

Urban mobility, particularly via the subway, was a signature feature of the early days of hip hop in New York City (Forman 2004, 1), and Philip Bohlman (1993, 413) recounts how Chicago rappers responded to the beating of Rodney King and the subsequent Los Angeles riots by taking to the city's elevated trains and performing the news for passengers—something hard to imagine in the age of Twitter. A memorable aspect of my trajectory across Havana with my companions was the improvised rap contest on the bus, apparently not uncommon in Havana: Zurbano (n.d.a, 7) describes rap improvisations as a regular feature of his journey into the city when he lived in Alamar. My nocturnal journey illustrates how rap also stimulates and accompanies movement around the Cuban capital. Rappers talk about their scene as *el movimiento* (the movement), a word which refers to a sociocultural community but also evokes the physical engagement of rappers with the city. Hip hop events draw young habaneros from diverse neighborhoods, providing them with the motivation and opportunity to explore the urban environment and to participate in the social life of the city (Condry 2001; Sansone 1995). For rappers, many of them unemployed in a formal sense, concerts, rehearsals, meetings, and recording sessions are prime stimuli to get out and about. Engaging with the city is particularly important to the residents of Alamar, a vast concrete suburb on the easternmost extreme of Havana. Frequently described as the home of Cuban rap and arguably the dominant place in the Cuban rap imaginary, Alamar has been the source of many leading groups and rap devotees. Their participation in the scene has counteracted their geographical marginalization: not only are they drawn into the city by concerts at central venues, but also, during the boom years of rap in the late 1990s and early

2000s, rappers and fans from other parts of the city were attracted to Alamar for peñas and especially the annual rap festival.

Rap facilitates a particularly dynamic engagement with the city, for it is a music that is often on the move. Impromptu freestyling frequently takes place in public places—on buses or in the street—contesting the uses and meanings of such spaces. Rappers create instantaneous new roles for themselves on the urban stage, contesting their relative invisibility (or inaudibility) in the city and, in the case of residents of Alamar, their spatial marginalization. Movement itself thus opens up new platforms for self-expression.

Freestyling, because it needs no equipment or preparation, is ideally suited to the temporary, instantaneous appropriation or "poaching" of public spaces; it is a characteristic urban "guerrilla" strategy, a facet of the subcultural urban nomadism found in contexts of intensive spatial regulation that has been aptly described as a "performative mode of inhabiting the city" (Fielder 2001, 280). However, spatial appropriation through sound carries risks in Havana. The only time that I witnessed the police act with force was at a freestyle outside a party in Vedado. A concert had been canceled earlier that the evening, so the sizable audience descended instead on a house party in Linea Street. The occupants were charging an entry fee, so many people decided to stay out on the street. Soon there were some seventy people outside, and a freestyle began, some people making percussion sounds as an improvised backing track, others taking turns to compose rhymes. Suddenly four police vans screeched up, thirty policemen piled out, and within seconds there were batons flying and people running in all directions.

This event illustrates not simply the spatialized practices of Cuban hip hop but, more important, that it is precisely in the spatial and performative domains that much of its political challenge can be found. I never witnessed any reaction when rappers criticized the police in songs performed in government venues and distributed on CDs, yet improvisers of harmless "strings of nonsense" in the street were violently dispersed. The principal rap venues are in isolated, self-contained locations such as the middle of urban parks (like the Parque Almendares and the Quinta de los Molinos) or in distant Alamar. Rap peñas have generally been authorized at times and places that were unlikely to pull in casual passersby. The challenge of rap appears to be directly related to its visibility and audibility, and thus to be at its greatest either when outsiders are watching—particularly during the annual international rap festival—or when it spills out of its prescribed spaces into public places. Yet even official venues are contested zones: the struggle over regular access to performance spaces has been central to the history of hip hop in Havana, which is usually charted less by stylistic developments than by the flowering and then frequently abrupt end of activities in a series of locales. Negotiations and confrontations between the state and the Havana rap scene have been as much about territory as self-expression; the issue has been less what rappers are allowed to say than where they are allowed to say it. On repeated occasions, popular rap peñas have been terminated with little notice or reason, and the scene has thus been regularly uprooted, creating a sense of impermanence and uncertainty. The fractured state discussed in chapter 1 has been concretized in hip hoppers' spatial victories—and defeats.

An event in mid-2004 illustrated the degree to which the precarious status of rap was directly related to place. After the last-minute cancellation of the rap festival in August 2004 due to Hurricane Charley, the enterprising DJ and promoter Alexis D'Boys persuaded the director of the Teatro Mella to allow him to put on a series of afternoon rap shows in the theater's garden to provide a performance outlet for the frustrated groups. This garden, however, opens directly onto a busy street in the relatively upmarket Vedado neighborhood and faces a military building, and the rappers could be heard clearly on the street. Although it had been used in the mid-1990s, this was no longer a normal venue for rap, and the theater official in charge of the event was clearly nervous, hovering near the stage and, on several occasions, literally pulling the plug on the sound system. The songs were no more contentious than those performed at nocturnal peñas at isolated official venues, but they were apparently beyond the pale in a central public place during the day. This event illustrated differing understandings of the proper places for rap performances and the appropriate uses of public spaces, underneath which lie conflicting perceptions of urban space.

Representing the City

A focus on urban imaginaries is a feature of much recent work within the field of urban studies.[13] Urban experience is mediated by representations of the city that form an integral part of its reality: "The city is an understanding of itself. To make it work, to make it operate, to make it liveable, all manner of ideologies, schema, concepts and images are required" (Miles, Hall, and Borden 2000, 2). Urban space is multiply imagined and inflected, contested rather than fixed, framed by "a series of discourses, which involve ways of picturing the local and one's relation to it" (A. Bennett 2000, 63). Underpinning these conflicting discourses or representations are the radically unequal opportunities of urban environments: "The city is something akin to a vast and variegated whirlpool replete with all the ambivalence of a space full of opportunity, playfulness and liberating potential, while being entwined with spaces of oppression, exclusion and marginalization. . . . Cities seem to hold the promise of emancipation and freedom whilst skilfully mastering the whip of repression and domination" (Merrifield and Swyngedouw 1996, 13–14). Such a perspective is central to Forman's (2002) account of the development of rap, which in the 1980s began to express critiques of the uneven distribution of power in U.S. cities. As Tricia Rose (1994, 102) writes, at this time rap began to articulate "the chasm between black urban lived experience and dominant, 'legitimate' (e.g., neoliberal) ideology regarding equal opportunity and racial inequality." The sociospatial divisions of New York City shaped rap's oppositional narratives and were famously articulated in landmark tracks by Grandmaster Flash and the Furious Five such as "The Message" (1982) and "New York, New York" (1983).

The image of the divided city, a place of opportunity but also of marginalization, has been particularly apposite to Havana in recent years. The Cuban government's embrace of tourism during the Special Period required an image overhaul: the dour, politicized images of Soviet-era Cuba were augmented by classic Caribbean marketing icons—sun, sea, sex, and music. The repackaging of the country as both heritage site and tropical playground included representing Havana through the twin lenses of colonial architecture and nightlife.[14] Central to this re-imaging of the city have been the revamping of music venues and, above all, the project to restore Habana Vieja. The capital's architectural heritage has been commodified in order to create a distinctive and attractive place-image for the city. The urban "text" is thus increasingly drawn up in anticipation of what tourists want to read (Álvarez-Tabío Albo 2000, 18).

The combination of joint ventures with foreign capital and the "Plan

Maestro" have turned parts of the city (above all in Habana Vieja, Vedado, and Miramar) into picturesque places of opportunity, but largely for foreigners. The Cuban government's socialist rhetoric of equality has thus come to look ever more disconnected from reality, especially for many Afro-Cubans, who are widely perceived to have been disproportionately disadvantaged by these recent changes (de la Fuente 2008b) and who watch their neighborhoods slowly collapsing as funds are poured into a few visually appealing blocks of the city. Havana is increasingly a "city of illusion" (Christine Boyer, quoted in Low 1999a, 16), an assemblage of enticing images and proclamations of equal opportunity that bear little relation to most residents' everyday lives.

Many young habaneros are unimpressed by living in "an imagined community for others" (Jeffrey Sissons, quoted in Foster 1999, 268). In the documentary *Hasta Siempre*, a young rapper flicks through a tourist guidebook and claims that he has not been to any of the places in it. When Aldo of Los Aldeanos accompanied me to the Viazul tourist bus station to buy a blank CD, he snorted with derision as he looked through the postcards for sale. In songs such as "Hotel Nacional" and "Playa" (beach), Los Aldeanos explore the harassment, exclusion, and psychological dislocation that Cubans can face when trying to access iconic local places. The former song describes Aldo's stay at the famous hotel when Juanes was in Havana in September 2009 and his incredulity at experiencing the other side of the Cuban/tourist divide; the latter recounts an imaginary day out at the beach when El B is twice picked up by the police, first because a foreigner talks to him and second because a fight erupts next to him. The gap between Caribbean illusion and reality, paralleling the gulf between dominant ideologies and urban lived experience described by Rose, is nicely captured in one of Aldo's verses ("Mi país"): "Magnificent, enchanted island of dreams / Whose treasure is a frustrated youth." In trying to persuade Cubans that the tourist imaginary was key to the nation's economic future, Fidel Castro argued: "We are not . . . an oil-producing country . . . the sea, the climate, the sun, the moon, the palm trees . . . are the natural wealth of our country, and we have to take advantage of them" (quoted in Schwartz 1997, 205). But Aldo's verse suggests that this focus on such stereotypical (if enchanting) images has meant neglecting the human capital of Cuba's youth, the island's real (but lost) "treasure."

Rappers like Aldo explore the disjunctures between the global city of the imagination and local realities. If, as discussed above, hip hoppers embody alternative visions of urban life through their social and spatial practices, the social construction of urban space also takes place on a symbolic plane (Low 1999a, 1999b; Forman 2002): oppositional narratives of locality take the more literal form of discursive redefinitions of city spaces. Young Cubans who have been largely written out of the tourism script have found in rap an opportunity to construct their own representations of urban reality.

Remapping the City: From "New York" to "the Village"

As a tool for imagining the city in new ways, rap has been described as a form of alternative urban cartography (Forman 2002, 60), its lyrics "providing maps upon which young artists and their wider audiences might trace patterns of dominant hegemonic power and locate spaces where alternative or oppositional potentials can cohere and thrive" (ibid., 71). Employing the same metaphor rather differently in an Australian context, Maxwell (2001, 265) describes hip hop as "a map preceding, and making, a new place, in which it is possible for the agents to think and experience their own being in a manner or modality that previously had left them feeling denied." Hip hop's globalization has thus led to a kind of local remapping. In Havana, hip hop provides a frame for naming and connecting marginal places—Alamar, Cojímar, Cerro, 10 de Octubre— allowing rappers to create meaningful cognitive maps of the city that contrast markedly with those in guidebooks, with their focus on Habana Vieja, Vedado, and Miramar.[15] This rewriting of the city may also take more literal forms: graffiti in the barrio of Buena Vista contests the neighborhood's contemporary association with elderly soneros by connecting it instead with modern urban culture via the word "crew," borrowed from U.S. hip hop.

Alamar, in particular, was transformed by this hip hop cartography. Suburban rappers contested the peripherality of their barrio by resignifying it as a cultural center, the home of Cuban rap, drawing on its physical similarities to the housing projects of New York so central to the origin story of U.S. hip hop. Havana's geography was thus re-imagined by young residents of Alamar, who drew on the spatial imaginary of U.S. hip hop. In the 1990s, rap fans in Alamar divided the suburb in two and named one half "New York" and the other "Los Angeles." According to Edgar González, fans identified with hip hop styles according to which side of the imaginary line they lived on: those in "New York" listened to East Coast rap, those in "L.A." to West Coast rap, and rappers took on fashions, mannerisms, and flow accordingly. Geographical location thus determined musical taste, and when hip hoppers began to play out this U.S.-derived rivalry at rap peñas, real communities were forged around imagined places. This direct imitation of U.S. hip hop rivalries in Alamar gave way to a more Cubanized, citywide version, with groups identifying themselves as Costa Norte, Costa Este, and so on. Rivalries developed between Alamar and Vedado, sparked off by Amenaza and Grandes Ligas's song "Costa norte." Feuds made their way into lyrics and led to minor outbreaks of violence as hip hoppers defended their (imagined) turf with words and, on occasion, fists. Soon, though, the arrival of hip hop artists and activists from New York gave the urban imaginary a further twist: turn-of-the-millennium Havana as the 1970s South Bronx. Globally circulating urban music was thus key to the generation of new urban imaginaries, vividly illustrating Maxwell's description of hip hop as "a map preceding, and making, a new place."

More recently, a loose community has coalesced around a different imagined place: *la aldea*. Literally meaning "the village," and a play on the name of the rapper Aldo and his duo Los Aldeanos, it is used regularly to refer to the social and artistic world built up around this group. The reduction in scale of the urban imaginary from the global metropolises of New York and L.A. to "the village" is telling, as it reflects Havana hip hop's passage from optimistic boom to sobering decline and also its shift from the internationalism of the Black August years to the localism of a decade later.[16] However, it also conjures up the more positive idea of a small, tight-knit community. As El B explains at the start of the documentary *Revolution*, "for us the basis of la aldea is that of a small place where everyone—though it may seem utopian—helps each other, collaborates with each other, where everyone has the same objective." Although its epicenter is in Nuevo Vedado (in Aldo's house and, until April 2009, the neighboring club Barbarám), la aldea is movable: it goes with Los Aldeanos wherever they go. This word underlines the capacity of music to foster communal spaces and interaction, and, paradoxically, of urban music to create a social village within the city.

A typical apartment building in Alamar. Photo by Alex Lloyd.

In his famous essay "The Metropolis and Mental Life," Georg Simmel analyzes the effect of the city on the human psyche, making numerous comparisons between urban and rural or small-town life. He argues that due to the excess of stimuli in the city, "the metropolitan type of man . . . develops an organ protecting him against the threatening currents and discrepancies of his external environment which would uproot him. He reacts with his head instead of his heart" (1950, 410). Simmel argues at length that "metropolitan man" has a rational, objectivist, calculating character, while emotions and personal relationships are of greater importance in small settlements. Metropolitan man's intellectual mentality is intimately connected to the city's role as the seat of the money economy. In the city, "money, with all its colorlessness and indifference, becomes the common denominator of all values; irreparably it hollows out the core of things" (414). Simmel identifies a "blasé attitude" or reserve in interpersonal relations stemming from the metropolitan money economy: "The development of modern culture is characterized by the preponderance of what one may call the 'objective spirit' over the 'subjective spirit' . . . at some points we notice a retrogression in the culture of the individual with reference to spirituality, delicacy, and idealism" (421–22).

It is worth citing Simmel at length because of the parallels between his critique of urban mentalities and the vision of "the villagers"—Los Aldeanos—and their close associates in La Comisión Depuradora. Underlying their lyrics is a moralistic vision of an urban "retrogression" in spirituality and idealism, just as Simmel argues. In particular, they focus on the power of money in sociocapitalist Havana to "hollow out the core of things," and on the preponderance of head over heart, calculation over feeling. One of Aldo's demos is tellingly named *Poesía y corazón* (poetry and heart), and his critique of Havana society in "Miseria humana" culminates in the line "you know, it's more a matter of the heart than the government." Cold hearts, the absence of love, and calculated sex are recurring tropes (e.g., "La papa"; "La Rosi"): in "Crisis de fe," Los Aldeanos rap that "nothing motivates or moves us, love's just for films and TV"; they claim that "no one thinks about romance / The speed of thought doesn't allow love to advance." Los Aldeanos' songs are populated by boys sporting symbols of the new money economy—cellphones, the latest fashions—and girls with fake breasts offering love for sale. "El palla" unmasks such urban imposters, exposing the deceits and pretensions of the wheeler-dealer in the barrio and the girlfriend "with a big ass and a small heart" whose attentions he buys. In "Noches perdidas," Aldo raps: "Everything is calculated / There's not much difference between you and your MP3." His proposed solution? "Operation Rehabilitation of Feelings" ("Aldito el guzanito").

The idea that habaneros have become heartless gives rise to an imagined word peopled by robots ("La niña robot"), puppets ("Crisis de fe"), ghosts ("El joven fantasma"), and vampires ("Vampiros"), all metaphors for the kind of urban depersonalization analyzed by Simmel. In "Llorar es un lujo espiritual" (crying is a spiritual luxury) and "Retrato hablado" (police description), Aldo unveils a world of "plastic" people; the chorus of the former song begins: "You've got to make more room for the heart and less for money." "La niña robot" (the robot girl) tells of a girl who is "programmed" to go with anyone who has money, a cellphone, or a car; she has no heart, no feelings, no principles. In Papá Humbertico's "Vivencias," urban dwellers "are like androids, they give no sign at all of real life," and in "En esta ciudad," he reveals a dehumanized and desensitized city of the dead, blind, deaf, and dumb "where it's all about having, not being."

On the one hand, Simmel's "blasé attitude" is evident in these dehumanized creatures, transformed by the city into automatons; on the other hand, Havana rappers go even further, for the alienation that they describe leads to a form of urban psychosis. In "Mi barrio es loco" (my barrio is crazy), Aldo paints a cartoonish picture of local corruption, gossip, surveillance, violence, and hustling, based on "psicosis monetaria, esquizofrenia miqui" (monetary psychosis, materialist schizophrenia). "Resurrepción" by Escuadrón Patriota and El Aldeano riffs on a well-known line by Manolito y Su Trabujo (discussed below) as they claim that "en La Habana hay una pila de locos y muy pocos psiquiatras" (in Havana there are loads of crazies and very few psychiatrists). The idea of an urban-induced sickness is found in many rap songs. The "virus of human misery" is infecting the streets of Havana in "Miseria humana"; the rapper is thus cast in the role of healer in Papá Humbertico and Los Aldeanos' "Equipo," curing the infected mind of the subject by injecting it with intelligent music. If the urban subject is mentally ill, it is because the city itself is divided. Randee Akozta, in "Mi ventana," describes "minds that live in Miami while their body is in Havana"; similarly, in "La naranja se picó," El B raps that "their bodies are here, but their minds are ninety miles away, in a trance." Hermanos de Causa desire "a single capital that's the same for everyone" ("San Cristóbal de La Habana"); Havana reveals "a thinking that contradicts its own behavior / Miramar doesn't want to be like Cuba."[17] In "El chico pillo" (the clever boy), a song about the dangers of thinking too much, Aldo warns: "with your body here and your mind there / Stop that, boy, that'll get you nowhere." A society divided in two by the Florida Straits and under intense economic pressure is symbolized by the trope of a split subject.

Los Aldeanos and their collaborators thus expound a critique of urban society, attitudes, morals, and behaviors from the metaphorical space of "the village." Echoing Simmel, they urge habaneros to use their hearts more and their heads less: *el corazón* (the heart) is the key organ for underground hip hop today, having superseded *el pulmón* (the lung).[18] For Simmel, the economic context plays a crucial part in determining the "metropolitan" spirit, and hip hop in Havana came of age, of course, during a period of great economic changes. Rappers' urban critique focuses not just on urbanization but also on its effects on urban dwellers, who have supposedly embraced superficial metropolitan values and are thus held responsible for the city's decline. Havana is the center of Cuban sociocapitalism, and Los Aldeanos and other members of La Comisión Depuradora scrutinize the effect of the new money economy and new materialism on the urban psyche. Their dystopian anti-urbanism carries strong echoes of the jaundiced view of the city on the part of the original young rebels of the 1959 revolution, for whom the city represented the seat of all vices and agrarian reform was the highest priority. Not for the first time, underground hip hoppers and old school Cuban socialists seem to be coming from the same place.

La aldea may thus be seen as promoting village values in the face of the dehumanizing effects of modern urbanization—the anti-urban face of urban music. Underground rappers call for change and revolution, yet they are already living in times of rapid change, which they criticize harshly: they want change, just not *this* change.[19] The values they espouse are those of an earlier period, as evidenced by their veneration for Martí, Che, and Camilo Cienfuegos—a nostalgic "dreaming backward" for which hip hop is the perfect vehicle. Today, urban cool is out (U.S. hip hop fashions are much less prevalent in the scene than a decade earlier) and rural emotions are in. There is a dramatic contrast between this critical view of urbanization and reggaetón's embrace of the "metropolitan" spirit—its open glorification of money and appearances.

This picture needs to be qualified in one important way. Aldo's song "Cerebro de tivol" (shit-head) mocks the police for their predominantly rural origins and includes the repeated line "guajiro!" (peasant) in its chorus. This is a snapshot of an urban-rural tension felt every day on the streets of the capital: the mutual incomprehension of figures of authority from the *campo* (countryside) and urban youth "tribes." As Zurbano (n.d.a, 12) notes, policemen from rural areas tend to confuse members of urban subcultures on the streets of the capital with delinquents. The urban-rural tension has played an important role in the rap scene, since provincial bureaucrats have been in charge of the AHS since 2001; this is sometimes cited as one factor behind the association's declining support for rap since 2002. At a higher level of authority, to quote the off-the-record words of a well-known intellectual, the revolution was carried out by "a bunch of resentful peasants" who had little sympathy for urban culture. The trouble with the AHS and the police are just pointers to the broader difficulties that urban culture has faced under the rural-focused revolution. La aldea is not, then, about simple praise of the rural: Los Aldeanos want village emotions but also urban freedoms. As Simmel noted, despite his generally critical view, the city is the source of new forms of individuality, and for all the scathing views of today's rappers on urban life, the emergence and survival of a youth subculture like hip hop depends on this kind of urban ethos.

"The Havana You Don't Know"

The city itself is a significant presence in rap lyrics—in some cases, the protagonist. As previously discussed, rappers share many of the state's concerns in the realms of morality and ideology, but a more oppositional aspect of their art can be found in their urban portraits, which reveal the material evidence of the widening gulf between this ideology and day-to-day experience, between glittering appearances and gritty reality, in (post–)Special Period Havana. In "La Habana que no conoces" by Papá Humbertico, the two faces of Havana are revealed through a description of Havana after midnight, "the Havana you don't know":

Here I am in the streets of Havana, can't sleep,
Going nowhere, don't want to do anything.
I watch the whores and pimps making a living,
No respect anywhere.
You can hear the cops' siren in the distance,
People running, trying to avoid the police.
The situation cools down, everything goes back to normal,
Peeping toms give free rein to their instincts,
That's how my city emerges after midnight.
This is the side of Havana you don't know, my friend,
Voices that draw you in, moments that get out of control,
Cowards who get brave after a couple of shots.
They don't forgive, those professionals of the small hours-
If you're not all there you lose, they'll do their business.
In every corner a bit of corruption,
While planning the attack, you flirt with a queer,
The driver's in league with the bag-snatcher,
The night bus is easier: it's a sitting duck,
Taxi-drivers fiddle the fare, they're making love in the security room,
Scammers dressed up as shop assistants behind the counter.
It's a big mistake to go there, some neighborhoods are no-go areas by
     night around here.
Up there at the window a four-year-old kid is lost in his sobs
While his mother sells her charms.

[Chorus]
This is my Havana, the Havana you don't know,

The Malecón at night. Photo by Alex Lloyd.

The Cuban capital after midnight.
Enjoy it if you're foreign, struggle if you're from here.
How I love my Havana, what would I do without you?

This song reveals the other face of Havana, the hidden side that the listener does not know because she or he is "asleep." It sounds a dissonant note by exposing the dark side of Havana never shown on TV or in tourist brochures. The rapper, like the Cuban tourist industry, draws on sexualized imagery, yet it is not the alluring figure of the sensual dancer or the macho drummer that is conveyed here, but rather images of prostitution, illicit sex, and perversion. The dual city of Havana is described through a markedly binarized imaginary: before midnight/after midnight; awake/asleep; pleasure/struggle; ignorance/knowledge. Papá Humbertico continues a long line of literary depictions of Havana that focus on uncovering the city, especially by night, a line that can be traced back through the novelists Cabrera Infante and Carpentier (Álvarez-Tabío Albo 2000) to the nineteenth century, when "Cuba is figured in a Manichaean visual imaginary alternating between the heterotopic nighttime of Habanero creole decadence, on the one hand, and the clear daylight of a patriotic and pastoral utopian interior, on the other" (Dopico 2002, 457).

The chorus also carries echoes of a more recent source—Grandmaster Flash and the Furious Five's "New York, New York," with its famous evocation of the insider's perspective:

You might get fooled if you come from out of town
But I'm down by law and I know my way around.

Suggesting that the true city remains invisible to outsiders and those who are "asleep," Papá Humbertico's verses may be seen as a valorization of local awareness and thus evidence of a nuanced urban perspective rather than a simple dystopian vision. In Havana, where the tourist is often treated like a king, this linking of pleasure with ignorance, and of struggle with knowledge, has particular resonance. As El Aldeano raps in "Tiranosaurio," "I know things about my Havana that not even Eusebio Leal knows," referring to the city historian and man behind the Plan Maestro: Aldo sets himself up here as a source of underground urban knowledge and an alternative authority on the city.

An implicit critique of the "tourist gaze" (Urry 1990) is also articulated in the following verse by Randee Akozta ("Los Paisanos con The Foundation Movement"):

My Havana isn't just beaches and palm trees
Like in the videos made by foreign companies,
Why is it that the truth is always hidden?
The more you ask, the fewer people reply.
Havana is the place, I keep wondering,
On every corner a committee,[20] everyone going about his own business,
Havana isn't just unusual for its scale-model-
It's also got the cheapest whores on the planet.
Here it's not just all parties like they show on TV,
Here you can see cops getting really stoned.
The truth hurts, the truth tends to
Be deeply wounding to certain people
Who think they're King Midas
But everything they touch turns to rotting garbage.
Go on! That's how we live in this city,
Tourism is for you, ours is another reality,
Go on! Here we do whatever to get by,
Huevo knows I'm not lying, everything else is just talk,[21]
Go on! How many businessmen are behind bars?
People have died when buildings have collapsed in Habana Vieja.
Havana is the ideal place for immigrants,
Most of them are from where the singers come from,[22]

"Car 8 to Car 7,"[23] sellers on the streets,
Big fish, gamblers, and even drug dealers.

Randee Akozta, like Papá Humbertico, juxtaposes the enjoyment of foreigners with the struggle of city residents. Whereas the government and tourist industry project images of beaches, palm trees, and fiestas, Los Paisanos paint a picture of prostitution, drunken policemen, rotting garbage, rising crime and immigration, and collapsing buildings. The issue of representation is itself foregrounded: the eye of the video or TV camera is aligned with the tourist gaze and contrasted with the piercing vision of the rapper, who seeks the "truth [that] is always hidden" and "another reality." Particularly notable is the reference to the *maqueta de La Habana*, a scale model of the city that is a tourist attraction in Miramar: the totalizing, dehumanizing vision and all-seeing eye of the urban planner is juxtaposed against the rapper's particularized, localized vision of the inequities of human life on the street corner. This is not just an alternative urban vision but also a critical reflection on ways of seeing and the power that they encode.

While the tourist industry prefers to focus on the restoration of Habana Vieja, Akozta alludes to the wider decline of the city's infrastructure. Indeed, it was estimated in 1997 that more than half of the city's buildings were in poor condition, while more than 5,300 collapsed between 1993 and 1996, leading Rutheiser (2000, 231–32) to claim that some sections of the city looked like wartime Beirut or Sarajevo. The trope of the ruined or collapsing city is a particularly potent one in Havana, for it is also a central focus of the tourist gaze, which tends to romanticize urban decay as an aesthetically pleasing metaphor for a vanishing yet authentic past: Havana as the city that time forgot. Akozta may be seen as contesting the meaning of ruins, as de-aestheticizing them and showing the human reality behind and within. This view of the collapsing city is a highly condensed critical reflection on both the anti-urbanism of the first three decades of the Cuban Revolution, with its neglect of the city's fabric, and the exclusive, tourism-driven urbanization of the Special Period.

Both songs, then, are exposés of the underside of city life; their creators are chroniclers of the other Havana. These artists disrupt the re-imaging of the city as an attractive tourist playground, challenging Kapcia's (2005b, 2, 213) optimistic view that "with restoration under way, Habana Vieja is a beautiful city in the re-making" and that this project is "a

A collapsing building in Habana Vieja. Photo by Alex Lloyd.

genuine moment and process of self-discovery and quiet confidence." These rappers are implicitly questioning the idea of a cultural identity for Havana based on romanticized colonial imagery and a Plan Maestro for Habana Vieja with which they do not identify and which brings them little benefit. Forman (2002, 26–27) has noted that if the city provides the frame for much black popular culture, the spatial scale in hip hop is often reduced to a more localized perspective. This focus on microlevels of space and experience makes rap a particularly useful tool for countering the homogenization of the city that occurs with tourism-oriented "imagineering" (Low 1999a, 16). Akozta's juxtaposition of the scale model of the city with its infamous prostitution is a perfect illustration of these contrasting spatial scales. Rappers' close observation of urban conditions resists the reduction of Havana to a limited set of simple, positive, easily consumed images. Their spatial critique may be seen as a form of resistance to "touristification" and creeping capitalism in Havana, and to the romanticization of place that underpins both.

A complicating factor in this analysis is that the image of Havana in ruins is one that sells globally in photographs, films, and literature. The BVSC film is set in the more crumbling parts of Havana, but it is also, in a metaphorical sense, about a search for ruins: "The 'Buena Vista Social Club' does not exist anymore, but its traces remain in the wrinkled faces and the hyperexpressive voices of half-forgotten masters" (Medina 2007, 16). The novelist Pedro Juan Gutiérrez rocketed to international fame and fortune on the back of portraits of the city, for example in *Trilogía sucia de La Habana* (Dirty Havana trilogy, 1998), that are very close to those provided by rappers. Hermanos de Causa's vision in "San Cristóbal de La Habana" of a city that "is suffering from slow erosion, with its monuments, empty or collapsing buildings, excrement, people from all over" is one familiar to many readers around the world. Although artists like Papá Humbertico and Akozta have neither courted nor achieved anything like the same level of exposure as Gutiérrez, it cannot be ignored that the other face or dirty side of Havana that they show has been thoroughly commodified, and that literary representations only feed the tourism boom that they critique (Whitfield 2008). Gutiérrez, too, promises to show the reader the unknown Havana—the "real Cuba" that many tourists seek.

Antonio José Ponte, another writer with a fixation on ruins, airs the conspiracy theory that Havana's dilapidation is in fact by government design, providing material justification for its policy toward the United States (ibid., 147). For Ponte, both the restoration and the neglect of the city's ruins are instruments of the revolution—a viewpoint that casts rappers' urban portraits in a slightly different light, since they would then be unwittingly bolstering rather than critiquing government policy. In the context of the global market for images of Havana's dilapidation and "notes from the underground," and the various interpretations of who might benefit from both ruination and its representation, rappers' portrayals of "the Havana you don't know" are not quite as straightforwardly opposed to government or tourist strategies as they might seem at first; their Havana has been sold to many real and armchair tourists. The resistance attributed to rappers is thus complicated by the unwitting overlap of their vision with an alternative tourist and literary gaze. The major difference between the urban tales of Gutiérrez and the lyrics of Havana's underground rappers is that the former are published, translated, and sold in the international marketplace and thus promote the voyeuristic, touristic watching that both critique (ibid., 125–26).

There is little danger that Los Aldeanos' "Mangos bajitos" could be accused of feeding transgressive tourist desires or promoting alternative tourism, despite its apparently seductive refrain "this is the land of easy pickings." The tourist gaze that Esther Whitfield identifies as a subplot of Gutiérrez's novels is elevated to the central theme of this song, in which the (imagined) foreign audience invoked in the introductory shout-out is invited, less than politely, to see Havana through Cuban eyes:

What does my spying eye see?
Tourists in cars and the people with broken soles and riding bikes—it makes me angry.
The fun is over, fatty, show respect, now the sun, the rum, and the *mulattas* are on the ration card.
Take off your T-shirt and your flip flops, come and walk around Havana like we do,
Wake up at five to go to work with forty cents in your pocket, so you can sweat and enjoy a Cuban sunrise,
Take my hand and see how my country is developing, stop by my house so I can cook for you,
Forget rice, black beans, tomatoes, and onion, it's rice and minced soya, classic Creole food.
The foreigners smelling dazzlingly brand-new, with their modern cameras and their huge backpacks,
Driving around Havana, spending the night in bars, paying for Cuban sex with leftovers and diseases.
They invade our city as if it were theirs, showing off their gear and their skinny white legs full of veins.
It's a shame that our tourism would be weaker without the mulattas
And that those foreigners aren't here to fish or to play jacks,
But if we respected ourselves, if we were different, they would sleep with the pigeons in the Plaza San Francisco,

But here they are treated like gods from Olympus, and not just Cuba but even hell is beautiful that way.[24]

Both the material inequalities and the psychological damage that they cause are exposed: as in Gutiérrez's novels, it is not just the marginalized local people who are left feeling demeaned but also (and intentionally) the foreign reader, listener, or tourist, and the message is driven home by the mocking intro and outro ("Where are the people from France?"), and the fact that El B raps the opening lines of this verse in a fake foreign accent. The presence of (distorting) foreign eyes and lenses in all three songs discussed here provides a self-reflexive dimension that (as in the case of Gutiérrez) undercuts any attempt to read these texts as simply fulfilling a different kind of tourist desire, the urge to consume Havana's dark side. The watcher is exposed in the act of watching, and these songs underline the fact that the dual city of Havana does not just have two realities, it is gazed upon from two different perspectives. These rappers do not simply represent the city: they also illuminate the issues of seeing ("what does my spying eye see?"), representation ("with their modern cameras"), and the mutual constitution of viewer and viewed.

In *Music and Urban Geography*, Adam Krims (2007, 12) defines the "urban ethos" as a "set of representations detailing which subjects move through the urban landscape, which parts of that landscape they traverse, and the extent to which that landscape imposes its constraints on those subjects." Rappers define the urban ethos of Havana as one of tourist freedom and no-go areas for ordinary locals (including many hotels, restaurants, nightclubs, and beaches). Urban space is fought over: "They invade our city as if it were theirs." Elsewhere in the song, Los Aldeanos invoke the city's colonial history even more explicitly:

I've lost count already, I don't know how many times
My Havana has been captured by the English.

The equation of tourism with European colonial expansion is a potent one, underlining the contests for urban space rather than the pleasures of cultural contact. A particular feature of Los Aldeanos' verse is the issue of transportation: foreigners drive or are driven, while habaneros walk, cycle, or take the bus.[25] Long, uncomfortable journeys to or from Alamar or to Papá Humbertico's studio Real 70 in the small town of Barreras are part of the lore of Havana hip hop. It is not just a question of where you can go but how (or indeed whether) you can get there.

Pace Kapcia, behind the urban renewal program—the fruits of which so many visitors to Havana enjoy—lie struggles, frustrations, and limits on access. Hermanos de Causa begin "San Cristóbal de La Habana" with the words "I walk, conscious that I don't have access to places where I'm of no value or interest," and later they allude to the effective ban on darker-skinned Cubans entering hotels:

> There's a situation with Cubans and hotels that I don't understand
> For all that the manager explains it to me.

In "Ya nos cansamos," Los Aldeanos rap:

> Many places today are closed off to me
> Since I'm poor and Cuban, I'm stuck here.

Alongside the increasing privatization of public space is the emergence of apparently calm zones where Cubans and foreigners in fact walk together at their peril. As Merrifield (2002, 13) notes, "the desperate pursuit for an improved place-image has led to a *purification* of some of the more unpalatable and problematical internal spaces of cities," and this cleansing takes the form of intensified police presence and intervention. Few foreign visitors to Havana will realize, as they stroll across the pleasant Parque Central, that this is contested terrain. However, one of my Cuban friends was questioned by police two nights running simply for chatting with me on one of its corners; another refused to cross the square with me and said "see you on the other side." In their critique of "voluntary" (i.e., obligatory) labor, Clan Completo rap:

> Grab your broom and your containers and your wash rag
> You've been allocated the Parque Central.

Their presence in the square is justified only by cleaning up after others. The video to "Es un sueño" (it's a dream) shows Aldo jumping around outside the Hotel Nacional and Papá Humbertico strolling across the Parque Central: only in their dreams do they have unfettered access to these landmarks—a standard part of the tourist experience—that remind them of the inequitable distribution of freedom across the urban landscape.

Putting the City to Music

Papá Humbertico's description of Havana after dark contrasts starkly with the portrayal of the nocturnal city in a 2006 government tourist brochure: "Party rooms, cabarets, discotheques and bars fill the tropical nights with the sound of sones, guarachas, mambos, catchy Cuban rhythms and international music." Havana is well known as a musical city, so music is central to its representation. Rappers are countering not just such glamorous images of the city's nocturnal life, but also sunnier depictions of the city in other musical genres: the representation of the city in music—even *as* music—is itself a contested field. This is one of the themes of Hermanos de Causa's song "San Cristóbal de La Habana," with its chorus:

San Cristóbal de La Habana is much more than rumba,
Much more than cathedral, rum, cigars, and partying.

In the first line of his verse, Soandres del Río claims there are "1,636 songs which talk about Havana's virtues," and he goes on to make an ironic, intertextual reference to one of them, Manolito y Su Trabuco's famous salsa song "Locos por mi Habana": "Que en La Habana hay una pila de locos y una tonga de frescos / Y cantidad de pencos disfrazados de violentos" (in Havana there are a bunch of crazies and lots of guys with no shame / and a load of cowards who act all violent). He thus invites the listener to contrast his gritty urban vision with the more playful one by Manolito and the more traditional one epitomized by rumba.

Since musical sounds and metaphors are central to the polemics about representing Havana, it is instructive to pay attention to the relationship between urban music and lyrics. Musicians working at the alternative/ fusion end of the urban-music spectrum may challenge stereotypical notions of the city in music or lyrics, but rarely in both at once. For Telmary, who raps on Síntesis' "Habana a flor de piel," Havana is "an enchanted city, a city of rhythms," described in sonic and emotional, rather than spatial, terms. For X Alfonso, in "Habana 8:00 p.m.," the capital has a natural swing. Both songs underline difference musically, with international styles like rock, funk, and electronica predominating over Cuban elements; yet in the lyrical realm, they construct softer, more "musicalized" depictions that concur with the traditional notion of Havana as a beguiling city of rhythms.[26]

In "Medio siglo después" (half a century later), the alternative/fusion rapper Kumar adopts the reverse approach, with intriguing results.[27] This song begins innocuously enough with a catchy bolero-chá instrumental, transporting the listener to the 1950s; the hip hop beat comes in later, followed by Kumar, who describes the city of that decade through the eyes of his grandfather. Although the song begins with a vision of pre-revolutionary Havana in which "the night was a fiesta," it soon goes on to allude to gambling, prostitution, drugs, and social inequalities. In the second verse, it is the grandson who speaks:

> Half a century later I'm walking
> Down the same streets that my grandfather told me about,
> Frozen in time, the big American cars keep going,
> Laden with stories, contaminating lungs.
> When the sun has had enough of frying our skin,
> Havana puts on its lipstick and spills its honey,
> And like a faithful photograph
> The same scenes are seen again.

This is, then, a critical version of nostalgia: instead of evoking the "good old days" that are long gone, Kumar suggests that that the "bad old days" of the 1950s have never gone away, and he brings the past, with all of its unresolved problems, into the present. Kumar is not at the most controversial edge of Cuban rap, and—on the surface, anyway—he draws some of the sting in his chorus:

> It's not about politics,
> It's not about the government, man.
> Human beings have always been the same,
> Now and back then.

Yet despite Kumar's protestations to the contrary, his suggestion that fifty years of revolution have changed nothing, either materially or spiritually, is a politically resonant statement in Havana. After all, what is a revolution without change? "Human beings have always been the same" may seem like an uncontroversial line, but not if one recalls that the revolution was supposed to create the hombre nuevo (new man). The listener to Kumar's song cannot help but be reminded that the social problems of the 1950s—ones that the revolution supposedly solved—

returned to haunt the city again in the 1990s, when the boom in foreign tourism at the expense of the local population brought back unpleasant memories of pre-revolutionary times (Pérez 2006, 310; Schwartz 1997, 208–9). Tracing connections between the 1950s and the present day, in both music and lyrics, is thus a subtly potent statement; Kumar evokes a face of the "repeating island" (Benítez-Rojo 1996) that many hoped had gone for good.[28]

He thus raises important questions about the popular notion of Havana as a city that time forgot. As nostalgic foreigners, with BVSC ringing in their ears, go to Havana to travel back in time, the city is reverting to conditions of inequality and social problems that pertained during the years when the oldest soneros were launching their careers, to a significant degree as a consequence of the tourism boom that facilitates those very nostalgic imaginings. The interplay and growing tension between the bolero-chá instrumental and the lyrics reveals a darker side to Havana's groovy retro feel, foregrounding the social tensions that underpin the neotraditionalism of Cuban tourism and cultural production, and countering the rose-tinted view of the past (and of its revival in the present) that played such a large part in the BVSC phenomenon. The musical background begins as a comforting index of tradition but evolves into a discomfiting reminder of the durability of Havana's problems. For all that Kumar's Havana swings, it does so to an increasingly disconcerting beat.

Underground rappers are more direct, arguing through music against existing musicalized representations of Havana. Both lyrics and instrumentals drive home the key message that "San Cristóbal de La Habana is much more than rumba." Papá Humbertico, Los Paisanos, Los Aldeanos, and Hermanos de Causa perform their underground visions of the city through music as well as words, choosing a hard, dark sound with no obvious Cuban inflections, which mirrors their uncompromising lyrics. Idealized, tourist-centered images of Havana are contested by music designed to challenge the characterization of the city in terms of the soothing, nostalgic sounds of the BVSC or the body-centered, hedonistic vibrancy of salsa or rumba. Given their opposition to tourist imagery and their mission to show the other face of the city, it is hardly surprising that their music does not, as the brochure claims, "fill the tropical nights with the sound of sones, guarachas, mambos, [and] catchy Cuban rhythms." In "San

Cristóbal de La Habana," Hermanos de Causa show keen awareness that music plays an important role in constructing urban identity, but they argue, both sonically and lyrically, that salsa and rumba misrepresent the city; only hip hop tells it like it is.[29]

From a spatial perspective, the predilection for underground sounds within Cuban rap is notable. While studies of global hip hop have tended to favor an adoption-adaptation model, musical nonadaptation can also be revealing, especially if viewed in terms of the construction of locality. To take a counterexample, the indigenized Cuban rap of Orishas' song "537 C.U.B.A." may be more appealing to general listeners, the music industry, and music critics, for the image of Havana that it encapsulates in both music and text is much closer to that of the BVSC and the tourist industry:

> Where are you, my Rampa?
> The sun that sings, the cathedral,
> The Capitol, rise up when you hear our voices,
> 23 and 12, Vedado, Paseo del Prado
> Your lions side by side
> Are part of my traditions,
> My emotions,
> You are my Cuba.

This is not hip hop cartography, but a versified cross between a Lonely Planet guidebook and the conservative nostalgia of the émigré. That it is accompanied by a lightly "urbanized" cover of "Chan Chan," one of the signature hits of the BVSC album, drives home the point that this song is not designed to overturn any urban stereotypes.

It is worth comparing the musical styles of Orishas' "537 C.U.B.A." and Papá Humbertico's "La Habana que no conoces" because there has been a marked tendency among scholars and critics to value the former style and ignore or disparage the latter. Concerns over the possible homogenizing effects of cultural globalization have led many commentators to cheer for forms of localization that involve conspicuous adaptation or indigenization, and to dismiss less distinctive musical adoptions as unimaginative or lacking in creativity (see, for example, Mitchell 2001c and 2004). Indigenization is seen as brave resistance against the oppressive forces of globalization. The problem is that, as Santiago Castro-Gómez notes, "the present global reorganization of the capitalist economy depends on the production of differences. As a result, the celebratory affirmation of these differences, far from subverting the system, could be contributing to its consolidation" (quoted in Medina 2007, 7). Adam Krims (2007) convincingly illustrates that the celebration of localism and place in the Caribbean is in fact intimately connected to the movements of global capital that it supposedly resists. In the case of Havana, this can be seen in the overlap of Orishas and the BVSC (both highly successful products of the transnational music industry) and tourist imaginaries. Orishas' "537 C.U.B.A." and the BVSC film participate in the kind of celebration of place that Krims discusses, drawing on an imagined preglobalization authenticity while thoroughly entwined in the postmodern practices of imagineering and nostalgia-driven tourism and commodification.

From this perspective, then, it is in fact the defiantly "un-Cuban" sounds of Papá Humbertico that might be seen as resistant, hesitant though I am to repeat that overused word: he is sonically rejecting a nostalgic, capitalism-driven celebration of place. Since global capital works so well with local difference—which may paradoxically be regarded as "a politics of conformity" (Wade 2004, 282)—sameness may be the only way to resist. The local, insider's view is expressed through globalized sounds, while the "distinctively Cuban" rap of Orishas (actually created in France) strikes a chord with music executives and armchair tourists around the globe. Given that Havana's local color is a global currency, it is of little use to most rappers for expressing obscured local realities. The question of whether underground Cuban rap is imitative, and whether this makes it less authentic, is thus misplaced.

If Papá Humbertico's song does not immediately transport the foreign listener straight to Habana Vieja, that is precisely the rapper's objective: the critical relationship to place is heard musically as well as lyrically. Underground sounds bear a distinctive message about place, evoking the city that the rapper—not the average tourist (or Ry Cooder)—knows, and forcing the listener to question typical associations of Havana with tradition, nostalgia, and pleasure. Krims shows music and tourism working together in Curaçao; Havana hip hop shows them in stark opposition, in both lyrics and music, even though tourism has provided economic and material support for the rap scene.

Underground rappers are revealing "human misery" on the streets of

Papá Humbertico at work in his studio, Real 70. Photo by author.

Havana, and the music that accompanies such visions is not simply derivative but rather stokes the debate over urban geography, tourism, and the
construction of place, and above all, the Buena Vista-ization of Havana.
In the film *Pa'lante*, Aldo says that contentious topics are rarely raised in
Cuba, especially in the media, "to protect the image of this so-called
paradise": rappers see their role as questioning that image. Given that
writers such as Pedro Juan Gutiérrez and Antonio José Ponte are doing
the same (to international acclaim) in the textual sphere, it may be in the
generally ignored or maligned sphere of underground beats where hip
hop's most distinctive challenge lies.[30]

"Is There Anyone in Havana Who Doesn't Dance?"

I describe the sound of these songs as "hard" and "dark" because of their
use of the sonic vocabulary of international underground rap, their lack
of obviously Cuban musical features, and the fact that they are designed
not to be dance music. At underground peñas that I attended, audiences

rarely danced to live rap, yet Cuba defines itself through dance like few other countries. John Charles Chasteen (2002, 66) observes: "A discourse making dance central to Cuban national identity reaches back into the mid-nineteenth century, well before independence. . . . A special Cuban penchant for music and dance is today widely and unreservedly affirmed by Cuban *vox populi*." Orishas draw on this to justify their catchy rhythms in "Represent," where they ask: "Is there anyone in Havana who doesn't dance?" The answer lies on their doorstep, in the hip hop scene from which they emerged.

It is worth underlining that it takes a lot to stop Cubans from dancing at live music events, and that many of those who endorse the antidancing rhetoric of underground hip hop are good dancers of other styles, such as rumba and salsa. Indeed, audiences and some artists themselves dance enthusiastically to the recorded U.S. hip hop played after the live section at rap concerts and peñas. A nondancing audience at a live music event thus sends out a clear signal. Underground rappers, like nueva trovadores before them, challenge this hallowed link between music and dance to appropriate music as a political space in a politically closed society. An antidancing rhetoric is regularly expressed in recordings and interviews by underground artists, in which dance music is seen as inhibiting a genuine challenge to the status quo because of its focus on pleasure and the body rather than on the mind. Most underground rap in Havana is deliberately designed to force listeners away from stereotypical bodily reactions and into an intellectual mode of reception. This disruption of common corporeal responses correlates to the disruption of habitual mental patterns: it is a physical stimulus to wake up to the disjunctions between appearances and reality described in lyrics—"stop moving your ass and your mind will follow," one might say.

It is partly through musical sounds that underground rappers challenge images of their nation as a tropical paradise and place of carefree pleasure, and the social critiques in rap lyrics are endorsed through audience performance which reinforces the idea of a genre centered on a serious message rather than sensual pleasure. In other words, not dancing is politically significant: it provides affirmation for the performers as they seek to reshape the national imaginary. If dance clubs may be considered as ritualized spaces (Washburne 2008, 148), not dancing in places where dance would be considered a normal response may also be consid-

ered a form of ritual; and indeed, there are characteristic physical responses at live rap events, most typically a one-arm wave above shoulder
height or a raised fist. By rejecting dance and adopting other forms of
physical response, the audience becomes involved in the performance
and creates a communication or feedback loop with the performers, one
in which the disruption of standard modes of physical pleasure is central.

In the context of live underground rap performances, I would argue,
dancing is associated with the "city of illusion," whereas not dancing
embodies the views of urban society and culture expressed through rappers' lyrics and music. Both production and reception at live rap events
reveal a marked element of delocalization or denationalization; music
and movement constitute performances of allegiance to música americana and the Hip Hop Nation alongside nonconformity with dominant
conceptions of Cuban culture and society. The nonlocalization of most
Havana hip hop is not, then, something to be overlooked: the deliberate
avoidance of "catchy Cuban rhythms" is designed both to redefine urban
space and to alter ways of inhabiting it.

In her study of music in Cali, Colombia, Lise Waxer (2002, 261) describes salsa as a cultural practice "through which Caleños [residents of
Cali] have made explicit their own sense of being together. . . . [S]alsa has
served as the sonic cue for the participatory framework of the rumba that
is the hub of Caleño collectivity, suturing the wounds of daily struggles
and banishing the shadows of urban violence. Through dancing, listening, and performance, Caleños have forged activities that get them in
sync and that reinforce and indeed structure the deeper synchrony of
social life itself." The content and two-part structure of Cuban rap concerts—not dancing to live Cuban rap, followed by dancing to recorded
foreign music—suggest a rather different dynamic. Both the lack of audience movement and the lyrical topics during the live part suggest that
underground rappers are pulling apart the appearance of Cuban collectivity, exposing wounds and shadows rather than healing or banishing
them. It is a deliberate breaking away from the traditional synchronicity
of Cuban social activity centered on dancing. But in the second part of
the concert (and in house parties afterward), when recorded U.S. rap is
played, by dancing a nonnative style to foreign music, Cubans reformu-
late the social bonds in a new way, countering the widening fissures of
local society with a close-knit subculture and affective links to an imag-

ined global hip hop community, the Hip Hop Nation. The not-dancing-then-dancing dynamic combines resistance to local dance-music cultures with a connection to a global one. Cuban rappers and audiences deconstruct dominant discourses of collectivity and then, by embodying a kind of imaginative transformation (Wade 2000) through dancing to U.S. hip hop, they enact a new urban narrative while simultaneously and symbolically taking their place in a wider world that most of them have never seen.

Conclusions

Hip hop is distinguished from other forms of popular culture by its spatial practices and narratives. It emerged in the South Bronx in the 1970s in part as a reaction to the deterioration of the urban residential infrastructure, which contrasted with the concentration of funds in business and tourist districts. Hip hop thus has its roots in the context of major urban change and is the music of urban inequality and sociospatial polarization par excellence. Rap has connotations that are lacking in other adopted musics in Cuba, such as rock; it is not simply music of youthful protest, for it carries historical echoes of dissent against the unevenness of urban development. It is thus an ideal lens through which to observe the emergence of a dual city. The adoption of hip hop is highly suggestive in a rapidly changing urban environment like Havana since the early 1990s, which has seen a rising differentiation of the cityscape under the influence of booming tourism and foreign investment, leading to an increasing segregation of urban space. This is particularly contentious in socialist Cuba, for the core ideology of equality has been undermined in a public, concrete, and visible manner. Rappers have reacted by shining a harsh light on the racialization of urban space and on the spatialized discrimination evident in de facto no-go areas and police harassment of Cubans in tourist districts. With its history of analyzing the articulation between race and space, rap has been a particularly sharp tool for documenting these new spatial conditions, just as it has been for examining the shifting sociospatial inequalities resulting from deindustrialization, urban decay, and postindustrial urban renewal in the United States. Merrifield (2002, 14) insists that "truth claims about cities must be conceived from the bottom upward, must be located and grounded in the street." Hip hop engenders precisely this bottom-up, from-the-street view of the city.

Many studies of global rap have focused on the use of the genre to open up debate on ethnic or racial issues, yet it would appear that rap's association with the exposing of spatial inequalities has been retained in some of its major global manifestations. If U.S. rap is a new lexicon and medium through which young people may describe the spaces and places of urban landscapes (Forman 2002, 343), it appears to have been readily translatable, above all to contexts which have seen significant urban changes. It may be no coincidence that some of the cities which have generated the most vibrant rap scenes outside the United States—such as Paris, São Paulo, and Havana—are also places in which discourses about polarized urban spaces (banlieue, periferia, or dollar zones) have loomed large in popular imaginaries.

Hip hop may be seen as a form of critique of urban development: urban culture does not necessarily reflect changes in urban space, it may also produce critical urban discourses that represent, analyze, and imagine alternatives to spatial restructuring (R. Bennett 2003). In hip hop, this deconstructive reading of urban space is both enacted and written: hip hoppers reconfigure spaces as well as producing critical urban discourses, and the two often overlap, for example in impromptu freestyles. Hip hop provides frameworks and practices which allow marginalized youth to impose meaning on the urban environment and to challenge dominant discourses of the city. Hip hop thus exemplifies Merrifield's (2002) "dialectical urbanism," as practitioners respond critically to urbanization through their words, musical choices, and actions. The tension between urban policies and experiences that Merrifield describes provides the raw material for many rap songs; hip hop may thus be seen as the result of a dynamic, productive relationship between the city and its residents.

Crucially, however, hip hop does not just form one half of a dialectic with urbanization; it also incorporates an array of dialectics within itself, something often overlooked by scholars of "global noise." As Whitfield (2008) details, the dollar looms large over urban life and cultural production in Special Period Havana, and hip hop has been both a way for young people marginalized by the dollarization of Havana to vent their frustrations and a means for them, as the U.S. expression goes, "to make a dollar out of fifteen cents." Havana rappers have excoriated tourism in lyrics and musical style, yet, particularly during the boom years, they depended to a significant degree on tourist dollars and donations. The fixity of hip hop's explicit morality is counterbalanced by the fluidity of its social and economic improvisation. Hip hop symbolizes the modern and the urban, yet it has a critical relationship to modern urban realities, as revealed by Los Aldeanos' echoing of Georg Simmel and their veneration of Che and Camilo Cienfuegos, two long-dead leaders of Cuba's antiurban revolution. Havana's underground rappers foreground a love-hate relationship with the city, embracing hard-edged urban sounds, language, clothing, and practices while critiquing urban values and the urban environment.

The dialectical nature of both urbanism and hip hop points up the latter's urban quality and suggests that the tensions at the heart of urban music, reflecting the contradictions of city life, are a vital part of its makeup. Merrifield claims that the dialectic between urbanization and urbanism needs to be harnessed, not resolved, and the same is arguably true for hip hop: rather than viewing the improvised side of hip hop—its street flow—as something that needs cleaning up (often discursively, through its omission from written accounts), we might instead understand the tensions within hip hop as productive, and attempts to resolve them as potentially weakening this cultural form. Through its struggle with the contradictions of urban life, and its logocentrism and improvisational aspect, hip hop is tied in with the creation of a vibrant, if limited, public realm.

The consideration of music and urban place in this chapter has revealed that globalization and its most visible face in Havana, tourism, are complex topics when seen through the lens of underground hip hop. While the adoption of foreign sounds with minimal adaptation might be viewed as evidence of the power of globalization to homogenize culture, it might also be seen as resistance to the nostalgic celebration of place and local difference that is a hallmark of globalization. Tourism has been strongly critiqued in underground rap, yet it has provided an economic lifeline to the hip hop scene. Socioeconomic improvisation and the rejection of musical indigenization are topics that observers of Cuban hip hop have preferred to sweep under the carpet, with the result that the picture is often either one-dimensional (portraying Cuban rap simply as a fusion with local traditions) or two-dimensional (the polarization of hustling versus moralism, commercial versus underground). Such dichotomies have tremendous popular (and academic) currency and must therefore be taken seriously, but in reality, the elements of Havana hip hop are bound together in more dialectical, less adversarial relationships. Too much global hip hop research, by adopting rather than analyzing such binary frameworks, simply repeats at greater length what hip hoppers say in condensed form. If ethnographic research is to bring anything to the table, it is surely to probe beneath the surface of popular constructions and uncover the complexity beneath.[31]

Under the influence of globalization and tourism since the mid-1990s, Havana has shown increasing parallels with other "postmodern cities" (Low 1999a, 16). Although postmodern cities are normally associated with late capitalism, Low's emphasis on imagineering and the repackaging of cities as commodities has many resonances with late socialist Havana; the marketing of the Cuban capital has, I have argued, created a distinctively postmodern "city of illusion." Cuban hip hop, too, has been characterized as postmodern for its capacity to undermine modernist constructions of the nation (M. Perry 2004, 74). Maxwell (2003, 122–24), however, has noted the conservatism of hip hop and suggests that its central discourses of community, nation, culture, truth, and representation are evidence of an Enlightenment worldview and thus the opposite of a postmodern sensibility. Other writers have remarked upon the conservatism underlying the progressive stances of conscious rap groups in the United States (e.g., Baldwin 2004; Boyd 2004). The work of Cuban underground rappers supports such viewpoints and suggests that hip hop in Havana is a decidedly modernist cultural project: a self-defined movement, with a strong sense of history and a fixation with ideas of truth and falsehood, which is mistrustful of surface appearances and rejects the postmodern play of consumable images characteristic of sociocapitalist Havana, seeking instead to represent the "reality" behind media illusions and asking: "Why is it that the truth is always hidden?"

4

CUBAN HIP HOP ALL STARS

Transnationalism and the Politics

of Representation

My Havana isn't just beaches and palm trees
Like in the videos made by foreign companies.
—RANDEE AKOZTA, "Los Paisanos con The Foundation Movement"

They want to be rappers when there's a festival with foreigners.
—SILVITO "EL LIBRE" RODRÍGUEZ, "La etiK"

The location for the meeting was ideal: the Casa de la Amistad (house of friendship), a grand old building in leafy Vedado. There were two delegations present on this steamy evening in early July 2008. The Cubans hosting the meeting were representatives of the Cuban Rap Agency and the hip hop collective La FabriK; their guests were members of the Pastors for Peace Caravan to Cuba, a group that had traveled from the United States and Canada bringing medical supplies and moral support, defying the U.S. blockade and ban on travel to Cuba. The caravan included hip hop

artists who arrived with a bus and musical equipment for the rap agency,
and plans to perform with local rappers as part of a project called the Hip
Hop without Borders Exchange.

The meeting began with informal presentations by the Cuban hip hoppers. Some discussed the social issues that they tackled in their lyrics and
community work, such as racism and sexism. Two independent artists
spoke of the material difficulties of creating hip hop in Cuba and the
struggles to gain institutional support, and in response La FabriK talked
about their strategies for approaching Cuban state organizations. After a
while, Lucius Walker, the founder of Pastors for Peace, stood up in the
audience. To the considerable surprise of those present at this fraternal
meeting, he was unhappy: he protested that all he had been hearing were
complaints about social and material problems in Cuba. Why were they
not focusing on anticonsumerism, antimaterialism, antiglobalization?
Why had they not even mentioned the "genius of the revolution" or the
positive things that made Cuba unique? They wanted equipment, they
wanted money, but they had said nothing about defending the Cuban
Revolution—an "unparalleled gift to world."

The Cuban hip hoppers were visibly shocked: they were used to being
showered with praise by North American visitors as paragons of "real hip
hop." On the defensive, they drew attention to the international respect
for Cuban hip hop and its positive effects as a role model. Another member of the caravan stepped up: the Cubans needed to look critically at
their society, he said, but also to be aware of how it is seen from outside
and how certain words or deeds may be interpreted abroad. Walker con-
curred. He argued that the hip hoppers' claim to have put the topic of
racism on the table in Cuba was both erroneous (because it had long been
a matter of concern for the state) and irresponsible (because it paralleled
the strategy of the U.S. State Department, which makes strenuous efforts
to play up social problems in Cuba in order to disparage the island internationally). As the debate continued, it became clear that there were
more ways in which Cubans and North Americans were talking at cross-
purposes. For the North Americans, the music industry was the root of
hip hop's problems and greater independence was the way forward. Yet
the Cuban hip hoppers, long hampered by a lack of resources, had expressed the need for more institutional support. The North Americans
saw Cuban hip hop as a beacon of hope and brotherhood; the independent Cuban rappers revealed the frustration and lack of unity in the

scene. The evening ended on a tense note, and the local rappers left looking grim.

When the groups reconvened at the same venue five days later for the final concert, it seemed as though bridges had been mended. If there was something strange in the air this time, it was due more to the layout of the space with tables and chairs and the rather sparse attendance. Since the event was by invitation only, it felt more like an exclusive cabaret than an underground hip hop concert. On the Cuban side, the attendees were primarily rap agency members and minor officials, supplemented by a few handpicked members of the scene. A number of local hip hoppers were denied entrance—this was an event primarily for foreign consumption. The performance consisted of three short sets by the ACR groups Anónimo Consejo, Doble Filo, and Obsesion, who struggled valiantly with the somewhat lukewarm atmosphere. The Pastors for Peace hip hoppers came on next—unlike the Cubans, they used a live backing band—and after performing a few numbers, they called out to the Cuban rappers to join them for a freestyle. The event started to liven up as Cubans and North Americans flocked to the stage. One of the latter led chants against the U.S. government and its blockade of Cuba. Then the two rappers of Juventud Reverde grabbed the microphones and launched into a routine which sounded suspiciously rehearsed and distinctly confrontational. Magia López, the director of the ACR, quickly seized the microphones and declared the freestyle, and the show, over. Once again, things had ended on a slightly sour note.

The event had ended early, and it was the peña of Los Aldeanos around the corner at Atelier that night, so a few of us wandered down there. Papá Humbertico shook his head at the recent events: he was not impressed by foreigners who lecture Cubans about the revolution, often on the basis of what they have read in books or seen on red-carpet tours. He dismissed the performance we had just witnessed as a "show": for him, Atelier was the main event of the night. We paid the doorman and entered the dark, smoky club for a dose of "real hip hop."

The drama was not yet over, however. It turned out that Anónimo Consejo, who had opened the exchange concert, had sung a track that had not pleased López, the organizer of the event (and, as part of Obsesion, a fellow rapper), and three days later she called Anónimo Consejo to a meeting and reprimanded them. The Casa de la Amistad was not the place

Juventud Reverde seize the microphones at the July 2008 Hip Hop without Borders Exchange concert at the Casa de la Amistad. Photo by author.

to sing those lyrics, she said; this was not an ordinary peña but an event for the Pastors for Peace. They had potentially damaged relations between the ACR and the Cuban Institute for Friendship between Peoples, with which the hip hop exchange had been negotiated over many months. Anónimo Consejo were concerned that they might be expelled from the agency, but their sanction consisted "only" in having their ICM engagements for August canceled.

Hip hop in Havana has transnational origins, of course, but one of the most distinctive features of the Havana scene, in comparison with other regions of the Hip Hop Nation, is the degree to which this transnational dimension has persisted: performances to foreigners, for foreigners, or by foreigners have marked key moments in the development of Cuban hip hop. As Havana became a spiritual home for political hip hoppers from around the world, the scene's boom years were distinctively international in flavor.

The two events involving the Pastors for Peace illustrate the benefits and challenges of the transnational connections and visions that have underpinned the scene since the late 1990s. The exchange brought material benefits to the ACR, and despite the tensions, it fostered potentially productive cross-cultural relationships. But leading Cuban hip hoppers also came face to face with the complexities of representing their scene in a transnational context. At the first meeting, they gave an honest, uncensored view of their situation and were harshly criticized by a distinguished foreign guest; López's censoriousness after the concert was surely at least partly a reaction to the difficult meeting five days earlier, in which Cuban hip hop had been publicly tarred as excessively critical. One of the issues that came out at the meeting was that the Cubans did not feel it necessary to foreground the revolution, precisely because it was such a fundamental part of their way of thinking. The hyper-revolutionary discourse that Walker was demanding would not have gone down well with the majority of local hip hoppers, who walk a finer line between broad support for the aims of the revolution and their belief in hip hop as a culture of resistance. This was a lesson—far from the first—that representing their work to foreigners required a different strategy.

Walker's criticism reminded me of a conversation I had had a few months earlier with Gustavo Borges, the director of the Venezuelan organization Hip Hop Revolución (discussed below) and the organizer of an annual hip hop summit in Caracas. He had begun inviting Cuban artists to the summit several years earlier but had stopped because he found their discourse, particularly that of Randee Akozta, too critical for a pro-revolutionary event. Akozta's line plays well with local audiences in Havana but less so with idealistic supporters of the Cuban Revolution overseas.

The world's eyes are on Havana—a "symbolic capital" (Quiroga 2005, 3) for leftists, progressives, and revolutionaries around the world, and especially for Latin Americans and African Americans. The issues of seeing and being seen, representing and being represented, are thus central. Rappers must look inward to construct a vision of their society, yet also outward to consider how this vision will be perceived overseas. The importance of presenting a good face to the world was the underlying message of the two Casa de la Amistad events. "Representing," that core hip hop term, is thus complicated in Havana by its transnational dimension; if scholars are to analyze it rather than simply repeat it, we need to ask questions such as who is doing the representing, to whom, and why. Being represented (visually or verbally) is equally fraught with problems, though considerably harder to control. Foreign fascination with Cuban hip hop has produced a mountain of representations, the vast majority of them destined for overseas consumption, and these representations have had an impact on the Havana scene.

Misunderstandings and mistranslations have been an inevitable consequence of this transnationalism—the tense debates in the House of Friendship symbolize the two sides of the coin. For all the excitement around the Black August exchanges, there were also problems. Black Star's performance at the 1998 festival saw most of the audience get up and leave; the hard core of local hip hoppers was impressed by these U.S. legends, but the general public did not get the lyrics. Sujatha Fernandes (2006, 91) writes that "African American rappers such as Paris, Common Sense, Mos Def and Talib Kweli spoke a language of black militancy that was appealing to young Cubans," an interesting turn of phrase given that they literally spoke a language that young Cubans could not understand. Tanya Saunders (2008, 266) draws on Fernandes to claim that "from its beginnings in Cuba, Cubans were listening primarily to socially conscious, and socially critical hip-hop." This contention is highly debatable, given that commercial and danceable forms of rap were not just popular but necessary for the break dancers who dominated the early days of the Havana scene, and that for much of the 1990s, U.S. gangsta rappers were widely viewed as models and favorites (e.g., Pacini Hernandez and Garofalo 1999–2000, 29–30). Even if this were true, it would raise serious questions about what Cuban hip hop fans took from such music sung in English. There is a certain irony in the fact that Havana hip hoppers later adopted message rap from New York without, in many cases, understanding the message. My experience was that most hip hop fans' tastes were catholic—those who claimed to be underground often cited mainstream U.S. hip hop and R&B artists as their idols—and their grasp of lyrics was limited at best. Both were illustrated one evening at an underground peña where the DJ put on the Ludacris track "Move Bitch," with the chorus "Move bitch, get out the way / Get out the way, bitch, get out the

way." Three young women—two of them outspokenly feminist performers from the underground scene—were dancing close by, chanting the
chorus enthusiastically. They looked quite shocked when I told them
what they were singing.

In 2000, Black August handed out fliers with information and lyrics in
Spanish (M. Perry 2004, 210–11), though one wonders how many of the
audience digested this information in the festive atmosphere and the
dark. Visual codes thus took on great importance; Cuban rappers often
mention that U.S. artists made a big impact on them, but mainly through
skin color, clothes, attitude, and energy. Alexánder Guerra of Familia's
Cuba Represent told me that he chose his favorite rappers by studying
their physiognomy on album covers, while Pacini Hernandez and Garofalo (1999–2000, 29) report moñeros' attraction to U.S. rappers' "pos-
ture of assertiveness." In the film *Cuban HipHop: Desde el Principio*, Roberto Rossell and Alexey Rodríguez describe the positive effect that seeing
dead prez live had on them but admit they did not understand anything
the Americans said. There is plenty of evidence, then, that the message of
message rap was the first element to get lost in translation. Yet even
visual codes are not necessarily transparent: Yrak Saenz told me that in
the late 1990s, many Cubans followed U.S. hip hop fashions (bandannas,
gang signs and colors, rolling up one pants leg) without understanding
what they meant. Despite all the contact, exchanges, and goodwill, U.S.
hip hop is thus not always readily comprehensible to Cubans. There is a
revealing scene in the documentary *La FabriK* in which the Cuban hip hop
delegation to the United States meets the legendary Afrika Bambaataa:
despite their high expectations, they look bemused as he launches into a
monologue about Mars and Venus and the supreme creator (the director
even puts a couple of question marks on the screen to underline the
point). In a subsequent scene, there are notable misunderstandings between the Cuban rappers and The Roots about how to organize their joint
performance. Alan West-Durán (2004) uses this concert as an example of
"diasporic dialogue": as the film reveals, turning this metaphorical dialogue into real communication was not always easy.

In the previous chapter, I discussed freestyling in terms of individual
liberation and group solidarity; at the Casa de la Amistad, its performative instability emerged, challenging attempts to control the event. The
fleeting moment when Juventud Reverde seized the microphones was

pregnant with politics that went far beyond the rappers' words. It unveiled the performance as stage-managed for an invited audience, with the desire to project the right image to the foreign visitors more important than "representing" a democratic community. In this moment, the freestyle placed the question of freedom center stage, and López's reaction revealed the hidden constraints; it was the North Americans who invoked the freestyle, blissfully unaware of the delicate political balancing act that their hosts were performing and the double-edged sword that improvisation could be in such a situation.

The aborted freestyle, along with the subsequent sanction of Anónimo Consejo, brings us to questions of freedom of speech, constraint, and censorship, and their relationship to transnational scrutiny; it also provides a window onto the way that responsibility for representing (and therefore controlling heterodox representations of) the rap scene has been passed to leading rappers, above all those running the rap agency. One of the evening's ironies was that Los Aldeanos performed later on, just a few blocks away, free to vent their much more controversial lyrics with no consequences, since there was no official North American delegation present. The difficulties that Anónimo Consejo faced recall the sanctions taken against Papá Humbertico after the 2002 festival, and in both cases it was the presence of foreign observers (however well intentioned) that catalyzed official reactions. The foreign gaze is, in some ways, complicit with censorship, and it may stand as a proxy for the scrutiny of the state.

The ACR, now with a rapper as its director, is responsible for representing the rap scene, and since this means presenting a good face to the world, it leads to segregation and sanctions. Many non-ACR hip hoppers do not feel represented by the agency, regarding it as an exclusionary organization serving mainly as a shop window; the Pastors for Peace event seemed to confirm their view that the agency's face is turned primarily to foreign visitors rather than to the local hip hop scene. That the donations brought by the Pastors for Peace were destined for the ACR did not help matters. Juventud Reverde, a controversial duo, had not been invited to the concert, but they decided to protest by gate-crashing the show and seizing the microphones. Hovering over their guerrilla action was the question of (in)visibility, above all to foreign eyes, and contests over the self-representation of the hip hop scene. Not for the first time,

Raúl of Juventud Reverde. Photo by Oscar Castillo.

the sincere efforts of foreign visitors to support the Havana hip hop scene ended in transnational and local discords, as disputes erupted over how to represent the scene, to whom, and to what ends.[1]

The Transnationalization of the Havana Hip Hop Scene

Much writing about global hip hop has focused on local uses of globalized cultural tools, but what is distinctive about the Cuban context is the personal involvement of foreigners, particularly North Americans. Ian Condry (2001, 222) writes of the arrival of hip hop in Japan as "a flying spark that traveled from the Bronx across the ocean to light a fire. This image of a flying spark is important, for it reminds us that although popular music styles travel on the winds of global capitalism, they ultimately burn or die out on local fuel." Though there was plenty of fuel in Cuba, it was not just the spark of rap that flew from New York to Havana but a host of rappers, journalists, activists, political sympathizers, academics, and documentary makers who came in its wake to fan the flames with political inspiration and material support, and to document the results.

While isolated foreign visitors to Havana undoubtedly encountered the nascent hip hop scene during its earliest years, there was little for them to notice. It was focused primarily on dancing to African American music (la moña) and thus of little interest to outsiders. The French producer and DJ Manu Cartano told me that when he first went to Cuba in 1994, he came across dance events but few rappers. However, the summer hip hop festivals beginning in 1995 provided a focal point for local hip hop practitioners and a window onto the emerging scene for outsiders. Several figures who were to play key roles in the development of the Havana scene, all of them from New York, converged at the 1997 festival: Nehanda Abiodun, an American political activist who was living in exile in Havana; Clyde Valentin, the senior editor at *Stress* magazine; the legendary hip hop pioneer Fab 5 Freddy; and the actor and activist Danny Hoch. Struck by the intelligence and social commitment of the lyrics, they began to swap notes. The group soon expanded to include another Havana-based U.S. exile, Assata Shakur (Tupac Shakur's aunt and godmother); the activist and journalist Kofi Taha; and Lumumba Bandele of the New York–based Malcolm X Grassroots Movement. In 1998 the Black August Hip Hop Collective was born, its name paying homage to an activist tradition begun in the 1970s in the California prison system and spread by members of the New Afrikan Independence Movement. The frame for transnational hip hop exchange between New York and Havana was thus provided by the radical black U.S. politics of the 1960s and 1970s. A fundraising concert was organized in New York, and in the summer of 1998 the first U.S. delegation arrived in Cuba, bearing musical equipment, political attitude, and leading conscious hip hoppers.

The Black August Hip Hop Collective sent delegations to Havana over three successive summers and provided a major stimulus to the local scene during some of its most vibrant years. Havana's hip hoppers were able to see live performances by, and in some cases meet, leading figures from the U.S. conscious hip hop world: Black Star (Mos Def and Talib Kweli) in 1998, Common in 1999, and dead prez in 2000. At the time when Orishas were bursting onto the global scene, singing about rum, cigars, and mulattas to the sounds of a son–hip hop hybrid, the U.S. artists provided Havana hip hoppers with an alternative model: harder, more Americanized beats, and a more politicized, racialized worldview. The timing was crucial.

Meanwhile, Havana's resident American political activist, Nehanda

Abiodun, found herself drawn into a year-round commitment to the rap scene. According to Abiodun, an American student who was a regular at moña events got fed up with local fans asking her about Malcolm X and said: "Why are you asking me when you've got the Malcolm X expert here in Havana?" Abiodun agreed to a meeting with half a dozen local hip hoppers, and one gathering led to another. Soon she had thirty or forty young people from Cuba, the United States, Latin America, and Europe visiting her house for weekly meetings to talk about political issues and local realities. Like Pablo Herrera, a Cuban who spent time in the United States and could easily pass as Bronx-born, she used her command of both English and Spanish and her knowledge of New York and Havana to help overcome the hurdles of translating U.S. message rap into a non-English-speaking context. The intellectual sphere that developed in conjunction with the local hip hop scene thus had at its center an African American figure of authority, who catalyzed a shift toward regular critical discussion and provided a living link to, and insights about, the black American history, culture, and radicalism that underlie the political branch of hip hop.

One of the distinguishing features of the Black August period was the way that foreign visitors did not just take their favorable opinions back home with them but also transformed them into words and actions which had a significant impact on the Havana scene. At the heart of their efforts was their conviction that Cuban hip hop embodied the genre's original spirit, now seriously diminished back in the United States. Fab 5 Freddy said of his visit in 1997: "It reminded me of the spirit of hip-hop here in the early days when it was really raw, in the parks, with guys literally hooking up to the light posts for electricity" (Smith n.d.). Mos Def recalls his impressions of Alamar: "There was this theater in the projects. It reminded me of the theater you see in *Wild Style* when they perform at the end" (*East of Havana* n.d., 4). Like so many visitors to Havana, they felt they had traveled back in time, though to a very specific time and place: the Boogie Down Bronx. Several of the Black August delegates were journalists and writers, and when Danny Hoch, Kofi Taha, Cristina Verán, and Raquel Z. Rivera published articles back in the United States and Puerto Rico, launching a wave of journalistic interest in Havana hip hop, the old-school talk gained momentum. Brett Sokol (2000), echoing Hoch (1999), wrote of rap in Havana: "it was hard not to be reminded of the beginnings of American hip-hop. Not unlike the American groups that gave birth to rap in the South Bronx in the late 70's and early 80's."

These positive foreign perceptions of Cuba as retaining a link to the original spirit of hip hop fed back into the Havana scene, legitimating local artists, boosting their self-confidence, and shaping discourses around their music. The Black August delegations led to a boom in negritude and revolutionary rhetoric, and they had a particular impact on key intermediaries such as Pablo Herrera and Ariel Fernández, who helped to translate (both literally and metaphorically) the concerns of the New York–based activists to the local scene. Herrera began not just to produce music for many of the leading Havana rap groups but also to mentor them, channeling Black August philosophies into local rap production. The interest in the Havana scene on the part of foreign journalists was not matched by the local press, however, and thus its discursive construction flowed largely from foreign pens during these crucial years.

Black August's influence was multilayered. It provided U.S. models for the local scene and a vision of Cuban hip hop as überauthentic which began to take root in the self-representations of local intermediaries and artists; and the evidence of international admiration seems to have helped to cement state institutions' acceptance of hip hop. Cuban elites have a history of accepting their country's popular music only after approval from abroad (R. Moore 1997, 104–5; 2003, 21). International interest in Cuban rap increased further with the worldwide success of Orishas' first album, released in 1999, and the world's press started attending the annual rap festival in increasing numbers. The culmination of this transnational intervention was undoubtedly the visit of Harry Belafonte to Havana in December 1999. As described earlier, Belafonte took his positive vision of hip hop from a meeting with local representatives to an epic eleven-hour "lunch" with Fidel Castro. Leading rappers are unanimous that Belafonte opened official eyes to their culture and helped to give legitimacy to the Havana scene.

José Quiroga (2005, 11–12) writes of Havana in the 1960s as "a player on the world stage, a beacon of solidarity for liberation struggles throughout the Third World, a model for a new Latin American culture": writers, painters, and filmmakers traveled to Havana "to escape capitalism and get a dose of what the world could look like." If those days seemed long gone as the Special Period dawned, just a few years later the hip hop festival began to attract idealistic, revolutionary artists and activists from overseas, and it is surely not coincidental that there was a major boost in state funding for the festival in 1999 (Hoch 1999), once local officials had seen the first

Black August delegation in action the previous year and the international interest it had generated. Havana was becoming a beacon again, this time for the revolutionary wing of the Hip Hop Nation, and state officials sat up and took notice.

Although the rapid expansion and internationalization of the hip hop festival around the turn of the new millennium was driven primarily by Havana- and New York–based nongovernmental organizations, it gained the financial and ideological backing of government institutions. Black August's activities were a gift for the Cuban government, which has long wanted to avoid the issue of race domestically but at the same time uses it as a stick with which to beat the United States: these activists focused their critiques on U.S. racism and capitalism and saw local hip hoppers as allies in this struggle. One interpretation of the Havana hip hop festival's rapid development from a marginal event to a state-supported international showcase is that it served Cuban officials for the hip hop scene to "externalize," as Mark Sawyer (2006, 62) puts it—shifting the focus of attention from domestic to international (primarily U.S.) problems, and giving a platform to hip hop's internationalist anti-imperialism and anti-capitalism. Conscious American artists could be relied on to express solidarity with Cuba—which was much safer than a purely inward-looking local scene. The Roots criticized the American government and the materialism of American society in their Cuban press conference, and they referred to a crisis in U.S. hip hop as a result of excessive commercialism, all topics that were eagerly digested in Havana ("The Roots en Cuba" n.d.).

The nationalization of hip hop in Cuba and the emergence of the Havana hip hop scene as a distinct, localized phenomenon were thus underpinned by extensive, hands-on North American intervention. The apparent paradox that hip hop was officially nationalized in Cuba at the same time that it was Americanized via Black August is less contradictory if we remember that this Americanization, which drew on the historically close relationship between the Cuban Revolution and black American radicals, consolidated a shift from dance music to message rap. Key Cuban intermediaries had their consciousness raised by Black August; U.S. intervention thus boosted the convergence between hip hop thought and national ideology that led to a flowering of state involvement.

North American involvement in the Havana hip hop scene of the late 1990s was both practical and discursive, and these two dimensions were

intimately linked. The journalists and activists connected to Black August
created and disseminated the nostalgic image of Havana as the new South
Bronx and the conceptualization of local hip hop as a black movement,
and these perceptions had a major influence on leaders of the scene and
on the next wave of written accounts, some produced by these same
leaders and others by foreign and local intellectuals. The rest of this
chapter will be devoted to analyzing the dominant ways of understanding, constructing, and representing Havana hip hop (in print, recordings,
and films) and to the sentiments and ideologies that underlie them,
always keeping in mind the constant circulation of these visions and their
incorporation back into the self-perceptions and self-presentation of Cuban hip hoppers, which blurs the line between representation and reality.

Constructing the Movement:
Nostalgia and Cuban Hip Hop

The street jams back in the day were real street jams, no one had anything,
You went there in what you were wearing and that was it,
And if there was money then great, if not it didn't matter,
The girls back in the day liked you for who you were,
And it didn't matter if your clothes were better or worse,
The love of music was everything.
—ALEXEY RODRÍGUEZ, "Como fue"

At El Proyecto, a Cuban hip hop event organized by Tanya Saunders at
Lehigh University in April 2008, Ariel Fernández stated that Cuban hip
hop was influenced by sociopolitical movements in the United States
such as the Black Panthers. He went on to say, though, that hip hop was
never a movement in Cuba itself. Instead, it had been "marketed" as a
movement by idealistic, nostalgic outsiders who thought it would change
the world. The foreign media—like CNN, the *Washington Post*, and the
New York Times—sold the idea of Cuban hip hop as a Black Panther–like
movement, but it wasn't: "People never understood what was happening
with us." They failed to see the contradictions, the disunity: "People
thought we were the Che Guevaras and Fidel Castros of global hip hop,
but we weren't. . . . This is the truth: we were young, black people trying
to do something positive with our lives, trying to occupy our time, because we didn't have to pay bills in Cuba." Joshua Bee Alafia, the director

of the documentary *Cuban Hip Hop All Stars*, stood up. Cuban hip hop *was* a movement, he insisted, since it was a unified group of artists who articulated similar themes and critiques.

This exchange, between an "insider" who claimed the "movement" was a romanticized creation of outsiders and an "outsider" who riposted that it *did* exist, illustrated the extent to which the ideologies and the very language used to construct the Havana hip hop scene derived from the late 1990s exchanges between New York and Havana, which in turn harked back to U.S. musical and political mobilizations of the 1960s and 1970s. While the argument remained unresolved, it is clear that the idea of Cuban hip hop as a movement was consolidated at a time when North Americans became involved in Havana, that it evokes the U.S. civil rights era, and that it is a contested term. There are certainly skeptical voices in Havana: Papá Humbertico dedicated an entire song, "El movimiento," to the topic, and his view can be summed up in the line: "You are you, I am me, we're not us." In "Algunos consejos," he states: "The stuff about 'the movement' is made up, unity is made up / Fists in the air is hypocrisy, friendship is a means to an end." Soandres del Río told me: "People have always talked about the movement, about unity, but it has never existed." It was a utopian vision that was never realized and a word that he avoided: "I never wanted to be part of a lie." It was certainly fashionable, but "if you want to see a real movement, you should see a foreigner come here with a suitcase full of T-shirts. See what happens to the movement." In his jaundiced view, foreigners both created and undermined the idea of "the movement." When I met Fernández in Havana in 2004, he told me that the title of *Movimiento*, the Cuban hip hop magazine of which he was editor, was intended to encourage the consolidation of a hip hop movement rather than describe the existence of one. In his eyes, the movement was a project rather than a reality. While there are also plenty of proponents (in both Havana and New York) of the movement discourse, two clear issues emerge: first, there are disjunctures between the language used to frame Havana hip hop and the experiences of some of those who have been framed; and second, language and representation are more than just a sideshow, since much of the interest and energy generated by Cuban hip hop derive from its symbolism, particularly to non-Cubans, which in turn rests on its linguistic construction as more than just a group of young people rapping to pass the time.

In 2009, a year after his diatribe over the word "movement," Fernández was still offering a public lecture that "examines the place of the rap cubano movement within the landscape of Cuban national culture and heritage, and its similarities to other Hip-Hop movements throughout the African Diaspora," and another that described rap cubano as "one of the most powerful black social-cultural movements ever born in the island."[2] This illustrates the extent to which the currency of the Cuban hip hop "brand" in North American academic and activist circles depends on the perpetuation (rather than critical analysis) of key linguistic tropes. Despite his skeptical view of foreigners who idolized Cuban hip hop, Fernández offers to explain that "while Hip-Hop may be dead in mainstream America, it remains a dynamic force in Latin America and Latino communities in the U.S." He has to walk a thin line: his cultural and economic capital depends on selling to eager U.S. audiences ideas about which he is privately skeptical. In a further twist, Pablo Herrera told me that Fernández, while still living in Havana and working in the media, had "pushed the button on the race issue by pursuing the word *movimiento* as the motto signature of Cuban hip hop culture." It is an ideologically loaded word that is pregnant with historical and political connotations; its unproblematized adoption in the Cuban hip hop literature obscures a host of controversial issues and thus deserves to be questioned.

Underlying the media tropes of Havana as the new South Bronx and the hip hop scene as a Black Panther–like movement lay a good dose of nostalgia for the interweaving of music, politics, and race in the United States of earlier decades. The tropes of nostalgia and blackness also came together in academic responses to the Havana hip hop scene, which played their part in constructing this transnational discursive sphere along lines derived from 1960s U.S. cultural and identity politics. Fernandes (2006, 4) writes that her book captures the views of ordinary Cubans and "records the poignant voices of these Cubans, desperate to hold on to meaningful and deeply held values from the past." There is no mention in her book, however, of timba or reggaetón, the two dominant musical styles in Havana of recent years. Certainly, some Cubans are nostalgic for the past, but timba in the 1990s encapsulated an urge for change, and the reggaetón generation is anything but nostalgic: both genres are fully engaged with the globalization, materialism, and hedonism that were resisted for so long in Cuba. The viewpoint of Fernandes's book is more representative of nostalgic currents in hip hop activism and North American scholarship, and in foreign views of Cuba more generally, than of Cuban youth culture of the new millennium. These currents can also be felt in the work of Marc Perry (2004, 13), who reveals that "Cuba's position as a one of the last remaining bastions of popular revolutionary promise coupled with its long-standing resistance to western capitalist hegemony continues to evoke a considerable level of political resonance for me."

In a penetrating article, Alberto Medina (2007, 15) describes Havana as "a space of nostalgic recovery," and his particular insight is to identify this space as one constructed and shared by academics as well as tourists and artists (including the BVSC director Wim Wenders). The urge for the "restoration of the real" in third-world Havana derives from a sense of lack or loss in the first world. Havana provides a stage where the other becomes a locus of nostalgia and "the monument can come back to life. Both the intellectual and the consumer turn a loss in the space of the self into a recovery and a hope in the space of the other" (ibid., 9). In the case of Havana hip hop, academic and journalistic responses have echoed those of activists and fans in reacting to first-world individualization and the splintering of the racial struggle since the 1960s by identifying Havana hip hop as a "movement" or "community" focused on black struggle. Much of the foreign engagement with the scene, including that of scholars, may be understood as "exercises in the restoration of the real" of the kind that Medina identifies, a reality or truth that lies in the past (in the U.S. black radicalism of the 1960s or New York hip hop of the 1970s) but, it is hoped, may live again in the present (in Havana). Randee Akozta's line "enough already . . . with your 'Cuban rap has found what was lost in New York'" ("Basta ya") underlines that the trope of loss and recovery was a common one among visitors to the Havana scene, and it echoes Medina's (2007, 11) remark: "The space of the other is the space of survival for something that the self has lost. It gives us the promise of a recovery."

Cuban hip hop has appealed to North American–based academics and activists as a space not just of "escape from the American self" (Brennan 2008, 12) but also of recovery of the self. The resulting representations have been shaped by utopian desires and the placing of "hope in the space of the other," leading Roberto Zurbano to talk of intellectual mythification and Ariel Fernández to claim that "the view that the world has of Cuban hip hop is a wrong view." At the heart of both Rivera's individual and collective redemption (as discussed in the introduction) and Medina's space of recovery lies the double-edged sword of myth-making and nostalgia, which may be productive in artistic and activist spheres but may also, when they determine representations of those spheres—above all scholarly ones—prove more problematic. Havana hip hop is an extremely well-documented topic, both in print and on film, but its representations need to be approached with a degree of caution. While most are underpinned by progressive aims, these representations tell us as much about nostalgia and race consciousness in U.S. activism and academia as they do about Havana hip hop.

The dominant perspectives of Cuban hip hop scholars are rooted in the Black August exchanges, organized by a collective with its roots in late 1990s New York nostalgia and named after a tradition begun in the 1970s. According to Rivera, the late 1990s witnessed a re-legitimation of Latinos in the United States as core participants in hip hop: "By 1998, not only had they been accepted and legitimized within hip hop, but Latino images and artists had become somewhat of a fad" (2003, 116). Simultaneously, there was a "rediscovery and romanticization of 'old-school' hip hop. The latter half of the 1990s saw a renewed interest in early hip hop as a site of authenticity" (ibid., 115). This celebration of *latinidad* and old-school hip hop in New York at the end of the decade sets the scene for the Black August Hip Hop Collective, created in 1998—the very year that, according to Rivera, latinidad peaked in U.S. hip hop. The "Cubaphilia" that Clyde Valentin describes in the film *Cuban HipHop: Desde el Principio*—generated by articles in U.S. hip hop magazines from June 1997 onward—was stoked by a more widespread Latinophilia.

Davarian Baldwin discusses the old-school element in more detail, describing the emergence of a "third position" in the late 1990s as an alternative to conscious and gangsta/ghettocentric rap. Articulated by KRS-One, this third position "is rooted in nostalgia, not for Africa's golden era, but for a hip hop golden age. In the midst of hip hop's international growth and change, this 'reaching back' for better times attempts to figure out 'what went wrong, and why did hip hop become the revolution that failed?'" (2004, 160). Baldwin identifies "a decline-and-fall narrative that understands hip hop to be over-commodified and calls for a return to the roots of street parties and the 'yes yes y'all' freestyle rhyme, which exemplifies a pre-commodified, undiluted era" (ibid., 161–62). This narrative is exemplified by KRS-One's 1997 hit, "Rapture," the video of which invokes the South Bronx of the early 1980s, "performing a corrective memory of the old-school concert as a utopic space" (ibid., 162).[3] According to Baldwin, New York hip hop in the late 1990s was seen as in need of correction, and New York purists were trying to redefine "real hip hop."

The context for the discovery of Cuban hip hop by foreigners in 1997 was thus one in which the New York scene was celebrating latinidad and the old school and searching for roots, for a lost golden age, perhaps for a revolution that had not failed. At this precise time, influential figures from New York found in Havana a Spanish-language hip hop scene, steeped in revolution and symbols of the past, which reminded them of hip hop's early days in the South Bronx, and subsequent developments in and representations of Havana may be seen as rooted in this New York–centered ideology. New York nostalgic purism was played out in Havana, with the disillusionment with U.S. rap transmuting into the glorification of the Cuban version. Medina's (2007, 17) observation that, in Havana, "the other is conceived as a supplement that provides what is missing in the self, a passion made possible, in the third world, by closeness to the real, and denied to the first world by the omnipresence of simulation and privatization" sheds light on the transnational construction of the Havana scene as "real hip hop" and on the strong emotions that it aroused in visitors from the first world. The search for the real in and through Havana hip hop may be read as a microcosm of the twentieth century "passion for the Real" (Slavoj Žižek, quoted in ibid., 15), and Medina's observation that Fredric Jameson sees in Havana "the possibility of recovering a certain proximity to the real" (ibid., 16) is equally relevant to many who were drawn to experience, film, or write about the city's hip hop scene.

Havana provided the perfect conditions for a hip hop renaissance, its socialist context the ideal foil for the hyperconsumerism of U.S. rap that so disillusioned purist New Yorkers. As Pablo Herrera told me, "I kind of have the feeling now that we were fulfilling a paradigm of what certain people in the U.S. wanted to achieve through hip hop in the United States, and that had a projection in Cuba." If the Havana scene was constructed discursively as the idealized Other of New York hip hop, its development amply illustrates Ana María Dopico's (2002, 452) description of Havana as "the projection screen for Western fantasies."[4]

At the crux of this U.S.-Cuba relationship, then, lies a multilayered nostalgia, for New York hip hop heads' reminiscences of the Boogie Down Bronx overlapped with the globalized nostalgia for Cuba and its music generated by the late-1990s BVSC project, which itself fed into the booming, retro-focused tourist industry in Havana, all of which was analyzed through a nostalgic first-world academic lens. As Quiroga underlines, nostalgia and romanticization inform most foreign approaches to Cuba: it is an island "where the capitalist and the consumer are offered a kind of unspoiled site where there is no capitalism. It brings up a kind of self-hatred of capitalism—hence its allure—as if the hunger for that which is not 'ours' were also manifested in the displeasure with what actually belongs to 'us'" (2005, xvi–xvii). Specifically, it is a place to flee from the commercialized culture of U.S. music, the object of the kind of displeasure Quiroga mentions. Where Cuban exiles see loss, foreign musicians and activists find fulfillment. In Cuba, Ry Cooder felt that he had recovered "artistry and music that is nothing to do with money. It is not a money-based, power-based culture. . . . What can you look at that isn't saturated with commerce?" (quoted in Bromley 2001, 107–8). Similarly, and also in the late 1990s, Fab 5 Freddy stated: "Art's a lot purer across the board there, in terms of goals and aspirations. Here, we get caught up in how many records we can sell" (quoted in Smith n.d.).[5] The idea that Cuban music embodies values of the past that have been lost in the United States underlies the appeal of BVSC and Havana hip hop; much of the discourse around Cuban music revolves around its meaning to outsiders and its position as the first world's Other. The Havana hip hop scene and the BVSC project both fed off a first-world search for lost purity and authenticity in the music of other times and places.

Cuba had something that North Americans wanted, spiritually rather than materially. As a result, the balance between center and periphery was substantially altered. In most manifestations of global hip hop, the economic and cultural might of the United States ensures a more or less one-way flow (Mitchell 2001c, 2), but Cuba is one of the few countries that has been taken seriously in North American hip hop and has had a demonstrable influence, specifically on conscious or underground rap.

Havana, as much as New York, is invoked in one way or another as the source—a thread that runs through the interviews in the book that accompanies the *East of Havana* film. Mos Def reveals: "I cried like a baby when I went there too. East Havana and everybody was so happy. You know these people are good people. . . . You know you're not going to see a McDonald's in Cuba. There's something very pure and comforting in that" (*East of Havana* n.d., 4). He claims that his visit to Cuba "was one of the highlights of my artistic career. It was also one of the highlights of my life as a traveler." It is not just the impact but the idealism that are striking: Havana is evoked as the United States' noncapitalist, nonmaterialist Other, a counterweight to the cultural imperialism symbolized by McDonald's. The dead prez rapper M1 made an even more dramatic statement about his Black August trip in *Cuban HipHop: Desde el Principio*: "I arrived in Cuba and that's when my life changed."

Another theme of the *East of Havana* interviews is that of Cuban rap as teacher as well as pupil. For Marinieves Alba, Cuban hip hop is a kind of beacon: "Hip hop heads from all corners of the earth look to Cuba for a trace of sonic light: hip hop without the industry-imposed packaging. The raw shit" (ibid., 202). Abiodun discusses the historical relationship between Cuban and U.S. music: "I think it's important that U.S. rappers come here, because they can learn a great deal. They can almost take a step into the past in terms of renewing their commitment to what rap really is. Or what it was, I should say. You know, about being a voice of protest" (ibid., 184). She argues that Cuban rap is not a peripheral reflection but a center of authenticity. American rappers are seen as taking a step into their own past: instead of a dichotomy of center and periphery, there is actually one of present and past, with Cuba's location in relation to the United States seen as temporal more than spatial. Cuba is perceived to be at an earlier stage in history than America: the clock stopped in Cuba in 1959, so those in the United States who were depressed at the trajectory from Malcolm X to 50 Cent could turn back the clock by going to Cuba.

Nostalgia is a common response to Cuba and its music, and it is particularly concentrated in the case of hip hop. "Hip hop is incredibly nostalgic music," writes Imani Perry (2004, 54–55), and this is particularly true of the militant, problack rap of the late 1980s, which, as Jeff Chang (2005, 269) underlines, was backward-looking from the start. The

godfathers of political rap, Public Enemy, were nostalgic black revolutionaries, hence the attraction of Cuba—a revolutionary "time warp" and
"racial paradise"—to their successors is multiply obvious. This nostalgia
is not only a response to commercialism but also a product of "the post-
civil rights and black power movement generation, trying to find symbol-
isms from those eras that can translate to more elusive contemporary
struggles by romanticizing an epoch of political movement and social
defiance" (I. Perry 2004, 55). Perry's comments find considerable resonance in foreign-produced representations of Havana hip hop, both verbal and visual, which have generally borrowed from the politicized discourses of an earlier era. This has been encouraged by important figures
including Nehanda Abiodun, Assata Shakur, and Lucius Walker, representatives of an older generation of African American radicals that, historically, has perceived the Cuban Revolution as an ideal toward which North
Americans should strive. Abiodun, for example, has said that she has
supported the revolution since 1960, when she was ten years old and
Castro met Malcolm X; she expresses a continued belief in and willingness to engage with the Cuban state.[6] The positive view of Cuba of such
figures, and their attachment to the revolutionary struggles of earlier
decades, has informed the New York–Havana hip hop link that was established in the late 1990s. Nostalgia thus provided an important spur to the
transnational activism of these years and also to the documentation of
this period in print.

Nostalgia is not the preserve of North Americans, of course: hip hop's
nostalgic streak manifests itself in Cuba too. The Havana scene has been
viewed from within as well as without through a nostalgic lens. Alexey
Rodríguez's "Como fue," a rose-tinted look back at Havana hip hop in the
1980s, quickly became one of the canonic songs of Cuban hip hop, regularly sung in front of North American audiences who thought that
even Obsesion's more forward-looking work was a throwback to hip hop's
early days. Kokino (Anónimo Consejo) commented on the tentative re-
appearance of the other elements of hip hop around 2000: "It was time to
recover the atmosphere of the '80s in Cuba. That thing of dancers and
lots of DJs putting on music in their houses" (quoted in Fernández n.d.,
10). The lyrics to "Como fue" and Kokino's remark both appear in the
first edition of *Movimiento*, alongside an article on KRS-One, launching
Cuba's brand-new hip hop magazine with a backward-looking flourish.

Since 2005, harking back to the glory days of the Havana hip hop festival has been a favored activity among older members of the scene. More broadly, a lot of underground rap production in Havana can be seen as resisting the socioeconomic changes of the Special Period and recalling the days before sociocapitalism dismantled Havana's value systems. There have certainly been local stimuli for local nostalgia, then, but the framing of Alexey and Kokino's reflections (and particularly the quotation from "Rapper's Delight" in the former's song) suggests that they had also learned a thing or two from the North American visitors about harking back to the old school.

A Black Space? Race and Cuban Hip Hop Studies

The Parque de los Policías—
A battle!
We went down there, the whole group,
And made a circle, all of us, white, brown, black
—ALEXEY RODRÍGUEZ, "Como fue"

One principal characteristic of the Black August project was nostalgia; another was its emphasis on race.[7] The group's very name encouraged local hip hoppers to focus on blackness, and as it was backed up visually, this was the part of the visiting American rappers' discourse that translated most readily across linguistic boundaries. Academics subsequently picked up the baton: the three scholars who have written most extensively on Cuban hip hop to date all place race at the center of their vision, with Sujatha Fernandes (2006; Fernandes and Stanyek 2007) focusing on the Cuban leadership's "fear of a black nation" and hip hop's "black public sphere," Alan West-Durán (2004) on "Cuba's redefinition of blackness," and Marc Perry on "revolutionizing blackness."[8] While race is undeniably an important lens through which to view Cuban hip hop, I believe that the theorization of the issue of blackness merits revision and some new questions need to be asked.

To begin with, the issue of race needs to be historicized. Hip hop has been present in Havana since the early 1980s. In the first years, it was primarily a racially mixed dance culture, as Alexey Rodríguez records in "Como fue"; hip hop was all about movement, not "the Movement." In the 1990s, the Special Period was particularly hard on the Afro-Cuban population, and many of those who took up rap were darker skinned. To what extent they considered themselves "black" before the appearance of Black August and its dichotomized view of race is harder to determine, since almost all academic research postdates the first Black August visit in 1998. Only Deborah Pacini Hernandez and Reebee Garofalo took soundings before 1998, and as we shall see below, their conclusions imply a shift in thinking on race in the late 1990s, one that subsequent studies have overlooked, making the projection back in time of views prevalent around 2000 rather problematic.

Furthermore, in Cuba, "black" is a term generally reserved for people with very dark skin, supplemented by a smaller number of people of color who identify themselves as "black" as a political statement. The Cuban categorization of skin color, according to which many different skin tones have their own descriptor, is much more complex than the North American view. *Negro* is just one of seven words commonly used to describe different shades of dark skin. According to the 2002 census, only 11 percent of the Cuban population described themselves as black; but if the U.S. definition were used, the number might be five times greater ("A Barrier for Cuba's Blacks" 2007). In other words, someone who understands race in North American terms is much more likely to see blackness than a Cuban, something that Marc Perry (2004, 152) acknowledges in referring to his "North American-attuned, black-seeking eye." The application of U.S. race models to Cuba is therefore a theoretical minefield, and the term "black" needs to be handled with great care.

Although there were also prominent light-skinned rappers such as Athanai, SBS, and two members of Primera Base, a nascent sense of blackness in the emerging rap scene of the mid-1990s was magnified by the involvement of Black August, which introduced a more Americanized conception of race from 1998 onward. Most listeners could not understand what the visiting U.S. artists were saying, but they could see dead prez and grasp their chant of "I'm a African," and the more committed could turn to the translations and explanations of English-speaking intermediaries like Pablo Herrera and Nehanda Abiodun. In the late 1990s, as Cuban rap became more aesthetically and politically radical, discourses of blackness came to play an increasingly prominent role, audiences became darker skinned, and the racially mixed break dancers faded from view. The years 1998 to 2002 were key from the point of view of the racial politics of Cuban hip hop, and they are the years on which most scholars have focused, but Cuban hip hop did not start or end there. Rebeld' Malcoms—who was a break dancer in the 1980s and then a founding member of Obsesion, Justicia, and Onda Livre, and who is today a leading hip hop producer—reminisced with me about the early days: "Many people think that at that time it was black people's music but everyone was dancing break dance—whites, *chinos*, blacks, *jabaos*—everyone was there and everyone went to the parties. . . . It was never a black movement or anything like that. . . . There wasn't that division, that whole 'this is for blacks, this is for whites,' no, no, no."[9] He gave a list of prominent white break dancers and went on: "The audience that went to those places, it was a diverse audience as well. . . . But then there was a moment when you looked around and the audience was almost all black . . . around 2000." Malcoms's comments underline both the differences over time and the tendency to obscure them.

The most detailed treatment of the question of race in Cuban hip hop is Marc Perry's doctoral thesis, which creates an overarching race-based narrative of the scene. He identifies his contribution in terms of illuminating the issue of blackness, "which all too often is either downplayed or whose complexities have been largely obscured by previous treatments" (M. Perry 2004, 146). His argument rests on the claim that the early hip hop scene was "almost exclusively black" (157), and he singles out as an example of "black space" the Parque de los Policías. Yet the break-dance battles there, as described by Rebeld' Malcoms and by Alexey Rodríguez in the lyrics of "Como fue," were racially mixed. Rodríguez is a leading figure of problack ideology within the Havana scene; if even he describes the break dancers as "white, brown, [and] black," then there would appear to be little basis for Perry's claim. From this debatable starting point, Perry goes on to state that "active engagement with U.S. rap music by way of radio and other resources like records, cassettes and videotapes signified, I maintain, a form of racial politic; one that involved significant levels of racial identification and racial self-meaning making" (ibid.). This argument appears to be based on the opinion of Ariel Fernández, certainly a figure of authority; however, in the remarks that Perry quotes, Fernández says nothing to support this view of the early scene. When I asked him about this, he told me: "This hip hop movement didn't start really conscious to be a black movement or to be a social movement, we were just trying to kill time." Black consciousness took some years to develop, he said, starting to emerge around the mid-1990s, and "even for myself, it took me a long time to really understand what was going on." It is reasonable to suggest that exposure to hip hop led a number of young people connected to the scene, like Fernández, to identify themselves as black—though much more research would be required to verify this as a broad social phenomenon—but this occurred primarily in the later 1990s, above all as a result of Black August. Perry's attempt to frame the history of Cuban hip hop in terms of race thus elides crucial historical differences and contradicts the testimony of Rodríguez and Fernández, two of his key informants; its apparently diachronic perspective is only a synchronic perspective (and a race agenda) projected back into the past, obscuring the key issue of the gradual racialization of Havana hip hop during the 1990s.

Two of those guilty of downplaying the question of blackness, in Perry's eyes, are Deborah Pacini Hernandez and Reebee Garofalo. Yet the title of their article indicates their interest in race, and they repeatedly discuss this topic, though in terms quite different to Perry's: on the basis of conversations with hip hoppers in the late 1990s, they describe rap in Havana as a "youth thing" rather than a "black thing" (Pacini Hernandez and Garofalo 1999–2000, 22) and as multiracial (ibid., 27). They add that "the moñeros with whom we spoke did not feel they were more subject to these [social] problems than other ordinary Cubans, and certainly not because of their race" (ibid., 31) and that "raps about racism were likely to be denunciations of the evils of racism in general rather than pointed critiques of its presence in contemporary Cuban society" (ibid., 35). While Perry (2004, 147) claims that this article "falls short in grasping the extent and political significance of race and racial identity in the making of Cuban hip hop," it would seem that it was actually hip hoppers themselves who were downplaying the race angle—which is rather more interesting and begs the question why. The difference between the two visions may rather reflect just how quickly perceptions of race were changing at the time in the hip hop scene. Pacini Hernandez and Garofalo carried out their research from 1997 to 1999, while Perry conducted his from 1999 to 2003. To my mind, the discrepancies between these studies support the notion, expressed to me by many hip hoppers, that the Black August exchanges, starting in 1998, were a turning point in understandings and articulations of race. The Cuban consciousness of race that Pacini Hernandez and Garofalo describe was losing ground to more Americanized views at the end of the decade, but its observance by two experienced researchers should perhaps not be dismissed as mere shortsightedness. Indeed, Pacini Hernandez and Garofalo (1999–2000, 37) appear remarkably prescient, predicting that as "Cuban rap finds a voice on the international stage, it is inevitable that Cuban conceptions of identity and racial unity will be put to the test."

If one flaw in Perry's argument derives from his failure to grasp that hip hop was racialized in phases, another is spelt out at the start of his study: his decision to focus exclusively on informants who identified themselves as black (M. Perry 2004, 9).[10] In essence, he first reached his conclusion—that blackness is key—and then chose informants who would bolster that view. His project was "unapologetically political; one directed towards advancing transnational kinds of critical black dialogue" (ibid.) and thus concerned as much with changing Havana hip hop as describing it. Scholarly discussions of Cuban hip hop tend to depend on the same small number of problack "usual suspects" such as Pablo Herrera, Ariel Fernández, Obsesion, and Anónimo Consejo. This is not to dismiss or disparage their views in any way, since they have been key figures in the scene, but rather to open up the idea that their accounts of Havana hip hop are based on their own Afro-centric ideological positions, and that they did not speak for everyone on the question of race. Because of Perry's unapologetically political stance, we do not hear the voices of Havana hip hoppers who did not identify themselves as black or who did not embrace (or even actively rejected) problack political stances, and the possibility that race was contested terrain is thus elided. Alexánder Guerra, a brown-skinned rapper who had been part of Familia's Cuba Represent, told me: "The rap movement in Cuba wasn't a movement of black people, because there were white rappers, jabaos, blacks, mulattos—everyone rapped, and you saw white kids rapping in the street." While Guerra dismissed the racialization of hip hop in the 1990s, Malcoms, who is also brown-skinned, took a stronger line in our conversation: "There was a very strong strand [of negritude] here and I was one of the first to criticize it . . . that racism, because for me that's racism. It's one thing if someone gives you trouble, but there's no reason to go dividing things like that, you can't go around saying 'this is music for blacks' when you've got fans who aren't black . . . [laughs] you can't say that. But yes, there

Alexánder Guerra. Photo by Alex Lloyd.

were people who were into that . . . lots who said 'black people, we're black,' and they went out with white girls . . . [laughs] so I don't know how far they really believed all that . . . for me, they were just another bunch of racists."

This raises the question of how the undoubted racialization of Havana hip hop in the late 1990s was perceived by hip hoppers. Both Malcoms's and Guerra's use of language was revealing: after many years at the heart of the hip hop scene, and a decade after Black August, both used the word "black" in its restricted Cuban sense (i.e., someone with very dark skin). They had not imbibed the Americanized view of race, so to describe the Havana scene as a "black space" was, in their eyes, simply incorrect. Malcoms saw negritude as marginalizing not just white but also brown Cubans. Some mixed-race hip hoppers adopted U.S.-style views and proclaimed themselves "black," but others maintained the centuries-old Spanish classification system used in Cuban society at large, with its array of terms for people of color: the pro-black strand was prominent, but not universally accepted. Given that Malcoms was an early member of Obsesion, a group that went on to become the embodiment of Afro-centrism, his views may be indicative of the unevenness of the supposed revolution in racial identity. He is brown-skinned and outspokenly antiracist, yet his and Guerra's rejection of the idea of hip hop as a race-based movement reveals that blackness was not redefined in a consistent manner even within the relatively tight circles of hip hop, much less in wider society. Osmell Francis, the director of Cubanos en la Red and another brown-skinned rapper, claims: "When I joined the ACR I did songs that weren't about black people or the police, that wasn't my reality, I didn't have those problems; so I wasn't well regarded by people within the Movement" (quoted in Castillo Martiatu n.d.b, 19). Like Malcoms, Francis alludes to a more discriminatory aspect of the growing racialization of the scene around 2000, and scholars have played their part by glossing over artists like these who did not embrace the hegemony of blackness.[11]

The difficulties in writing about race and the Havana hip hop scene were brought home to me in conversations with Pablo Herrera and Rebeld' Malcoms. Intriguingly, both brought up the topic of early U.S. hip hop films such as *Breakin'* and *Beat Street*, but to make diametrically opposed points. Herrera, who is a proponent of the "black space" viewpoint, told me that the films were about black people, whereas Malcoms claimed that many of the protagonists were white or mixed race as he described the early Havana scene in similar terms. If these two reliable figures of authority can disagree over something apparently so simple, determining the racial realities of 1980s Havana hip hop in retrospect is a difficult task. Nevertheless, it may be significant that Herrera has spent time in the United States and thus uses the word "black" in a much more Americanized way than Malcoms does. What is clear is that different ideological starting points produce contradictory visions and that if we also bear in mind the testimony of early participants, both black and brown, there is good reason at least to question the idea of the first phase of Havana hip hop as a "black space," with the exclusivity that it implies in a Cuban context.

The academic focus on blackness appears to be prescription as much as description, reflecting a desire to "advance black dialogue" rather than to analyze the (inconsistent) attitudes toward race within the Havana hip hop scene.[12] Marc Perry (2004, 291–92) describes his unsuccessful attempts to engage Susana García, the former director of the ACR, on the question of race, and concludes that "her avoidance and then fairly unsophisticated negotiations around the racial question was telling." Telling of what, though? That she and Perry did not see race in the same way?

That Cubans and Americans are drawing on quite different traditions of thinking about race? Perry's labeling of García's views on race as "unsophisticated" is perhaps more telling: García is not only black, but she had previously worked on questions of race in Cuban literature, so she was hardly a newcomer to the issue. Perry records García as saying that all Cubans are racially mixed (and therefore talking about race is difficult), and that while most rappers are darker skinned, some are lighter skinned; since both points are reasonable and widely heard, it seems that García's lack of sophistication was simply not to share Perry's view. Joaquín Borges-Triana (2009, 123), a leading authority on Cuban popular music, criticizes a certain tendency within hip hop to copy North American ideas on race, suggesting that García is not alone among Cuban intellectuals in defending the local particularity of race. Perry's response—echoing early anthropologists' attitudes about supposedly primitive beliefs—shows the challenges of trying to study a cause and advance it at the same time, particularly in an alien culture in which advancing may require riding over divergent local opinions.

If there was a crescendo of negritude during the 1990s that peaked in the early 2000s, the seven years of my research (2003–10) were marked by a slow but steady erosion of the primacy of blackness: certainly, there are groups who have maintained this line up to the time of writing (such as Anónimo Consejo and Obsesion), but others have de-emphasized racial discourses as they have focused more on commercial viability. Race may be a process, a question of identification rather than identity—as Perry (2004, 141) notes—but in that case it is a two-way street: individuals can become racially demobilized as well. Furthermore, the Afrocentric groups that scholars have highlighted have declined in importance in the Havana scene in comparison with the early 2000s: Anónimo Consejo and Obsesion have performed more regularly in the provinces than in the capital in recent years, while others (Instinto, Los Paisanos, Explosión Suprema, Hermanos de Causa, Cuarto Imagen, Reyes de la Calle, Las Krudas, Alto Voltaje, Papo Record, and many more) have left the country or disbanded. However, the biggest phenomenon has been the emergence of a new school of hip hop in their place, epitomized by La Comisión Depuradora, the large collective that dominated the Havana scene in 2007–8, and Los Aldeanos, the leaders of the Comisión and the current brand leaders of Cuban rap.

Los Aldeanos, Aldo (El Aldeano) and Bián (El B), might be regarded as light-skinned persons of color in the United States, but they are not considered black in Cuba. Their audience is increasingly heterogeneous, and—in contrast to the late 1990s—a significant proportion is light skinned. Finally, and unsurprisingly, race plays little part in their lyrics. Lest this seem to be too great a focus on one group, it should be underlined that Los Aldeanos were playing an increasingly large role in defining the hip hop scene by 2008. They ran two of the three weekly peñas in Havana; they were easily the biggest audience draw among rap groups; and they created new music at many times the rate of any other group (some fifteen demos in five years), ensuring that they were the most listened-to and talked-about rappers in the city.

Furthermore, Los Aldeanos were the heartbeat of La Comisión Depuradora, the large collective that was the most significant development in the Havana scene during my research years. Since it includes other light-skinned rappers, such as Silvito "El Libre," El Discípulo, Maikel Extremo, El Enano, and El Loko, this new school is more racially heterogeneous than the old. More of the rappers articulate a kind of cultural marginality (based on musical tastes, hairstyles, and tattoos) rather than racial marginality: Zurbano's comparison of the new school of hip hop to punk in the film *Revolution* is illuminating, not least because of its racial implication. Although there are earlier examples of rappers who collaborated with rock musicians, the formation of La Comisión Depuradora coincided with the forging of new musical and social connections between different underground scenes. Mala Bizta Sochal Klu is evidence of this kind of link: a musician who emerged from the rock scene yet cites rappers like Los Aldeanos and Papá Humbertico as key influences. The collaboration between Aldo and controversial rockers Porno Para Ricardo on "A mí no me gusta la política" is another example. La Comisión Depuradora is closely associated with the underground dance-music collective Matraka, which organizes the Puños Arriba hip hop awards and the Rotilla Festival, an annual three-day event devoted primarily to electronic dance music and hip hop. These developments have had a significant impact on the racial composition of the Havana hip hop scene, since the rock and electronic dance-music scenes are predominantly white. Several white DJs— such as Rasiel, Edgaro, Dark, Wichy, and Vans—move easily between hip hop and dance music. Hip hop peñas now attract more white youths, students, and fans of alternative culture who are not necessarily die-hard hip hop heads. Doble Filo, one of Havana's longest established and currently most active rap groups, now includes two white electronica DJs (Edgaro and Dark), collaborates with the white rock band Qva Libre, and increasingly targets an alternative-music audience.

The shift from an exclusive, race-based scene around 2000 to a more open one drawing on a shared, colorblind, underground sensibility is exemplified by the increased mixing of hip hoppers with alternative-music fans and artists on a small strip of grass in the middle of the broad G Street in Vedado, known as Parque G. Artists and young people of all stripes head in their hundreds to the park late at night for hours of drinking and talking, creating a socially mixed environment in which underground or alternative—rather than a particular musical style—is the tie that binds. Parque G began attracting more hip hoppers in 2007–8, particularly after peñas at nearby Vedado clubs like Karachi and Atelier, illustrating how hip hop's geographical shifts have had significant effects on the scene's social contours. Most notably, the growing prominence of Parque G in the hip hop scene reflects changing racial dynamics since, as Matthew J. Reilly (2009, 2) notes in a detailed study, the young people who frequent the park are overwhelmingly white or light skinned. The common description of the Parque G scene as *miqui* (a term used for the fashion-conscious children of families with money or influence, usually white, often fans of electronic music) is also revealing, suggesting how far hip hop has shifted since its Alamar heyday.

Parque G's atmosphere and ideology can be detected in recent rap lyrics. El Aldeano's "Friki incomprendido" shows a sympathy for the urban tribe known as *frikis*. In "Que sería," El Enano (a white rapper who emerged from the underground rock scene) begins: "Parque G brings them together, makes them a strange race which doesn't work on Mondays, the dark side of the moon"; El Aldeano goes on to say that his allegiance is "to the poor, the people, rappers, rockers, long-hairs, dreads." Papá Humbertico ("Pluma y micrófono") displays the ambivalence of a rapper who sits between Havana hip hop's old and new schools: "Down with the miqui, down with the slave to cash / Down with the numbskull and up with the rebelliousness of the friki."

A decade after Black August, Havana hip hop had become more insulated from transnational currents of race politics and was shifting toward a more heterogeneous scene, connected to the broader, whiter, local underground. In this sense, hip hop has been undergoing a process of localization on a social level as it has moved away from Cubanization on a musical level. Most of the new school are less interested in transnational political or racial alliances than in connecting with other local underground music scenes. This shift has been fed in part by the splintering of the hip hop scene with the creation of the ACR; many of today's new-school amateur rappers display more ties to the Parque G, rock, and electronic dance-music scenes than to the old-school, professional rappers of the Black August years.

Some older participants (such as Soandres del Río and Escuadrón Patriota) embrace strong problack positions, but others are lighter skinned, and while they sympathize with Afro-centrism, they do not "represent" it. Papá Humbertico, one of Havana's most respected rappers, has only one black pride song in the four demo CDs that he gave me between 2004 and 2008: "Tu propia lucha" (your own struggle) encourages Afro-Cubans to be proud of their heritage, yet, significantly, it is written in the second person. He criticizes racism and supports the struggle of black people, but he does not articulate it as his own, even though he would be identified as a person of color in the United States. He is also skeptical of public declarations of black pride within the rap scene, for example in his song "El Movimiento," which echoes critical comments by Rebeld' Malcoms:

> Many of them talk about our African roots
> And they say that they defend them at all costs—black people!—
> So why do they chase around after white European girls, who understands
>   them?

If leading rappers like Papá Humbertico and Los Aldeanos do not identify themselves as black in their lyrics, one must question sweeping characterizations of the hip hop scene as a black space or a black community, and wonder how deeply Black August–style racial discourses penetrated into the hip hop scene, let alone into Havana society at large.

There is also the musical evidence to consider. While music critics and scholars have constructed an image of Cuban rap as markedly indigenized, the musical productions of La Comisión Depuradora are typical of the Havana scene in recent years in generally shunning Afro-Cuban musical history. Although they draw on African American music, producers

such as Papá Humbertico, Aldo, Randee Akozta, and Lápiz often foreground European classical music, piano and strings, Spanish-style guitars
and pop music, and electronic sounds. Of course, some of these musics
contain African elements and aesthetics, as does their transmutation
into hip hop, but in general terms, surface musical markers of blackness
(such as African-derived percussion instruments) are downplayed or,
more often, absent. The prominence of classical music, in particular, is
significant. Some would mark hip hop itself as "black music"—a problematic term (Tagg 1989)—but the samples used by La Comisión Depuradora
tend to elide race as a musical theme, and the characteristic sound of live
hip hop in Havana in recent years has been neither overtly Cuban nor
black.

When I asked El B in 2008 about this decline in the prominence of
blackness, he replied: "What happened before was a process of identification, because really the roots of hip hop are there [in blackness], and in
those days, ten or eleven years ago, we were trying to create a Cuban hip
hop, you understand? So we had to go through all of that. Now it's not the
same thing that's happening, now if you go to a rap peña, you find whites,
you find blacks, in fact our biggest achievement in the last couple of years
is that if you go to a rap peña, there aren't just rappers, there are rockers,
all sorts of people." This idea of blackness as a phase through which
Cuban hip hop needed to pass in order to find itself closely echoes comments made to Marc Perry (2004, 188) by Alexey Rodríguez, who said:
"This is a stage of rap. One must first announce 'I am black.' And when
you acknowledge this we can then move forward from there." Perry interprets to "move forward" as "to act," but in fact, from today's perspective,
Rodríguez's words might be seen as prophetic—an understanding that
explicit race consciousness was, as he said, "a stage of rap."

Thus, for all the academic obsession with blackness, the dominance of
negritude was a phase of Cuban hip hop—the most important phase, for
some, but not the whole story. In Havana, as in New York, the centrality
and explicitness of blackness was a feature of the middle period, not an
original essence. The blackness of U.S. hip hop was, in some ways, a
construction of the mid-1980s, when "hip-hop culture realigned itself
and reimagined its roots, representing itself now as a rap thing, a serious
thing, a Black thing" (Chang 2005, 229). The black nationalism of Public
Enemy, for example, did not reflect the early days of hip hop so much as

its precursors in the late 1960s. The current dominance of Los Aldeanos and other light-skinned rappers in their circle makes any description of Havana hip hop in 2010 as a black culture, space, or community highly problematic.

If there is a need to historicize the question of race and hip hop, many scholars' central claims are also problematic for their hyperbole. Although West-Durán subtitles his article "Cuba's Redefinition of Blackness" (2004), as I have shown above, this redefinition did not even permeate the Havana hip hop scene in a consistent way, much less the entire island (recall the census in hip hop's peak year, 2002, with only 11 percent of Cubans identifying themselves as black). This is one example of the blurring of Havana hip hop's liberation mythologies and its realities that I discussed in the introduction. Indeed, West-Durán's article is based on a foreign-produced CD (*The Cuban Hip Hop All Stars, Vol. 1*) that was released on the New York label Papaya Records and had minimal circulation in Cuba; both the CD and the resulting article tell us more about the transnational construction of Havana hip hop than they do about local realities. If anything has been "revolutionizing blackness" since the start of the Special Period, meanwhile, it has been the interlinked spheres of tourism (Roland 2006), rumba, and timba. Ariana Hernandez-Reguant (2006, 250) argues: "An embryonic rap movement was in the works in marginal urban neighbourhoods, but it was timba, the most popular dance music of the period, which loudly put forth a counternarrative of race." These spheres have witnessed not the kind of intellectualized, politicized race debates that rap scholars have studied but rather "the revolution of the body," to quote the title of a song by Ogguere. It is a revolution based on the enhanced capital of black bodies in an increasingly internationalized cultural economy centered on fascination with all things Afro-Cuban. This revolution was far more widespread than anything that took place in rap. Going on day and night in front of large crowds in Havana's top music venues, it claimed a significant space in the media and music industry, and it touched, in some way, most foreign visitors to the capital as well as many local residents.

The comments made to me by several leading (black and brown) rappers, echoing Papá Humbertico's lines above, illustrate that two "revolutions" in blackness—tourism and hip hop, the revolution of the body and the revolution of the mind—came not only into contact but into conflict.

Rubén Marín expressed this in a published interview, in which he described his loss of faith "when I saw people getting up on stage saying one thing and then getting down and saying another, when they said 'hands in the air, *mis negros*' and then were with a white foreign girl" (quoted in Matienzo Puerto n.d., 15). The 1990s were the decade not only of hip hop's boom in Havana, but also of the explosion in Cuban tourism. Furthermore, travel restrictions for Americans were relaxed in 1998, and the following few years saw increasing links and exchanges (cultural, activist, academic, and athletic) between the United States and Cuba. Black August was just one manifestation of this new openness, part of a specifically North American tourism and exchange boom. As the journalist Alex Berenson (2008) wrote recently: "A decade ago, Cuba was paradise for a certain kind of young, hip American. Cuba was Puerto Rico, with fewer bachelorette parties and more propaganda posters. . . . In a word, Cuba was cool." Given that the renewed possibilities for activist and political exchanges coincided with an influx of American visitors and the BVSC-driven rediscovery of Cuban music, it is clear that the Havana rap scene was suddenly riding two waves at the same time in the late 1990s: the Black August–inspired hip hop revolution and the music-inspired tourist boom.

Hip hop events thus become an alternative tourist attraction as well as sites of social and political consciousness raising. Havana presented particular advantages: as well as being "cool," it is also—unlike many of the big cities or suburbs around the world where hip hop thrives (such as São Paulo and the cités of outer Paris)—an important tourist destination, with safe and, post-Alamar, accessible hip hop venues; since CD sales to tourists were for some time the main source of income for many hip hoppers, foreigners were welcome. There was a double-page spread on hip hop in the *Time Out* guide to Havana that I took with me in 2004. The hip hop festival had made underground culture a significant draw, and rappers were the stars of the show. In fact, interaction with hip hoppers became a formal part of exchange programs organized by pro-Cuba organizations like Global Exchange and Pastors for Peace: conscious Cuban hip hop and alternative or political tourism were drawn together.

The topic raised by Papá Humbertico, Rubén Marín, and Rebeld' Malcoms is a delicate and controversial one. Foreigners can open doors that Cubans cannot, and a number of hip hoppers from Havana have left the island on marriage visas, some of them resulting from attachments made within the hip hop scene. Like other rap researchers, I have heard rumors that certain individuals sought out a foreign fiancée as a way of leaving Cuba. While such rumors are unverifiable, Katrin Hansing (2002, 193, 196) discusses hustling in the Rasta scene, to which a few participants have been tempted by the opportunity to *pescar* (fish for) tourists; she states that many Rastafarian Cubans were successful in that quest and can now be found living all over Europe. Since "fishing for" tourists can also be seen every weekend at rumba peñas at El Palenque and Callejón de Hamel, it is unlikely that it has passed by hip hop altogether. At the 2004 festival, Los Aldeanos unveiled a critique of the hip hop scene in which they asked: "Tell me, my friend, what the hell do you do? / Perform so that you can sweet-talk all the girls afterwards?" They claimed that their aim was "to place ourselves on the shrinking list of true MCs / Who don't create hip hop just so that they can leave the country." "P'al que se va," a collaboration between Los Aldeanos and Papá Humbertico, is a bleak warning of the emotional and economic torments that await the male *jinetero* who catches a foreign woman as a way out of Cuba. It is unusual because of the reversal of the usual stereotype of female jinetera and male tourist, but rather more relevant to the male-dominated hip hop scene.

Leaving aside all moral judgments, it is clear from rap lyrics and comments by several leading rappers that issues of sex and emigration have swirled around the scene and that romantic attachments between dark-skinned hip hoppers and white foreigners have caused tensions and disillusionment with the problack strand of Havana hip hop. Two transnational dynamics thus came into conflict, pointing to the dialectical aspect of hip hop (morality and hustle) and of the race revolution (explicit identity politics and the implicit politics of black bodies). An in-depth study of race and hip hop in Havana would need to include both these aspects of race in Cuba and examine how the tourism-driven revolution in blackness came to undermine its hip hop counterpart, leading to an exodus of rappers and a loss of faith among some who remained.

This revolution of black bodies in the 1990s notwithstanding, recent years have shown a downgrading of the theme of blackness within the broader field of urban popular music. The blackness of timba has dissipated somewhat since the late 1990s as groups have become more commercially focused and less confrontational, as exemplified by La Charanga

Habanera's increasingly pop direction and concomitant whitening of its frontline singers. Above all, the meteoric rise of reggaetón, increasingly coded as a "Latin thing," has taken the edge off expressions of blackness in popular music: a number of leading reguetoneros who were formerly rappers have in effect deprioritized their own blackness by eliminating explicit racial discourses and aligning themselves with a broader musical culture in which latinidad overshadows *negritud*.

Nevertheless, scholars' exaggeration of the saliency of blackness continues. Marc Perry's claim that rap is (or was) "revolutionizing blackness" invites comparison with Robin Moore's pathbreaking *Nationalizing Blackness* (1997), yet the difference between the two cases could not be starker. Moore's study explores the role of Afro-Cuban music in a major paradigm shift in Cuban national culture and identity in the 1920s and 1930s, something that is glaringly lacking in the case of hip hop seventy years later. The rise of reggaetón suggests that, in some cases, those who pronounced racial discourses did not revolutionize even their own sense of blackness, and race was not consistently on the agenda of the hip hop scene, let alone on that of Cuban society at large.

Although leading politicians have been more willing to discuss the question of race since the mid-1980s, hip hop has caused no broad change in thinking on the part of the government or the wider Cuban population. The key to this failure, and to the success of the soneros of the early twentieth century, was the media. Son became the mass-mediated music par excellence in 1930s Cuba, and the mass media were at the core of the nationalization of blackness, as the rise of the recording industry and radio led to a blackening of national culture. In more recent times, the door to the media has opened only a crack for Cuban rap, and as a result the music has had little impact outside those who attend live performances—who number perhaps in the thousands rather than the millions who were exposed to son. The only group to buck the trend in the last decade, reaching a large audience through the alternative routes of the digital revolution, is Los Aldeanos, whose discourse is not race focused. Not only is rap rarely seen on the small screen, but TV is in general still a white preserve: the only rapper with a regular presence on TV is Edgar González, who is white. The continued resistance to the attempts of rappers, and of black people more generally, to make inroads into television is a clear example of the absence of a notable revolution in elite conceptions of blackness. However revolutionary the racial discourses of rappers may have been, their limited diffusion means that their impact on national culture and identity cannot be compared to that of the soneros that Moore describes, nor to that of rumba, timba, or reggaetón musicians. In terms of ethnic or racial identity, the real revolution of the last decade has been the Latin-Caribbean revolution of reggaetón, which has put rap's race agenda in the shade.

Reading Cuban hip hop through the twin lenses of race and Moore's book is thus problematic, for all the excellence of the original model, since it squeezes this cultural form into a historical mold into which it does not easily fit. Yet Fernandes (2006, 119) also follows this path: her interpretation of the state's involvement with hip hop as "harness[ing] the energy of these rappers to bolster the image of Cuba as a mixed-race nation with African roots" is explicitly modeled on Moore's thesis, without providing any evidence to suggest that the same dynamics were at play more than half a century later. Fernandes argues that "given the increasing racial disparities in Cuba's special period and growing cynicism among Afro-Cubans about the ability of the revolution to continue to address their needs, the state draws on articulations of blackness in Afro-Cuban cultural expression to reconstruct national unity and regain popularity" (120). Yet, as Fernandes herself notes, the articulations of blackness in rap have generally taken the form of criticisms of nationalist discourse with regard to race (184). Her claim that the state "appropriate[s] rappers' calls for a 'black nation' in an effort to rebuild popular support and national unity" (133) begs the question: how do rap's outspoken racial critiques boost national unity or bolster the official image of Cuba as a place of racial harmony?

There are close parallels to Brazil, where imported African American musics have challenged the national ideology of racial democracy (Pardue 2008, 46–47). It makes little sense to suggest that the Cuban leadership has actively embraced this kind of challenge to a national ideology on race that has remained fundamentally stable for half a century. If it were true that "the Cuban state bolsters its power among young blacks by associating itself with images of the black nation" (Fernandes 2006, 184), then race would not be elided from the official forums in which hip hop is discussed. Fernandes does not present any evidence to support her arguments, relying instead on Moore's theories and an assumed equivalency between the 1930s and 1990s. Yet the cases of son and hip hop could hardly be further apart: the former served as a productive symbol of national identity because it was unambiguously Cuban and avoided topics that could be considered socially divisive, whereas the latter was widely perceived as an American import and challenged hegemonic unifying discourses on race—hardly a recipe for national unity.

Underneath Fernandes's confusion over whether the Cuban leadership fears a black nation or embraces it lies an a priori urge, shared with other Cuban hip hop scholars, to provide race-based answers to key questions. Race was undoubtedly an important topic in hip hop around 2000, but exclusive interest in problack voices has led scholars to overplay the importance of discourses of blackness and exaggerate their impact on Cuban society. Cuban leaders have been acknowledging the persistence of racism since at least 1986 (well before Cuban rap emerged) and have become comfortable with praising rappers for highlighting instances of prejudice, but this is a far cry from constructing cultural policy around the question of race. The lessons from the 1960s, discussed in chapter 1, are that the Cuban leadership can be quite willing to engage with black radicals without engaging at all with the blackness of their radicalism.

The idea of Cuban hip hop as part of a "black public sphere" (M. Perry 2004; Fernandes and Stanyek 2007; Saunders 2008) also needs to be treated with care. Fernandes and Stanyek's essay is based on the idea that hip hop is a "black culture" that links "black communities" to create "black public spheres," flattening out much of the complexity and historical variation of the Havana scene (and indeed of hip hop per se) and begging questions about the implied relationship between skin color and cultural forms (Tagg 1989). Similarly, Marc Perry (2004, 272) poses the rhetorical question (with regard to Alamar): "Where else in Cuba today can one gather publicly before anywhere from one-hundred to three-thousand black folks and engaged in relatively opening critique of systematic racial exclusion let along racially-directed police harassment?" [sic].

What we see here is the assumption of an equivalency, and therefore a blurring, between terms—black public sphere, culture, space, community, and folks—that in fact lie at quite different points on a continuum from fictional to real, political project to physical entity. As Michael Warner (2002, 50–51) suggests, a public is a fiction, a product of the imagination: "A public is a space of discourse organized by nothing other than discourse itself. It is autotelic; it exists only as the end for which books are published, shows broadcast, Web sites posted, speeches delivered, opinions produced. It exists *by virtue of being addressed*. The circularity is essential to the phenomenon. A public might be real and efficacious, but its reality lies in just this reflexivity by which an addressable object is conjured into being in order to enable the very discourse that gives it existence." Warner is at pains to distinguish between a public as brought into being by texts and their circulation and a public as concrete audience.

As a result, one could argue that when a rap group like Anónimo Consejo performs an Afro-centric song, it creates a black public sphere, irrespective of the skin color or racial identifications of its audience. In Warner's terms, the black public is conjured into being by virtue of being addressed. Ascribing to that same audience membership of a black community or participation in a black space or culture is more problematic since it would seem to involve potentially overriding the attitudes and perceptions of individual audience members such as Rebeld' Malcoms and Alexánder Guerra, who regard such descriptions as false. There are still arguments that could be made in favor of such a proposition: for example, that the majority of people present regard themselves as participating in a black culture or that many people *not* present (i.e., in Cuban society at large) regard hip hop concerts as black spaces (without necessarily having been to one). However, one would have to research beyond a few core members of the scene, acknowledge the existence of complicating factors and alternative views, and spell out the grounds on which those arguments are made, all elements that have been conspicuously lacking in analyses of Cuban hip hop.

To describe that audience as made up of black folks is more problematic still, since it goes even further down the path of disregarding individual audience members' potentially complex self-identifications in favor of a simple reliance on how they looked from afar and imposing a U.S. definition of blackness over a local one. Marc Perry (2004, 268) argues that "identities of blackness are realized in their most tangible and active of forms through the ways in which they are enacted through their performance. To 'be' black in this context is to 'act' as such not simply in the dramaturgic sense, but rather in the political sense of moving or *acting* consciously from critically positioned kinds of black identity. For raperos/as, the political *enactment* of black-self is ultimately exercised through lyric voicings of race-based social critique." Given this, it is clear how blackness can be ascribed to an individual rapper but not to an audience of three thousand. If blackness is generated from within and manifested through action, then the fact that many people in wider Cuban society regard hip hop as *una cosa de negros* (a black thing) is of little relevance. What matters is how hip hoppers act and what they believe—and that requires talking to more than just one sector of the scene.

Ultimately, then, defining the Parque de las Policias or the amphitheater at Alamar as "black spaces" is not so much erroneous as an ideological operation that involves ignoring abstaining or conflicting voices, and scholars have participated in this operation rather than analyzing it. To borrow Warner's phrase, academics have participated in "conjuring into being" a black public for Havana hip hop. Behind this lies a problack political position and an Americanized view of race, which concord with some dominant perspectives in the Havana scene but also overlook others that, in more traditional Cuban style, focused on the presence of people of different skin colors and identified hip hop spaces as racially mixed. The blackness of Havana hip hop has been uneven and disputed territory, yet since the pioneering work of Pacini Hernandez and Garofalo, scholars have painted a monochrome picture; as the political projects of black hip hoppers and foreign-based academics have become entwined, the space for conflicting voices has vanished, complications have been smoothed over to make a more powerful argument about race, and the line between artistic liberation mythology and reality, political project and fact, has become blurred.

At the heart of the matter are the questions of who defines a space, community, or culture as black and how. As I hope to have shown, there are many different ways of thinking about "black space," but existing studies simplify the question. Is a black space defined by the presence of dark-skinned people? By the presence of people who self-identify as black? By the circulation of discourses of negritude? By light-skinned people in wider society who may know next to nothing about hip hop but who regard it as *una cosa de negros*? By intellectuals who want to incorporate it into the academic field of race studies? Is the blackness of black space a visible fact or a political aim? Is blackness something that one ascribes to oneself, or is it something one ascribes to others (whether they like it or not)? There is no simple answer to these questions, but nevertheless I believe them to be important, all the more so since they do not appear in the normalized field of Cuban hip hop studies in which the cracks and tensions have been smoothed over.

To be clear, I am not arguing with the racial makeup of the hip hop scene around 2000 nor with the existence of prominent and novel race discourses in rap lyrics. Race is an important issue in Cuba and in hip hop; race-based social problems are real, and public explorations of them are significant. What I am questioning is the intellectual framing and analysis of this material and the suggestion of a broad and even spread of ideas of blackness that has never been proven. If the sample is limited to those who espouse a particular outlook, then an exaggerated, one-sided view is going to emerge. Hermanos de Causa, often cited in discussions of negritude, told me that some of their fellow rappers were guilty of crossing the line from problack stances to the exclusion of nonblacks, ignoring the fact that Cuba is a mixed-race nation; academic constructions of Havana hip hop show a similar tendency.

There is a huge gulf between Cuban and North American understandings of blackness; the internationally circulating academic constructions of Havana hip hop are built on the latter and thus have shakier local foundations than is usually admitted. For all that Marc Perry (2004, 18) and Fernandes (2006, 89) are well aware of the different meanings of "black" in U.S. and Cuban contexts, they fail to heed their own warnings: both describe and analyze Cuban culture using terms and theoretical constructs derived from the study of people of color in the United States, contributing to the hardening of racial categorization in a fluid context and covering up as much as they reveal. Perry (2004, 18) defends his decision to override local racial terminology with his own (of U.S. derivation) as an inclusive political move; yet Malcoms's reaction to the discourse of blackness (echoing that of Charlie Chase quoted in chapter 3) reveals that such a move was perceived as divisive by some on the ground, given the more restricted connotations of the word *negro* in Cuba. Perry's stated intention to effect change through his discursive choices illustrates the tension between activism and scholarship in Cuban hip hop studies. The advancement of a political agenda can lead to simplification, exclusion, and contradictions: for example, between Perry's view of early Havana hip hop and that of his two principal informants, Ariel Fernández and Alexey Rodríguez, or between his theoretical cornerstone that to "be" black in this context is to act consciously from a critically positioned

black identity and his description of the Parque de los Policías break
dancers or Alamar audience as black.

Since self-identification and subjectivity are vital to the meaning of
"black" in a Cuban context, any postulation of a black space or community would have to be backed up by research on the reception and impact
of problack discourses. It would be necessary to undertake a more systematic survey of audience responses than has been done. Scholars have
formed their theories on the basis of the discourses of a limited range of
self-identified black figures, the presence of majority dark-skinned audiences in the years around 2000, and the assumption of a correlation
between the views of these two groups (and their relevance to earlier
periods). In Cuba—indeed anywhere, if one takes seriously the notion of
race as performed or socially constructed—one would need to know a lot
more about the self-identifications of the audience to make the leap to
theories based on blackness. Instead, the views of a few are projected
onto audiences of hundreds or thousands. The 2002 census data, however, was based on self-identification, and it suggests that a significant
proportion of the "black folks" in Alamar might have actively excluded
themselves from that category and chosen to call themselves mixed race.
People of color who were exposed to discourses of blackness did not
necessarily adopt or agree with them, rendering the language and concepts of the Cuban hip hop literature too totalizing and exclusionary to
use in describing the Havana scene. Malcoms and Guerra were leading
brown-skinned rappers who headlined at the festival, but they do not
subscribe to the idea of a black culture; how many of the racially mixed
audience, many of whom were probably less committed to hip hop than
these rappers, really identified themselves as black? How many of the
light- and brown-skinned Parque de los Policías break dancers would have
identified themselves as black, a decade before Black August?

It is worth asking whether the ideology of blackness had the same
impact on Havana audiences as it did on scholars. For that matter, how
widely and deeply was it internalized by rappers themselves? Rubén Marín, one of the founding figures of Cuban rap, told me that the Havana hip
hop scene declined because audiences lost trust in rappers as they saw
contradictions between what was being said on stage and what was being
lived off it, again referring to rappers who proclaimed problack slogans
while dating white foreigners. Marín's tone was bitter, but Yrak Saenz,

another legendary first-generation black rapper, laughingly described some of the stages of Cuban hip hop: "There was race, then the police, now it's more about politics . . . there was an 'ancestors' phase when everyone was saying 'I'm a *mambís*, I'm a *lucumí*, I'm a *carabalí*.' "[13] Aside from underlining the variations in the articulation of race, he hinted that scholars sometimes need to take questions of music and identity with a pinch of salt. Like Malcoms and Marín, he raised doubts about the degree of consistency between words and deeds during rap's heyday. Even leading black rappers question the extent to which expressions of black pride, for all that they became popular and fashionable, should be taken at face value. If the "black public sphere [is] predicated on the assertion of black political difference," as Marc Perry (2004, 3) suggests, then it may be more of a mirage than scholars have allowed, since black rappers themselves point out that talk is cheap.

This is not to deny the existence of a black public sphere, but rather to question its location and constitution. As Perry (273–77, 288) himself notes, race has become a topic of discussion within intellectual circles in Havana. Hernandez-Reguant (2009b, 83) argues that discussions of race in the late 1990s usually took place behind closed doors; the public projection of local notions of blackness came not so much within Cuba as via academic and cultural exchanges with the United States, and thus the promotion of a black Cuban identity was intertwined with North American activism and academia. At the heart of the black public sphere, then, lies a small, transnational group of activists and intellectuals who actively seek it out and promote it. In a sense, the label "black public sphere" says as much about hip hop scholars' own world as it does about Cuban hip hop: it has seen its fullest expression in transnational intellectual and activist circuits rather than on the streets of Havana. U.S.-based academics have remade Cuban hip hop in their own image, reinforcing U.S. discourses of the civil-rights era and downplaying elements that do not fit with the idea of a noncommercial, race-based movement. They have focused on the performance of race by groups like Anónimo Consejo and Obsesion and have failed to account for conflicting views and responses (a vital part of the social construction of race), preferring to focus on (and advance) their own views. As a result, the catchy label "black public sphere," an apt description of the circles in which they move, has ended up being applied to the Havana hip hop scene that they study, despite being much more problematic in Cuba than in the United States. The black public sphere of Cuban hip hop is a project and a desire—one shared by scholars.

It is important to underline the extent to which the production of knowledge about Cuban hip hop has been primarily (though not exclusively) in foreign hands and the way that this knowledge has circulated in Havana. U.S.-based researchers and journalists imported both race consciousness and models for analyzing it from the United States, and given the lack of local media interest and the small sums of money circulating in the rap scene, they became part of the "market" for Havana hip hop by interviewing, filming, and recording; sometimes paying; helping to resolve problems; and bestowing prestige. Fernandes, Perry, and West-Durán all participated in rap festivals, contributing their opinions in formal and informal settings; all three have published articles in Cuban magazines; Fernandes was even a festival judge. North American visions of race thus fed into the Havana hip hop scene from two sources: Black August and research. While one can only speculate about the role of researchers—who interviewed the most race-conscious groups, asked race-focused questions, and talked about race in public and private forums—in consolidating the racialization of the Havana scene, it is clear that scholars helped to keep blackness on the table at colloquia, conferences, and debates, as well as in more private, everyday conversations. It is hard to imagine that repeated, extended conversations on race with several hip hop scholars have not in some way sharpened Obsesion's thinking on the topic. With numerous foreign filmmakers and journalists also a notable presence, many of them activists as well, the dominant tropes of the Havana scene cannot be divorced from the priorities of those who sought to document them.

Foreign intellectuals and activists have participated in the construction of a black public sphere on the ground in Havana but also on the pages of their resulting reports. We have already seen Marc Perry's redefinition of the early break dance scene as a black space. Another example of the scholarly invention of a black public sphere can be found on the first page of his dissertation, setting the tone for things to come. Perry launches his thesis on race and hip hop with a description of Papá Humbertico's performance at the 2002 festival: "His lyrics vividly recounted the daily lives and struggles of people in his working-class, predominantly black barrio of Guanabacoa, touching on themes of poverty, crime, imprisonment and prostitution. . . . Collective energies peeked [*sic*] as Papa Humbertico riffed critically about Cuban police and their frequent harassment of black youth. 'Police, police, you are not my friend; For Cuban youth, you are the worst nightmare . . . *You* are the delinquent . . . ,' the MC exclaimed" (M. Perry 2004, 1). It is immediately apparent, to judge from Perry's report, that Papá Humbertico did not actually rap about race: he rapped about various social problems and the police, while the race angle is provided by Perry, who transforms Papá Humbertico's "Cuban youth" into "black youth" and his mixed neighborhood into a "predominantly black barrio." The absence of race in the performance is little surprise: as mentioned above, I found only two examples of explicit discussion of race in the forty-odd songs on four of Papá Humbertico's albums, and of these, one is critical of negritude in Havana hip hop. According to Perry's (2004, 268) own definition, discussed above, Papá Humbertico should not therefore be considered black.

This example is clearly important in Perry's mind since it constitutes his opening paragraph, yet it in fact says nothing about race and Havana hip hop and everything about the kinds of assumptions that underpin his and other studies. The centrality of race is taken for granted to such an extent that scholars pay little attention to the detail. This example amply illustrates my point that the black public sphere of Cuban hip hop has been properly documented in only a few cases and then expanded out to cover the scene as a whole without ascertaining its broader relevance. The black public sphere in this case is forged by Perry's description, not Papá Humbertico's lyrics. A public sphere, like Warner's public, is discursive; and scholarly studies need to be recognized as among the texts on which Cuban hip hop's black public sphere is based. If a public is brought into existence by being imagined and addressed, it makes sense to describe academics as co-creators, rather than observers, of a black public sphere.

The race current has now faded somewhat in Havana hip hop, thanks to the departure or retirement of many of its key proponents, the suspension of the Black August exchanges, and the return of race-focused scholars to the United States, but the intellectual black public sphere that feeds on it continues to exist in the international academic arena; in the light of the historicizing perspective presented here, however, it appears self-referential and self-perpetuating. To take an example, Fernandes's (2006,

120) interpretation of state policy on hip hop springs from de la Fuente's (2001) analysis of Cuban foreign policy in the 1970s, an imaginative leap that is undermined by studies (C. Moore 1988; Sawyer 2006) that underline the radical disjunctions between foreign and domestic policy at the time. De la Fuente (2008a) has in turn drawn from Fernandes's work the belief that a "national hip hop movement" provides evidence of a "new Afro-Cuban cultural movement," even though each of the key terms—national, Afro-Cuban, and movement—is in fact highly questionable in relation to Cuban hip hop, certainly today. For all de la Fuente's excellence as a scholar, his essay says more about the received wisdom of Cuban hip hop scholarship, where the language of Black August lives on, than it does about contemporary realities in the hip hop scene, and it illustrates a kind of "Chinese whispers" effect in which simplifications and exaggerations by observers of hip hop become amplified as they become further removed from the source.

Another example: Hermanos de Causa's song "Tengo" has been circulating for a good few years between academic studies, but no one has stopped to ask how many young people in Havana know this song (which was released in New York and has never been widely available in Cuba) nor what impact it might have had on local conceptions of racial identity. Scholars love it because it is based on a classic Nicolás Guillén poem and includes some Cuban musical elements, and it therefore checks all sorts of academic boxes—even though it is not typical even of Hermanos de Causa's work, much less of contemporary hip hop aesthetics. But how might we weigh its influence against a Gente de Zona reggaetón video like "Tremenda pena" in which the dark-skinned former rapper Alexánder Delgado appears alongside pale-skinned models? The activist strand to Cuban hip hop scholarship has ensured a slippage between what scholars would like to see and what actually exists. Rap has been drawn into a self-perpetuating, scholarly black public sphere that gives academics plenty to talk about but has come loose from its moorings in Havana, where Hermanos de Causa— excellent rappers though they may be—have not produced a demo in six years, and where for each young person who knows "Tengo" there are probably a hundred who know "Tremenda pena." "Tengo" is of course worthy of study in its own right, its relative obscurity in no way diminishing its aesthetic value, but to form theories about changing notions of blackness in Cuba on the back of it is more problematic, as is ignoring the much more prominent elision of blackness in recent commercial popular music. When I asked Soandres del Río of Hermanos de Causa whether hip hop had changed people's thinking about race, he replied: "Only a minority—hip hop has changed rappers and the people around them and the few people who come across them." Where has the revolution in blackness taken place—in Cuban society, Cuban hip hop, or Cuban hip hop studies?

Cuban hip hop scholars could learn much from Derek Pardue's (2008) work on hip hop in São Paulo: Pardue stresses diversity, fragmentation, and contests with regard to racial discourses, and his historicized view traces how blackness fell in and out of favor among hip hoppers in the city. Race emerges as a dynamic theme in Brazilian hip hop, in contrast to the somewhat static, synchronic, and thus exaggerated depictions of race in Havana. A serious study of race and hip hop in Havana would investigate the invention of blackness; when, how, and why it became a central topic; who listened to it; who accepted it, who opposed it, and why; and when, how, and why it started to fade. The theoretical models and terminology that have been borrowed from U.S. scholarship have exaggerated the impact of rap's blackness discourses on wider Cuban society, a tendency exacerbated by taking hip hop out of the context of other Cuban musics. Had scholars paid more attention to what was going on with timba and reggaetón, they would have seen a growth in internationalized Latin aesthetics at the expense of overt expressions of blackness—which, while a real and interesting phenomenon, were becoming the preserve of just a few within a small hip hop subculture in Havana. This is a paradox rarely acknowledged by race-focused scholars: there has been a small opening for discussion of race issues within intellectual circles, yet in the wider sphere of mass-mediated popular culture, articulations of blackness have been in decline in recent years. Marc Perry (2004, 273) wrote optimistically at the end of 2004 that "the Cuban hip hop movement is emerging as a key player in an evolving black public sphere," yet by this point, both the circulation of discourses of blackness in popular culture and hip hop itself were clearly past their peak.

Far from being downplayed, then, the issue of blackness has actually been overplayed but underanalyzed in Cuban hip hop scholarship. An investment in promoting the problack strand of Havana hip hop has hindered a clear-sighted analysis of race and perpetuated the kind of mythification that is an important tool for artist-activists but more problematic in academia. Studies that focus on blackness are still appearing and shaping the terms of the transnational debate today, even though things have moved on a long way in Havana, illustrating how the race lens is somewhat divorced from the phenomena on which it is supposedly trained. As a gap increasingly opens up between what Cuban hip hop was and what it has become, the nostalgia underpinning both scholarly and documentary representations becomes increasingly apparent.

Representing Cuban Rap on Record

The release of the BVSC album in 1997 and its Grammy award in 1998 stoked international excitement about Cuban music at the same time the Black August exchanges were set up. This, and the fact that many of the first foreigners to become involved in the Havana hip hop scene were journalists, ensured that the buzz around Cuban hip hop expanded rapidly in the international media, almost immediately attracting a steady flow of foreign music producers and documentary makers. One of the first was the French producer Manu Cartano, who had been keeping an eye on developments in Cuba since 1994. When he returned to Havana, he met Pablo Herrera, who at the time was managing Amenaza, the forerunner of Orishas. Together they informally auditioned a number of local groups and made a compilation demo in 1998, which Manu took to France, mixed, and brought back to Havana. The demo was copied and passed from hand to hand, and within six months the songs were being heard widely in Havana. One of the songs, Junior Clan's "Una guerra entre dioses," won the grand prize at the 1998 festival before it had even been released. Meanwhile Manu persuaded a subsidiary of Virgin France to invest $15,000 in the project, which allowed him to return to Havana in 1999 to record the CD *Cuban Rap Ligas: La Crema del Hip-Hop Made in Cuba* in the EGREM studios. One particularly notable aspect of Manu's project was that he brought about twenty-five instrumentals to Cuba with him, some of them made specifically for this project but others created without thinking about Cuba at all. He left the groups entirely free to choose which backgrounds they wanted to use, and he remarked that most rejected those that mixed hip hop with Cuban traditional music in favor of those which sounded more *yuma* (American). During the course of this protracted project, two members of Amenaza had left for

France to form Orishas, and most of the Havana-based groups wanted to distance themselves from the commercial son–hip hop formula. As Obsesion rap in their song "Quisás" from this compilation: "I have a rhythm which doesn't wear a guayabera [Cuban shirt]":

> Perhaps it doesn't sound like cha-cha-cha
> But this is the rhythm that identifies me most.
> Let it be known from Tokyo to Havana
> This is my way of making Cuban music.

Manu left the groups free to choose an underground direction, even though he knew it would make the CD harder to sell in Europe. The fact that he paid an advance of $1,100 per song, an astronomical sum in the context, may also have encouraged the artists to express themselves in their choice of instrumentals: their financial reward was not dependent on the final product, so, as Manu presents it, they were led by their own tastes, and no doubt those of their Havana audience as well. The results are essential listening for anyone who believes that Cuban hip hop is synonymous with fusions of Cuban tradition and American modernity.

Another very significant recording project took place in 1999: *The Cuban Hip Hop All Stars, Vol. 1* (CHHAS). As Pablo Herrera tells the story, the producer Michael Esterson turned up in Havana with an MPC sampler/drum machine in August that year, and within ten days Herrera had not only learned to use the equipment but had created all the instrumentals for the project. Herrera, Ariel Fernández (the project director), and a number of leading rap groups went into the Abdala studios and recorded the tracks for the compilation with the participation of several live musicians.

It is instructive to compare these two foreign-produced compilations, significant landmarks that marked the beginning of a major new phase in the Havana hip hop scene, in terms of local creativity and international exposure. To begin with, neither provides a straightforward snapshot of Cuban hip hop in 1999, so it is risky to draw conclusions from them without some knowledge of the conditions of their production. The artists on Manu's project chose their own instrumentals from a range of preexisting options (made in France), and the resulting musical aesthetic is, in most cases, not markedly Cuban. This avoidance of surface Cubanisms by most of the rappers involved is reflected in the CD cover art. Much more strikingly "Cuban" is the cover of the CHHAS CD, with its cartoon-style

Havana hip hopper wearing a shirt and cap each emblazoned with the Cuban flag, superimposed over a third, larger national flag. Along with the word "Cuban" itself (in the title), Cuba is thus referenced four times. The other major symbol is a record turntable, an object as rare as a hen's tooth in the Havana scene at that time. The images for foreign consumption continue on the inside cover with a large, forbidding "CENSORED" sign. It is not clear who or what is supposed to be censored, but the CD was recorded with official permission in the far-from-underground surround-ings of the Abdala studios. The writer of the sleeve notes drew on the old-school New York discourse that was circulating in the scene at the time: "Habana, Cuba in the 21st century: Crumbling architectural relics, stray dogs and proud people. With a powerful vibrant culture. Not much dif-ferent from the South Bronx in the '70's and '80's."

The musical contents of this compilation are rather subtler: Herrera managed to create musical textures that were distinctive and appealing without reproducing the Orishas formula. For all the artistic value of the project, however, this CD is not representative of late 1990s Cuban hip hop, which was still primarily dependent on backing tracks borrowed from U.S. hip hop. The CHHAS instrumentals were made with foreign equipment, and the studio time and live musicians were paid for by a foreign producer: this was all exceptional at the time. The results were a Cuban creation, but one demonstrating foreign production values and destined for the overseas market. The fact that this became the most easily available Cuban hip hop compilation overseas is partly responsible for the widespread view that Cuban hip hop is a mixture of Afro-Cuban music and rap, whereas in fact live instruments and fusions with Cuban traditional music are rare, controversial, and often produced (or talked about) with foreign listeners firmly in mind. Cubanized hip hop is thus much more than just a "natural" local response to globalized cultural currents.

Without knowing the details of their production, it would be easy to misunderstand the different aesthetics of these two albums, produced in the same year in Havana, and assume that CHHAS sounds more localized than *Cuban Rap Ligas* because it was produced by a habanero rather than a Frenchman. Yet Herrera's ear was markedly globalized. Pionero Pando, one of Amenaza's founders, had invited Herrera—at that time his lan-guage teacher—to see the group perform at the Café Cantante. Herrera recalls his amazement: "I was like, wow, if there's anything close to what I have studied in *Rolling Stone* and *Spin* and all these different magazines, this is it." His immediate frame of reference was U.S. hip hop. Yet he felt that Amenaza were simply copying their North American models, and when he joined the group as its mentor and manager, he advised them to adopt a more Cuban aesthetic. He spent four months in New York in 1998, so by the time of the 1999 CHHAS project, he was even more immersed in the U.S. "source." His input was crucial to the two most "Cubanized" hip hop projects of the late 1990s, Orishas and CHHAS, precisely because he was the most globally aware figure in the scene at that time: it is no coincidence that the Cubanizing turn in Havana hip hop took place largely in the hands of someone who could, and often did, pass as a New Yorker. The influence of Herrera's global outlook was to go local, whereas the preferences of the majority of Havana rappers can be heard in the yuma sounds of *Cuban Rap Ligas*.

The making of CHHAS is a snapshot of the way that the Havana rap scene, in its heyday, depended on outside interest to sustain it, given the local lack of technology, record label interest, or market; it is significant that Herrera started making beats in earnest only when given equipment by a foreign producer for a foreign compilation, and live musicians were incorporated because there was a foreign producer on board, thinking about an overseas audience. A publicity flier for CHHAS describes it as "the only 100% Cuban product in existence," but like the Buena Vista Social Club, it is an imagined, freshly constructed "authenticity" for export, and it was led by Cubans with a particularly Americanized vision, since both Herrera and Ariel Fernández were unusually well informed about U.S. hip hop. As with Ry Cooder's project, the artistic ideas and talent were there in Havana, but a foreign producer was required to catalyze them and provide the investment and marketing vision; in both cases, artists who did not normally work together were united for a recording project to create something new that nevertheless bore the stamp of authenticity for foreign listeners.

Havana Hip Hop under the Lens

One of the most extraordinary aspects of the Havana hip hop scene is that, since Joe Wentrup's *Más voltaje—más volumen, rap en Cuba* (1997), it has been the subject of more than two dozen documentaries in a decade, almost all of them made by foreigners. As the Cuban media and record labels have shown little interest in hip hop, non-Cubans have played an important role in its diffusion, and while there have been a few further recording projects (such as *Flow Latino*, *Soy Rapero*, and *Calle Real 70*), the prime medium for documenting (or constructing) the Havana hip hop scene has been the camera lens. Some leading groups have never formally released an album yet have appeared in a fistful of documentaries; the visual has almost taken precedence over the aural in the mediation of Havana hip hop. There are obvious reasons for this: two of hip hop's four elements (dance and graffiti) are purely visual, and thus film is a more effective medium than an audio recording for capturing the interplay of the culture's different strands. In addition, in transnational contexts the visual aspect of hip hop is vital: as U.S. hip hop crosses linguistic borders, the first thing to be lost is language, while the visual is retained. The moving image was crucial to the adoption of hip hop in Cuba via TV programs beamed from Miami, and it has also been vital to its rediffusion from Havana back to the outside world. With local media and recording industry interest so low, foreign-made documentaries were transformed into key outlets of self-expression for many Havana artists, and visuality helped to recross the language barrier, above all to North America. With documentary, much more than audio, the verbal message could be translated (as subtitles) or its importance played down in favor of other aspects.

Soandres del Río is a top rapper who has never released an album or been legally paid to perform. However, he has appeared in numerous documentaries and is one of the three leads in the glossiest of them all, *East of Havana*. He saw the proliferation of documentaries in generally positive terms, despite some bad experiences. Because of the general lack of access to the Internet in Cuba, they are almost the only form of promotion available to some groups, and the main way to surmount the metaphorical wall surrounding Cuba and have their work heard abroad. In Cuba no one is interested in this kind of project, del Río said; foreign documentaries are the prime way for Cuban rappers to broadcast their existence and their art to the world.

Many other hip hoppers, however, hold more equivocal views, and it is clear that the filming of Havana hip hop has not been without its complications. Rapping is a form of representation (of oneself and one's environment), and the power to represent takes on particular importance in a context where dominant representations are often far removed from most people's reality. Rappers thus see themselves as a truthful lens on Cuban reality. El B, in his song "El periodista" (the journalist), raps about his "sharp vision": he describes his track as a "documentary," an alternative to the official media, in which "we show reality with sincerity, we talk about what lies behind Rafael Serrano's mustache" (referring to a well-known TV news reader). Yet as rappers started turning to documentary makers as the principal way of getting their messages out, their representations were mediated by a foreign lens, and they thus lost control of the act of representation. As Randee Akozta's epigraph to this chapter reveals, the camera does sometimes lie; indeed, the images of Cuba broadcast at home and abroad are almost all viewed as untrustworthy. The documentary thus becomes a double-edged sword: visual media are both coveted and distrusted by rappers, who proclaim the superiority of their own vision over the camera, yet in many cases are forced to hand over representational responsibility to a foreigner wielding a camera in exchange for greater exposure.

Furthermore, as several scholars have discussed (Dopico 2002; Quiroga 2005; Whitfield 2008), visuality and the camera lens are politically charged in Havana. However positive the intentions and fine the artistic results, the relationship between the foreign eye behind the camera and the "tourist gaze" (Urry 1990) is uncomfortably close. Almost all documentaries have been made with foreign audiences in mind (there is virtually no outlet for them in Cuba), and most filmmakers mix rappers' perspectives with more stereotypical touristic images in order to make the final product more digestible (and marketable) overseas. But even an underground vision replicates the desire for authenticity and the urge to uncover "the real Cuba" that lies behind contemporary tourism (Whitfield 2008, 26–27). Since getting beneath the surface of a foreign city or country is a commonplace touristic desire, training a lens on Havana's underground is intimately connected to the tourist gaze. Underground hip hop may explicitly refuse to play the BVSC game, with its celebration of place, and yet, via its mediation on film, it becomes the other side of the BVSC coin, offering up the city's underside—"the real Havana"—to foreign viewer-consumers just as Wim Wenders's film did for the "overside." Many underground hip hoppers are skeptical about tourism and its ways of seeing, yet their repeated representation on film has offered them up to the tourist gaze, drawing foreign visitors to Havana and fueling their expectations, just like BVSC.

Many of these documentaries share with academic representations and the BVSC the "nostalgic recovery" and "restoration of the real" of which Medina (2007) writes. For all the apparent urge to cut through the rose-tinted nostalgia and get underground, underpinning the filmic production of the Havana scene is the nostalgic assumption that it harks back to an earlier, more real phase in the history of hip hop. The book that accompanies the documentary *East of Havana* is described as "introducing one of the last pure youth movements in the world . . . While rap in the U.S. has been losing its voice of struggle to the pressures of commerce, Cuban artists defend their voice using their music not as a vehicle of fantasy, but of survival."[14] Medina's (ibid., 16) comment that "for Wenders, the very meaning of cinema is restoration, the recovery of a reality whose truth has somehow been lost" is also an apt description of many hip hop films.

Filming has also brought practical problems and frustrations. Foreign production brings an extra degree of distancing, since the editing and screening of the films take place primarily overseas, beyond the reach of those who star in them. In some cases, artists have never seen the films in which they appear; in other cases, films have filtered back to the island sporadically. Yrak Saenz described his irritation at seeing early video footage of himself included in a documentary, footage that he had never previously seen. Being captured on film has thus left many Havana hip hoppers feeling simultaneously possessed and dispossessed. Even the most honorable filmmakers have struggled with the difficulties of traveling to and working within Cuba. Charlie Ahearn (the maker of the legendary hip hop film *Wild Style*) was always concerned about where he screened his work, presenting it in the projects, in clubs, for the people who appeared in it, seeing "representation as liberation" (Chang 2005, 186). In Cuba, this is much more difficult, so most films have played almost entirely to foreign college and film-festival audiences, and local hip hoppers have had little opportunity to see them or experience the liberation of which Ahearn speaks. The politics of representation is thus complicated by the difficulties in ensuring that the representations circulate freely back at the source.

The power of film directors is occasionally manifested in other concrete ways. Jauretsi Saizarbitoria recounted the problems that she encountered when she was in Havana in August 2004 to film the hip hop festival as part of her *East of Havana* project. The festival was canceled at the last minute due to a hurricane; Jauretsi needed live footage, so she organized a concert at the Acapulco Theater for the collective that appears in the film, El Cartel. But because of the festival's suspension, Havana was full of rappers (foreign, local, and from the provinces) who were desperate to perform. Every rapper in town wanted to be part of the Acapulco concert, and Jauretsi found herself responsible for determining the lineup of what had almost become the alternative Havana hip hop festival. Unsurprisingly, many tensions were generated that day, as far more artists were left out than included; the creation of authentic-looking material for the documentary had real-world effects on the hip hop scene, whether the director liked it or not, illustrating how the construction of Havana hip hop by overseas visitors has not been restricted to its representation on film.

Filming the hip hop scene has thus brought practical and political problems as filmmakers have found themselves enmeshed in both the everyday complexities of working in Cuba and broader questions about representation, nostalgia, and tourism in post-BVSC Havana. If the practical problems are formidable, the political problems can seem almost insoluble. How is a foreign filmmaker supposed to avoid duplicating the tourist gaze in an environment that has been so comprehensively visually commodified? The "beaches and palm trees like in the videos made by foreign companies" are ruled out, yet the underground vision of the gritty urban reality behind the facade circulates around the globe in the novels of Pedro Juan Gutiérrez: the desire to get beneath the surface of Havana is as much a voyeuristic, touristic desire as any other. I would suggest that it is those films that tackle the issue head on—like Gutiérrez's novels—that provide some response to this devilishly tricky question. With some two dozen documentaries in existence, an overview, much less a critical discussion, is impossible: I will thus focus on a few films that illuminate the question of visuality and the process and politics of representation.

One of the earliest documentaries was *Cuban Hip Hop All Stars*. In a mirror image of the BVSC, it was filmed in conjunction with (but two years after) a recording project of the same name. Both films thus mix a documentary premise with a commercial or promotional intent and are partially fictional. Like the CHHAS compilation discussed above, the film is a construction of the Havana hip hop scene, but in this case, since it was filmed after the recording had been made, it is a visual reconstruction of and support for the musical world constructed by the album. In a sense, then, it is at two removes from the hip hop scene that it portrays. The director, Joshua Bee Alafia, makes no secret that this is an artistic creation, not a simple mirror of reality: he includes several prominent docudrama sections, and in other places (such as Papo Record's performance in the street) the constructed nature of the scene is made perfectly clear. This artificiality is underestimated by Alan West-Durán (n.d., 39), however, who writes of "an extraordinary segment of rappers and *rumberos* in the street. The scene with the *rumberos* is great, because without a word—thereby avoiding any kind of didacticism or explanatory notes— one can see the 'natural' symbiosis between rap and rumba." For all the author's enthusiasm, it is worth underlining that there is little "natural" about this supposedly chance meeting of rappers and rumberos in the street, which not only bears all the hallmarks of a manufactured scene but is also hardly representative of Havana hip hop, in which the symbiosis between rap and rumba has been minimal. While such meetings do occasionally happen, far from being natural they are generally instigated by special events (festivals, important concerts, and film shoots), particularly those organized by or aimed at foreigners.

The purpose of this scene is in fact to legitimate the somewhat "unnatural" combination of rappers and traditional musicians in the Abdala studios in August 1999. At the same time that this scene was filmed, Alexey Rodríguez (Obsesion) and Kokino (Anónimo Consejo) were complaining about generalized prejudice toward rappers from Cuban musicians ("Encuentro entre amigos" n.d., 20–21). More often than not, the relationship between rappers and musicians has been characterized by tensions and mutual suspicion rather than comradely jamming. As the editorial to the sixth edition of *Movimiento* magazine admits, musicians' interest in rap has been intermittent and "a true dialogue between rap and other forms of our popular music has not been produced"; the editor blames this lack of dialogue on prejudice on the part of musicians. However, there is also a long history of hip hop skepticism toward musicians (see Baker 2012). Obsesion have talked about how it took touring overseas to convince them to put their recorded instrumentals aside and work with live musicians.[15] The scenes of *Cuban Hip Hop All Stars* that include a spontaneous rap-rumba jam in the street, a freestyle with saxophone accompaniment, and rappers having a singalong with a *tres* player old enough to be their grandfather should not therefore be confused with research footage: the recording (atypically) features Cuban drums and live musicians, so, as with the BVSC, the documentary retrospectively conjures up a musical world to provide a visual context for the album. The rumba scene recalls Omara Portuondo singing as she wanders through the streets of Old Havana in BVSC; both scenes are striking, but they are primarily symbolic and aimed at projecting a particular vision of Cuban culture—not necessarily an accurate one—to the outside world.

In one sense, *Cuban Hip Hop All Stars* illustrates the perilous path that all documentary makers seem to face. The rumba scene is musically and dramatically satisfying, and it gives the film a great splash of local color; but in its artificiality, it also echoes the playing up of Afro-Cuban music, dance, and religion so central to the marketing of Cuban culture to foreign audiences (Hernández 2002, 64; Fernandes 2006, 46). This localizing highlight of the film is thus virtually indistinguishable from the commodifying processes of touristic production and consumption, for all that the film's director and protagonists may be skeptical of such processes. However, before we cry neocolonialist foul, we also need to note the scenes in which first Papo Record and then Kokino speak to the camera about the talent in Havana that is just waiting to be discovered. They call out through the lens to music entrepreneurs, almost saying "come and get us." This plea to be noticed, to have the opportunity to show their talent to the world, upsets any simple characterization of the unequal relationship between lens and subject. If the rappers are the raw material in a film for overseas consumption, they also use the film as a platform for international promotion. The camera is thus revealed as a protagonist in the film and part of the machinery of the international music business, its complicity exposed by the rappers' direct address to the lens.

Another film that provides ample scope for rappers to voice their views is *La FabriK*, which makes Cuban-U.S. exchange its central organizing principle. While the Cuban rappers use the camera to voice their criticisms of the U.S. government, social conditions in American cities, and the obsession with bling in U.S. hip hop, the director's implicit criticism of the Miami media is perhaps the most memorable. He allows the Miami reporters to hang themselves by simply filming their frantic, exaggerated reactions when the hip hop delegation arrives—some of the Miami media claimed the rappers were anti-Castro and the voice of resistance, others that they were pro-Castro and the voice of the Cuban Revolution. Apart from underlining the liminality and multivocality of Cuban rap, these scenes also highlight the distorting power of the lens and the word; there is a certain self-reflexivity in inviting the watcher to ponder the pitfalls of mediating Cuban hip hop. As with many of the films, these pitfalls are also in evidence in the subthemes of Santería and rumba. The film plays up the spiritual or mystical side of the preparations for the tour, suggesting that divine intervention led to the granting of visas, and providing perfect fodder for the exoticizing tourist gaze. The discussion of Obsesion's turn from pure hip hop to Cubanized fusion is also mystifying rather than enlightening, presenting the change as a natural, inevitable return to their roots rather than a consequence of the kind of international touring documented in this film.

There is a brief scene in the film *Inventos* which captures a group of Cubans scrutinizing an English-language magazine with illustrated articles about Cuban hip hop groups including Orishas, Grandes Ligas, and Sexto Sentido. This captures wonderfully the multiple layers of representation and translation that have gone on in the Havana scene: the foreign director films Cubans consuming foreign-made representations of themselves. This implicit self-reflexivity—training a foreign lens on a foreign lens—is developed into a fully fledged theme in Ryan Fleck and Anna Boden's *Young Rebels*, a film about filming Cuban hip hop.

The lens is first thrust in front of the viewer when Los Paisanos discuss the fact that tourism is important not just for the nation but for poor people like themselves: they do not work since state jobs are so poorly paid, and they make a living instead from selling their demo CDs to foreigners. Randee Akozta turns to the camera, grinning, and says: "If you folks didn't come to Cuba, nobody would buy our CDs, and we wouldn't have U.S. dollars." In these few seconds, the mutual relationship between filming, tourism, the underground scene, and the rap economy is laid bare. For Akozta, documentary makers are a subspecies of tourist-consumer: they are all people who buy CDs and keep the rap scene (and Akozta's household) going. The lens is revealed as a two-way passage that allows foreign consumers access to Havana's hip hop scene and vice versa, and thus a mediator of economic transaction. Any illusion that the filmmaker is a fly on the wall, capturing an untouched underground scene, is stripped away as the mutual dependence of filmmaker and subject is exposed. This fleeting moment underlines the fact that documentaries are not windows onto Havana hip hop but part of its construction and economic foundation, highlighting the merging of cultural production and the dollar that is so characteristic of Havana since the mid-1990s.

Now that the camera has become a protagonist in the film, it rarely goes away. As Las Krudas are performing at Almendares, another foreign cameraman appears in front of the stage, pointing his lens up at one of the members of the group; she leans in close to the camera, throwing the gaze straight back into the lens. The Havana scene is under close observation, but so are those who wield the cameras. Las Krudas made their living as carnivalesque performers on stilts in Old Havana, providing colorful subject matter that appears in numerous hip hop films. But Boden and Fleck do not leave it at that: they also capture tourists filming the act and Pelusa MC passing a hat around, asking for contributions, and thus the film foregrounds the economic-touristic exchange—money in return for film footage—rather than just the local color.

In a later scene, Familia's Cuba Represent are captured in a meeting with a music video director about a possible shoot. Let's break away from the traditional images—the *solar* (courtyard), Havana streets, city rooftops—says the director. The visual clichés of Havana found in most films and videos are thus laid out before the viewer, airing the problem of how to film an already visually commodified city. The director continues: "We need a camera. We need a good camera. Something professional. [*In English, looking at the camera*] Like this [*laughs*]." Again, a lot is condensed into this moment: what does it mean to make a documentary about Cuban hip hop when the subjects of the film do not have a camera to shoot their own video, vital for their continued existence as a group? The documentary makers' material advantage over their subjects is exposed, and by implication, the unequal foreigner-local relationships of which it is a microcosm. Once again, it is the relationship between the foreign lens and the economics of cultural production that is foregrounded; the filmmakers' power to wield a lens is set into relief by their subjects' powerlessness to make a video.

The foreigner may provide money or equipment; what else can she or he help to resolve? What FCR really need—says the girlfriend of Warner, a member of the group—is an overseas trip to move their career to the next level; she grins and looks straight at the lens, or rather, through the lens to the foreigners behind it who might be able to make such a thing possible. There follow a number of scenes in which the self-reflexivity becomes subtler: a discussion among friends of how there are no good new films about ordinary Cuban life (in a film about ordinary Cuban life); some young Americans interviewing DJ Alexis D'Boys (one of the protagonists of this American, interview-based film); FCR making phone calls as they try to borrow a camera for their video shoot, and then the video shoot itself (with a lot of joking about the artifice [sunlight reflectors] required to make the image look natural); and a cat-and-mouse joke about the need to speak two languages to work in tourism (in a bilingual film shot by foreigners). But there is one more crowning scene. Randee Akozta explains that the rap festival is the most important event of the year, so it has more eyes on it—in other words, TV and documentary crews from around the world. There follows a rapid sequence of camera shots, cutting between images of several different camera crews that were also present at performances that appear in the film, and zooming in on a camera with CNN emblazoned on the side. Again, the notion of the hip hop scene as heavily scrutinized is brought to the forefront. Akozta says that as a result, rappers have to be careful about what they say, because their views can be manipulated or misinterpreted abroad. This scene completes the problematization of the status of the foreign lens, which mediates not just between Cubans and foreigners but also between hip hoppers and the state. The foreign camera is revealed as a surveillance apparatus that constrains what it films and indirectly serves the Cuban government.

As the aftermath of the 2002 festival showed, state officials do not need access to the tapes: the mere knowledge that Papá Humbertico's denuncia social gesture was caught on film was enough to precipitate official consternation and retributive action (Henríquez Lagarde 2002). Alpidio Alonso stated clearly that the problem was the presence of foreign media, whom he accused of parroting stereotypes, searching out controversy, and twisting messages. The foreign gaze is not invisible: both state officials and rappers know they are being watched, and their behavior is affected accordingly. One of the principal messages conveyed by cultural and political leaders at the prefestival meeting I attended in 2004 was that the presence of the foreign press necessitated extra care and responsibility. A senior politician warned rappers about foreign journalists' attempts to manipulate their lyrics. He took out a piece of paper and read aloud a few phrases about dissent and oppositional youth from the international press reports on the previous year's festival. As Soandres del Río points out in the *East of Havana* film, rappers' words had more impact at the festival because of the presence of the international media. Similarly, at a meeting before the Almendares hip hop festival in 2004, the festival organizers told participants to watch their words as there would be a lot of attention from outside. They also announced that no film cameras could be used without permission, since they had had bad experiences in the past with foreign producers and documentary makers. I was also told about a peña organized by Papo Record in 2003 at which an unknown foreign journalist had appeared; nervous about how the journalist might react and the possible local consequences, and with Papá Humbertico's ban still fresh in his mind, Papo told all the invited artists to watch their tongue.

There is little question, then, that being observed and filmed by foreigners had become a key issue by 2004, though whether this did indeed restrict artists is another matter: in conversation with me, Roberto Zurbano questioned whether the presence and attitude of the world's press may have encouraged some rappers to act in a *more* controversial manner, as a form of self-promotional strategy. Be this as it may, the lens is neither innocent nor inconsequential, and its gaze transforms the object being viewed. In Havana, Akozta implies, cameras functioned as an instrument of censorship on hip hop performances. It has been suggested that the denuncia social incident was the turning point in the fortunes of the hip hop scene and the beginning of the end of the festival; if so, the foreign lenses that were pointed at the festival were complicit in its demise. Many filmmakers raise the issue of state censorship, but few admit their unintentional collusion in the process.

Young Rebels provides numerous insights into the complicity between the filmmaker, tourism, and the state, and their complex relationship with the rap scene. It provides an illuminating critique of the visuality and voyeurism that have been identified as of central importance in

Havana and its artistic representations since the Special Period. If, as Esther Whitfield (2008, 125) suggests, Pedro Juan Gutiérrez exploits the proximity between reader, tourist, and voyeur "to unmask special period Cuba watching as fundamentally sordid," *Young Rebels* does the same, exposing the connections between filming, money, power, and surveillance. The boundaries between filmmaker, film watcher, and tourist are blurred: "watching and the desire to do so unremarked are constitutive of the essentially liberal quest for authenticity that . . . drives the tourist experience" (ibid.), and yet the film's directors constantly remind us that we are *not* doing so unremarked, as its subjects stare back into the lens and make repeated appeals through the camera to the watcher, thus unsettling the tourist-viewer. That the appeals all concern material needs underlines the fact that the relationship between watcher and subject is fundamentally economic, and that the watcher is consumer as well as armchair tourist. *Young Rebels* underlines just how much the filming of documentaries by foreigners became an integral part of the hip hop scene; while most filmmakers are careful to edit each other out lest the supposedly hidden, underground scene they were filming look more like a press conference, Boden and Fleck gleefully focus on other camerapersons. The viewer is left in no doubt about the power of the lens (and the people behind it) to shape the phenomena that it captures.

In many cases, this power is wielded benignly, since the camera is held by a hip hop fan or Cubaphile with a deep attachment to the local scene; still, Boden and Fleck reveal that the politics of representation, surveillance, and touristic consumption lie far beyond the control of any individual, however well intentioned. Furthermore, the poor circulation of information between the United States and Cuba and, in some cases, misunderstandings on the part of Cubans about the logistics and economics of independent film production, lead to widespread suspicions within the rap scene. Many rappers believe that people who made documentaries about them have gone on to make a fortune back in North America or Europe without giving anything back to participants, and the backlash against filmmakers has started to make its way into print (e.g., Sáez Rodríguez n.d.b). While not all the complaints are equally justifiable—some misunderstand the shoestring economics of independent documentary making—the film *Guerrilla Radio* stands out for the questionable intentions that seem to underpin it.

Guerrilla Radio is the one film that appears to be a deliberate attempt to undermine its subjects and distort their words, making heavy use of voice-over in order to impose the directors' vision. In one of the first scenes, the narrator says that if rappers cross the line, they will be denied the right to perform or thrown in jail: in reality, even bans are very rare and short-lived and jailing rappers is unheard of, and the narrator's words are undermined by the footage that plays underneath them, which shows Anónimo Consejo and Doble Filo—both employed by the ACR—performing at the prestigious Casa de la Música. The directors Thomas Nybo and Simon Umlauf at no point mention that Kokino, one of their principal subjects, is employed by the state, or that even critical rappers are more likely to benefit from state support (via the AHS) than to suffer sanctions. The film then moves on to Las Krudas: while not referring specifically to them by name, the narrator remarks in this section that "the only sure way to make money is to sell your body," despite the fact that Las Krudas illustrate precisely the opposite with their tourist show in Habana Vieja. He labels Alexánder Guerra "the hustler," despite filming him in his (perfectly legitimate) job at a department store. In true conservative fashion, the Cuban state is personalized: owners of bed-and-breakfasts have to pay "a hefty fee to Fidel's government" (in other countries, this is known as a tax); "Fidel is watching your every move" (scary music plays in the background at this point); and Fidel has a monopoly on the word "revolution" (the directors fail to mention that Anónimo Consejo created the slogan "¡Hip hop, revolución!," which has been appropriated by the AHS and has spread across Latin America).

The directors claim that some Cuban rappers dare to criticize Castro and then segue into a scene lifted from CHHAS in which Etián's freestyle on the beach includes the phrases "counterrevolution, no!" and "go on Fidel!" They later say that Papá Humbertico criticizes Castro (untrue), and they illustrate this with the song "El Movimiento," which is in fact a criticism of the rap scene itself. Nybo pushes Papá Humbertico to say something critical about the government, but the rapper resists, his mistrust palpable (and eminently justified). When asked about the denuncia social incident in 2002, Humbertico says: "Nothing happened. I was banned for four months, that was it." Undeterred, the narrator forges ahead, claiming that "these musicians are risking their lives to be heard." And he finishes on the equally dramatic (if risible) note: "Remember

these faces. They might be thrown in prison, killed by firing squad, relegated to a life of obscurity on the streets of Havana, or they might ignite a
new Cuban revolution." Or they might carry on making critical hip hop,
as they have in fact done, often in spaces provided by the state.

While an extreme example, this film amply illustrates the risks that hip
hoppers run by collaborating with filmmakers. When I visited Havana in
2008, I talked to several protagonists of the film: none had seen it or
heard a word from the directors since filming had finished, and they were
less than amused to hear how their words had been twisted. The irony is
that a film like this could turn out to be a self-fulfilling prophecy: if one
thing is likely to derail the career of artists like Anónimo Consejo or Papá
Humbertico, it would be association (even unsuspecting) with the political positions espoused in the film's voice-overs and on-screen titles. This
documentary illustrates, if in extreme form, the disempowering potential
of the foreign lens. No wonder many hip hoppers are now highly circum-
spect when a lens is pointed at them.

The Cuban Gaze

Since the focus has thus far been firmly on foreign representations, it is
worth highlighting three Cuban-made documentaries that provide insights into local perspectives.[16] The first, *Mano Armada*, is a short film by
the group of the same name, made up of Papá Humbertico and El Discípulo. This is as close to an insider's view as one could hope for: a documentary made by two of the scene's most respected figures. The tone is serious,
and the camera style is "talking head," focusing repeatedly on the speak-
er's mouth: this is all about words, about ideas. It is not a beautiful film—
they are working with basic, borrowed equipment—but it is clearly not
meant to be beautiful. It is made up mainly of interviews, interspersed
with fragments of music videos, and there is no padding, no pandering to
the tourist imagination: no rumba, no Santería, no 1950s cars or crumbling city streets. Looking through the eyes of Mano Armada, one becomes
more aware of the visual clichés interspersed throughout foreign-made
films to appeal to foreign viewers.

The second, Ricardo Bacallao's *A Short Radiography of Hip Hop in Cuba*,
uses hip hop as a vehicle for discussing the broader question of race in
Cuba. It is perhaps more significant as an example of its own central

thesis—that race was increasingly a topic of debate by Cuban intellectuals and artists around the beginning of the millennium—than for its detail about the hip hop scene, in which the director was not heavily immersed. A polemical film, it contributes to the debate on race but somewhat bends reality in order to make its overarching point, since (as happens with academic analyses) the urge to see Cuban hip hop through a race lens entails overlooking significant nuances (for example, the music accompanying the opening titles of this film about "black culture" in Cuba is provided by Edgar González, a white rapper).

Bacallao presents the takeover of the rap festival's organization by the AHS in 2001 and the removal of Grupo Uno as a white coup directed against a black movement, with the AHS president Alonso and his assistant Luis Morlote (both white) usurping an event started by Rodolfo Rensoli and Balesy Rivero (both black). The reality is more complex. As discussed in earlier chapters, the AHS had been involved in the festival since 1997, and Alonso did not take over the festival from Rensoli but rather from his predecessor as president of the AHS, Fernando Rojas, who is white; responsibility had thus lain in the hands of a white president since 1997. Furthermore, it was not Alonso who took Rensoli's place, but Ariel Fernández, a self-identified black Cuban with a problack agenda. If anything, the festival took on more of a racial character after 2001, as Fernández and Pablo Herrera (also markedly problack) played leading roles. The changes came as much from an internal power struggle between black figures of authority within the hip hop scene (Rensoli and Fernández) as from intervention by white officials. *A Short Radiography* is thus an insider's view of the black Cuban experience, rather than of the hip hop scene. The director knew Rensoli and Rivero before starting to make the film, and we see the Havana scene largely through their eyes, despite the fact that Rensoli had been sidelined two years before. There is no mention of Fernández or Herrera, two (black) figures at the heart of the hip hop festival by this time (whom Rensoli unsurprisingly resented). The overall point of the film—that the story of Cuban hip hop is all about race and government power—is one that many people would agree with, but the argument used to make it is more questionable.

The third film presents a broad vision of contemporary Havana society but gives hip hop a significant role. *Pa'lante* takes up the self-reflexive theme of *Young Rebels*. Los Aldeanos and friends are recorded discussing how they will come across in the documentary, revealing their awareness of the lens's distorting potential. Aldo addresses the camera: "When you develop your idea, when you have your documentary, when you do your job, you are going to do it in a way, unwillingly, that when you show it to anyone, we're going to look like gusanos. People who don't agree with the government or anything. No, no, no, it's unavoidable." Aldo implies that the lens almost has a power of its own; simply appearing in a film may make rappers look more like dissidents than they actually are. Filming, then, is political, and representation inherently problematic. Tellingly, however, they immediately joke (to the camera) about being thrown in jail for saying the wrong thing, laughing heartily—hardly the state of fear that Nybo and Umlauf describe. The camera becomes a protagonist again when we see a group of tourists crossing the road; one turns to face the film camera, points his camera straight at it, and pretends to take a photo. Tourist and Cuban lenses gaze at each other for a brief moment. This cues the song "Mangos bajitos" by Los Aldeanos, discussed in chapter 3, which begins: "What does my spying eye see?" Later in this track, in which the rappers throw the foreigners' gaze back in their faces, they rap to their imaginary tourist listeners:

Accompany me to see more than just the Havana Malecón,
Take your camera, buy two or three rolls of film,
I'll invite you to take photos in El Fanguito [a notoriously run-down
    barrio].

They foreground the role of the lens in mediating foreigners' experiences of Havana and the circulation of a limited stock of "classic" images. As with *Young Rebels*, the references to the lens, tourism, representation, and state power ensure that the issues of filming and being filmed are never far from the surface.

Cuba Represents

Orishas' debut album *A lo Cubano* begins with a two-minute drummed invocation of the gods of the Santería pantheon and segues into the track "Represent," in which the group emphasizes its roots in rumba, son, and guaguancó. In a line reminiscent of a tourist board advertisement, they rap: "I represent salsa and the sun of Cuba." The opening minutes of *A lo*

Cubano were Orishas' chance to "represent" on the global stage. If we compare their lyrics with Los Aldeanos' "Mangos bajitos," it is clear that "representing" in hip hop requires making artistic and political choices. Just as the camera lens is not a mirror of reality, neither is the rapper's eye: both construct, omit, and proselytize.

There is a tendency to assume that the representations of underground rappers are more reliable than those of their commercial counterparts and therefore need no discussion qua representation. It is worth pointing out, therefore, the tension between the notion of conscious rap as a faithful mirror of social realities, and its proselytizing intention, which implies a more interventionalist stance. Zurbano (n.d.b) contrasts conscious rap with reggaetón, which "does not aim to go into reality in depth, but just to describe it, often reproducing alienating aspects of culture." In other words, it is precisely the interpretive, even exclusionary, aspect of hip hop representation that gives it value, according to this view; mirroring does nothing to make the world a better place, since much of what is reflected is not worth seeing. Imani Perry (2004, 39–40) provides a welcome reminder that realist movements in art still involve choices about how to represent reality. Too often in accounts of global hip hop, conscious rap lyrics are perceived simply as mirrors of reality, but "representing" is both a political and an artistic act, and it thus invites critical reflection.

This is particularly true in Havana, where "representing" takes place under external influences. Robert Neustadt (2002, 153) discusses the tendency of Cuban artists "to skew their own social reality so that it conforms to tourists' expectations." He draws on the studies of Louis Pérez, who focuses on how foreign visions of Cuba (and foreign money) have long shaped the ways in which Cuba represents itself. Pérez underlines the existence since the early twentieth century of "a complex transaction by which the North American notion of 'Cuban' acted to change or otherwise modify Cuban self-representation as a means of success and advancement" (quoted in Neustadt 2002, 153). The relevance of these remarks to Orishas is clear enough: the first song on the album begins with the chant "represent, represent," yet their vision of Cuba—sun, rum, cigars, mulattas, rumba—is clearly conditioned by the expectations of non-Cuban tourists and consumers. Of course, the case of Orishas is not typical but rather reflects the most successful bid for commercial success by any Cuban rap group. Nevertheless, it points usefully to the transnational politics of representation in Havana hip hop.

The market for Cuban hip hop is complex, because it consists not just of foreign producers and record labels but also, and indeed in large measure, of foreign documentary makers, activists, journalists, and scholars. As the popularity of rap started to decline, around 2003, underground rappers became increasingly aware that their music was consumed more enthusiastically by foreigners than locals. When I met groups like Explosión Suprema and Los Paisanos in 2004, they made no bones about their target audience: foreigners were more excited than Cubans about underground hip hop, and they promoted the groups back home, raising the possibility of foreign tours. As Randee Akozta points out in *Young Rebels*, foreigners also provided crucial economic support via the purchase of CDs. Yet even for the previous five years, ever since the Black August exchanges began, North American expectations had played a big part in shaping the hip hop scene in Havana. Neustadt's basic point, that outsiders' gaze has long had an impact on the production of Cuban popular music, thus remains true.

Explosión Suprema. Photo by Alex Lloyd.

Of course, there were many other factors involved, but the fact that the foreign delegations in the late 1990s brought and sought out political, race-conscious, underground rap undoubtedly reinforced its newfound primacy over the more commercial, dance-centered styles prominent just a few years earlier.[17] This underground orientation was further strengthened by those who came to interview hip hoppers; foreign visitors wanted to see an underground, black movement, with its fists in the air.

We need to be aware of the competing transnational forces at play in the Havana hip hop scene in the late 1990s, the pull of Orishas (in France) in one corner and that of dead prez in the other. Cuban artists were "representing" within this transnational sphere, and many were keen to attract one of two sets of foreign listeners: the global fusion crowd and the revolutionary hip hop crowd. When legendary figures of Cuban hip hop like Rubén Marín and Yrak Saenz raised questions about the boom years, they implied that what some of their colleagues "represented" on stage reflected fashionable ideologies more than lived realities. The ideological leanings of Black August and many of the foreigners who came in their wake hang over the issue of "representing" in Havana hip hop; it wasn't just where you were from, it was where you were hoping to go. The potential benefits of hip hop thus destabilized "representing," and this is reflected in the many songs about fake rappers, such as Papá Humbertico's "Real MC" or Los Paisanos' "Está de moda ser rapero" (it's fashionable to be a rapper). Running through such songs is the concern that it is easy, and advantageous, to look like a rapper. The first and last "commandments" of Anónimo Consejo's "Ley 5566" concern truth and appearances, illustrating the centrality of such concerns: "put the truth first, NO to falsehood" and "underground hip hop is not a facade: it is an approach to life. Grow and develop yourself, there is no room for empty words here." The line between "representing" and mimicry is thin, and the temptation to cross it is greater when the foreign gaze is more prominent: as El Libre raps in "La etiK," another song about false MCs, "they want to be rappers when there's a festival with yumas [foreigners]." Thanks to its transnational dimension, Havana hip hop, like tourist Cuba, "lives off the compulsive imitation of its own authenticity" (Medina 2007, 17), leading to continual anxiety over realness. The "passion for the Real" that underpinned foreign interest risked "culminat[ing] in its apparent opposite, in a theatrical spectacle" (Slavoj Žižek, quoted in ibid., 15).

Questions about art, mimesis, and representation surfaced with the emergence of Los Aldeanos. Their work has been acclaimed by old- and new-school hip hoppers alike, yet (as they admit) they are not always, to speak in the strict hip hop sense of the word, "representing" (i.e., speaking about their personal experience), since they are from the upmarket neighborhood of Nuevo Vedado and Aldo lives in relatively comfortable circumstances. When they say *somos de la calle* (we're from the street), they don't actually mean that they are from the street. While this irritates a few of the Havana old school, particularly those who come from humble backgrounds, it is worth remembering that the archetypal political rappers, Public Enemy, were middle-class kids from the suburbs (Chang 2005, 232, 236). They would visit relatives in Harlem and the Bronx, but they lived on Long Island and described their trips to the city as living vicariously: they knew the street but did not live in it. They had the time, space, and economic advantages to think through and map out their course. "Representing" in political rap is thus a transformative process, for all that it might appear otherwise. Los Aldeanos are representing realities that are close, but not identical, to their own, and one might ask whether there is a connection between the unparalleled power of their lyrics and the greater degree of artistic invention involved. Aldo wrote poetry before he started rapping, so he thinks of rap as an art form, not just a mirror. For all that Los Aldeanos may evoke metaphors of the video camera and the spying eye, to quote the title of one of Aldo's albums, their raps come from "poetry and the heart." The gap between representation and reality can thus be a source of strength as well as weakness.

The politics of vision and representation is itself a topic in much rap production, and a recurrent theme is that twenty-twenty vision depends as much on where you look as who is looking—hence Los Aldeanos' offer to take tourists to shoot photos in El Fanguito. Randee Akozta ("Mi ventana") evokes the world that he sees from his window:

> If I could, I would make more windows
> Not with a sea view but onto Cuban reality.

Hermanos de Causa rap in "San Cristóbal de La Habana":

> You need to see the social chronicle as I've seen it
> I don't take photos or go cross-eyed.

The lens as distortion, in this case of racial realities, reappears in Hermanos de Causa's "Lágrimas negras":

> Whites and mulattos in 'Sun and Son' magazine for tourists while on TV
>   practically the same
> In a Cuba where there are loads of black people, you see, what a
>   contradiction.

The camera lens links the tourist industry, tourists themselves, and the media, all of them misrepresenting local realities.

While the camera can lie, hip hop opens up the possibility of clear-sightedness: as Aldo stated in an interview, "hip hop removed the veil from my eyes" (quoted in García Freyre 2009). Many of his lyrics, such as those of "Nos achicharraron," aim to uncover harsh realities behind shiny appearances—a kind of x-ray vision. He criticizes his generation for

> Paying who knows how much to see who knows who singing
> While your mother is washing by hand,
> Having ten twenty-four-carat gold chains
> And a son who doesn't go to school because he doesn't have any shoes.

His image of "a packet of Hollywood with some Titanics inside," contrasting expensive hard-currency cigarettes with the cheapest in local pesos, sums up his vision of a young generation in which appearances rarely tell the truth. The rapper's role is then to see through the cover.

Nevertheless, the rapper too can lie and can give the tourist what she or he wants to see. The auto-exoticization of Orishas is punctured by El Libre and El B in "Mi sociedad," in a line that parodies the opening of "A lo cubano":

> The Cuban way, a bottle of cheap rum and a stick to smoke
> You can use your sore throat again tomorrow for your hangover.[18]

Most accounts of the Havana scene have been written by commentators for whom the central hip hop discourses of "representing" and "keeping it real" are self-explanatory; as a result, questions raised by acts of (self-)representation and anxieties over realness have been paid minimal attention. But numerous rappers, in songs and interviews, have underlined that misrepresentations may come from within hip hop as well as without. "Representing," an artistic act that may be aimed at foreigners, is therefore potentially suspect.

"The More National You Are, the More Universal You Will Be"

In her study of Romanian socialist cultural production, Katherine Verdery (1991, 303–4) writes that "bargaining for resources from the center was basic to politics in command systems. For cultural producers seeking the resources to sustain their activity, much of this bargaining consisted of claims about 'cultural representativeness.' . . . 'Representing' one's culture need not automatically entail invoking national identity, but in the Romanian context this was the form often taken by contests for attention from the center."

Verdery's analysis is useful here in two key ways. First, she illustrates the external motivations behind "representing," that key hip hop term that is so often taken to stem only from within. The questions of to whom and why rappers represent are important for Cuban hip hop studies, which have tended to focus on the content rather than politics of representation. The idea of representing as a "contest for attention" is relevant, since in Havana, bargaining for resources took place not just with the state but also with foreign cultural activists and entrepreneurs. Representing is thus a terrain of negotiation rather than a simple mirror. Second, Verdery makes the link between representing, national identity, and expediency, which questions the positive moral value often granted to distinctively nationalized cultural forms.

In the introduction to his influential anthology *Global Noise*, Tony Mitchell (2001c, 11) sets out an adoption-adaptation model for hip hop around the world: he describes two phases, an initial negotiation with U.S. rap and then a "return to the local" (ibid., 32), which he interprets as syncretism or the incorporation of local features. The second phase, indigenization, is presented as moving beyond the first, simple appropriation. James Lull (2002, 242) too, sees a two-stage process of transculturation (the movement of cultural forms in time and space) followed by hybridization or indigenization. The "imported cultural elements take on local features as the cultural hybrids develop" (ibid., 244); taking rap as his example, Lull states that "the sounds become indigenized at the same time" (ibid.). Elsewhere, Mitchell (2004) expresses anxiety over music that does not show any local or national characteristics, dismissing Swedish rappers for their "bland, homogenized Americanisms" (ibid., 120).

Lull's and Mitchell's evolutionary views have been influential, and others have followed in labeling nonsyncretized hip hop with negative terms such as "simple" and "mimicking" (Tickner 2008, 122), and implying that such music is developmentally stunted, since it is supposedly associated with an initial stage.

Underlying Mitchell's vision are the laudable aims of the "preservation of ethnic autonomy" and the "survival of the local" (2004, 121). However, that vision is inadequate to explain the complex politics of hip hop style in Havana, and it fits poorly with what I have seen on visits to Caracas and Bogotá. The kind of syncretism that Mitchell describes is rarely found on a musical level; it is located more commonly in language and the depiction of local realities. Certainly, exceptions can be found, often quite prominent ones, since groups that hybridize their music (such as Orishas or the Colombian Choc Quib Town) tend to be more commercially and critically successful; but theorizing on the basis of such atypical examples is a dubious policy. Mitchell's view is ultimately exclusionary and moralistic since it assigns greater value to adaptation than adoption and refuses to take the latter seriously, and since it misses some important points about local versions of globalized cultural forms. Accepting this simplistic "the more indigenized, the better" ideology would entail dismissing perhaps 80 percent of the hip hop created in Havana in the last few years and 95 percent of what I heard, week in week out, in live peñas. The obsession with syncretism does not allow for the reality that a lot of hip hoppers, in Cuba and across Latin America, identify more closely with U.S. rap than with their officially recognized national culture and musical genres. While academics and music executives seek difference from the global norm, many hip hoppers seek difference from the local norm; it is not clear that an academic discourse that dismisses the majority of Latin American hip hop is a particularly useful one.

Most Havana rappers have little time for Mitchell's view of indigenization, and many urban music producers and consumers are not at all bothered about his idea of musical localization (much less the resistance to global currents that underpins it). For many, sounding yuma is precisely the point. La Comisión Depuradora incorporated dozens of Havana's most active rappers in 2007–8, yet it does not fit at all with Mitchell's picture. Its producers make hip hop out of samples of classical music, Spanish pop, film scores, and anything else that may be at hand, but very rarely Cuban music. The first step is to recognize that such nonlocalized sounds are central to and characteristic of Havana hip hop since 2004, not the productions of an unevolved minority; the second is to ask why this might be the case and what it might mean.

Let us go back to the late 1990s, when a new wave of transnationalism affected hip hop in Havana. From 1998 to 2000, a selection of the finest conscious rappers from the United States performed live in the city. Meanwhile, in 1999 Orishas released their first album, *A lo Cubano*, in Spain. These developments encapsulated two major strands of hip hop that had been in the air in Havana for some time, categorized as underground and commercial. Orishas were far away in Europe, but Mos Def, Common, and the rest were in Havana: as a result, the ideology of the hip hop scene was becoming more politicized, more underground. Mitchell's vision does not allow for these local circumstances, in which indigenization was associated with the blatant commercialism of Orishas in Europe and authenticity was attributed to underground stylistic purity.

Peter Wade (2004, 277) critiques a common academic model of globalization and localization "in which the global is 'out there' as a series of external influences which then impinge on a ready-made local scene and are adapted and resignified there, creating a diversity which goes against ideas of simple cultural homogenization through globalization." A central part of Wade's work on music has been to underline the fact that the local musical culture in Colombia, and elsewhere in Latin America, was in fact already global. This is eminently true of music in Havana, a cultural crossroad since the sixteenth century and an avid consumer of American music since the nineteenth. Equally, in the case of Cuban hip hop, the global was already local: the incoming global culture was a hybrid mixture that included musical and ideological elements derived from the local context (as discussed in chapter 1).

By using Black August and Orishas as examples, we can see globalization taking place on the local stage and localization on the global stage. The kind of indigenization that Mitchell champions has generally occurred, in the field of Cuban hip hop, through the mediation of foreign producers, foreign record labels, or Cubans with a distinctly transnational outlook. This raises the question of precisely what Mitchell means by "the survival of the local": according to his definition, the epitome of local Cuban hip hop style would be Orishas, based in Europe for a decade and backed by the international corporation EMI. The soundtrack of the Havana scene, rooted in the city's clubs where the locals go, is global in its aesthetic orientation. "The local" is thus something of a misnomer when applied to indigenized music, since it inverts the relationship between style and location. In Cuba, as in other parts of Latin America, the embracing of global musical styles plays an important role in producing and intensifying local (sometimes called neotribal) identities, as evidenced in strong local music scenes such as Havana hip hop; if one focuses on identity rather than aesthetics, global music like underground rap may be more linked to the survival of the local than is localized music produced in a transnational context for international consumers.

As Borges-Triana (2009, 141–42) notes, Cuban "localization" often takes place outside the island in the hands of émigré artists, as a form of nostalgia; island-based groups that tour overseas are also drawn toward Cubanization. Localization also takes place in dialogue with the market, which further complicates the implied link between syncretism and authenticity, given that within the world of "real hip hop," the market is a symbol of everything to be avoided. Thanks to Orishas, and to SBS before them, mixing hip hop with local styles became linked to commercialization; as the Havana scene became more underground under the influence of Black August, musical localization became representative of inauthenticity, or a desire to insert music into the market, rather than authenticity.[19] The latter was associated with heavy, hard, uncompromising beats —"bland, homogenized Americanisms," as Mitchell would call them—to accompany the hard-hitting lyrics. Since, during the Black August period, the identity of the Havana scene revolved around the idea of being more authentic than the original, of being the guardian of hip hop's spirit, there is considerable logic behind the gravitation toward stylistic conservatism and a purist stance. Such a stance needs to be understood as a choice underpinned by a coherent ideology, not dismissed as evidence of a lack of creativity.

The relationship between musical adaptation and the market is significant. The indigenization argument is upheld by Mitchell and others largely because it is seen as a form of resistance to globalization, with the local pitched against the global in a fight for survival. In fact, the celebration of local distinctiveness and autonomy is a product of globalization that meshes perfectly with the global movement of capital (Robertson

ence is closely aligned with the interests of the capitalist music and
tourist industries: Orishas, the most localized Cuban hip hop, was the
most appealing to a major international record label, and the localization
evident in its music and lyrics is one that sells readily to a global audience
of real and armchair tourists. Cheerleading for the local thus raises difficult questions.

Furthermore, in the Cuban hip hop context, to equate localization with
mixing hip hop with son or rumba is simplistic because it implies a clear
distinction between local music and global music. As all students of Cuban music know, American music has been a staple for Cuban listeners
for over a century, and many of my informants grew up listening primarily to funk, soul, and hip hop. Few would argue with the idea of
baseball as the local sport in Havana, or 1950 Chevys as the characteristic
local form of transport; why, then, might música americana not be considered as a local form of music? As Lise Waxer (1994, 163) points out,
Cuban music that traveled to the United States in the first half of the
twentieth century was already influenced by jazz; Humberto Manduley
López (2007) argues that there has not been such a thing as pure national
music in Cuba for at least fifty years. If Cuban music has long been mixed
with American, what sort of autonomy or local essence is there to preserve? Equally, hip hop, like most of the main forms of popular music to
emerge from New York in the twentieth century, had some Cuban roots.
If hip hop is in fact partly Cuban, then why should rappers have to adapt
it in order to localize it?

The pro-indigenization viewpoint would not be worth so much discussion were it not so common—indeed, virtually universal—in Cuban and
global hip hop studies. It coincides with the nationalist discourse of
Cubanization and the music industry–driven ideology of "difference
sells" to send a powerful message that fusion is the only authentic path.
As a result, many of the most admired figures among hip hoppers are
sidelined or studied only as producers of verbal texts, creating a distorted
image of the hip hop scene.

This view seems to rest on an outdated, essentialist vision of the relationship between music and identity, ignoring the fact that scholars have
been arguing for a more flexible picture for some time. Stuart Hall (1996,
2–3) prefers the term "identification," with its emphasis on process,

contingency, and strategy, while Simon Frith (1996) also takes an anti-essentialist view, dissecting the fallacies of looking for direct reflections of identity or place in music. For Frith, musical practices need to be interpreted as processes through which identity is actively imagined, created, or constructed: "Identity . . . comes from the outside not the inside; it is something we put or try on, not something we reveal or discover." He goes on to cite Mark Slobin: "We all grow up with *something*, but we can choose just about *anything* by way of expressive culture" (quoted in Frith 1996, 122). If we take such anti-essentialist conceptions of music and identity seriously, then there is no reason to accord greater value or authenticity to musical expressions that exhibit surface features of national identity, or to dismiss other kinds as "mimicry."

Scholars of U.S. hip hop generally embrace the idea of sampling as constructing a musical history, connecting to roots in time and space. What, then, are we to make of the prevalence of classical music samples in underground hip hop in Havana? What sort of history is being constructed here? It is rather an antihistory: a break with hegemonic conceptions of place and identity, a rejection of a national musical history focused on pleasure and dance that is seen as a poor reflection of the contemporary city. In a society in which the pressures of cultural nationalism are so great, such aesthetic choices are not to be dismissed as evidence of immaturity.

Although for many, the dominant vision of Cuban identity is something to celebrate, for others it is restrictive and homogenizing at best, and distorting at worst. Edgar González is one of the more eclectic figures in the Havana hip hop scene, but even he described cubanía as a kind of small box into which everything had to be squeezed. The hallmark of Cuban music brings great advantages on the global stage but complicates the lives of artists on a local level. In recent popular music, *lo cubano* is heavily colored by BVSC and Orishas; Quiroga (2005, 164) describes the late 1990s as a time when " 'Cuba' became almost a kind of franchise within the capitalist music scene," illustrating why avoiding Cubanization was a logical step for those who were ideologically opposed to that scene. If representing national identity is linked with expediency and the market, rejecting indigenization may be seen as a strong statement of identity and ideology, not a failure to progress to a second, more authentic phase.

There is, of course, some truth in the broad adoption-adaptation posi-

tion espoused by Mitchell and Lull and propounded by many commentators on Cuban hip hop, since examples of indigenization clearly exist.
However, it is misleading (because it represents only a small proportion
of hip hop production) and judgmental (in the implication that the aesthetic preferences of most Havana hip hoppers are primitive). In the
Cuban case, it is often expounded by commentators with only limited
experience of the week-in, week-out hip hop scene, whose judgments are
based on selective listening to recordings and occasional attendance at
showcase hip hop events. The first rap in Havana was made over instrumentals borrowed from the United States, and it is undoubtedly true that
once local producers started creating beats, some groups were interested
in pursuing a more overtly Cuban aesthetic. Nevertheless, the combined
influence of Black August and Orishas muddied the waters considerably.
Herrera recounts in the film *Cuban HipHop: Desde el Principio* that Orishas
led to a crisis in the way rap was produced in Cuba, making people think
that Cuban rap had to be mixed with elements of traditional music and
"made with nostalgia"; but the aesthetic and political influence of Black
August ensured that Orishas imitations were looked down upon and few
in number, as evidenced by the *Cuban Rap Ligas* compilation and much of
the hip hop produced since. The dominant sound of Havana hip hop has
been moving away from cubanía, not least because key rappers who were
more interested in fusion, such as Telmary and Kumar, have moved out of
the hip hop scene and eventually out of the country.

Changes in musical style have continued to take place within the hip hop
scene, with Obsesion shifting to a more Africanized sound and 100%
Original changing not only their musical identity but also their name (to
Ogguere), but by and large these shifts have been the result not of a
natural process but rather of exposure to (or the desire for exposure to) the
global music scene. Tours overseas, starting in 2001, seem to have convinced several artists of the need to have something distinctively Cuban to
show, in order to have any chance of making an impact internationally.
Alexey Rodríguez (Obsesion) told me that an important lesson he had
learned from foreign exchanges was the importance of working with live
musicians—something he had earlier resisted (Borges-Triana n.d., 7). A
tour to Europe with the rumba group Clave y Guaguancó in 2002 was key
to changing his mind, and he was blown away by a performance by the
multinational group Ska Cubano in London in 2007: "They'll put us out of

work," he joked. Having defended nonlocalized sounds in their lyrics on *Cuban Rap Ligas*, Obsesion went on to become one of the groups most associated with the use of live instruments and African-derived sounds. Like many other artists, they found that having a rhythm that "wears a guayabera" was actually quite important for Cuban musicians in New York or London, if not in Havana, where audiences are more skeptical; their exposure to the global music scene catalyzed their conversion to the local. Ogguere's more Cuban sound brought them long-awaited success, attracting the attention of British producer Gilles Peterson and leading to invitations to perform in the United Kingdom as part of the Havana Cultura project. Rubén Marín was quite open to me about the need to Cubanize to capture attention overseas: "I need training in Cuban music, because otherwise when you go overseas or they hear you there, they will say: 'If you're going to make rap that's the same as in the U.S. you've got nothing to say to us.'" He quoted approvingly Guillén's aphorism: "The more national you are, the more universal you will be."

Leading hip hoppers have thus been pulled in two directions, aware that national and international recognition and commercial viability required a profusion discourse, while local "real hip hop" ideology required the opposite. The mixed feelings of key figures in the scene at this time is evident in Fernández's landmark article, in which he both praises and criticizes fusion. He underlines the fact that the pressure to indigenize was both commercial and external in origin: "Foreign entrepreneurs generally come to impose their criteria, coming with money in hand and trying to buy Cuban talent on the cheap. Promoting the fusion of rap with Afro-Cuban music, with son, with salsa and timba. . . . That doesn't mean one can't create a fusion with our rhythms, as long as it's done well, but we shouldn't have to be saturated with the 'SBS tumbao,' nor is this kind of mixing necessary to give Cuban rap its identity. You can imagine 150 groups making timba-rap, with commercial lyrics, going on about cigars and Guillén—it would be a cultural catastrophe" (2000, 10).

The reference to "cigars and Guillén" would seem to invoke Orishas and CHHAS (which included three reworkings of texts by the Cuban national poet), and yet Fernández goes on to praise these two projects: further evidence, I would suggest, of the contradictory forces operating on him. Be that as it may, his anxious comments reveal that the scene was under pressure from forces emanating from outside the island, and that

Obsesion performing in London. Photo by Alex Lloyd.

mixing with Cuban music was far from a straightforward option, since it was tainted by commercialism and not well regarded by many fans; the result was that many artists rejected indigenization. In an interview, Pablo Herrera said, "I only sample Cuban music, nothing else," yet he stressed that congas were not an option: "The youth that listens to hip-hop wants to listen to something that resembles where the music comes from. . . . If you overdo [the percussion], people say, 'That's salsa; I've already had enough of that'" (Sokol 2000). The ambivalence and contradictory pressures felt by Fernández and Herrera, two of the architects of the scene, have not been reflected in the Cuban hip hop literature.

The contradiction between what most Havana rappers wanted to do and what most foreigners wished they would do is perfectly encapsulated by a remark made by a member of the U.S. hip hop group The Roots during a press conference to accompany their performance in Havana ("The Roots en Cuba" n.d., 37): "I've just seen four musicians who are looking for technology, and here I am looking for musicians; the musicians who were playing in the lobby of the Hotel Nacional were like DJs— The Beatnuts, a very popular group in my country, would pay thousands of dollars to sample them." Similarly, at the Pastors for Peace concert, the North Americans performed with live musicians whereas the three Cuban groups did not; attempts to work with live bands are rarely greeted with enthusiasm by the core Havana hip hop audience. I am thus wary of any suggestion that it is natural for Cuban rappers to want to incorporate Cuban music. Intellectuals like to underline the connections between traditional and imported musical forms, but the artists themselves—though they may learn to talk the talk—have generally been resistant to making such links in practice.[20]

In a recent article, two journalists (Carroll and Schipani 2008) under-line the fact that foreigners are the primary purchasers of culture in Havana, and so foreign tastes dominate. They quote one artist who said bluntly: "The tourists are the only buyers, and they want shit, so we give them shit. We get money in our pocket, everyone is happy." It is therefore interesting to note how, some years earlier, Fernández had rallied the troops against "music industry adventurer-entrepreneurs": "Don't let them think that, just because things are tight economically, we're going to do whatever they feel like. There's a consensus, a union among the majority of groups, to demand respect, not to sell their ideas and their work for pennies" (2000, 10). This resistance to international pressures was paradoxically boosted by the New York–based Black August collective, an important counterbalance to these adventurer-entrepreneurs and an alternative market for real hip hop. As a result of these transnational connections, Cuban rap was validated as underground hip hop, aligned more with dead prez than with Cuban music. The localization of the music was thus not so crucial because the lyrics were regarded as authen-tic, distinctive, and a significant contribution to the global Hip Hop Na-tion. If the localization discourse is often not reflected on the ground in Havana, it is partly because many artists are interested in locating them-selves more as representing underground hip hop than as representing Cuban music. The pro-indigenization scholarly stance locates authen-ticity only in local adaptation, whereas in many hip hop scenes outside the United States, being true to hip hop is of paramount importance; departing musically from the canons of hip hop means abandoning hip hop itself, as exemplified by Free Hole Negro's invention of the term "free hop" to describe their eclectic fusion. (The group's days within the Ha-vana hip hop scene were numbered.)

Many hip hoppers regard Cuban popular music as a term against which to define themselves, something that Mitchell's model cannot countenance. The cheerleading for adaptation ought to make room for a more nuanced perspective that takes full account of local producers with a more jaundiced view of local traditions, for whom imitation is not a sign of poverty of imagination but a positive, conscious alignment. Globalized sounds mean more than just an absence of creativity, ability, or maturity; they are full of messages about imagined connections, about place, and about local visions of local society. If we take the refiguring of American music too literally, we will miss a lot of significant cultural production. There are already forces lined up against the musical preferences of underground hip hoppers in Havana—above all the state and the global music market, both of which actively promote indigenization. The last thing that these rappers need is for academics to do the same.

Rather than ignoring or dismissing nonindigenized musical sounds, we would do better to try to understand them. What does it tell us that, during my visit to Havana in 2007, the most popular rap group in Havana was Los Aldeanos, the most popular reggaetón artist was Elvis Manuel (whose instrumentals were copies of Puerto Rican music), and the Caimán Rock festival was dominated by thrash and death metal sung in English? It seemed as though after decades of official resistance and limited access to globalized musical currents, Havana audiences were now swallowing them whole. I had to look hard at the rap, reggaetón, and rock scenes to find the hybridization so beloved of musicologists. Some observers saw this as evidence of an unprecedented crisis in Cuban music; whether that is true or not, something was certainly going on that could not be ignored.

The new school of Cuban hip hop, epitomized by La Comisión Depuradora, has almost without exception rejected musical Cubanization, placing the adoption-adaptation model in further doubt. Rather than putting this down to inexperience (Los Aldeanos have made nearly twenty demos at the time of writing), we should acknowledge a strong anti-Cubanization ideology at work, one rooted in a perception of localization as commercially oriented self-exoticism. The views of Herrera, a leading figure of Cuban hip hop's old school and the producer widely credited with making the greatest steps toward Cubanization, are worth noting. Talking to me about Los Aldeanos in 2008, he said that Cubanness in music no longer mattered, and he saw this as a major leap forward: "we were part of the old norm . . . we thought the best way to make this Cuban was by having a Cuban tag to it, a traditional and historical tag that we could put onto it—if we mix with son, salsa, that's going to make us Cuban . . . that was important and relevant for that time, but now it's like, we don't really need to do that, we're past that stage, we're being Cuban." In the documentary *Calle Real 70*, the rap group Soldier Squad claims: "Before, rap was more . . . there was more son, more you know, more Cuban stuff, it was 'Ah, I'm Cuban, whatever, fiesta,' now it has changed. . . . Now it's deeper, much more critical, rigorous." Here, then, we see an evolutionary perspective, but one directly opposed to that of Mitchell and Lull. Both Herrera and Soldier Squad, representing old and new schools, associate surface Cuban-isms with an initial stage in which anxieties about cultural identity are at the forefront, while they perceive the second stage as more authentic since it is marked by simply "being Cuban."

Conclusions

This chapter has examined how hip hop fans, activists, and commenta-tors from around the world, particularly New York, fell in love with Havana, and how this has generated a huge amount of documentary material for a cultural form that had a relatively limited space in Cuban society. Rather than seeing the films and articles and theses (and this book) simply as windows onto processes of globalization and localization, I see them as an integral part of those processes. Hip hop as music of resistance, as "race music," as a "movement": these ideas and many oth-ers circulate globally and are localized by all sorts of intermediaries, including scholars. Hip hop in Cuba started out as dance music for a racially mixed crowd, and its transformation into a problack "hip hop revolution" by the end of the 1990s illustrates glocalization ("think glob-ally, act locally") in action—yet not simply because global currents were re-interpreted by local artists. Foreign filmmakers, writers, activists, and producers, including myself, have all been part of the cultural flows of Havana hip hop, and our cultural production has played a significant part in localizing the global Hip Hop Nation and globalizing the local Havana hip hop scene.

Underpinning both the Havana scene and the production of knowledge

about it has been the special relationship between the United States and 329
Cuba, above all between New York and Havana. Cuban hip hop boomed at
a moment when many North Americans were attracted to Cuba, in particular to its music and politics. The historical links between the Cuban
Revolution and figures such as Malcolm X and the Black Panthers paved
the way, with Harry Belafonte acting as a key intermediary between past
and present, and the Black August collective serving as a bridge between
New York and Havana. Cuban hip hop became intensely important for
many North American visitors and for U.S. exiles in Havana, such as
Nehanda Abiodun and Assata Shakur, who found in Havana hip hop (and
the Black August exchanges) a way to reconnect with and breathe new life
into the struggles of their earlier years. In the eyes of some Cubans, the
kids were just rapping like kids all over the world, and it was the foreign
observer-participant-activists who turned Cuban rap into a movement.
Be that as it may, its significance was clearly constructed transnationally.
For U.S. artists and activists, going to Cuba was a big deal: they felt that
they were going home in some sense, and that they had a lot to learn (as
well as to give) there, one of the principal ways in which Havana hip hop
differs from other outposts of the Hip Hop Nation.

An example of the international respect accorded to Cuban hip hop can
be seen in a connection forged between the revolutionary allies Cuba and
Venezuela. Anónimo Consejo's slogan "¡Hip hop, revolución!" has inspired a Latin American political hip hop organization of the same name,
based in Caracas. Its creators describe this organization in the following
terms: "Hip Hop Revolución is a concept that was conceived in that small,
great island named Cuba. It was created by Anónimo Consejo and picked
up by other artists, not only Cubans. It is a [web]site, and a tribute, which
tries to disseminate Hip Hop that is engaged with our People's realities,
taking a special stand in Latin America. Beginning from the site, HHR is
becoming a web of artists that understand Hip Hop as a tool of struggle
and social change" ("Hip Hop Is a Weapon" 2005). Havana is transfigured
from periphery to center of a web of progressive, grassroots cultural politics
articulated through hip hop. Hip Hop Revolución and Obsesion helped to
organize a series of concerts across the Americas to protest against the war
in Iraq, symbolically linking revolutionary hip hoppers across the hemisphere. This NGO connecting revolutionary artists in Venezuela and Cuba
is notable for representing an independent validation of government-level

solidarity: it is an enactment of neo-Bolivarianism, the Hispanic Caribbean alternative to U.S.-centered neoliberal pan-Americanism, modeled on Bolívar's vision of Latin American unity under Latin American leadership (Erisman 2004, 313). This organization promotes transnational solidarity within the hemisphere, with the Cuba-Venezuela axis at its center, and it has organized several international hip hop summits in Caracas, uniting artists and activists from across the Americas.[21]

The idea of Cuba as center rather than periphery, leader rather than follower, has circulated since the 1959 revolution, and it has been periodically reinforced (for example, by Castro's leadership of the nonaligned movement from 1979 to 1983).[22] The Cuban Revolution has been a global figurehead, an example and inspiration to many, and Cubans are used to the idea that their nation has an international importance and historic mission out of proportion to its size. Cubans are the last people to have an inferiority complex—"a significant facet of their national psyche is an extraordinary self-confidence" (Brenner et al. 2008, 278)—and pride in local hip hop grows out of this. Underlying the transnational relationships discussed in this chapter is thus an interesting dynamic between Cuba and the United States. If African Americans have a long history of admiration for Cuba, Afro-Cubans have long felt solidarity with the United States, but from a position of assumed superiority: they commiserate with their U.S. brethren for the perceived greater social inequities that they face. Despite the apparent centrality and position of power of the United States, within the realm of African American and Afro-Cuban relations the story is more complex, and Cuban hip hop reflects that fact.

In some cultural spheres being up-to-date is everything, but in the nostalgic world of hip hop where the old school is venerated, being behind the times can be a major advantage. Thus, since Cuba was behind the United States, it was actually ahead. For all that rap was considered by many as post-BVSC music, it ended up being framed in a very similar way, in terms of nostalgia, a time warp, rediscovered authenticity, and noncommercialism. As foreign observers saw it, isolation had kept Havana hip hop in an old-school bubble, untainted by the commercialism affecting the U.S. version—a story very similar to that of the BVSC. Son was the modern, commercial popular music of its time, yet it made a comeback in the late 1990s packaged as premodern, anticommercial music. In a similar way, rap represented modernity to Cuban youth in the mid-1990s, yet it appealed to foreigners largely because of its perceived old-school, anti-modern vibe.

Foreign nostalgia and fascination with the combination of politics and anticommercialism have been behind the proliferation of documentaries about Cuban hip hop; the unabashedly modern, commercial (and far more popular) timba and reggaetón scenes have provoked much less interest from filmmakers, with Jennifer Paz, director of *Popular!* and *Animals of Cuban Music*, a notable exception. A similar dynamic has been at play in the academic field: the millions of listeners to timba and reggaetón have had fewer scholarly defenders than the thousands of rap fans. In comparison to other cities where hip hop has been studied in detail, the ratio of filmmakers and researchers to hip hoppers has been very high, and our impact has thus been significant. Most of the leading hip hoppers in Havana have appeared in foreign-made documentaries, been interviewed by foreign journalists or researchers, and appeared on foreign-produced compilations: La FabriK even included a spoof interview by a foreign journalist as an interlude on their album of the same name. Although hard facts are impossible to come by, it seems that before the recent proliferation of videos on YouTube, the international audience for rap made in Havana was small, but a significant proportion of that audience was made up of journalists, photographers, filmmakers, researchers, and students. Interested foreigners helped transform Havana hip hop into something it could not otherwise have been, given the paucity of local resources and the lack of interest on the part of local media and record labels, and into something they wanted it to be. The sheer volume of the production of knowledge illustrates that the multivocal character of Cuban hip hop that I discussed in chapter 1 goes far beyond the sphere of Cuban rappers and officials.

It may be in the international sphere that Cuban hip hop has had its greatest successes: Orishas in Europe, triumphant concerts in New York, and Hip Hop Revolución in Caracas. Certainly, there were high hopes that Cuban hip hop could catalyze change far beyond the island. Danny Hoch, one of the organizers of the 2001 International Hip Hop Exchange tour that brought Cuban hip hoppers to New York, revealed that "his hope is to steer young Americans back to hip-hop's earlier social awareness, which he said exists today in a growing minority marginalized by the major labels or by the news media" (Navarro 2001). Perhaps its greatest failures, too, have been in the international arena, in the sense that so many of its leading figures have left the island, both legally and through defection. The 2001 tour to New York showed both sides of the coin: the Cuban artists were heralded as a symbol of hope for U.S. hip hop, yet Julio Cárdenas skipped the flight home to seek his fortune in the United States. In Cuban hip hop's finest hour, the cracks were already apparent. Cárdenas had grown up in Alamar, dreaming of being a famous rapper in New York; in *Young Rebels*, as he washes dishes in New York, he dreams of being a famous rapper in Alamar. Nostalgia for the old days of the Havana scene is spreading as its participants disperse across the globe. As Orishas sing in "Emigrante":

> He's sad, he left behind
> His sun, his people, his shirt
> Without realizing that distance changes everything
> And nostalgia tears you apart.

The list of names of those who have left Cuba is long and illustrious, but their success outside the island has so far been limited. There have been exceptions: for instance, Eli Jacobs-Fantauzzi, the director of *Inventos*, has supported the transnational female hip hop collective Omega Kilay, which was formed in 2005 to link Cuban artists still in Havana with émigrés in the United States. Jacobs-Fantauzzi's Clenched Fist Productions organized the Mujeres de Hip Hop Cubano tour in the United States in 2007, and the participants Las Krudas have been making small waves in the United States. Randee Akozta achieved a loyal following in Caracas, and marriage to La Mala Rodríguez opened doors in Spain and further afield for Reynor Hernández (Explosión Suprema). Still, the fact that by 2009 all the members of Omega Kilay had left Cuba, depriving the Havana scene of many of its most charismatic female artists, illustrates that such international openings have come at a local cost. Furthermore, many in the Cuban hip hop diaspora have struggled artistically and economically. As Ariel Fernández said at Lehigh University in 2008, hip hoppers had been "trying to do something positive with our lives, trying to occupy our time, because we didn't have to pay bills in Cuba"; the constraints of life in capitalist cities were a shock to many of them, as were the difficulties of translating Havana's hip hop culture into new social and linguistic contexts.

The significance of Cuban hip hop has thus been as much international as national: it came to be seen as a symbol of what hip hop really was and what it could be again. This message continued to resonate overseas even as local audiences abandoned hip hop for reggaetón and local hip hoppers abandoned Cuba for North America and Europe. There are echoes of Robin Moore's (2003, 32) contention that "the most consistent support for first-generation trovadores [nueva trova singers] is now among non-Cubans abroad rather than at home." Similarly, conscious Cuban rap has maintained its international profile largely through a continued interest on the part of idealistic non-Cubans for whom the revolution has kept its appeal, and for whom politically committed Cuban music therefore occupies a special position.

CONCLUSION

The Rise and Fall of Havana Hip Hop

In July 2007, to coincide with the Hip Hop Symposium, the Cuban newspaper *Granma* ran an article titled "Cuban Hip Hop Exists." If local and foreign efforts had combined a decade earlier to turn Havana into one of the most vibrant outposts of the Hip Hop Nation, this headline illustrated the decline of more recent years. The pessimism and loss of belief among rappers, particularly between the end of the rap festival in 2005 and the emergence of La Comisión Depuradora in 2007, is clear in Papá Humbertico's songs from Mano Armada's 2006 demo *Revolución dentro de la Revolución*, such as "Fundido":

> I'm done in, the stress is getting to me, I can't do this anymore,
> I can't relax in the peñas any more, they do me in as well to tell
> the truth.

In "Mi historia," he raps:

> Time passes and doesn't come back,
> The glory days are behind us.

Certainly, this nostalgic, "rise and fall" frame, reflecting a modernist conception of time, is a common one in cultural movements, particularly in hip hop narratives. Furthermore, the involvement of North Americans in the Havana scene from 1997 on ensured a double dose of nostalgia, even at a relatively early stage: when Cuban hip hop was still on the upswing, Alexey Rodríguez's "Como fue" looked longingly back to the old days. Nevertheless, there really has been a rise and fall in Havana hip hop. Around 2000, the hip hop festivals attracted big-name rappers from the United States and audiences of thousands; today, the Hip Hop Symposium attracts an audience of a few hundred at most, and the foreign invitees are mainly low-profile activist-artists from Canada and Latin America. The opportunities for rap performance in Havana have shrunk, and hip hop has declined in prominence as reggaetón has usurped much of its cultural space. Many leading figures switched to the new style or left the island: despite the optimism at the beginning of the millennium, the biggest "movement" turned out to be the exodus of rappers from the scene and the country. Rappers' big hope, the ACR, turned out to be divisive and disillusioning, and within five years, half of its original groups had left. Hip hop is far from dead—indeed, some regard 2008–9 as one of its most exciting phases—but no one in Havana denies that it fell a long way between 2003 and 2007. The rise and fall narrative thus reflects subjective visions and objective factors, and I aim here to summarize and analyze both.

The state has played a significant role in both the rise and the fall of hip hop in Havana, most obviously via the AHS, which began to support the showpiece festival in 1997 and dropped it in 2005. The creation of the ACR in 2002 was an ambiguous move, since it grew out of hip hoppers' desire for greater representation, but it also split the hip hop scene, promoted reggaetón groups, and "sent rappers off into the mountains" on ICM tours, as one of my informants told me, weakening their base in the capital. There was a poor fit between the multifaceted hip hop scene and the structure of the commercial music agency, and the limited exposure of rap in the media and the absence of public access to the Internet ensured that rappers' efforts to reach a broad audience, whether through official or independent channels, largely failed even as the live scene was booming, with only Los Aldeanos recently bucking the trend.

Several leading Cuban hip hop figures see these combined factors as evidence of a state conspiracy to bring down hip hop. Ariel Fernández lectures on "the subliminal framing used by Cuban cultural officials and institutions to shut down one of the most powerful black social-cultural movements ever born in the island."[1] Alpidio Alonso, president of the AHS from 2001 to 2006 and a politicized and polarizing figure, is often held partly responsible. Alonso is considered rigid, risk averse, and predisposed against urban cultural scenes, and the 2002 festival may have been a tipping point in convincing him that the festival's risks outweighed its potential benefits: after all, given that he considered its prime purpose to be sending a positive message about the Cuban Revolution to the outside world, it would have been little wonder if the negative responses of the world's press in 2002 had made him rethink the festival's usefulness. Nevertheless, it should be noted that the festival at first grew under his stewardship, and even after the denuncia social incident in 2002, it continued for another three years. Given that some of the key architects of Cuban hip hop believe in the conspiracy theory, it needs to be taken seriously; but to my mind, there was less of a coherent plot than a series of factors, only some of them the result of institutional decisions and loss of faith, that combined to weaken the hip hop scene.

A crucial question is how much power to attribute to the state. Fernando Rojas portrayed institutional efforts such as the creation of the ACR as well intentioned but defeated by circumstances beyond the state's control: he blamed rappers themselves and the globalization-induced commercialization of culture in Havana for the agency's disappointing results. In his eyes, the ACR, and Havana hip hop more generally, were, as he told me, "contaminated by the market," and the hip hop festival was weakened by the increasing turn toward reggaetón on the part of both rappers and audiences. For Rojas, the death of the festival was the result of a loss of purpose and coherence among hip hoppers and a loss of interest by audiences; the AHS's response—the abandonment of the festival—was thus a consequence, not the cause. However one may view Rojas's opinions, rap's travails in Havana in recent years need to be considered in the context of broader shifts, including the steady commercialization of the cultural sphere in Cuba and the international explosion of reggaetón. Rap's influence has also been declining in the United States, and thus the rise-and-fall narrative is not simply a local one.

To attribute Cuban rap's problems solely to deliberate neglect or state conspiracy elides the influence of these broader national and international trends, and places too much responsibility in the hands of the state. I have emphasized that the nationalization of rap was driven to a large extent by hip hoppers and intermediaries, and if these actors are to be credited with hip hop's successes, they must also take some responsibility for its subsequent failures—which they indeed do. While some of the older hip hop pioneers believe that the government conspired to bring down hip hop, they all emphasize that the decline of recent years also stems in large part from internal discords and disunity, organizational failures, and the inability to agree on clear objectives. Pablo Herrera argues that the hip hop scene grew too fast, asked for too much too soon, and ended up self-destructing; he summarized his view as "we let it slip through our fingers, we are all responsible, we should have responded to the challenge" (quoted in Castillo Martiatu n.d.a, 15). Yrak Saenz told me that "the biggest mistake by Cuban rappers was to beg for help from the institutions," and Obsesion blame hip hoppers for allowing the festival to die. As Fernández told his audience at Lehigh University, "we were weak, we weren't strong enough, we weren't smart enough, we didn't organize enough." These leading figures also felt that Cuban hip hoppers came up short in comparison with their Venezuelan or Brazilian counterparts: the Venezuelans had clear political objectives that were lacking in Cuba, while the Brazilians were more united and developed all four elements of hip hop (whereas rap dominated in Havana). Most observers placed the threat to hip hop as coming from without, and above all from the state, but it actually came to a significant degree from within.

The strategies adopted by leading figures in the mid- to late 1990s, bolstered by the involvement of the Black August Hip Hop Collective, were at the root of both Havana hip hop's successes and its failures. The framing of hip hop as revolutionary culture opened doors to institutional recognition and international adulation, and it was very effective for a few years. However, this strategy also carried the seeds of future problems, as hip hop, at first a dance and party culture in Cuba, was reframed as serious, moralistic, and increasingly antidance.

The shift toward socially committed lyrics and a focus on race led Havana hip hop down some exciting but perilous paths. On one level, as many rappers told me, the public adoption of moralistic discourses invited scrutiny of their private behavior, which sometimes came up short; Rubén Marín is convinced that the scene was weakened because many artists talked the talk, but fewer walked the walk. Serious, moralistic rappers are bound to be judged by the same ethical principles they foreground in their raps, and they are thus more susceptible to criticism and disillusioned rejection than the ludic, ambiguous figures of commercial hip hop. Furthermore, a shift toward more overt racial politics was arguably, for all the radical political rhetoric, a move in a conservative direction, as it was in the United States (Gilroy 1993, 100). Todd Boyd (2004, 332–33) labels the rise of the Afro-centric group Arrested Development "an unconscious co-optation of regressive class politics" and "the death of an earlier revolutionary agenda." If Ariana Hernandez-Reguant's (2006) observation of a class difference between moña and timba fans in the late 1990s is accurate, this may be evidence that the "revolutionary conservatism" of U.S. hip hop (Paul Gilroy, quoted in Mitchell 2001b, 4) fed into its Cuban counterpart and distanced rap from its broad popular audience, which was soon to embrace reggaetón. On another level, the embrace of overt blackness was politically risky. The percussionist Alfredo "Punta de lanza," who has worked with several of Havana's top hip hop groups, expresses the view in the film *Hip hop cubano* that the Black August exchanges led Cuban rappers to start speaking out more about race and political issues, provoking the government to take greater control. Herrera, too, believes that the adoption from the United States of the idea of hip hop as a black movement eventually backfired in Havana; in his eyes, this overclarification of racial and political objectives became a recipe for disaster, given the government's suspicion of supposedly divisive positions on race.

Revolución sin pachanga

You are nostalgic, magic like childhood,
A pity that many feel you only with their feet
—LOS ALDEANOS, featuring El Adversario, "Amada mía"

Che Guevara reportedly characterized the Cuban Revolution as a *revolución con pachanga*, referring to a Cuban dance rhythm, yet in the late 1990s Havana hip hop started to morph into a revolution without pachanga. With hip hop focusing increasingly on the lyrics, a certain conservatism, even austerity, set in on the musical plane. Although Pablo Herrera and a small handful of others produced first-rate instrumentals, they were working in a scene in which creating catchy, danceable, eclectic music was viewed ambivalently. While the hip hop scene's racial and political positioning eventually caused trouble at the top, its distancing from dance, and pleasure more generally, had an impact at the street level. As a result, hip hop's appeal began to narrow, and while North Americans fleeing Puff Daddy were impressed, Cubans looking for good-time music saw their options shrinking. A significant portion of hip hop's audience was left on the sidelines, and the door was thus left wide open for reggaetón.

As Herrera told me, Cuban hip hop went down a conscious, under-ground line, aiming to fill a gap in the Cuban musical spectrum and leave dance to more traditional Cuban genres: "Every time something more danceable appeared, people were like 'that's not hip hop—hip hop is this other thing.' . . . In some ways we were very responsible for that, and it backfired on us." Dance came to be seen as suspect, as a form of opium for Cuban minds; the identity of Havana hip hop was increasingly constructed in opposition to salsa, and the former thus moved away from most Afro-diasporic musics (and their audiences), in which dance is part of the solution, not the problem—a form of liberation, not oppression. As Greg Dimitriadis (2004, 422) argues, dance is key to African-derived musics and was central to the communal ethos of early hip hop, for all that its role in hip hop history is often downplayed in favor of rap lyrics. In Havana, however, a focus on text over dance was made concrete in the scene from the late 1990s onward, and indeed in reports and studies of it, which have tended to treat hip hop as "social anthropology with rhythm" (Lusane 2004, 357) but then have forgotten about the rhythm. The pleasure prin-ciple was neglected not just by intellectuals but by all those who wanted to construct Cuban hip hop as the new nueva trova, as the vanguard of the revolution, as the savior of U.S. hip hop. Moña and rap cubano, once almost inseparable, were slowly driven apart, and two competing visions emerged: moña as a space to dance, dream, and forget; and rap as a social chronicle aimed at the mind rather than the feet. Ten years after Black August, there was little overlap between those who went to moña club nights and those who attended live rap.

What was lost in Havana, to a degree, was the understanding of hip hop as a dialectical culture. Imani Perry (2004, 4–6) conceives of U.S. hip hop in terms of binaries of high and low, respectable and rough, sacred and profane, and (importantly) she views the interplay between terms as central to the culture. I would add further dualities to this list: composed text and improvisation, morality and hustle, seriousness and play—and, to draw from studies of Cuba and beyond, the politics of passion and the politics of affection (D. Fernández 2000), official ideology and operative ideology (Pekacz 1994), and the politics of fulfillment and the politics of transfiguration (Gilroy 1993).

The iconic song "The Message," often seen as the launchpad of conscious rap, was, according to David Toop (2000, 120), "a hardcore dance track [that] cut straight across the stagnation in rap lyricism." Numerous writers have argued that the success of Public Enemy, the paradigmatic group of message rap, was crucially dependent on the balancing of politics and pleasure (Boyd 2004, 328; I. Perry 2004, 51–52). Mark Anthony Neal (2004a, 374–76) claims that the reason why Public Enemy's first album, *Yo! Bum Rush the Show* (1987), was not a big hit was because it was undanceable. *It Takes a Nation of Millions* (1988), however, got the balance right—the journey toward the apex of political hip hop involved not a retreat from dance but an embracing of it. Neal attributes the album's success to its appeal as a dance record, and he claims that the subsequent decline of political hip hop was due to an inability to find the equilibrium between lyrical content and danceability. Crucial to Chuck D's messages, therefore, was the counterweight of Flavor Flav's antics: "He keeps it from being so serious, keeps it from being like straight vodka with no chaser. It's the chaser that makes it lighter, easier for people to handle. That's necessary when you're trying to get something across" (Dery 2004, 411). Public Enemy grasped fully that it is precisely its dialectical aspect that gives hip hop its strength. They knew that Flavor Flav was vital, the yang to Chuck D's yin. Chuck D wanted to make political music but realized the risks of alienating his audience: "It was impossible to put that type of shit in your rhymes. It was like, you better rock the fucking crowd" (Chang 2005, 247).[2]

Public Enemy also depended on a highly developed media strategy, recognizing that being underground was no way to make an impact on society. As George Lipsitz (1994, 34) insists: "Oppositional practices among diasporic populations emerge from painful experiences of labor migration, cultural imperialism, and political subordination. Yet they are distinguished by an ability to work within these systems. . . . It is their desire to work *through* rather than *outside* of existing structures that defines their utility as a model for contemporary global politics." Mass mediation and mass appeal have given popular music its power in the

United States, where artists like James Brown, Stevie Wonder, and Public Enemy had such an impact because they moved both minds and bodies on a mass scale. Conversely, there has long been ambivalence about message rap among U.S. artists and critics; many rappers are concerned by the "political" label, since it often means being sidelined into a niche market and "condemned to preach to a very small choir" (Chang 2005, 448). Talib Kweli, one of the U.S. rappers who went to Cuba, worried that being marketed as political would mean he was not promoted to the general hip hop market. The music critic Aaron Fuchs described message rap as "a capitulation to the adult norm who can't accept the music on its own terms" (quoted in Toop 2000, 120). Yet this ambivalence was lost in translation to Havana, with unfortunate long-term consequences. Conscious rap was thus an ambiguous gift from the United States to Cuba; it opened up doors to state support and international acclaim, but it limited local appeal.

It is worth recalling what was going on at the U.S. end of the Havana–New York hip hop bridge of the late 1990s. Alongside the celebration of latinidad and old-school hip hop, there was a "moral panic" over the issue of commercialism, one centered on New York: "The panic wanted to assert a kind of progressive politics, and a kind of aesthetic politics too, not unlike the efforts to exert conservative politics through other moral panics the United States has witnessed in recent times. . . . The moral panic does not simply respond to forces from without but also to the sensibilities from within hip hop. . . . On one level, the moral panic marks an attempt to excise a difficult part of the hip hop self" (I. Perry 2004, 192–94). I would argue that the construction of an axis of authenticity between New York and Havana from 1997 on was shaped partly by this ideology. New York desires to "excise a difficult part of the hip hop self" were realized in Cuba, a place where, as noted in chapter 4, "the intellectual and the consumer turn a loss in the space of the self into a recovery and a hope in the space of the other" (Medina 2007, 9).

In Havana, hip hop was reconstructed as a cleansed alternative (for both young Cubans and idealistic foreigners) to the muddy, complex disappointments of Special Period Cuba and the commercialization of hip hop in the United States. In Havana, overseas visitors could dream that hip hop did not have a "low" side and could fall in love with it again. Havana became a screen on which to project alternatives to mainstream

U.S. music, just as occurred with the BVSC. The result was a distillation in Havana of many progressive aspects of hip hop: political commitment, anticommercialism, an old-school vibe. But as with the BVSC, this also led to a certain degree of marginalization of those musical currents that did not conform to the newly dominant templates. This became evident in the increasingly virulent debates over underground versus commercial rap, which morphed into hip hop versus reggaetón; the supposedly negative elements of hip hop—commercialism and hedonism—were excised rather than held in productive tension, and with the loss of this dialectical balance went hip hop's strength and a considerable part of its audience. By 2005, most of Havana's underground rappers were indeed preaching to a very small choir.

It is interesting to listen to the first Cuban rap album to be released, Primera Base's *Igual que tú*, which represents the group's style in the mid-1990s, before the Black August exchanges. It is an eclectic album which mixes social and political themes with lighter, party songs, over beats that are more commercial (i.e., lively, danceable) than those that came to dominate the scene in the following five years. It illustrates the dialectical aspect of hip hop, even of message rap, through its balance of the urges to rock the crowd and to say something. The gradual separation of these two faces of hip hop was induced by the reframing of the Havana scene as a sociopolitical movement. The producer and rapper Rebeld' Malcoms confirmed to me that the early days of Havana hip hop saw a mixture of conscious texts with more up-tempo music, and that both lyrics and instrumentals became "heavier" under the influence of U.S. artists. Underground and commercial rappers moved in opposite directions, and a decade after the release of *Igual que tú*, the urban music scene was characterized by the hypercommercialism of leading reggaetón groups in one corner, and the deep-underground stance of new-school rappers in the other. The productive tension had become all-out war.

Isnay Rodríguez (DJ Jigue), a prominent hip hopper who moved from Santiago to Havana and became the deputy director of the Cuban Rap Agency as well as Obsesion's DJ, felt that the Black August–inspired craze for underground hip hop led to a narrowing of vision and a loss of diversity: an excessive focus on rap (to the detriment of the other three elements of hip hop), on text (to the detriment of music), and on political topics (to the exclusion of other themes like love or humor). In adopting the Black August paradigm, Havana hip hoppers rejected anything that departed from it, saying "that's not real hip hop." As a result, Rodríguez saw rap becoming monotonous and catering mainly to male rappers, pushing away female fans and those who enjoyed dancing and saw live music as a night out, not a cause. For all that he is a conscious hip hopper himself, he lamented the lack of commercial rap in Havana. In other words, he saw rap's decline as stemming from a failure to maintain its dialectical balance; idealists tried to prune the "low" branches off hip hop and ended up stunting its growth.

One of the most interesting aspects of Havana hip hop, to my mind, is the way that foreign visions helped to construct local realities, creating a cultural scene that had tremendous international currency but became somewhat disconnected from local popular culture. It was a canvas on which to project various ambitions, quests, and agendas. Despite its minority status in Cuba's cultural scene, hip hop's multivocality made it the perfect subject matter for dozens of written and filmed treatments from overseas perspectives, in a way that the far more popular timba and reggaetón were not. The same tendency to elide the dialectical aspect of hip hop can be found in both the Havana scene and representations of it. In the field of global hip hop studies, and particularly within the Cuban subfield, scholars have done a better job of grasping the first term in each of the binaries that I presented above than the second. The focus of scholarly approaches has been the serious, self-conscious, moral discourses of official texts (above all, lyrics), not least because these fit neatly with academic agendas centered on questions of politics and identity, race and gender. The free-flowing side—the verbal, ideological, social, and economic improvisation—has been largely ignored.

But the escape from dialectics to purity turned out to be an illusory path, because the tensions within hip hop are, as Imani Perry argues, a source of strength. Hip hop needs the "low" in order to prosper. As Isnay Rodríguez pointed out, rap came to dominate in Havana at the expense of the other elements of hip hop, and this was partly because foreigners were excited about the revolutionary lyrics. With the focus firmly on politics and words, dance and graffiti and spinning records took a back seat, making hip hop no longer a balanced, multifaceted culture. Above all, the reunion of high and low was discarded, so when the latter reared its head again in the form of reggaetón, it was regarded as alien and radically opposed to hip hop, rather than the other side of the same urban music coin. For all the polemics that have raged between defenders of roots reggae and dancehall, or message and gangsta rap, only extremists would argue that these are not debates within reggae or within hip hop. In Havana, however, as in many Latin American hip hop scenes, reggaetón is considered to be a different genre altogether rather than simply hip hop over a Latin or Caribbean beat. Hip hop thus loses half of its dialectic and much of its cultural space.

In *The Hip Hop Wars*, Tricia Rose (2008, 243–44) argues that the espousal of overt politics worked against hip hop as a progressive culture, as conscious artists were separated from the mainstream and relegated to a niche. Political artists had little chance when gangsta rappers looked like they were having all the fun. Rose believes that for hip hop to progress in the United States, conscious artists have to deal with a wider range of topics and make themselves sexier and more marketable. What happened in Havana was almost the opposite. The politics of U.S. conscious rap was imported into the Havana scene in the late 1990s and early 2000s, but without the economics. While Rose may be generally correct, conscious artists who criticize capitalism still have a certain impact in the United States since capitalism can happily sell and sell to its own detractors; but in the more limited economic system of Cuba, groups which steered toward underground lyrics and music ensured their marginalization by the media and local record companies (the Cuban recording industry is too small to deal with niche markets). The success of artists like Common and Mos Def, even if modest in comparison with that of 50 Cent, has depended on their ability to combine conscious lyrical elaboration with commercially appealing music, to be socially engaged while advertising suvs. The complexities and ambiguities of life as a conscious artist in the United States were lost in the purified Havana version, and with them went the opportunity to make either money or a broad social impact. The divide between conscious and commercial rap in the United States is in many ways rather minimal on a practical level, since underground artists tend to operate through the mainstream commercial economy, and their supposedly independent labels are usually distributed by major corporations (Marshall 2009, 38). But in Havana this small and somewhat illusory gap was taken literally and became an ideological chasm. As rappers jostled to be the most underground, many artists who aspired to make a living from music had to leave either hip hop or the island, pushed by the lack of interest from Cuban record labels but also by the extremism of the local scene.

The underground or political orientation of Havana hip hop ensured that its most significant outlets would shift over time to the international sphere. Leading conscious rappers from Alamar went on tour and were feted in New York; but back in Cuba, Alamar was rapidly transforming itself from Rap City into Reggaetón City. Cuban hip hop became a great topic for newspaper articles and university theses, but it was losing ground in the streets of Havana. Foreign writers and researchers joined the wave of approval from outside Cuba and helped nudge the Havana scene further down the conscious path, but in many cases, that led to local dead ends. As a result, many hip hoppers eventually felt they had little choice but to leave the country, and those who stayed behind and stuck to their line struggled to make an impact—my interview in 2008 with Anónimo Consejo, darlings of foreign filmmakers and writers for a decade, but by then disillusioned and marginalized in Havana, was sobering. In the long term, then, Havana hip hop turned out to be more successful in the international arena than locally. It lost the battle with reggaetón for young hearts and minds in Havana, but its appeal to the progressive-minded outside the island continues.

"The Wider Public We Talked about Still Doesn't Acclaim Me"

Havana hip hop's rise and fall may have more than a little to do with the raising and deflating of expectations. Papá Humbertico provides a disillusioned snapshot of his career and Cuban hip hop in "Si los ves":

> If you see them, tell them that I'm still at it,
> Stuck, though, screwed, drowning,
> That I haven't succeeded, that fame never arrived,
> That the wider public we talked about still doesn't acclaim me,
> That producers and labels aren't calling me,
> That I'm still stuck out there in Barreras.

Soandres del Río, too, exudes a sense of disappointment: one of the stars of *East of Havana*, he told me he had few hopes for the future, because his expectations had been raised too many times in the past, only to be dashed. If these artists expected much more, it was because there had been so much hype in the earlier years. While the local media and music industry were always wary, Papá Humbertico's dreams of success and a wider public were stimulated by the foreign activists, journalists, researchers, producers, and filmmakers who could not get enough of Cuban hip hop. Roberto Zurbano told me that rappers started to believe the hype and thought they were going to change the country. By the early 2000s, many people both inside and outside Cuba had a lot invested symbolically in Havana hip hop—"people thought we were the Che Guevaras and Fidel Castros of global hip hop," as Ariel Fernández told the Lehigh University audience—and there was a feeling that it might go on to achieve great things on the domestic front.

Arguably, behind these high expectations were misreadings and misunderstandings. At the Cuban end, the fact that hip hoppers expected producers and labels to be calling them suggests an excessive belief that foreign enthusiasm would be converted into career-changing action. At the visitors' end, too, appearances could be deceptive. For example, the festival concerts in Alamar, with their audiences of thousands, looked amazing, but the reality is that many present were young, bored local residents who did not know a huge amount about hip hop but saw this as good cheap entertainment in their barrio. Hip hop was undoubtedly fashionable at the time (see M. Perry 2004, 208), but as soon as reggaetón came along and fashion changed, almost all of them switched their allegiance; they were more interested in the entertainment than the messages. These audiences gave the impression that hip hop was a big social movement, but no observers attempted to gauge audience motivations or responses. Were these teenagers engaging with open racial critique, as Marc Perry (2004, 272) maintains, or were they hanging out, drinking, flirting, and showing off their hip hop gear, there because they had nothing better to do, stuck out in Alamar? My impression—admittedly formed after the peak years—was that for many people, it was primarily a social gathering. At regular hip hop peñas and concerts from 2003 onward, attendance was usually between 100 and 150 people: even the Hip Hop Symposium, which filled the gap left by the festival, attracted audiences of a few hundred at most. In other words, not many members of the young Alamar audiences of the late 1990s became committed fans.

With all the local buzz and foreign involvement, some local people who were less than completely committed to the cause hitched themselves to the bandwagon in search of personal advantage. They looked like they were into hip hop, but what were they really about? This question underpins several underground songs, with their concern that fake hip hoppers abound. In the film *Inventos*, Kokino of Anónimo Consejo expresses similar doubts, and he says "los falsos que andan por ahí" (the fakes out there) will be unmasked in time. The last "commandment" of Anónimo Consejo's "Ley 5566" proclaims that "underground hip hop is not a facade," underlining their anxiety that in some cases it was. If some who joined the hip hop scene were just along for the ride, then the stories of a huge explosion of interest need to be taken with a grain of salt.

This deep concern with the question of appearances and reality, or superficiality and authenticity, is one of the many reasons why I consider Havana hip hop to be a modernist reaction against an increasingly postmodern cultural context.[3] In musical terms, many hip hoppers resist the processes of hybridization that are characteristic of the postmodern era; and the political ideologies of global hip hop are based on Enlightenment-inspired Marxism, suggesting that both hip hop and the socialist state are modernist movements fighting against the postmodern tide, of which reggaetón is the loudest example in Havana.

One of the major misconceptions of foreign visitors in the late 1990s and early 2000s was that the Havana scene was old school solely by choice. Just as Ry Cooder read a noncommercial ethos into the music of older or retired popular musicians—even though Manuel Galbán, for example, had been almost as popular in Cuba as the Beatles during the heyday of his group, Los Zafiros—North American hip hop activists at the same time saw the undeveloped hip hop scene as evidence of an old-school sensibility —yet, just like the South Bronx of the 1970s, it was a scene in an early stage of development, and this was destined to change as soon as there was an influx of money and interest (something the North Americans provided). Of course, there were numerous artists and intermediaries who did represent this kind of ethos, but there were many others who did not disdain commercial aspirations nearly as much as their foreign admirers thought and were "old-school" primarily by necessity.

Alberto Medina (2007, 17), writing about the intersections between touristic consumption and foreign artistic and academic production, argues: "Authenticity and affect become the places of their own simulation. They are no longer 'discovered' but rather produced, either by the nostalgic first world citizen trying to experience again what he has lost or by the third world citizen, giving to the tourist what he asks for in return for survival." According to this view, the old-school aspect of Havana hip hop might be seen as a site of transaction and, in part, an invention by and for foreigners, who were much more interested in consuming underground hip hop than commercial fare. One former underground rapper told me that his colleagues acted up for foreigners: there was a lot of talk of union and "the movement," but when the yumas left, there were struggles over the equipment and donations left behind. He felt there had been a lot of invention and deception in order to gain access to material goods and foreign travel.

As Ariel Fernández told me, many rappers were eager to make money from hip hop—hardly a surprise, considering the straitened circumstances in which they lived. We only have to look at the careers of SBS, Orishas, Primera Base, Alto Voltaje, Papo Record, Familia's Cuba Represent, Justicia, Gente de Zona, Eddy-K, Insurrecto, and many other top groups to realize that commercialism was a big (if politically inconvenient) part of the story. Once these artists gained a local and international audience, they wanted to take their careers up a level, but the anticommercial ideology that ruled the scene hampered the development of a strong economic base, and without this necessary evolution, artists were pushed away and the long-term viability of hip hop was jeopardized (Matienzo Puerto n.d.).

Even if there were fake MCs mixed in with the real ones, there is no question that for a few years, large numbers of people were drawn to headline hip hop events, and to a degree the scene became a victim of its own success. Isnay Rodríguez told me:

> The hip hop movement in Havana reached a peak when lots of people were coming to Havana to nourish themselves on that spirit of hip hop that had been lost, for example in the U.S. Many people came and found in the movement in Havana that spirit that had been lost. But I felt (and many people felt) that in Havana the same process had started that had occurred in the U.S. That unity, that creativity, that community spirit, that commitment to the hip hop movement began to disappear for many reasons: people started to want to be protagonists, to be Number One or the best, or they had other interests as artists, like to be signed by a record label, or to have a CD on the market and commercialize their music, because they

realized they had a certain appeal to people, and this led to a degradation of the spirituality that the hip hop movement had in Havana.[4]

Rodríguez hints at the double process that occurred as outside interventions in the Havana scene invented a noncommercial ethos and, at the same time, undermined it. Ironically, it was the arrival of foreigners marveling at underground Cuban hip hop that created a market for it: selling demos to foreign researchers, songs to foreign producers, and interviews to foreign journalists became a good way to "invent." As the festival expanded with the foreign interest, it became more commercial, even though it was precisely the supposed lack of commercialism that appealed to foreigners. The trajectory of the hip hop festival and the boom of interest from foreign producers, filmmakers, and researchers illustrate perfectly Medina's (2007, 17) contention that the "passion made possible, in the third world, by closeness to the real . . . now becomes either an economic or an intellectual commodity, and in any case it is integrated into the dynamics of commodity fetishism, the system of value production driven by the market." As rap became a marketable commodity, the other elements withered: you couldn't sell graffiti or break dance to a foreign visitor. Dimitriadis (2004, 425–27) argues that the commodification of hip hop via rap recordings changed the rules of the game in the United States, and it is worth remembering that much of the impetus for recording Cuban rap came from foreign producers, who even provided equipment to make the beats. International interventions helped to construct the Havana scene in the late 1990s as a cohesive, black, noncommercial movement, but they also helped to deconstruct it, bringing in temptations of all kinds.

Veteran hip hop observers are well aware that the scene became weaker as it offered more illusions of success. Nehanda Abiodun, the godmother of Cuban hip hop, told me of her high hopes and the problems that deflated them: "I was so proud of those young people, and am proud of them, but my expectations for them and what they could have accomplished had they stuck together was so much that I was obviously was deluding my own self in that I left out the human factors. . . . They took a turn that I did not understand." She saw individualism, selfishness, and commercial motivations emerge, undermining her sense of the hip hop scene as a community. As a result, she withdrew from the scene for several years.

In essence, the urge to resolve communal problems was undermined by the need to *resolver* (solve problems) on a personal level. As Damián Fernández frames it, in a broader analysis of Cuban society, the politics of passion has been undermined by the politics of affection. He analyzes the tensions between these two forms of politics: "The crisis of Cuban socialism in the 1980s and 1990s has been accompanied by pervasive informality at the level of *la calle* (the street). Informality in turn exacerbates economic and political difficulties by chipping away at the tenets of the system and its effectiveness. Informality is, therefore, both a cause and a consequence of the problems facing the country since the 1980s" (D. Fernández 2000, 102). While Fernández is looking at the big picture, his analysis is of particular interest in our case since "the street" is a key index of authenticity, of "keeping it real," in hip hop. "We're from the street" means "we're the real deal." Yet, as Fernández underlines, the street is also the place of informality. If you are flat broke in Cuba, *sales a la calle* (you go out into the street) to try to sell or "invent" something. The street thus encapsulates the dialectics of hip hop: the moral authority and the hustle. In Havana, however, these two sides of the street came into conflict because hip hop was reconstructed in the late 1990s as a moral and political crusade, a revolution within the revolution; as a result, the microcosm suffered from the same problem as the macrocosm. The informal side of hip hop (the politics of affection) was not in a productive relationship with its formal side (the politics of passion)—as, for example, in the street flow of Biggie Smalls—but rather undermined its moralistic claims, becoming a source of destructive tension.

The rise and fall of Havana hip hop is thus encapsulated in the word "street." Like the street, hip hop has two faces: doing the right thing and doing your own thing. Hip hop's politics of passion enabled the rise of rap within the structures of the state, because it made hip hop understandable to officials and politicians—representatives of the large-scale politics of passion that is the Cuban Revolution. Hip hop's politics of affection lay behind rap's fall, undermining the grand claims and leading many artists to switch to reggaetón or leave the island to "resolve" their personal situations. The international success of Cuban hip hop created bridges that at first strengthened the genre as they brought material and moral support into Cuba, but later weakened it as they became a way out of the island. There have been numerous departures and defections, many of which resulted from connections between Cubans and foreigners that were made through the hip hop scene. Cuban hip hop is clearly a politics of passion, and that side of it has attracted a lot of attention; but it is also a politics of affection, and that side has been glossed over in most accounts, which also tend to overlook the intimate connection between this "informal" kind of politics and foreign observation and participation. The widespread attempts to construct Cuban hip hop as the triumph of passion over affection contributed to its fall because the inevitable compromises and messy realities of the street looked like betrayal rather than part of the game.

"We Need More Than MCs / We Need Hueys and Revolutionaries"

Almost as soon as the idea emerged that Cuban hip hop was, or would become, a sociopolitical movement, the Havana scene was imprisoned in a linguistic straitjacket of high expectations. Anything less than notable social change was liable to appear as a failure, and that change has not occurred. Herrera, one of the principal architects of Cuban hip hop, told me that the expanded space for race-conscious, politically aware art that hip hoppers created has shrunk again. The idea of a new, black urban subject had its moment in the sun, he said, but the Cuban ideology of the "mestizo nation" was never really disrupted. An important point that Herrera and others have raised is that this opening for black expression foundered on the lack of a sociopolitical base in Cuba. Hip hop has been a more powerful force in Brazil, for example, because of the traditions of community political organization on which it could build. In Havana, the musical "movement" flowered spectacularly but briefly, since it had no substantial, organized foundation. Ariel Fernández told me that Havana hip hoppers lacked concrete proposals or a plan of action; ultimately, for all the talk of a "movement," it did not have the cohesion of a sociopolitical organization because it did not have a clearly stated objective. When musical fashions changed, so did hip hop's fortunes. Even in the United States, Neal (2004a, 378) argues, "Public Enemy's efforts to create a political insurgency for the 1980s were destined to fail because they existed beyond an actual political movement rooted in legitimate political concerns." As dead prez rap in "We Want Freedom": "Tell me, what you gonna do to get free / We need more than MCs / We need Hueys and revolutionaries." The problems in Cuba are much more acute, since there is no history of civil rights or black power movements on which to draw. In many ways, the current situation of Havana hip hop reflects the broader one of Cuban race politics: Cuba is active on the international stage, but there is less happening back on the island. Cuba has succeeded in internationalizing its rap movement, just as it has become a global figurehead for antiracism, but in Havana the hip hop scene has withered, in part because of the government's nervousness about black activism at a local level.

This lack of impact in the social sphere is thus an important source of the sense of failure within the hip hop scene. Robin D. G. Kelley (2002, ix) is right to suggest that social movements should not be judged solely on their success but also on the power of their visions; nevertheless, that power has been more consistently felt outside the island than within, and disillusionment has stalked the scene in recent years. But perhaps those who feel this failure are looking for politics in the wrong place. As Imani Perry (2004, 197) argues, hip hop is "too flexible and too fluid to imagine that it might have one sort of political or social influence." Rap's politics should be sought not only in its lyrics but also in the distinctive spaces carved out by its practitioners. In line with the arguments of numerous music sociologists and jazz scholars (e.g., Frith 1996; Fischlin and Heble 2004), I have suggested that the politics of music is found as much in the performative moments and movements, in the temporary creation and recreation of community in live performance, as in the attempts to frame musical activities in terms of a coherent, explicit, long-term movement. Jolanta Pekacz's (1994) skepticism about the political influence of popular music under late socialism may be salutary, especially in its analysis of the way that academic accounts tend to overstate the political impact of popular musicians and feed their discourses rather than examining them critically. Both Cuban hip hoppers and foreign observers were burdened by expectations of macropolitical influence and change, but is the macropolitical level where the real action takes place with music? Is music any less political if its meanings are fleeting and evanescent?

Yordis (Grandes Ligas), one of Havana's legendary rappers, told me that he found freedom in performance, and above all in metaphor. For him, the interplay of restriction and liberty in the realm of language was key. Double meaning is freedom for rappers, who use language to create spaces

in a restrictive environment. This is micropolitics in action: the freedom of
words and fleeting moments. Is this where the politics of hip hop lies, in
the sense of flow in performance and the opening up of spaces for play and
ambiguity? I found that rappers were often quite dismissive when the
topic of politics came up: many did not see themselves as political figures
or even as interested in politics. Reynor of Explosión Suprema asked me
rhetorically "am I a rapper or a politician?" His focus was usually on more
immediate questions. He is a figure in the Biggie Smalls mould—an im-
proviser in all senses of the word, playful, ambiguous, all about the street
flow.

To return to Terry Eagleton and the meaning of life, the Buena Vista
Social Club is not held up as the answer because of any overarching,
permanent, or textual meanings that it expounds, but rather because it
enacts a meaningful life in the moment, through music. As noted in
chapter 1, in the documentary *From Mambo to Hip Hop*, the hip hop
pioneer Grandmaster Caz claims that he and his generation "were either
going to start hip hop or start a revolution." The key words here are
"either" and "or": the revolutionary energy of the late 1960s and early
1970s was subsumed into music, rather than put to music. The film
underlines the centrality of dance, capturing interviews with original
break dancers talking about how they did not care who was rapping.
Music was not a vehicle for revolutionary ideas—it *was* revolution.

For all the talk about the hyperauthenticity and old-school vibe of
Cuban hip hop, Havana rappers distanced themselves from hip hop's
origins in making politics explicitly rather than via music; by losing its
connection to dance music, hip hop's revolution began to lose energy. The
editorial in the first edition of *Movimiento* is subtitled "moving ideas,"
and it ends: "Moving feelings, ideas, images, ideas, sounds, ideas." Conspicuously lacking is any reference to the body. Havana hip hop appealed
increasingly to the mind, rather than the feet. The ideas that music and
dance were somehow restricting the revolutionary potential of hip hop
and that revolution was to be found primarily in lyrics had little to do
with the genre's origins, and the fact that dance music became a more
static "music for reflection," as it is often described by Havana underground rappers, was one of the major (mis)translations that occurred
when hip hop traveled to Havana.

However, Alexey Rodríguez's song "Como fue" suggests an implicit understanding of the politics of the body and the moment in the early days, when break dancing was the central element of hip hop, before rappers took over the leading roles and started "saying something." He evokes a multiracial community that would form spontaneously in the park: the dancers would chant together and "support the crazies who are polishing the concrete." It was competitive, but also communal: "You lost—never mind, my friend, take it easy." The love of music overruled that of fashion or money. Importantly, "you had to live it, you had to see it, feel it, know it": you had to be there in the moment to get what it was about. It could not be transcribed or recorded. However rose-tinted this account may be, it illustrates perfectly a conception of the micropolitical movements of hip hop before it became "the movement."

Foreigners, though, looked to Havana for macropolitical inspiration. To take one example, Gwendolyn Pough (2004, 286) wrote in 2001 that "the current re-birth of message rap is promising a rise in political consciousness and the possibility of a political project," drawing on Common's visit to Cuba in 1999, his interview with Assata Shakur, and his participation in the Havana hip hop festival. In the face of such expectation to catalyze a "political project," and to save U.S. hip hop from itself, the value accorded to music itself and its capacity for the spontaneous creation of community in Havana declined; only the articulated, activist "movement" counted. For all that Cuban rappers became admired around the world, the neglect of the micropolitics for the macro—a neglect in which intellectuals have been complicit—ultimately weakened the object of affection.

Hip Hop in Havana Today

With the exception of Los Aldeanos, hip hop today is a niche music in the capital, as perhaps it was always destined to be. The rapper Osmell Francis argues that hard-core rap was never going to be huge in Cuba; if not reggaetón, another dance genre would have come along to displace it (Castillo Martiatu n.d.b, 19). While the hip hop scene has indisputably declined from its peak around 2000, there are still a few optimists who feel that reggaetón and artists' departures from Cuba have stripped the scene of a lot of dead wood and that those who are left are truly committed to it. It may be that the rap scene had to shrink to progress, to pass through a crisis in order to renew itself.

There has been a major shift toward independence. The AHS, once the main champion of hip hop in Havana, has reduced its support: the festival ended in 2005, and in summer 2008 there were no hip hop events at La Madriguera and nothing about hip hop on the AHS website. Older groups like Doble Filo and Obsesion, however, see a silver lining to this cloud: they feel that hip hoppers allowed themselves to become too dependent on institutions, and they see independence as the future of Cuban hip hop (as it is for alternative scenes around the world). Institutionalization worked at first, but ultimately the AHS came to dictate the life and death of the festival, the ACR caused more harm than good, and the ICM transformed hip hoppers into "mere" musicians. Black August, by encouraging rappers to believe that solutions would come from outside the local scene, increased the paternalism of the late 1990s.[5]

The Hip Hop Symposium that La FabriK has organized since 2005 is a smaller-scale event than the festival, supported by institutions rather than run by them—a crucial difference in hip hoppers' eyes. The rise of Los Aldeanos with only minimal institutional acceptance has also been a good advertisement for independence; Yrak Saenz felt that the new school had taught an important lesson to the older generation about the importance of autonomy and hard work. The drive toward greater institutionalization that took place in the late 1990s and early 2000s has gone into reverse, and while this means a lower profile for hip hop, some artists find this a price worth paying. This signals an important shift in their approach to cultural politics: those who led hip hop's boom in the late 1990s—such as Rensoli, Herrera, and Fernández—were certain that working within institutions was the only way to progress in Cuba. While this may well have been true at the time, a decade later almost the opposite view was beginning to prevail, as more and more groups saw an independent future in digital technologies and semi-autonomous performance spaces on the margins of state authority.

Another important change in the new millennium has been in the field of mass mediation. Due to technological advances, far more people were listening to Los Aldeanos in 2009 than listened to Anónimo Consejo in 1999. As Herrera said, his music reached maybe 10,000 people, while with Los Aldeanos it might be closer to a million. The rap scene has undoubtedly shrunk, but rap listenership has grown with the explosion of digitalization. As a result, there has been a broadening of the audience base. A notable development of recent years has been the whitening of the hip hop scene, and as with son in the 1920s, technological changes mean that a music that became coded as black is now reaching a wide white audience that is not obliged to come into direct contact with the social environments in which the music is consumed live. Today more people are listening to rap cubano than at any time since Orishas released *A lo cubano*.

The audience for Cuban hip hop is not just national, and therefore its health must also be judged in an international perspective. Orishas have been a global success story for a decade now, and underground hip hop made in Havana has fans around the world. Even as rap declined in visibility in Havana and leading figures quit or sank into disillusionment, films and articles about it burst forth on the international scene, and a continuous round of overseas film screenings, conferences, panels, and concerts has kept the interest of American and European audiences alive. It may be that Cuban hip hop's destiny was to be like a smaller-scale version of roots reggae: a player overseas but more of a specialist interest back home. The story of Jamaican reggae and the rise of dancehall shows that combining conscious music with widespread local popularity is hard to achieve: message music may be respected nationally, but its real influence may be international. Cuba, like Jamaica, is a small island with a big musical voice, and hip hoppers from around the world have taken inspiration from Havana hip hop even as the local scene has struggled to keep going.

Another space of vitality in current Havana hip hop is the boom in freestyling, which has become a more significant part of live rap performances in recent years. Los Aldeanos' enthusiasm for and skill in improvisation—El B is two-time national Red Bull champion—has contributed to freestyling's growing popularity, which in turn may be seen as a return to the more social, communal aspect of hip hop now that the days of foreign producers, cameras, and press are largely in the past. The dreams of most rappers may have shrunk, but this has allowed them to focus more on the core elements of the scene. The vitality of Havana hip hop may be visible at the micro level in these fleeting moments of verbal skill, competition, and community creation, in which it is evident that the creativity and imagination of Cuban rappers has never been richer.

Nevertheless, the resilience of the hip hop scene was put to the test once again in mid-2009. A second rise, or renaissance, had taken place in

2007, under the auspices of Los Aldeanos and La Comisión Depuradora,
this time with minimal involvement from the state, and 2008 and early
2009 were something of a boom time: there were up to three peñas a
week, and the scene was awash with new demos and fans. But a series
of events in April and May 2009 led to Los Aldeanos being effectively
banned from performing for over six months, illustrating that the state is
still able and prepared to apply stiff sanctions. It is worth underlining the
fact that they had been making confrontational hip hop since 2003, so
this was not a simple question of offending government ears. Rather, it
was the complex interplay of foreign intervention, the camera lens, and
local politics discussed in chapter 4 that upset the delicate balance. First
of all, film footage shot without permission at Los Aldeanos' illicit club
night at Barbarám found its way onto a Miami TV channel, leading to the
almost immediate suspension of the gig (and the venue's manager). Then
the duo were interviewed on CNN, and a video of El B's incendiary song
"La naranja se picó," launched on a pro-Cuba U.S. website, was immediately pirated and broadcast by another Florida TV station, which gave it
a different spin. Finally, an interview with Aldo was published on an anti-
Castro website.[6] With Los Aldeanos catapulted to a new level of international prominence, and their work seized on by anti-Castro elements in
Florida and Spain, reaction in Havana was strong and swift, and Los
Aldeanos went from rising stars to untouchables in the space of a few
weeks.

This had an immediate effect on the hip hop scene. Not only were its
figureheads silenced, but the clubs that had hosted their peñas suddenly
wanted nothing to do with live rap, having seen what took place at
Barbarám, and so there were no regular hip hop nights by mid-2009.
Further pressure was applied in September, when Juanes gave a shout out
to Los Aldeanos and Silvito "El Libre" in front of a million people (and TV
cameras) at the end of his "Paz sin Fronteras" (peace without borders)
concert in the Plaza de la Revolución. A week later, Aldo's house was
raided by the police, and his equipment taken away (it was subsequently
returned, apparently after Silvito's father, Silvio Rodríguez, intervened).
Whereas the late 1990s and early 2000s revived a historically productive
Havana–New York connection that opened up spaces for hip hop in both
cities, in 2009 underground rappers were being drawn (against their
wishes) into the tense Havana-Miami axis, pushing Havana hip hop in a

dangerous new direction. At the heart of the controversy was a struggle for control of representation of Los Aldeanos: as their music began to circulate widely in digital form, it was increasingly reinterpreted and reused without authorization by figures inside and outside Cuba to support critical political positions, often ones with which the duo were not in agreement. This became less about Los Aldeanos "representing" and more about the uncontrollable circulation of representations.

At the end of 2009, the future of Los Aldeanos and the Havana scene seemed uncertain. Yet in a remarkable turnaround, the AHS decided to back Los Aldeanos at the start of 2010, initiating a new upswing. Thanks in large part to the efforts of the duo's international representative, Melisa Rivière, and AHS employee and hip hop supporter Jorge Rodríguez, Los Aldeanos were permitted to perform at an event at La Madriguera in January 2010 and then to put on their own concert at the Acapulco Theater in April, in both cases to sell-out audiences. The AHS also helped to organize the Puños Arriba hip hop awards in May, and it promoted and reviewed these events on its website. *Revolution*, a hard-hitting documentary about Los Aldeanos, won several prizes at an ICAIC film festival and was shown at two cinemas. Most significantly, the duo was allowed to leave Cuba for the first time, appearing at the Exit Festival in Serbia, Interrapción in Spain, and their own concert in Miami.

Since Havana hip hop has had so many ups and downs, it is impossible to predict where this latest renaissance will lead. Nevertheless, the AHS's decision to support the only group in Cuban popular music that combines a wide listenership with overtly confrontational lyrics seems to mark a significant shift in Cuban cultural politics, even though it harks back to 1997 when the AHS leadership saw its role to be working with cultural sectors seen as problematic by other institutions. The fact that a group with a discourse as critical as that of Los Aldeanos is not simply heard on every street in Havana but actively supported by a quasi-state institution is unprecedented in the history of Cuban music since 1959.

In 2007, Nehanda Abiodun, a key figure in the history of the Havana scene, told me: "Hip hop is not dead in Havana, it's just at a . . . calm waters or still waters right now, and I do believe that it will eventually take on another powerful period, not like it was before, but something that probably will be more useful and important to the growth of this process because it has had time to think. It's been wounded, you know,

it's licking its wounds . . . there's that expression, that which doesn't kill
you makes you stronger. And that's what I think is going to come out of
this. So I've got faith in Cuban hip hop." The jury is still out as to whether

the rise of Los Aldeanos represents this new "powerful period." On the
one hand, the group has attracted a huge number of new listeners to rap
and exposed them to many core ideologies of the underground hip hop
scene (though not that of blackness). They have charted an independent
path to national and international fame, providing a new model for Cuban underground and alternative musicians to emulate. And their capacity to generate excitement among young people in Cuba and beyond, to
attract the attention of Latin American superstars like Juanes and Calle
13, and even to carry an important cultural institution like the AHS in
their wake, illustrates that something powerful is undoubtedly occurring.

On the other hand, there is little evidence that rappers other than Los
Aldeanos generate anything like the same degree of excitement, begging
the question of what would happen to the hip hop scene if the duo left
Cuba. They have alienated some of those attached to the older Black
August–inspired ideologies because of their skin color, their nonracial
discourse, their Nuevo Vedado origins, and their vocal attacks on the
older generation of rappers. Their standoff with the ACR has further
damaged the reputation of the key hip hop institution and once again
pitted it against the AHS, underlining the institutional divisions that do
little to foster unity within the scene. Finally, their very success is likely
to bring complications, as their idealistic revolutionary discourse collides
with the pragmatism of the international music industry, which was
beginning to show considerable interest in Los Aldeanos by the time of
this writing. If photographs with Calle 13 and invitations from Juanes are
indicative of what is to come, Los Aldeanos' reputation as Cuba's most
underground and revolutionary rappers is soon to be put to the test.

Refiguring American Music

It is worth recalling the musical characteristics of the hip hop renaissance
in Havana from 2007 to 2009. The most active groups in this renaissance
embraced musical styles that threw into doubt the evolutionary narratives (adoption-adaptation, mimetic-authentic) that dominate Cuban
cultural criticism and global hip hop studies; indeed, there is evidence

that some of those closely involved with the Havana scene perceive an evolutionary counternarrative, regarding the move away from overt cubanía as evidence of greater maturity and authenticity. Los Aldeanos are the epitome of a postlocalization phase of Cuban popular music that is evident not just in hip hop but also in the majority of reggaetón and rock groups (as evidenced in the metal-heavy selection for the Agencia Cubana de Rock) and the current popularity of electronic dance music. Cubanization is popular with foreigners, record companies, and cultural institutions, but many artists and Cuban fans today prefer something else. Localization has been a battlefield. It was a key part of the nationalization discourse in hip hop circles and thus gained great currency as an idea, but nonindigenization was fundamental to the ideology of rap as resistance to the currents of commercialism, tourism, and Buena Vista socialization. Herrera, the principal architect of the Cuban rap sound during its heyday, sees overt cubanía as no longer relevant today—"we don't really need to do that, we're past that stage, we're being Cuban." He thus sees the current situation as evolution rather than regression. Cuban hip hop is now at a stage where its national identity does not need to be worn on its sleeve. Herrera has some of the sharpest ears in Havana's urban music scene, and he hears today's hip hop as simultaneously more global and more local. Nevertheless, I would add that the combination of localized lyrics and globalized musical style has always been an important strand in the rap scene; its domination today might be interpreted as an evolution from localization to postlocalization, but it could also be seen as the triumph of an aesthetic ideology that has been consistently present, as evidenced by the making of the *Cuban Rap Ligas* compilation.

Herrera's perception is quite different from that of X Alfonso—another musician with finely tuned hearing—for whom the lack of Cuban rhythms in hip hop is evidence that a true rap cubano has yet to be created (L. González n.d., 49). Indeed, one could argue that Cuban hip hop has failed to bring about significant change not only in the sociopolitical realm but also in the musical. Herrera once talked about his hope that hip hop would "springboard Cuban music to a new realm: a new type of rhythm, a new sound, and a new voice" (*East of Havana* n.d., 60), and for all the creativity shown by local producers, Herrera himself is clear that this leap has not happened. Cuban hip hop has achieved many things, but a new style of Cuban music is not one of them.

The evidence is ambiguous: Cuban urban music has not moved to a new
level, yet the postlocalization mind-set does indicate a significant shift,
though toward the more intensive absorption of global styles rather than
returning Cuba to the vanguard of Latin popular music. Even groups creating Cuban hip hop for export to Europe, such as Ogguere and Kumar,
rely on a jazz-funk-rock fusion that is distinctly retro in character. Perhaps it is on the level of ideologies about music that the real change has
occurred, as the Cubanization promoted by institutions and the music
industry has come under pressure from digital technology and the global
outlook of contemporary Cuban youth.

To what extent is it valid, then, to consider the history of hip hop in
Havana as a case of "refiguring American music," to refer to the title of
the series to which this book belongs? Given the transmission of U.S. hip
hop to Cuba and its growth with the conspicuous help of North American
activists and artists, the answer might have seemed straightforward.
However, the preceding pages have raised two important questions: Is hip
hop *American* music? And is its flowering in Cuba a case of *refiguring*?

The current post-localization musical phase undercuts the evolutionary narrative implied by the term "refiguring." In fact, the purist, nostalgic construction of Cuban hip hop suggests a process that is more akin to
"defiguring": a deconstruction of hip hop, pulling away the parts that
disturb (such as rampant commercialism) and leaving the "unadulterated
essence." It is an imagined step backward in the direction of the 1970s
South Bronx.

The music of hip hop, meanwhile, like so many African American musics of the twentieth century, has Afro-Cuban roots, undermining the
simplistic notion of Cuban rap as a reworking of American music. Although hip hop is widely considered as Caribbean music, with its well-
known Jamaican and Puerto Rican influences, the contribution of Cuba,
the third country in hip hop's Caribbean trinity, is rarely given much
attention. Jamaica provided sound systems, dub instrumentals, and DJs,
Puerto Rico contributed many early practitioners (especially break dancers) in New York, while Cuba left its mark on the musical style of break-
beat and the politics of message rap. The nationalization of rap in Cuba
was also, therefore, a kind of homecoming.

The idea of refiguring American music needs to be treated with care in
contexts in which musics of the African diaspora cross-fertilize one an-

other. A globalization-localization (or nationalization) model can be questioned anywhere within the Black Atlantic, since it depends on seeing one cultural form of the African diaspora as extrinsic to another part of it. This is particularly true in the Cuban case. The long-standing connections between African American and Cuban music and politics were reinforced in the 1960s and early 1970s, the years in which hip hop was gestating: one need think only of Castro's meeting with Malcolm X in Harlem, and the Che-worshiping Last Poets rapping about revolution over a conga beat.

That said, it is insufficient to argue simply that hip hop was already Cuban music. This is not the only reason for hip hop's incorporation into Cuba. In "Mi historia," Papá Humbertico recalls how as a twelve-year-old, he was "talking and gesticulating, believing I was from the Bronx." In other words, it was the Americanness, not the Cubanness, of hip hop that appealed to him, as it did to many others. As one Havana graffiti artist said: "My room has nothing to do with Cuba. I love my country, but this room is all about New York" (*East of Havana* n.d., 130). On an imaginative level, this attraction was all about difference, not sameness. The acceptance of hip hop drew on the similarities and shared roots of Cuban and African American musics; but at the same time, Cubans have a long history of welcoming and absorbing the latest form of U.S. popular music, if not always officially. As Ariel Fernández told me: "Hip hop didn't come from nothing—it came because it is a tradition that people are always trying to be on top of what is the new type of music coming from the U.S." He captures the paradox perfectly: a love of American modernity is a Cuban tradition.

We need to keep the image of the twelve-year-old Papá Humbertico in mind when we hear arguments from Cuban intellectuals (e.g., Paneque Brizuela n.d.) and well-trained hip hoppers that Cuban rap is based more on local traditions than on American hip hop; there is an obvious political and cultural nationalist agenda in these post hoc justifications via the connections with Cuban music. There is no doubt that Cuba's musical history contains forms that resemble rap, unsurprising given their shared Kongo ancestry. Nonetheless, Papá Humbertico did not get into hip hop because of its precedents in the declamation of Luis Carbonell or the poetry of Nicolás Guillén, but rather because the kids in East Havana tuned into Miami radio and TV stations to catch the latest trends in

American music and because they dreamed of living in the Bronx. Paying attention to musical style, clothing, and physical gestures, 1990s Havana hip hop was very Americanized in performative terms. Hip hop may be Afro-Cuban as well as African American music, but it was heard and performed in Havana as the latest in a long line of developments of música americana. As Alexey Rodriguez raps in "Como fue": "There were many people like me in Havana / Dancing and listening only to American music." This love for African American music has often been viewed with suspicion by Cuban officials and is sometimes downplayed in public discussions, but it is no less real for all that.

While hip hop may have been Afro-Latin-Caribbean-American music in the 1970s, when it arrived in Cuba in the 1980s, it no longer sounded Latin. This was the decade when Puerto Rican involvement in hip hop was largely erased from the picture. Although the Puerto Rican rapper Vico C was often mentioned in my conversations with hip hoppers in Havana, I never heard much made of the Latin connection more generally; the early hip hop spaces were known as la moña. Hip hop may have been Latin music in part, but it was understood primarily as African American music. It is thus important to separate out the musicological genealogies from the way that people heard hip hop in Havana. Whatever historical links—Kongo, Afro-Latin—may have unconsciously underpinned habaneros' attraction to hip hop, their conscious focus was primarily on the African American dimension.

Havana hip hoppers, like those around the world, had to play a balancing act: authenticity is defined simultaneously as "being yourself" (difference) and "being true to the culture" (sameness). Beginning in 1997, Havana's rap scene became valued internationally for its similarity to New York hip hop (in the past) and its difference from U.S. hip hop (in the present). It was Havana's imagined connection to the original source—one reinforced by African American visitors to Cuba, ranging from Harry Belafonte to Mos Def—that provided authenticity, at the same time that the distance between Cuban and mainstream U.S. rap was held up for admiration. At its most successful moment, Cuban hip hop achieved a perfect balance of sameness and difference, and a single word, valued in both New York and Havana, held the key to that success: revolution.

NOTES

Introduction

1. Since many of the people discussed in this book share surnames, I will frequently identify hip hoppers by their first names or artistic names.

2. For detailed discussions of the term "underground," see Baker 2011 and 2012.

3. On the BVSC and *timba*, see Neustadt 2002 and Perna 2005.

4. His comments appear on the inside back cover of the second edition of *Movimiento*, the Cuban hip hop magazine. All translations are by the author unless otherwise noted.

5. The bibliography on U.S.-Cuban musical relations is extensive: particularly useful are Roberts 1979, Waxer 1994, Sublette 2004, and Acosta 2005.

6. Brennan (2008, 8) notes four previous cycles of foreign infatuation with Cuban music, dating back to the nineteenth century.

7. *East of Havana* is the title of both a documentary and an accompanying book about Havana hip hop. Where page numbers appear, I am referring to the book.

8. The Buena Vista Crew, also known as the Buena Vista Plan, was formed to unite hip hoppers in this Havana neighborhood.

9. Like Pardue (2007, 704), I have opted for "hip hopper" as a catchall term since the alternatives are either long winded and ideologically loaded ("members of the hip hop movement") or excessively colloquial for repeated use ("hip hop heads").

10. The atmosphere at hip hop club nights is quite different from that at more commercialized venues where timba and reggaetón predominate: entry

is based less on the ability to pay, and social interaction is more pronounced since many who attend know each other.

11. The realities were a little more contradictory: the BVSC revived the commercial popular music of earlier decades when Cuba was a central node in the global music industry, and its music was a huge commercial success, while the BAHHC exchanges ironically opened up new commercial vistas for hip hop groups in Havana.

12. The title of this song recalls Ernesto Duarte's famous bolero of the same name, recorded by Ibrahim Ferrer on *Buena Vista Social Club Presents Ibrahim Ferrer*.

13. Wark's (1994, xiv) maxim "we no longer have roots, we have aerials" could hardly be more apposite to residents of Alamar, a postrevolution housing development where everyone had been relocated from somewhere else, leading to a melting pot of influences rather than local traditions, and where the combination of tall buildings and seaside location was ideal for rigging up makeshift antennae.

14. The influence of U.S. funk, soul, jazz, and pop on Cuban music in the 1970s and 1980s is captured on the compilation *Si, Para Usted: The Funky Beats of Revolutionary Cuba, Volume 1*. Those genres have remained influential, leaving their mark on 1990s timba and the alternative music scene of the past decade; many fusion artists, such as Ogguere, Free Hole Negro, Interactivo, and Kumar show distinct jazz-funk leanings.

15. The literature on the Special Period is vast: good starting points are Brenner et al. 2008 and, from a cultural perspective, Hernandez-Reguant 2009a.

16. One AHS official told me that the association's staff jokingly described it as an OSíG (*organización sí gubernamental*, or governmental organization), a pun that reverses the meaning of the Spanish acronym ONG (*organización no gubernamental*, or nongovernmental organization).

17. There is some mythmaking around Alamar's claims: it was undoubtedly a key site, but many leading groups of the 1990s and their followers came from more central barrios like Centro Habana and Vedado, parts of the city with longer established traditions of consuming *música americana*. However, Alamar's physical resemblance to U.S. housing projects lent weight to its claims of primacy.

18. The artists and activists involved in the Black August exchanges included Latinos as well as African Americans, and promoting good relations between these two constituencies was a priority of the supporting organizations.

19. The strong welfare state, free health and education, and subsidy of basic necessities reduced economic and practical pressures, thus freeing up individuals to devote time to hip hop (see Cushman 1995).

20. For all their independent rhetoric, however, Los Aldeanos have never cut themselves off altogether from institutions or the media. The AHS has played a key role in their history, and their songs have been played regularly on the radio program *La Esquina de Rap*.

21. In contrast, Pardue (2008) draws exclusively on a number of locally produced theses in his study of hip hop in São Paulo, revealing a quite different balance between national and international interest.

22. The preponderance of rap in this book reflects both the influence of such agendas on my own thinking at the outset of my research and the far greater production of knowledge—one of my primary interests—about hip hop than reggaetón.

23. In fact, political rap has always had a foot in universities. Three members of Public Enemy studied "The Afro-American Experience" at university summer programs in the early 1970s, and the group began to coalesce while they were in college (Chang 2005, 235–41). They found a mentor in a young African American studies professor, Andrei Strobert, whose classes on black music and musicians were a big influence on the group. Jeff Chang (2005, 422) also underlines the importance of college radio in nurturing underground hip hop: "If the city street was hip-hop nationalism's mythical wellspring, the college campus was its hothouse, the hub of the local underground."

24. This quotation is from a final draft of "New York *Bomba* and *Palos*: Liberation Mythologies and Overlapping Diasporas," forthcoming in *Black Music Research Journal*. A Spanish version has been published in *Boletín Música*: http://www.casadelasamericas.org/publicaciones/boletinmusica/26/temat icos.pdf.

25. Over the next seven years, I made eight subsequent visits to Havana, ranging in length from one week to two months.

26. The only significant exception to this statement is Orishas, a group which honed its style in France and aimed for the international market (and thus for audiences that might not understand Spanish).

27. My critical perspective with regard to language and the Cuban rap literature extends to my own previous work, in which, all too often, I used the terminology of the hip hop scene as though it were transparent. I know firsthand how easy it is to adopt unthinkingly the linguistic framework of those whom one studies—one of the dangers of an insider view. Here my aim is to question such terms and categories, even when I have previously used them, not to perpetuate them.

28. The recent success of Los Aldeanos, achieved through alternative channels opened up by the spread of digital technologies, has altered the picture somewhat; for the first time since Orishas' *A lo Cubano* was released, Cuban

rap can be heard blaring out of stereos (and now also cell phones and computers) across Havana and beyond. Nevertheless, this is really the success story of one group rather than the genre that it represents.

1. ¡Hip Hop, Revolución!

1. For a "rock perspective" on the fast-tracking of hip hop, see Olivera and González 2005.

2. The other elements of hip hop (DJ-ing, break dancing, and graffiti) have received less institutional support in Havana.

3. The restriction of my focus to Havana is justified by my contention that the nationalization of rap has been manifested not in the even spread of the music across the whole island, as in the case of reggaetón, nor in consistent institutional support, but rather in the incorporation of hip hop into conceptualizations of national culture. Nationalization has been a discursive process that has resulted primarily from the actions and negotiations of a small number of Havana-based figures. *Pace* Boudreault-Fournier (2008, 101), there is therefore no contradiction in seeing nationalization as a local process, or indeed a transnational one.

4. The full name of Grupo Uno was in fact Grupo Uno de la Asociación Hermanos Saíz, undermining accounts of Havana hip hop that credit cultural institutions only with the later co-optation of an originally independent scene.

5. I am very grateful to Laura García Freyre for sharing this information with me.

6. This phrase is still frequently invoked, for example by a senior Communist Party official at a prefestival meeting between rappers and AHS officers at La Madriguera in November 2004.

7. Robinson (2004, 118) noted the use of "politically correct" language: Fernández "framed the whole thing in impeccable official rhetoric, at times quoting Fidel himself."

8. Many of Los Aldeanos' lyrics in the original Spanish can be found online at websites like www.musica.com.

9. This appears to be the accepted way to frame social critique in contemporary Cuba (Pérez Sarduy and Stubbs 2000, xiii).

10. Los Aldeanos consists of Aldo Rodríguez Baquero (known as Aldo or El Aldeano) and Bián Rodríguez Gala (El B).

11. This technique of imagining José Martí or Antonio Maceo's response to contemporary realities has a long history in Cuban music (Borges-Triana 2009, 96).

12. A short definition of Che's hombre nuevo can be found at http://www.radiohc.cu/che/paginas/5heroes.htm.

13. Since the housing project of Alamar was conceived as the home of the hombre nuevo (Geoffray 2007), it was an appropriate place to emerge as "the city of hip hop."

14. Yrak Saenz told me: "I'm not against the revolution: I'm against everything that is *not* revolution, everything that is not revolutionary, in its essence, as in change. That which remains static is not revolution. Revolution in its essence is to change and to improve, and when things don't improve, well, then you'll see me having my say." Similarly, Nehanda Abiodun (*East of Havana* n.d., 182) states that rappers "are being more revolutionary because they are willing to point out the contradictions that exist. And in pointing them out they are saying that they want things to be better, they are not satisfied with it being the way that it is, and that's a revolutionary stand."

15. There are parallels with Hosokawa's (2002) study of Japanese salsa musicians, who see themselves as striking a blow for old-school *salsa dura* in the face of the mainstream popularity of (the supposedly degenerate) *salsa romántica* in the Americas; purity can thus be located away from the source if the source is perceived as contaminated.

16. This track appears on an unreleased compilation, planned as the second volume of *Cuban Hip Hop All Stars*.

17. A salsa-rap group in the 1990s.

18. The reality on the ground was often quite distinct from the theory: I regularly attended performances where both music and lyrics bore scant relation to the positions upheld by Herrera and Fernández. La Madriguera, for example, was a space where the boundaries of "constructive criticism" were sometimes pushed to the limit. I have seen a rapper waving a machete above his head on stage while leading the audience in a chant of "fucking police." But the key point is that, by expounding particular discursive positions, intermediaries made such performances possible in state venues; the macro-level negotiation of a space for criticism within the orbit of the state left considerable room for maneuver on the micro scale. With the party line fixed higher up the institutional chain, control over the details of rap concerts was often less than strict. In contrast, an example of what happens when an artist openly rejects discursive negotiation can be seen (or, to be more exact, not seen) in the case of the highly controversial and invisible punk group Porno Para Ricardo.

19. Fidel's attachment to ideas is evident in Castro and Ramonet 2008, 390–91, 401.

20. Underground rappers and state officials also share a distaste for reggaetón (see chapter 2). Officials like Alpidio Alonso and Fernando Rojas express opinions on reggaetón virtually identical to those of leading underground rap groups. This overlap in interests further suggests that their relationship can-

not be reduced to mutual appropriations or to a purely manufactured consensus. Both the Cuban political elite and the Cuban underground rap scene are predominantly masculine environments focused on the power of the spoken word, and both share an ideological preference for text- or intellect-centered music—rap, nueva trova—over body-centered genres such as timba or reggaetón.

21. The substitution for Fidel Castro of Che, Camilo Cienfuegos, or themselves is one of Los Aldeanos' favored and most controversial strategies. In one song, they transform Carlos Puebla's line "Se acabó la diversion / Llegó el comandante y mandó a parar" (the fun is over, the commander-in-chief is here and he's ordered it to stop), from the song "Y en eso llegó Fidel," into "Sí, la diversión se va a acabar / Llegamos nosotros y mandamos a parar" (yes, the fun is going to finish, we're here and we've ordered it to stop).

22. The only missing code is agrarianism. As argued in chapter 3, the revolution's long-held attachment to agrarianism gave way to a more urban focus with the advent of the Special Period and the need to boost urban tourism.

23. The full statement can be found at http://www.afrocubaweb.com/rap/blackaugustoo.html.

24. Fernández has spoken of hip hop as providing a path for him to become a journalist, activist, and cultural promoter at a time when the upheavals of the Special Period, which saw many professionals abandon careers to work in tourism, removed the logic of continuing in formal education. Hip hop thus provided him with the education that opened up a new career and purpose in life.

25. Quoted at http://www.thetalkingdrum.com/neh.html.

26. Some information about this meeting can be found in "Encuentro entre amigos" (n.d.), though my account draws primarily on my interview with Belafonte in February 2009.

27. This appears in an interview with Emetrece Productions, available at http://www.youtube.com/watch?v=C2OunPSsmy4.

28. As in the case of the other characteristic New York music of this time, salsa, the individuals were predominantly Puerto Rican, but their musical influences were markedly Afro-Cuban. Thanks to the U.S. embargo on Cuba, the line between Afro-Cuban music and break-beats was not direct but rather passed through a predominantly Puerto Rican–Nuyorican filter (Chris Washburne, pers. comm.). Emblematic of the ethnic and cultural mix of early hip hop is the half-Cuban, half–Puerto Rican, Bronx-born DJ Luis "DJ Disco Wiz" Cedeño, who created the Mighty Force Crew with Grandmaster Caz in 1975.

29. As Thompson underlines, the connection goes back to the Kongo ancestry of all these musical styles.

30. While the artists chosen to make up the ACR were already professional, they had been dispersed among other agencies. Thus the formation of the ACR did not create an amateur-professional divide, but it was a symbolically charged act that solidified emerging divisions within the rap scene.

31. This positive view of the first phase of the AHS's involvement with hip hop is shared by independent figures like Ariel Fernández (2002), Edgar González (2007), and Joaquín Borges-Triana (2009).

32. Boudreault-Fournier (2008) shows a reverse picture in Santiago.

33. This contradictory environment recalls Alma Guillermoprieto's memoir (2005) of Havana's modern dance school, founded in the early days of the revolution, where modern dance was given institutional support and recognition yet was placed under the control of bureaucrats who had very little sympathy for it.

34. In seeking parallels with the ACR, one might look at the Soviet-era Leningrad Rock Club (Cushman 1995). As Szemere (2001, 11) notes, through dividing rock scenes in the Soviet bloc into professional and underground, the state created conflicts and censored more extreme groups. While there are parallels with the Cuban case, I will argue in chapter 2 that this example of political control may be less relevant than the perestroika-era restructuring of organizations involved in cultural production that Cushman describes, which led to a sudden turn toward commercial imperatives. A closer parallel might then be the Son de Cuba agency for traditional music launched in Santiago in 2000 (Boudreault-Fournier 2008, 50). A comparison between Son de Cuba and the ACR suggests that the latter may be rather ordinary within the Cuban context of the new millennium, simply one among many commercial music agencies, a sign of the times rather than of a government plot. It is significant that by 2010 several groups had left (or were talking about leaving) the ACR and that their dissatisfaction stemmed not from issues of control but rather from perceptions that the ACR lacked the professionalism and promotional clout of other agencies of longer standing.

35. For a sober assessment of the challenges facing the ACR, see Magia López's (n.d.) own account.

36. Almendares Vivo was a cultural project run by the musician Gerardo Alfonso in the Parque Almendares; with DJ Alexis D'Boys as artistic producer for some years, it provided an important venue for hip hop concerts.

37. This refusal is sometimes point-blank; at other times, bureaucratic foot-dragging ensures that the necessary travel documents are not ready in time.

38. El B's unsurprisingly scathing view of this turn of events can be heard in his song "La naranja se picó," in which he describes bureaucrats who "sat in a chair, playing ping-pong with your future." He broadens out into stinging

criticisms of Cuba's policy on overseas travel and emigration, accusing the Cuban leadership of feeding the sharks in the Florida Straits: "Many are dead or in jail / They prefer to die for the American dream than live the Cuban nightmare."

39. Furthermore, there is the transnational angle to consider. Fernandes (2006, 9) argues for a mass media–arts dichotomy, with the arts supporting a public sphere that the mass media shun as result of government control; but rather than discounting the media, we need to be aware of the transnational mediation of the public sphere. Foreign journalists and film makers became a prime outlet for the Havana hip hop scene, providing Cuban rappers with a chance to reach out beyond their local live audiences and participate in a transnational, mass-mediated public realm. The resulting films played to audiences in festivals and universities around the world, and Havana hip hop's public sphere now includes a global array of conferences, panels, debates, lectures, and classes. The Internet is also playing an increasingly important role: El B's song "La naranja se picó" has received more than 400,000 hits on YouTube, leading Melisa Rivière to call Los Aldeanos "YouTube kings" (quoted in Israel 2010).

40. Olivera and González (2005) contrast the internationalism of the rap festival around 2000 with the provincial character of rock festivals (also organized by the AHS), underlining that the issue of visas implied an official vision behind this discrepancy.

41. Boudreault-Fournier (2008, 114–15) notes the elision of race in urban music workshops in Santiago's Casas de la Cultura, mirroring the state's "politics of silence" about race.

42. Certainly, the AHS, like any large organization, has its fair share of critics, but the responses to its suspension of the rap festival revealed that if there is one thing worse than the state's taking charge of culture, it is the state's *not* taking charge of culture.

43. On the issue of censorship in Havana hip hop, see Baker 2011.

44. Circular email from the AHS.

45. The supposed resistance of U.S. commercial rap has been critiqued quite widely (e.g., Krims 2000), but there has been much less questioning of rap outside the United States in this respect.

2. The Revolution of the Body

1. The clave is a fixed rhythmic pattern that underlies musical genres such as son and salsa. The clave cubana, or rumba clave, is very similar, but the different placing of one of the five attacks is crucial since it gives music a characteristically Cuban flavor.

2. See, for example, Padura Fuentes (2006), Martínez Molina (2007a), and two articles by Caballero, the first defending reggaetón (2007b) and the second, only a few months later, attacking it (2008).

3. See Coplan's (2005, 25) comments about academic preferences for rap over *kwaito* in South Africa. In contexts such as Cuba, South Africa, and Brazil, rap is widely perceived as logocentric and as contrasting with the body-centrism of dominant dance genres (reggaetón, kwaito, and funk, respectively).

4. See also Boudreault-Fournier's (2008) illuminating study of reggaetón in Santiago.

5. There is only one female reggaetón singer of any renown in Havana, La Fres_k.

6. Although El Micha had become a major star by 2010, during most of the period under consideration he could be considered underground due to his musical style and because he operated outside the mainstream music economy of artistic agencies, record companies, and the media. On the underground aspect of reggaetón, see Baker 2011.

7. It should be noted, however, that there has been a steady move toward ever more explicit language in Cuban popular music over the last century. Timba was similarly accused of debasing the language in the 1990s; today it is held up nostalgically as a paragon of poetry in comparison with reggaetón. The language of the soneros of the Buena Vista Social Club was perceived similarly in its time.

8. Boudreault-Fournier (2008, 144) takes issue with this idea, citing expressions of national pride in reggaetón. While examples of nationalism can be found, they are somewhat infrequent in Havana; and if one were to examine reggaetón through the lens of Kapcia's codes of national identity (see chapter 1), one would see just how small the overlap between reggaetón and national ideology really is. Reguetoneros' flaunting of state ideologies—verbally, musically, visually, and performatively—outweighs any nods they may make in the direction of national pride.

9. Indigenization may also be a matter of place: Boudreault-Fournier's (2008) research on reggaetón in Santiago suggests that the music produced there shows more evidence of Cubanization.

10. The documentary *Animals of Cuban Music* provides insight into the timba-reggaetón relationship, though I have heard stronger views expressed off-camera.

11. The value of studying (rather than dismissing) imitative music scenes is evident in studies such as Hosokawa (2002) on Japanese salsa and Avelar (2001) on Brazilian heavy metal.

12. The discourses around both rap and reggaetón as musics that started

out as authentic and were corrupted by the transnational music industry are useful in Cuba because they allow the possibility that Cuba (with its absence of the said industry) will rescue or recreate the authenticity of the original. While this possibility is seen as unfulfilled in the case of reggaetón, rappers are widely credited with just such a recuperative achievement.

13. Here there are distinct echoes of *afrocubanismo*, an artistic movement of the 1930s in which professional, conservatory trained composers "improved" and "polished up" the street sounds of rumba and son, converting this "raw material" into art music compositions (R. Moore 1997).

14. This is not to suggest that all Havana reggaetón productions are simple—though some undoubtedly are—but rather that they are created according to different aesthetic criteria than other forms of popular music. Indeed, Carlos of TC Records, one of Havana's most experienced producers, was adamant in our conversations that his home studio offered something unique: for him, mainstream studios like EGREM (Empresa de Grabaciones y Ediciones Musicales) did not have much experience with street music like reggaetón. He claimed that "street producers" had specialized knowledge of how to create the most appealing bass and percussion sounds for reggaetón, and he thus rejected the idea that home-grown productions were amateurish or inferior. Many reggaetón producers may have no formal musical skills, but their ears are highly attuned to the specific aesthetic requirements of reggaetón.

15. For more on timba and the despelote, see Perna (2005) and Hernandez-Reguant (2006); on reggaetón dancing and gender, see Fairley (2006).

16. See Hernandez-Reguant (2006, 267) on overt displays of sexuality in timba dance as a site of political challenge.

17. I have borrowed the phrase "the revolution of the body" from a song by Ogguere.

18. See, for example, Gente de Zona's hymn to a *farandulera*, "Le gustan los artistas."

19. Carroll's dichotomy is also played out in the musical sphere: tourists enchanted by BVSC often ask where to find music venues "where the locals go" and are usually disappointed to discover that in Havana, at least, the locals go mainly to reggaetón clubs while BVSC plays in the exclusive Hotel Nacional (where most locals are discouraged from entering).

20. In 2008, Gente de Zona finally released their first official CD, but their local strategies remained the same. They did not release an album until after they had become the biggest act in Cuba, and they released it on Planet Records in Italy.

21. Several people suggested to me that the name of this collective was ironic, considering their hypercommercialism and the rumors of their sharp business practices and underworld connections.

22. Mora was interviewed on TV by Carlos Otero the day after he arrived in Miami in April 2008; the interview can be seen on YouTube.

23. It is undoubtedly significant that I spoke to Rojas just a week after Alexánder Delgado had been dressed down for an incident of indecency in performance: cleaning up reggaetón was clearly the order of the day.

24. Esteban Israel, pers. comm.

25. Borges-Triana (2009, 64) quotes a rumor of a late-1970s report on rock by CIDMUC and the Ministry of the Interior, which reputedly concluded that the genre was neither music nor healthy for Cuban youth. Whether true or not, this rumor illustrates the connection between CIDMUC's research and the formation of cultural policy, suggesting that the 2005 reggaetón report's motivations were as much political as academic.

26. Esteban Israel, pers. comm.

27. For more in-depth discussion of the underground/commercial question, see Baker 2011b.

28. That the comedy agency set up by the AHS was equally "corrupted" (as Rojas admitted) suggests a problem with the institutional model rather than with urban musicians.

29. There has also been a process of softening and institutionalizing timba in the twenty-first century, which arguably left a space for a new, harder, more transgressive street style to take root. Whereas timba pushed the aesthetic and political boundaries in the 1990s, in the following decade its leading practitioners took a safer, more commercialized line. The pendulum swing to reggaetón may also be, therefore, an example of the domestication of one popular music style paving the way for the emergence of a brash new upstart.

30. Cooper's ideas, in particular that of slackness as "the antithesis of Culture," illuminate the gulf between reggaetón and state ideology discussed above (see note 8).

31. Papá Humbertico, in "Aquel niño que fuimos," raps about the impact of the Special Period on the hip hop generation: "That's how the present youth was formed and forged / The students, the emigrants, the delinquents / Youth that's combative, battle-hardened, brave / Our past helped us to be a little bit better."

32. For example, the meaning of the reggaetón hit "A ti te gustan los yumas" (you like foreigners) evolved from humorous critique to affirmation through constant repetition (CIDMUC 2005, 19); this is in marked contrast to the serious, moralizing treatment of the same theme in underground rap songs.

33. The widespread popularity of Los Aldeanos is a complicating, though exceptional, factor. However, since they have split off from the old-school hip hop "movement" and most of their audience listens to them only on record-

ings, one might argue that their music is simultaneously hyperpolitical (in lyrical terms) and apolitical (in its detachment from nonmusical projects). They push the political boundaries to new limits, but listening to Los Aldeanos seems to testify to youthful, middle-class rebellion more than political mobilization. Furthermore, I would argue that Los Aldeanos' success does not point to a significant resurgence of interest in hip hop as such; most of their followers are Los Aldeanos fans more than hip hop fans.

34. The home of Cuban reggaetón is normally considered to be Santiago, the country's second city. Santiago's location at the eastern end of the island places it directly in the path of musical currents—and radio signals—emanating from Jamaica, including the dembow dancehall rhythm that became an essential building block of reggaetón.

35. The distinction between African American and Caribbean music is arguably a false one, as suggested in chapter 1. Hip hop has clear Caribbean roots, while early reggaetón drew on U.S. commercial rap. Nevertheless, this kind of dichotomy often informs popular thinking and discussions.

36. El Micha is an exception, but—perhaps not coincidentally—he was also the outsider among leading reguetoneros for most of the period of my research, an underground star who did not belong to an agency and had little exposure in the mainstream media.

3. The Havana You Don't Know

1. Saunders (2008, 312–26) includes a useful discussion of CD album covers and T-shirts, though some key transnational questions are left unasked. Who was the cover of *Cuban Hip Hop All Stars, Vol. 1*, aimed at? The album was released in the United States, and insofar as it circulated in Cuba, it was only in pirated form without the cover. Where did rappers get their T-shirts? If North American hip hoppers donated them, as seems highly likely (such items cannot be purchased in Cuba), how does this affect the meanings generated by their display?

2. I am very grateful to Laura García Freyre for generously sharing with me a transcript of her interview with this employee.

3. In mid-2010, La Madriguera still belonged to the AHS, suggesting that the crisis had passed.

4. In reality, the Havana hip hop scene was not always quite as pacifistic as its proponents have claimed, as discussed below, though it is still very safe.

5. When they recorded the song a year later, Los Aldeanos reproduced the audience response, including samples of audience members cheering in the introduction, and saying "they've all left" when the shout-outs at the end are met with silence.

6. Commercial clubs had played a role in the hip hop scene since the 1990s, but primarily as places to dance rather than perform; live rap took place predominantly in cultural centers and outdoor venues.

7. Although concerts continued to be put on in Alamar, others were organized at the Salón Rosado de la Tropical, and the colloquia took place at central venues like UNEAC.

8. Even though both types of venue are ultimately answerable to the state, institutional venues are subsidized and thus charge low entrance fees, whereas commercial venues are run more like businesses.

9. An important detail is that such peñas were organized *al doble* (on the side), which made them more economically appealing to club managers and artists (see Baker 2011).

10. As ever, there are clear limits to hip hoppers' control over these spaces; within a year Los Aldeanos had crossed the line and all three of these venues had stopped promoting live rap, though negotiations with the administrator of Karachi (which I witnessed) saw one peña revived. Popularity can open doors, but political controversy can close them far more quickly.

11. See, for example, the report of the gentlemanliness of the battle between the old friends El Aldeano and El Adversario in the 2007 competition (Castillo Martiatu n.d.c, 25).

12. The foreign presence has varied over time: it became significant in the late 1990s and was a notable feature of the scene when I began my research in 2003–4, but it tapered off into insignificance again over the next five years.

13. For a comprehensive overview, see Bridge and Watson 2000b and 2002.

14. Among other sources here, I draw on the promotional brochure titled "Cuba" produced by the Cuban Ministry of Tourism in 2006.

15. This practice echoes Arsenio Rodríguez's *guaguancós* in praise of Havana barrios (García 2006, 61).

16. The duo frequently expresses a jaundiced view of the foreign presence and involvement in Cuba. For example, Aldo told Laura García Freyre (2009) that "here the foreigner comes before the Cuban. He or she has all the comforts, studies whatever he or she likes, and the Cuban is stuck in the background." Los Aldeanos have repeatedly distanced themselves from overseas political causes and emphasized that they are interested only in what is going on in Cuba; in the documentary *Revolution*, El B defends the localism of their texts, which, he says, are based on the only reality they know. The duo's "village" skepticism toward outsiders marks a distinct move away from the earlier embrace of transnationalism embodied by Black August. Indeed, the editorial on the inside front cover of the second edition of *Movimiento*, a magazine which is closely aligned with the older ideological strand of Havana hip hop, states that "we want to reject all *aldeanismo* [village-ism] and enter

into the original dimensions of hip hop culture." However, the tide was moving the other way.

17. Miramar is one of the wealthiest suburbs of Havana.

18. Pulmón signifies struggling and overlaps with inventar; it is thus more a feature of the middle phase of Havana hip hop, when there were more foreigners visiting the scene.

19. This skepticism is evident in Los Aldeanos' song "La gente cambia de la noche a la mañana" (people change overnight), in which change is equated to the abandonment of principles.

20. The reference is to the Committees for the Defense of the Revolution (state-sponsored neighborhood associations).

21. Huevo was Akozta's rap partner in Los Paisanos.

22. "De donde son los cantantes," the famous line from Trio Matamoros's "Son de la Loma," refers to the mountains of eastern Cuba. It is used here to address the issue of immigration from eastern Cuba to the capital, which is perceived as adding to the pressure on the city's overstretched resources.

23. The allusion is to policemen talking to each other over their car radios.

24. My translation is adapted from the documentary Pa'lante, with help from Pablo Herrera.

25. This distinction is translated into the kinds of camera shots used in the hip hop documentaries discussed in chapter 4: foreign-made films often include shots from moving cars, whereas the Cuban-made Pa'lante includes a scene shot on a public bus. Similarly, the video for El Aldeano's song "Miseria humana" opens with Aldo on a bus; when he appears in a car, it is in the fantasy world of "Es un sueño" (it's a dream).

26. For example, Manolito's "La Habana me llama" (Havana is calling me) is built on the idea that "La Habana tiene un swing" (Havana has a swing).

27. This analysis is based on a demo version of the song given to me in Havana by Kumar. The version later released in Spain contains minor differences.

28. Rutheiser (2000) subtitles his critical study of recent urbanization "the return of the repressed in a late socialist city."

29. The anti-Cubanization aesthetic of musical productions by Los Aldeanos and other underground hip hoppers, combined with the shift from the real and imagined New York–Havana transnationalism of the late 1990s to the localism of la aldea, reveals that localization, often sought in the music of Cuban rap, has taken place to a greater extent in the social, political, and imaginary realms.

30. For further discussion of musical style, see chapter 4 and Baker 2012.

31. For an analysis of the mythical dichotomy of underground and commercial and its perpetuation in Cuban hip hop studies, see Baker 2012.

4. Cuban Hip Hop All Stars

1. Soandres del Río and Clyde Valentin both told me about the tensions generated as Cuban hip hoppers jockeyed for access to equipment and other material goods brought to the island via the Black August exchanges, while the behavior of visiting artists did not always impress either the American organizers or their local hosts, as del Río discusses in *Cuban HipHop: Desde el Principio*. Valentin left the project after the 2000 exchange due to these tensions.

2. See Fernandez's website, http://www.arielfernandezdiaz.com.

3. It is thus significant that the first article in the first edition of *Movimiento* magazine was dedicated to KRS-One.

4. Writing about North American visions of Cuba a century earlier, Louis Pérez (2008, 22–23) claims: "The Americans came to their knowledge of Cuba principally by way of representations entirely of their own creation, which is to suggest that the Cuba that the Americans chose to engage was, in fact, a figment of their own imagination and a projection of their needs. . . . It has always been thus between the United States and Cuba."

5. Of the four groups that won the Grand Prize at the hip hop festival from 1995 to 1998, three went on to commercial music careers, two of them abroad, suggesting that the pure aspirations that Fab 5 Freddy detected had more to do with his own dissatisfaction with U.S. hip hop than with the local scene.

6. See http://www.thetalkingdrum.com/neh.html.

7. I am very grateful to Raquel Z. Rivera for her insightful comments on this chapter and in particular on this section, though her views should not be conflated with mine.

8. *Revolutionizing Blackness* is the provisional title of Perry's forthcoming monograph. Race is also a dominant theme of both older and more recent work, such as Pacini Hernandez and Garofalo 1999–2000 and Saunders 2008.

9. *Chinos* are people considered to be of oriental appearance, though they are rarely of oriental origin; *jabaos* are light-skinned people of color.

10. Pacini Hernandez and Garofalo's (1999–2000) findings may also have resulted, therefore, from interviewing a broader range of individuals than Perry, since they had no explicit intention to seek out problack informants.

11. In the documentary *La Ciudad del Hip Hop*, the white rapper Edgar González storms off after his complaints that he is discriminated against for being white are not taken seriously.

12. The desire to provide a race-based analysis has led scholars to extrapolate from a part of the story. For example, a focus on blackness seems not to have been spread evenly across all the elements of hip hop in Havana: while

rappers have been predominantly darker skinned, those who practice DJ-ing, break dance, and graffiti have been more racially mixed. To portray hip hop as a race-based movement therefore elides internal differences.

13. Mambises were black soldiers who fought against the Spaniards in Cuba's independence wars; Lucumí and Carabalí are ethnic groups of African origin found in Cuba.

14. The quote is from the publisher's website (http://new.neverstop.com/catalog/product_info.php?cPath=1&products_id=31&osCsid=5d0f2a0a0 21f4f8fe86).

15. A video of the interview is available online (http://www.havana-cultura .com/INT/EN/cultura.html#/677).

16. *Revolution*, a fourth Cuban-made documentary and the first full-length one, was released in 2010, unfortunately too late for analysis in this chapter.

17. The groups that dominated the 1995 festival were the hypercommercial SBS and Primera Base, who had a mixed repertoire of conscious and commercial songs.

18. "A lo cubano, botella de 30 pesos y fuma estaca / Recicla garganta de palo mañana pá la resaca."

19. Shuhei Hosokawa's (2002) study of Japanese salsa offers illuminating parallels. In this context, too, nationalization is seen as inauthentic, and niche audiences shy away from fusions, which are associated with commercial mainstream pop.

20. See Baker 2012 for further discussion of the polemics around live musicians and Cuban styles in Havana hip hop. Pardue (2008, 35) notes that in Brazil, too, rappers have been slow to incorporate national influences like *repente* and recognize them as authentic; and my own (more limited) experiences of hip hop peñas in Caracas and Bogotá is that localized musical styles are the exception rather than the norm.

21. A more recent link has been forged between Los Aldeanos, Silvito "El Libre," and Venezuelan rapper Gabylonia, who appears on songs such as "H1N1" and "A pesar de todo"; in the latter, she raps: "Listen up, Cuba and Venezuela don't just share doctors and petrol / There's also good art—hidden art on the streets."

22. Brennan (2008, 154) writes: "It is important to recall Ulf Hannerz's helpful revision of the center/periphery construct when he observes that there are actually many regional centers in the global arrangement of states: . . . For Latin America and the Caribbean, Cuba has acted as this sort of center."

Conclusion. The Rise and Fall of Havana Hip Hop

1. See Fernandez's website, http://www.arielfernandezdiaz.com/?page_id=129.

2. The nearest thing to Public Enemy to come out of Havana was Explosión Suprema. However, the group's riotous stage show and surreal lyrics did not sit easily with the serious paradigms of Cuban cultural institutions and intellectual constructions of Cuban hip hop, and despite remaining a firm favorite within the scene, this gifted quartet never achieved the wider success it deserved.

3. See also Maxwell 2003 and Mitchell 2001c, which draw on the work of Paul Gilroy and Martin Stokes to argue against hip hop as postmodern culture.

4. Rodríguez's first two sentences are uncannily close to Medina's (2007) argument and even wording, underlining the relevance of the latter's analysis to Havana hip hop.

5. Yrak Saenz had a running joke with me about an (imaginary) old-school Cuban rapper sitting at home on his sofa, day after day, explaining his inactivity by saying "Mos Def didn't call me today."

6. García Freyre 2009. I am grateful to Melisa Rivière for confirming these facts, which were circulating as rumors in Havana.

BIBLIOGRAPHY

Acosta, Leonardo. 2005. "Interinfluencias y confluencias entre las músicas de Cuba y los EE.UU." *Los que soñamos por la oreja: boletín de Música Cubana Alternativa* 13:5–18.

———. 2008. "Música *techno*, ruido y medio ambiente." *Gaceta de Cuba* 4 (July–August): 14–18.

Akpan, Wilson. 2006. "And the Beat Goes On? Message Music, Political Repression and the Power of Hip-Hop in Nigeria." In *Popular Music Censorship in Africa*, edited by Michael Drewett and Martin Cloonan, 91–106. Aldershot, England: Ashgate.

Allen, Ernest, Jr. 1996. "Making the Strong Survive: The Contours and Contradictions of Message Rap." In *Droppin' Science: Critical Essays on Rap Music and Hip Hop Culture*, edited by William Eric Perkins, 159–91. Philadelphia: Temple University Press.

Alonso, Alpidio. 2007. "Apuntes para una reflexión necesaria." *El Caimán Barbudo* 40 (338): 16–17.

Álvarez-Tabío Albo, Emma. 2000. *Invención de La Habana*. Barcelona: Editorial Casiopea.

Anderson, Jon Lee. 2006. "Castro's Last Battle." *New Yorker*, 31 July, 44–55.

Armstead, Ronni. 2007. "'Growing the Size of the Black Woman': Feminist Activism in Havana Hip Hop." *NWSA Journal* 19 (1): 106–17.

Askew, Kelly M. 2002. *Performing the Nation: Swahili Music and Cultural Politics in Tanzania*. Chicago: University of Chicago Press.

Attali, Jacques. 1985. *Noise: The Political Economy of Music*. Manchester, England: Manchester University Press.

Avelar, Idelber. 2001. "Defeated Rallies, Mournful Anthems, and the Origins of Brazilian Heavy Metal." In *Brazilian Popular Music and Globalization*, edited by Christopher Dunn and Charles A. Perrone, 123–35. Gainesville: University Press of Florida.

Baker, Geoffrey. 2011. "Cuba Rebelión: Underground Music in Havana." *Latin American Music Review* 32 (1).

———. 2012. "Mala Bizta Sochal Klu: Underground, Alternative and Commercial in Havana Hip Hop." *Popular Music* 31 (1).

Baldwin, Davarian. 2004. "Black Empires, White Desires: The Spatial Politics of Identity in the Age of Hip-Hop." In *That's the Joint! The Hip-Hop Studies Reader*, edited by Murray Forman and Mark Anthony Neal, 159–76. New York: Routledge.

"A Barrier for Cuba's Blacks." 2007. *Miami Herald*, 20 June. http://www.mia miherald.com/multimedia/news/afrolatin/part4/index.html.

"La Batalla de Ideas: Una revolución dentro de la Revolución." 2007. http://www.cha.jovenclub.cu/municipios/concepto/viewpage.php?page_id=12.

Benítez-Rojo, Antonio. 1996. *The Repeating Island: The Caribbean and the Postmodern Perspective*. Translated by James E. Maraniss. 2nd ed. Durham, N.C.: Duke University Press.

Bennett, Andy. 2000. *Popular Music and Youth Culture: Music, Identity and Place*. London: Macmillan.

Bennett, Robert. 2003. *Deconstructing Post-WWII New York City: The Literature, Art, Jazz, and Architecture of an Emerging Global Capital*. New York: Routledge.

Berenson, Alex. 2008. "Target: Castro." *New York Times*, 26 December.

Bohlman, Philip. 1993. "Musicology as a Political Act." *Journal of Musicology* 11 (4): 411–36.

Borges-Triana, Joaquín. 2009. *Concierto cubano: la vida es un divino guión*. Barcelona: Linkgua.

———. n.d. "La FabriK: Obreros de la construcción y embajadores de la creación." *Movimiento* 2:5–9.

Boudreault-Fournier, Alexandrine. 2008. "On the Beat: Composing with Cultural Policies and Music in Cuba." Ph.D. diss., University of Manchester.

Boyd, Todd. 2004. "Check Yo Self before You Wreck Yo Self: The Death of Politics in Rap Music and Popular Culture." In *That's the Joint! The Hip-Hop Studies Reader*, edited by Murray Forman and Mark Anthony Neal, 325–40. New York: Routledge.

Brennan, Timothy. 2008. *Secular Devotion: Afro-Latin Music and Imperial Jazz*. London: Verso.

Brenner, Philip, et al., eds. 2008. *A Contemporary Cuba Reader: Reinventing the Revolution*. Lanham, Md.: Rowman and Littlefield.

Bridge, Gary, and Sophie Watson. 2000a. "City Publics." In *A Companion to the City*, edited by Gary Bridge and Sophie Watson, 369–79. Oxford: Blackwell.

——, eds. 2000b. *A Companion to the City*. Oxford: Blackwell.

——. 2002. *The Blackwell City Reader*. Oxford: Blackwell.

Brock, Lisa. 1998. "Introduction: Between Race and Empire." In *Between Race and Empire: African-Americans and Cubans before the Cuban Revolution*, edited by Lisa Brock and Digna Castañeda Fuertes, 1–32. Philadelphia: Temple University Press.

Bromley, Roger. 2001. *From Alice to Buena Vista: The Films of Wim Wenders*. Westport, Conn.: Greenwood.

Caballero, Rufo. 2007a. "La honestidad nos salvará." *Juventud Rebelde*, 30 September.

——. 2007b. "Felicidades cubanos en el Día de la Cultura Cubana." *Juventud Rebelde*, 20 October.

——. 2008. "Dinero." *Juventud Rebelde*, 9 January.

Cabrera Cepero, Natacha. 2007. "De espaldas a la cultura." *El Caimán Barbudo* 40 (338): 18.

Carroll, Rory. 2009. "Cuba: Open for Business." *Guardian*, 14 April.

Carroll, Rory, and Andrés Schipani. 2008. "Cuba's Young Revolutionaries Fight for Their Art." *Observer*, 28 December.

——. 2009. "As Hard Times Bite, Cubans Show Little Appetite for Celebration." *Guardian*, 1 January.

Castillo Martiatu, Arsenio. n.d.a. "Pablo Herrera en el laberinto del hip hop." *Movimiento* 5:12–15.

——. n.d.b. "Estoy en buen camino." *Movimiento* 6:18–20.

——. n.d.c. "Gallos pelean en el ring, no quiero empates." *Movimiento* 6:23–26.

Castro, Fidel, and Ignacio Ramonet. 2008. *Fidel Castro: My Life; A Spoken Autobiography*. Translated by Andrew Hurley. New York: Scribner.

Castro Medel, Osviel. 2005a. "¿Prohibido el reguetón?" *Juventud Rebelde*, 13 February.

——. 2005b. "Se cruzan balas por el reguetón." *Juventud Rebelde*, 6 March.

"Castro the 'Lennonist.'" 2000. 9 December. http://news.bbc.co.uk/1/hi/world/americas/1062993.stm.

Chang, Jeff. 2005. *Can't Stop Won't Stop: A History of the Hip-Hop Generation*. New York: Picador.

Chasteen, John Charles. 2002. "A National Rhythm: Social Dance and Elite Identity in Nineteenth-Century Havana." In *Music/Popular Culture/Identities*, edited by Richard Young, 65–84. Amsterdam: Rodopi.

Chávez, Lydia. 2005. "Adrift: An Introduction to Contemporary Cuba." In

BIBLIOGRAPHY

Capitalism, God, and a Good Cigar: Cuba Enters the Twenty-first Century, edited by Lydia Chávez, 1–14. Durham, N.C.: Duke University Press.

CIDMUC (Centro de Investigación y Desarrollo de la Música Cubana). 2005. "Informe sobre el reguetón." Unpublished manuscript.

Cloonan, Martin. 2003. "Call That Censorship? Problems of Definition." In *Policing Pop*, edited by Martin Cloonan and Reebee Garofalo, 13–29. Philadelphia: Temple University Press.

Condry, Ian. 2001. "A History of Japanese Hip-Hop." In *Global Noise: Rap and Hip-Hop outside the USA*, edited by Tony Mitchell, 222–47. Middletown, Conn.: Wesleyan University Press.

———. 2006. *Hip-Hop Japan: Rap and the Paths of Cultural Globalization*. Durham, N.C.: Duke University Press.

Cooper, Carolyn. 1993. *Noises in the Blood: Orality, Gender, and the "Vulgar" Body of Jamaican Popular Culture*. London: Macmillan.

Coplan, David. 2005. "God Rock Africa: Thoughts on Politics in Popular Black Performance in South Africa." *African Studies* 64 (1): 9–27.

Corbett, Ben. 2004. *This Is Cuba: An Outlaw Culture Survives*. New York: Basic Books.

Cordero, Tania. n.d. "Persistir en Primera Base." *Movimiento* 3:21–23.

Cortés, José Luis. n.d. "Qué es el rap?" *Movimiento* 4:7.

Cushman, Thomas. 1993. "Glasnost, Perestroika, and the Management of Oppositional Popular Culture in the Soviet Union, 1985–1991." *Current Perspectives in Social Theory* 13:25–67.

———. 1995. *Notes from the Underground: Rock Music Counterculture in Russia*. Albany: State University of New York Press.

Dawson, Michael C. 2001. *Black Visions: The Roots of Contemporary African-American Political Ideologies*. Chicago: University of Chicago Press.

De la Fuente, Alejandro. 2001. *A Nation for All: Race, Inequality, and Politics in Twentieth-Century Cuba*. Chapel Hill: University of North Carolina Press.

———. 2008a. "The New Afro-Cuban Cultural Movement and the Debate on Race in Contemporary Cuba." *Journal of Latin American Studies* 40:697–720.

———. 2008b. "Recreating Racism: Race and Discrimination in Cuba's Special Period." In *A Contemporary Cuba Reader: Reinventing the Revolution*, edited by Philip Brenner et al., 316–25. Lanham, Md.: Rowman and Littlefield.

Del Río, Joel. 2002. "Amulatao, aplatanao, cubaneao." *Jiribilla* 67, August. http://www.lajiribilla.cu/2002/n67_agosto/1607_67.html.

"Democracy: The 10 Big Questions." 2007. *Observer*, 30 September.

Dery, Mark. 2004. "Public Enemy: Confrontation." In *That's the Joint! The Hip-Hop Studies Reader*, edited by Murray Forman and Mark Anthony Neal, 407–20. New York: Routledge.

Dimitriadis, Greg. 2004. "Hip-Hop: From Live Performance to Mediated Narrative." In *That's the Joint! The Hip-Hop Studies Reader*, edited by Murray Forman and Mark Anthony Neal, 421–35. New York: Routledge.

Domínguez, Jorge. 2008. "Cuba and the *Pax Americana*." In *A Contemporary Cuba Reader: Reinventing the Revolution*, edited by Philip Brenner et al., 203–11. Lanham, Md.: Rowman and Littlefield.

Dominguez, Maria Isabel. 2008. "Cuban Youth: Aspirations, Social Perceptions, and Identity." In *A Contemporary Cuba Reader: Reinventing the Revolution*, edited by Philip Brenner et al., 292–98. Lanham, Md.: Rowman and Littlefield.

Dopico, Ana María. 2002. "Picturing Havana: History, Vision, and the Scramble for Cuba." *Nepantla* 3 (3): 451–93.

Dos Santos Godi, Antonio. 2001. "Reggae and *Samba-Reggae* in Bahia: A Case of Long-Distance Belonging." In *Brazilian Popular Music and Globalization*, edited by Christopher Dunn and Charles A. Perrone, 207–19. Gainesville: University Press of Florida.

Eagleton, Terry. 2007. *The Meaning of Life*. Oxford: Oxford University Press.

East of Havana. n.d. Seattle: Neverstop.

Eckstein, Susan. 2007. "Dollarization and its Discontents in the Post-Soviet Era." In *A Contemporary Cuba Reader: Reinventing the Revolution*, edited by Philip Brenner et al., 179–92. Lanham, Md.: Rowman and Littlefield.

"Encuentro entre amigos." n.d. *Movimiento* 2:18–23.

Erisman, H. Michael. 2004. "Policy Changes and New Objectives in World Relations." In *Cuban Socialism in a New Century: Adversity, Survival, and Renewal*, edited by Max Azicri and Elsie Deal, 303–19. Gainesville: University Press of Florida.

Fairley, Jan. 2006. "Dancing Back to Front: *Regeton*, Sexuality, Gender and Transnationalism in Cuba." *Popular Music* 25 (3): 471–88.

Faya Montano, Alberto. 2005. "Algunas notas sobre el reguetón." *Cubarte: El portal de la cultura cubana*, 28 March. http://www.cubarte.cu/paginas/ac tualidad/opinion.detalle.php?id=12681.

Fernandes, Sujatha. 2006. *Cuba Represent! Cuban Arts, State Power, and the Making of New Revolutionary Cultures*. Durham, N.C.: Duke University Press.

Fernandes, Sujatha, and Jason Stanyek. 2007. "Hip-hop and Black Public Spheres in Cuba, Venezuela, and Brazil." In *Beyond Slavery: The Multilayered Legacy of Africans in Latin America and the Caribbean*, edited by Darién J. Davis, 199–222. Lanham, Md.: Rowman and Littlefield.

Fernández, Ariel. 1998. "Rap cubano: anatomía de un movimiento urbano." *El Caimán Barbudo* 31 (288): 31.

———. 2000. "Rap cubano: ¿Poesía urbana? O la nueva trova de los noventa." *El Caimán Barbudo* 33 (296): 4–14.

388 ———. 2002. "Los futuros inmediatos del hip hop cubano." *Juventud Rebelde-La Ventana*, 12 November. http://laventana.casa.cult.cu/modules.php?name =News&file=article&sid=623.

———. n.d. "Identidades e interiores de ciertos consejos anónimos." *Movimiento* 1:5–10.

Fernández, Damián J. 2000. *Cuba and the Politics of Passion*. Austin: University of Texas Press.

———. 2008. "Society, Civil Society, and the State: An Uneasy Three-Way Affair." In *A Contemporary Cuba Reader: Reinventing the Revolution*, edited by Philip Brenner et al., 92–100. Lanham, Md.: Rowman and Littlefield.

Fielder, Adrian. 2001. "Poaching on Public Space: Urban Autonomous Zones in French *Banlieue* Films." In *Cinema and the City: Film and Urban Societies in a Global Context*, edited by Mark Shiel and Tony Fitzmaurice, 270–81. Oxford: Blackwell.

Fischlin, Daniel, and Ajay Heble. 2004. "The Other Side of Nowhere: Jazz, Improvisation, and Communities in Dialogue." In *The Other Side of Nowhere: Jazz, Improvisation, and Communities in Dialogue*, edited by Daniel Fischlin and Ajay Heble, 1–42. Middletown, Conn.: Wesleyan University Press.

Flores, Juan. 1996. "Puerto Rocks: New York Ricans Stake Their Claim." In *Droppin' Science: Critical Essays on Rap Music and Hip Hop Culture*, edited by William Eric Perkins, 85–105. Philadelphia: Temple University Press.

———. 2004. "Puerto Rocks: Rap, Roots, and Amnesia." In *That's the Joint! The Hip-Hop Studies Reader*, edited by Murray Forman and Mark Anthony Neal, 69–86. New York: Routledge.

Foehr, Stephen. 2001. *Waking Up in Cuba*. London: Sanctuary.

Forman, Murray. 2002. *The 'Hood Comes First: Race, Space, and Place in Rap and Hip-Hop*. Middletown, Conn.: Wesleyan University Press.

———. 2004. Introduction to *That's the Joint! The Hip-Hop Studies Reader*, edited by Murray Forman and Mark Anthony Neal, 1–8. New York: Routledge.

Foster, Robert. 1999. "The Commercial Construction of 'New Nations.'" *Journal of Material Culture* 4:263–82.

Fraser Delgado, Celeste, and José Esteban Muñoz. 1997. "Rebellions of Everynight Life." In *Everynight Life: Culture and Dance in Latin/o America*, edited by Celeste Fraser Delgado and José Esteban Muñoz, 9–32. Durham, N.C.: Duke University Press.

Frith, Simon. 1996. "Music and Identity." In *Questions of Cultural Identity*, edited by Stuart Hall and Paul du Gay, 108–27. London: Sage.

———. 1998. *Performing Rites: Evaluating Popular Music*. Oxford: Oxford University Press.

Fuller, Mike. 2008. "Havana Hip Hoppers for Peace." http://www.cubanow .net/pages/articulo.php?sec=17&t=2&item=4210.

Galletti Hernández, Danay, and Adianez Fernández Izquierdo. 2007. "¿Adónde vas, edad de la inocencia?" *Juventud Rebelde*, 29 April.

García, David F. 2006. *Arsenio Rodríguez and the Transnational Flows of Latin Popular Music*. Philadelphia: Temple University Press.

García Freyre, Laura. 2009. "El hip hop me quitó la venda de los ojos." *Cubaencuentro*, 12 May. http://www.cubaencuentro.com/es/entrevistas/articul os/el-hip-hop-me-quito-la-venda-de-los-ojos-177231.

García Márquez, Gabriel. 2006. "The Fidel I Think I Know." *Guardian*, 12 August.

García Meralla, Emir. 2007. "La rumba del fauno: Discretos apuntes para entender la música cubana de fines del siglo xx." *Gaceta de Cuba* 4 (July–August): 3–6.

Geoffray, Marie Laure. 2007. "Cuba, de la subversion des normes révolutionnaires à la (re)création d'un espace public." Paper presented at the Second Biannual Congress of GIS, Rennes, France, 15–17 November. http://ha lshs.archives-ouvertes.fr/halshs-00203053/en.

George, Brian. 2007. "Rapping at the Margins: Musical Constructions of Identities in Contemporary France." In *Music, National Identity, and the Politics of Location*, edited by Ian Biddle and Vanessa Knights, 93–114. Aldershot, England: Ashgate.

Gilroy, Paul. 1993. *The Black Atlantic: Modernity and Double Consciousness*. Cambridge: Harvard University Press.

Giovannetti, Jorge. 2003. "Popular Music and Culture in Puerto Rico: Jamaican and Rap Music as Cross-Cultural Symbols." In *Musical Migrations: Transnationalism and Cultural Hybridity in Latin/o America*, edited by Frances Aparicio and Cándida Jáquez with María Elena Cepeda, 1:81–98. New York: Palgrave Macmillan.

González, Edgar. 2007. "Agencia Cubana de Rap: ¿Arte o mercado?" *El Caimán Barbudo* 40 (338): 15.

González, Liliana. n.d. "Equis Alfonso: Romper las barreras de los públicos." *Movimiento* 5:48–49.

Guillermoprieto, Alma. 2005. *Dancing with Cuba*. London: Vintage.

Guridy, Frank A. 2003. "From Solidarity to Cross-Fertilization: Afro-Cuban/ African American Interaction during the 1930s and 1940s." *Radical History Review* 87 (Fall): 19–48.

Gutiérrez, Pedro Juan. 1998. *Trilogía sucia de La Habana*. Barcelona: Anagrama.

Hall, Stuart. 1996. "Introduction: Who Needs 'Identity'?" In *Questions of Cultural Identity*, edited by Stuart Hall and Paul du Gay, 1–17. London: Sage.

Hansing, Katrin. 2002. "Rasta, Race and Revolution: The Emergence and Development of the Rastafari Movement in Socialist Cuba." Ph.D. diss., University of Oxford.

Haraszti, Miklós. 1988. *The Velvet Prison: Artists under State Socialism*. London: Tauris.

Henken, Ted. 2005. "Entrepreneurship, Informality, and the Second Economy: Cuba's Underground Economy in Comparative Perspective." In *Cuba in Transition: Papers and Proceedings of the Annual Meeting of the Association for the Study of the Cuban Economy (ASCE)*, 15:360–75. Bethesda, Md.: Association for the Study of the Cuban Economy.

Henríquez Lagarde, Manuel. 2002. "Rap cubano: Con la manga hasta el codo." *Jiribilla* 68, August. http://www.lajiribilla.cu/2002/n68_agosto/1629_68.html.

Hernández, Tanya Katerí. 2002. "The *Buena Vista Social Club*: The Racial Politics of Nostalgia." In *Latino/a Popular Culture*, edited by Michelle Habell-Pallán and Mary Romero, 61–72. New York: New York University Press.

Hernandez-Reguant, Ariana. 2006. "Havana's *Timba*: A Macho Sound for Black Sex." In *Globalization and Race*, edited by Kamari Maxine Clarke and Deborah A. Thomas, 249–78. Durham, N.C.: Duke University Press.

———, ed. 2009a. *Cuba in the Special Period: Culture and Ideology in the 1990s*. New York: Palgrave Macmillan.

———. 2009b. "Multicubanidad." In *Cuba in the Special Period: Culture and Ideology in the 1990s*, edited by Ariana Hernandez-Reguant, 69–88. New York: Palgrave Macmillan.

———. 2009c. "Writing the Special Period: An Introduction." In *Cuba in the Special Period: Culture and Ideology in the 1990s*, edited by Ariana Hernandez-Reguant, 1–18. New York: Palgrave Macmillan.

Herrera, Pablo, and Yesenia Selier. 2003. "Rap cubano: Nuevas posibilidades estéticas para la canción cubana." *Boletín Música* 11–12:96–101.

Hesmondhalgh, David, and Caspar Melville. 2001. "Urban Breakbeat Culture: Repercussions of Hip-Hop in the United Kingdom." In *Global Noise: Rap and Hip-Hop outside the USA*, edited by Tony Mitchell, 86–110. Middletown, Conn.: Wesleyan University Press.

"Hip Hop Is a Weapon: An Interview with Hip Hop Revolución." Translated by Jose Garciá. 2005. *Dynamic Magazine*, August. http://www.yclusa.org/article/view/1697/1/302.

Hoch, Danny. 1999. "Not Only Built 4 Cuban Bronx: La Revolución Embraces Hip-Hop—with Fidel's Blessing." *Village Voice*, 28 September. http://www.villagevoice.com/1999-09-28/music/not-only-built-4-cuban-bronx.

Hosokawa, Shuhei. 2002. "Salsa no tiene fronteras: Orquesta de la Luz and the globalization of popular music." In *Situating Salsa: Global Markets and Local Meanings in Latin Popular Music*, edited by Lise Waxer, 289–311. London: Routledge.

Hoyler, Michael, and Christoph Mager. 2005. "*HipHop ist im Haus*: Cultural Policy, Community Centres, and the Making of Hip-Hop Music in Germany." *Built Environment* 31 (3): 237–54.

Impey, Angela. 2001. "Resurrecting the Flesh? Reflections on Women in Kwaito." *Agenda* 49 (2001): 44–50.

Israel, Esteban. 2009. "Reggaeton Fever Shakes up Cuba's Culture." *Reuters*, 29 June. http://www.reuters.com/article/idUSTRE55S6EK20090629.

———. 2010. "Cuba's disaffected youth finds its voice." *Independent*, 18 May.

Kapcia, Antoni. 2000. *Cuba: Island of Dreams*. Oxford: Berg.

———. 2005a. "Educational Revolution and Revolutionary Morality in Cuba: The 'New Man,' Youth and the New 'Battle of Ideas.'" *Journal of Moral Education* 34 (4): 399–412.

———. 2005b. *Havana: The Making of Cuban Culture*. Oxford: Berg.

Kelley, Robin D. G. 2002. *Freedom Dreams: The Black Radical Imagination*. Boston: Beacon Press.

———. 2004. "Looking for the 'Real' Nigga: Social Scientists Construct the Ghetto." In *That's the Joint! The Hip-Hop Studies Reader*, edited by Murray Forman and Mark Anthony Neal, 119–36. New York: Routledge.

Kirk, John, and Leonardo Padura Fuentes. 2001. *Culture and the Cuban Revolution*. Gainesville: University Press of Florida.

Krims, Adam. 2000. *Rap Music and the Poetics of Identity*. Cambridge: Cambridge University Press.

———. 2007. *Music and Urban Geography*. New York: Routledge.

Lemelle, Sidney J. 2006. "'Ni wapi tunakwenda': Hip Hop Culture and the Children of Arusha." In *The Vinyl Ain't Final: Hip Hop and the Globalization of Black Popular Culture*, edited by Dipannita Basu and Sidney J. Lemelle, 230–54. London: Pluto.

LeoGrande, William M. 2004. "The 'Single Party of the Cuban Nation' Faces the Future." In *Cuban Socialism in a New Century: Adversity, Survival, and Renewal*, edited by Max Azicri and Elsie Deal, 183–205. Gainesville: University Press of Florida.

Leyshon, Andrew, David Matless, and George Revill, eds. 1998. *The Place of Music*. New York: Guilford.

Lipsitz, George. 1994. *Dangerous Crossroads: Popular Music, Postmodernism and the Poetics of Place*. London: Verso.

Loomba, Ania. 1998. *Colonialism/postcolonialism*. London: Routledge.

López, Magia. n.d. "La reconstrucción." *Movimiento* 6:27.

López Sánchez, Antonio. 2005. "Felices lágrimas negras." *Los que soñamos por la oreja: boletín de Música Cubana Alternativa*, no. 6. http://www.oreja.tro vacub.com.

Low, Setha. 1999a. "Introduction: Theorizing the City." In *Theorizing the City: The New Urban Anthropology Reader*, edited by Setha Low, 1–33. New Brunswick, N.J.: Rutgers University Press.

———. 1999b. "Spatializing Culture: The Social Production and Social Construction of Public Space in Costa Rica." In *Theorizing the City: The New Urban Anthropology Reader*, edited by Setha Low, 111–37. New Brunswick, N.J.: Rutgers University Press.

Lueiro, Marcel. n.d. "Movimiento cubano de hip hop." *Movimiento* 6:2–3.

Lull, James. 2000. *Media, Communication, Culture: A Global Approach*. 2nd ed. Oxford: Polity.

Lusane, Clarence. 2004. "Rap, Race, and Politics." In *That's the Joint! The Hip-Hop Studies Reader*, edited by Murray Forman and Mark Anthony Neal, 351–62. New York: Routledge.

Manduley López, Humberto. 1997. "Rock in Cuba: History of a Wayward Son." *South Atlantic Quarterly* 96 (1): 135–41.

———. 2007. "¿Se debería de morir quien por bueno no lo estime? Repaso incompleto por fundamentalismos en la música cubana." *El Caimán Barbudo* 41 (341): 2–4.

Marable, Manning. 2000. "Race and Revolution in Cuba: African American Perspectives." In *Dispatches from the Ebony Tower: Intellectuals Confront the African American Experience*, edited by Manning Marable, 90–107. New York: Columbia University Press.

Marshall, Wayne. 2009. "From Música Negra to Reggaetón Latino: The Cultural Politics of Nation, Migration, and Commercialization." In *Reggaeton*, edited by Raquel Z. Rivera, Wayne Marshall, and Deborah Pacini Hernandez, 19–76. Durham, N.C.: Duke University Press.

Martinez, Theresa A. 1997. "Popular Culture as Oppositional Culture: Rap as Resistance." *Sociological Perspectives* 40 (2): 265–86.

Martínez Molina, Julio. 2007a. "Los émulos del Daddy." *Juventud Rebelde*, 24 June.

———. 2007b. "El reguetón: de la legitimación popular a la venta al por mayor." *Juventud Rebelde*, 23 September.

Matienzo Puerto, María. n.d. "La historia es no quedarse atrás." *Movimiento* 6:13–15.

Matory, J. Lorand. 1999. "Afro-Atlantic Culture: On the Live Dialogue between Africa and the Americas." In *Africana: The Encyclopedia of the African and African American Experience*, edited by Kwame Anthony Appiah and Henry Louis Gates, 36–44. New York: BasicCivitas.

Mattern, Mark. 1998. *Acting in Concert: Music, Community and Political Action*. New Brunswick, N.J.: Rutgers University Press.

Maxwell, Ian. 2001. "Sydney Style: Hip-hop Down Under Comin' Up." In *Global Noise: Rap and Hip-Hop outside the USA*, edited by Tony Mitchell, 259–79. Middletown, Conn.: Wesleyan University Press.

———. 2002. "The Curse of Fandom: Insiders, Outsiders and Ethnography." In *Popular Music Studies*, edited by David Hesmondhalgh and Keith Negus, 103–16. London: Arnold.

———. 2003. *Phat Beats, Dope Rhymes: Hip Hop Down Under Comin' Upper*. Middletown, Conn.: Wesleyan University Press.

McClary, Susan. 1994. "Same as It Ever Was: Youth Culture and Music." In *Microphone Fiends: Youth Music and Youth Culture*, edited by Andrew Ross and Tricia Rose, 29–40. London: Routledge.

Medina, Alberto. 2007. "Jameson, Buena Vista Social Club and Other Exercises in the Restoration of the Real." *Iberoamericana* 7 (25): 7–21.

Merrifield, Andy. 2002. *Dialectical Urbanism: Social Struggles in the Capitalist City*. New York: Monthly Review Press.

Merrifield, Andy, and Erik Swyngedouw. 1996. "Social Justice and the Urban Experience." In *The Urbanization of Injustice*, edited by Andy Merrifield and Erik Swyngedouw, 1–17. London: Lawrence and Wishart.

Miles, Malcolm, Tim Hall, and Iain Borden. 2000. "Introduction." In *The City Cultures Reader*, edited by Malcolm Miles, Tim Hall, and Iain Borden, 1–10. London: Routledge.

Mitchell, Tony. 2001a. "Fightin' da Faida: The Italian Posses and Hip-Hop in Italy." In *Global Noise: Rap and Hip-Hop outside the USA*, edited by Tony Mitchell, 194–221. Middletown, Conn.: Wesleyan University Press.

———, ed. 2001b. *Global Noise: Rap and Hip-Hop outside the USA*. Middletown, Conn.: Wesleyan University Press.

———. 2001c. "Introduction: Another Root—Hip-Hop outside the USA." In *Global Noise: Rap and Hip-Hop outside the USA*, edited by Tony Mitchell, 1–38. Middletown, Conn.: Wesleyan University Press.

———. 2004. "Doin' Damage in My Native Language: The Use of 'Resistance Vernaculars' in Hip Hop in Europe and Aotearoa/New Zealand." In *Music, Space and Place: Popular Music and Cultural Identity*, edited by Sheila Whiteley, Andy Bennett, and Stan Hawkins, 108–23. Aldershot, England: Ashgate.

Moore, Carlos. 1988. *Castro, the Blacks, and Africa*. Los Angeles: Center for Afro-American Studies, University of California.

Moore, Robin. 1997. *Nationalizing Blackness: "Afrocubanismo" and Artistic Revolution in Havana, 1920–1940*. Pittsburgh: University of Pittsburgh Press.

———. 2003. "Transformations in Cuban *nueva trova*, 1965–95." *Ethnomusicology* 47 (1): 1–41.

———. 2006. *Music and Revolution: Cultural Change in Socialist Cuba*. Berkeley: University of California Press.

Navarro, Mireya. 2001. "Giving Hip-Hop a Cultural Beat; Rappers Visiting from Cuba Find a Welcoming Audience." *New York Times*, 24 October.

Neal, Mark Anthony. 2004a. "Postindustrial Soul: Black Popular Music at the Crossroads." In *That's the Joint! The Hip-Hop Studies Reader*, edited by Murray Forman and Mark Anthony Neal, 363–87. New York: Routledge.

———. 2004b. "' . . . A Way Out of No Way': Jazz, Hip-Hop, and Black Social Improvisation." In *The Other Side of Nowhere: Jazz, Improvisation, and Communities in Dialogue*, edited by Daniel Fischlin and Ajay Heble, 195–223. Middletown, Conn.: Wesleyan University Press.

Neate, Patrick. 2003. *Where You're At: Notes from the Frontline of a Hip Hop Planet*. London: Bloomsbury.

Neustadt, Robert. 2002. "Buena Vista Social Club versus La Charanga Habanera: The Politics of Cuban Rhythm." *Journal of Popular Music Studies* 14 (2): 139–62.

Olivera, Camilo Ernesto, and Tony González. 2005. "Agencia de Rock: Utopía o Realidad." *Los que soñamos por la oreja: boletín de Música Cubana Alternativa* 5:4–7.

Pacini Hernandez, Deborah. 2003. "Amalgamating Musics: Popular Music and Cultural Hybridity in the Americas." In *Musical Migrations: Transnationalism and Cultural Hybridity in Latin/o America*, vol. 1, edited by Frances Aparicio and Cándida Jáquez with María Elena Cepeda, 13–32. New York: Palgrave Macmillan.

Pacini Hernandez, Deborah, and Reebee Garofalo. 1999–2000. "Hip Hop in Havana: Rap, Race and National Identity in Contemporary Cuba." *Journal of Popular Music Studies* 11–12 (1): 18–47.

———. 2004. "Between Rock and a Hard Place: Negotiating Rock in Revolutionary Cuba, 1960–1980." In *Rockin' Las Américas: The Global Politics of Rock in Latin/o America*, edited by Deborah Pacini Hernandez, Héctor Fernández L'Hoeste, and Eric Zolov, 43–67. Pittsburgh: University of Pittsburgh Press.

Padura Fuentes, Leonardo. 2006. "¿Reggaeton, signo de nuestra época?" *Los que soñamos por la oreja: boletín de Música Cubana Alternativa* 23:51–52.

Paneque Brizuela, Antonio. n.d. "¿Está ocupando el rap su lugar en la vida?" *Movimiento* 3:16–19.

Pardue, Derek. 2004. "Putting *Mano* to Music: The Mediation of Race in Brazilian Rap." *Ethnomusicology Forum* 13 (2): 253–86.

———. 2007. "Hip Hop as Pedagogy: A Look into 'Heaven' and 'Soul' in São Paulo, Brazil." *Anthropological Quarterly* 80 (3): 673–709.

———. 2008. *Ideologies of Marginality in Brazilian Hip Hop*. New York: Palgrave Macmillan.

Pekacz, Jolanta. 1994. "Did Rock Smash the Wall? The Role of Rock in Political Transition." *Popular Music* 13 (1): 41–49.

Pérez, Louis A. 2006. *Cuba: Between Reform and Revolution*. 3rd ed. New York: Oxford University Press.

——. 2008. *Cuba in the American Imagination: Metaphor and the Imperial Ethos*. Chapel Hill: University of North Carolina Press.

Pérez Sarduy, Pedro, and Jean Stubbs, eds. 2000. *Afro-Cuban Voices: On Race and Identity in Contemporary Cuba*. Gainesville: University Press of Florida.

Perkins, William Eric. 1996. "The Rap Attack: An Introduction." In *Droppin' Science: Critical Essays on Rap Music and Hip Hop Culture*, edited by William Eric Perkins, 1–45. Philadelphia: Temple University Press.

Perna, Vincenzo. 2005. *Timba: The Sound of the Cuban Crisis*. Aldershot, England: Ashgate.

Perry, Imani. 2004. *Prophets of the Hood: Politics and Poetics in Hip Hop*. Durham, N.C.: Duke University Press.

Perry, Marc. 2004. "*Los raperos*: Rap, Race, and Social Transformation in Contemporary Cuba." Ph.D. diss., University of Texas.

Perullo, Alex. 2005. "Hooligans and Heroes: Youth Identity and Hip-Hop in Dar es Salaam, Tanzania." *Africa Today* 51 (4): 75–101.

Phillips, Emma F. 2007. "'Maybe Tomorrow I'll Turn Capitalist': Cuentapropismo in a Workers' State." *Law and Society Review* 41 (2): 305–42.

Plato. 1992. *The Republic*. Translated by A. D. Lindsay. London: David Campbell.

Pough, Gwendolyn. 2004. "Seeds and Legacies: Tapping the Potential in Hip-Hop." In *That's the Joint! The Hip-Hop Studies Reader*, edited by Murray Forman and Mark Anthony Neal, 283–89. New York: Routledge.

Quiroga, José. 2005. *Cuban Palimpsests*. Minneapolis: University of Minnesota Press.

Ramet, Sabrina Petra. 1994. *Rocking the State: Rock Music and Politics in Eastern Europe and Russia*. Boulder, Colo.: Westview.

Ramsey, Guthrie. 2003. *Race Music: Black Cultures from Bebop to Hip-hop*. Berkeley: University of California Press.

Ravsberg, Fernando. 2005. "Cuba: 'peligroso' reguetón." BBC Mundo, 15 March. http://news.bbc.co.uk/hi/spanish/misc/newsid_4350000/4350595.stm.

Reilly, Matthew J. 2009. "The Nocturnal Negotiations of Youth Spaces in Havana." Ph.D. diss., University of North Carolina.

Ritter, Archibald. 2005. "Cuba's Underground Economy." http://www2.carleton.ca/economics/ccms/wp-content/ccms-files/cep04–12.pdf.

Rivera, Raquel Z. 2003. *New York Ricans from the Hip Hop Zone*. New York: Palgrave Macmillan.

Roberts, John Storm. 1979. *The Latin Tinge: The Impact of Latin American Music on the United States*. Oxford: Oxford University Press.

Robertson, Roland. 1990. "After Nostalgia? Willful Nostalgia and the Phases of Globalization." In *Theories of Modernity and Post-Modernity*, edited by Bryan Turner, 45–61. London: Sage.

Robinson, Eugene. 2004. *Last Dance in Havana: The Final Days of Fidel and the Start of the New Cuban Revolution*. New York: Free Press.

Roland, L. Kaifa. 2006. "Tourism and the *Negrificación* of Cuban Identity." *Transforming Anthropology* 14 (2): 151–62.

"The Roots en Cuba." n.d. *Movimiento* 1:35–37.

Rose, Tricia. 1994. *Black Noise: Rap Music and Black Culture in Contemporary America*. Hanover, N.H.: University Press of New England.

———. 2008. *The Hip Hop Wars: What We Talk about When We Talk about Hip Hop—and Why It Matters*. New York: BasicCivitas.

Rutheiser, Charles. 2000. "Capitalizing on Havana: The Return of the Repressed in a Late Socialist City." In *A Companion to the City*, edited by Gary Bridge and Sophie Watson, 224–36. Oxford: Blackwell.

Sáez Rodríguez, Félix Mauricio. n.d.a. "Historia mínima sobre gallos y toros." *Movimiento* 5:9–11.

———. n.d.b. "Habana Blues, Inventos: Cuba, la música y el siglo XXI." *Movimiento* 6:42–43.

Sansone, Livio. 1995. "The Making of a Black Youth Culture: Lower-class Young Men of Surinamese Origin in Amsterdam." In *Youth Cultures: A Cross-cultural Perspective*, edited by Vered Amit-Talai and Helena Wulff, 114–43. London: Routledge.

———. 2001. "The Localization of Global Funk in Bahia and Rio." In *Brazilian Popular Music and Globalization*, edited by Christopher Dunn and Charles A. Perrone, 136–60. Gainesville: University Press of Florida.

Saunders, Tanya L. 2008. "The Cuban Remix: Rethinking Culture and Political Participation in Contemporary Cuba." Ph.D. diss., University of Michigan.

Sawyer, Mark. 2006. *Racial Politics in Post-Revolutionary Cuba*. Cambridge: Cambridge University Press.

Schwartz, Rosalie. 1997. *Pleasure Island: Tourism and Temptation in Cuba*. Lincoln: University of Nebraska Press.

Scott, James C. 1990. *Domination and the Arts of Resistance: Hidden Transcripts*. New Haven, Conn.: Yale University Press.

Sennett, Richard. 2000. "Reflections on the Public Realm." In *A Companion to the City*, edited by Gary Bridge and Sophie Watson, 380–87. Oxford: Blackwell.

Sharp, Joanne, et al., eds. 2000. *Entanglements of Power: Geographies of Domination/Resistance*. London: Routledge.

Silverstein, Paul A., and Chantal Tetreault. 2006. "Postcolonial Urban Apartheid." In "Riots in France." Brooklyn, N.Y.: Social Science Research Council, 11 June. http://riotsfrance.ssrc.org/Silverstein_Tetreault.

Simmel, Georg. 1950. "The Metropolis and Mental Life." In Simmel, *The Sociology of Georg Simmel*, edited and translated by Kurt H. Wolff, 409–24. Glencoe, Ill.: Free Press.

Smith, Shawnee. n.d. "Hip hop a la Cubano." http://www.afrocubaweb.com/rap/pabloherrera.htm.

Sokol, Brett. 2000. "Rap Takes Root Where Free Expression Is Risky." 3 September. http://www.afrocubaweb.com/rap/pabloherrera.htm.

Stephens, Simon. 2000. "Kwaito." In *Senses of Culture: South African Culture Studies*, edited by Sarah Nuttall and Cheryl-Ann Michael, 256–73. Oxford: Oxford University Press.

Stokes, Martin. 1994. "Introduction: Ethnicity, Identity and Music." In *Ethnicity, Identity and Music: The Musical Construction of Place*, edited by Martin Stokes, 1–27. Oxford: Berg.

Stolzoff, Norman. 2000. *Wake the Town and Tell the People: Dancehall Culture in Jamaica*. Durham, N.C.: Duke University Press.

Sublette, Ned. 2004. *Cuba and Its Music: From the First Drums to the Mambo*. Chicago: Chicago Review Press.

Szemere, Anna. 2001. *Up from the Underground: The Culture of Rock Music in Postsocialist Hungary*. University Park, Pa.: Penn State University Press.

Tagg, Philip. 1989. "Open Letter: 'Black Music,' 'Afro-American Music' and 'European Music.' *Popular Music* 8 (3): 285–98.

Thompson, Robert Farris. 1996. "Hip Hop 101." In *Droppin' Science: Critical Essays on Rap Music and Hip Hop Culture*, edited by William Eric Perkins, 211–19. Philadelphia: Temple University Press.

———. 2005. *Tango: The Art History of Love*. New York: Pantheon.

Tickner, Arlene B. 2008. "*Aquí en el Ghetto*: Hip-hop in Colombia, Cuba, and Mexico." *Latin American Politics and Society* 50 (3): 121–46.

Toop, David. 2000. *Rap Attack 3: African Rap to Global Hip Hop*. London: Serpent's Tail.

Torna, Miranda. 2007. "Doble Filo, reparmofereando por La Habana." *Esquife* 56, April–May. http://www.esquife.cult.cu/primeraepoca/revista/56/05.htm.

Urry, John. 1990. *The Tourist Gaze: Leisure and Travel in Contemporary Societies*. London: Sage.

Valdés, Reynier. 2007. "El reguetón: la noches, cazadores y una fiera que espera." *Gaceta de Cuba* 4 (July–August): 7–11.

Vázquez Muñoz, Luis Raúl. 2006. "Los olvidos del reguetón." *Juventud Rebelde*, 4 November.

Verdery, Katherine. 1991. *National Ideology under Socialism: Identity and Cul-*

tural Politics in Ceausescu's Romania. Berkeley: University of California Press.

Vizcaíno Serrat, Mario. 2006. "Música hecha en Cuba: ¿Todo es culpa de la mala difusión?" Gaceta de Cuba 6 (November–December). http://www.uneac.org.cu/index.php?module=publicaciones&act=publicacion_numero&id=25&idarticulo=146#articulo_top.

Wade, Peter. 2000. Music, Race and Nation: Música Tropical in Colombia. Chicago: University of Chicago Press.

———. 2004. "Globalization and Appropriation in Latin American Popular Music." Latin American Research Review 39 (1): 273–84.

Wang, Jimmy. 2009. "Now Hip-Hop, Too, Is Made in China." New York Times, 24 January.

Wark, McKenzie. 1994. Virtual Geography. Bloomington: Indiana University Press.

Warner, Michael. 2002. "Publics and Counterpublics." Public Culture 14 (1): 49–90.

Washburne, Christopher. 2008. Sounding Salsa: Performing Latin Music in New York City. Philadelphia: Temple University Press.

Waxer, Lise. 1994. "Of Mambo Kings and Songs of Love: Dance Music in Havana and New York from the 1930s to the 1950s." Latin American Music Review 15 (2): 139–76.

———. 2002. The City of Musical Memory: Salsa, Record Grooves, and Popular Culture in Cali, Colombia. Middletown, Conn.: Wesleyan University Press.

West-Durán, Alan. 2004. "Rap's Diasporic Dialogues: Cuba's Redefinition of Blackness." Journal of Popular Music Studies 16 (1): 4–39.

———. n.d. "El cine y el hip hop cubano: espacio social, reflexividad e identidad." Movimiento 6:36–39.

Whiteley, Sheila, Andy Bennett, and Stan Hawkins, eds. 2004. Music, Space and Place: Popular Music and Cultural Identity. Aldershot, England: Ashgate.

Whitfield, Esther. 2008. Cuban Currency: The Dollar and "Special Period" Fiction. Minneapolis: University of Minnesota Press.

Wilk, Richard. 1995. "Learning to Be Local in Belize: Global Systems of Common Difference." In Worlds Apart: Modernity through the Prism of the Local, edited by Daniel Miller, 110–33. London: Routledge.

Wunderlich, Annelise. 2001. "Cuban Hip-Hop, Underground Revolution." http://journalism.berkeley.edu/projects/cubans2001/story-hiphop.html.

Young, Cynthia. 2006. Soul Power: Culture, Radicalism, and the Making of a U.S. Third World Left. Durham, N.C.: Duke University Press.

Young, Robert. 2003. Postcolonialism. Oxford: Oxford University Press.

Yúdice, George. 1994. "The Funkification of Rio." In Microphone Fiends: Youth Music and Youth Culture, edited by Andrew Ross and Tricia Rose, 193–217. London: Routledge.

Zamora Céspedes, Bladimir. n.d. "El hip hop en la isla de las utopías." *Movimiento* 3:55–56.

Žižek, Slavoj. 2007. "Resistance Is Surrender." *London Review of Books*, 15 November: 7.

Zurbano, Roberto. 2009. "El Rap Cubano: Can't Stop, Won't Stop the Movement!" In *Cuba in the Special Period: Culture and Ideology in the 1990s*, edited by Ariana Hernandez-Reguant, 143–58. New York: Palgrave Macmillan.

——. n.d.a. "Se buscan: Textos urgentes para sonidos hambrientos." *Movimiento* 3:6–12.

——. n.d.b. "¡Mami, no quiero más reggaetón! O el nuevo perre(te)o intelectual." *Movimiento* 6:4–12.

INDEX

Geoffrey Baker

is a senior lecturer in the department of music at the University of London.
He is the author of *Imposing Harmony: Music and Society in Colonial Cuzco* (2008), also published by Duke University Press, which won the American Musicological Society's Robert M. Stevenson Award in 2010.

Library of Congress Cataloging-in-Publication Data
Baker, Geoffrey, 1970–
Buena Vista in the club : rap, reggaetón, and revolution
in Havana / Geoffrey Baker.
p. cm.—(Refiguring American music)
Includes bibliographical references and index.
ISBN 978-0-8223-4940-2 (cloth : alk. paper)
ISBN 978-0-8223-4959-4 (pbk. : alk. paper)
1. Rap (Music)—Cuba—Havana. 2. Reggaetón—Cuba—Havana.
3. Buena Vista Social Club (Musical group)
4. Music—Political aspects—Cuba.
I. Title. II. Series: Refiguring American music.
ML3531.B35 2011
782.421649097291—dc22   2010041681